4

11/21

D0843385

Air War D-Day

Volume 5

Gold - Juno - Sword

Other volumes in this series

Gold-Juno-Sword

Air War D-Day

Volume 5

Gold - Juno - Sword

Martin W. Bowman

Pen & Sword
AVIATION

First Published in Great Britain in 2013 by
Pen & Sword Aviation
an imprint of
Pen & Sword Books Ltd
47 Church Street, Barnsley, South Yorkshire S70 2AS

Copyright © Martin W Bowman, 2013
ISBN 9781781591796

Typeset in 10/12pt Palatino
by GMS Enterprises

Printed and bound in England by
CPI Group (UK) Ltd, Croydon, CR0 4YY

Pen & Sword Books Ltd incorporates the Imprints of Pen & Sword
Aviation, Pen & Sword Family History, Pen & Sword Maritime, Pen & Sword
Military, Pen & Sword Discovery, Wharncliffe Local History, Wharncliffe
True Crime, Wharncliffe Transport, Pen & Sword Select, Pen & Sword
Military Classics, Leo Cooper, The Praetorian Press, Remember When,
Seaforth Publishing and Frontline Publishing.

For a complete list of Pen & Sword titles please contact
PEN & SWORD BOOKS LIMITED

47 Church Street, Barnsley, South Yorkshire, S70 2AS, England
E-mail: enquiries@pen-and-sword.co.uk
Website: www.pen-and-sword.co.uk

Contents

Acknowledgements

I am enormously grateful to the following people for their time and effort and kind loan of photos etc, not least to my fellow author and friend Graham Simons, for getting this to press-ready standard and for his detailed work on maps and photographs: My thanks to Ray Alm; Ed 'Cotton' Appleman; James Roland Argo; Peter Arnold; John Avis; Les Barber; Harry Barker; Mike Bailey; Carter Barber; Neil Barber, author of *The Day The Devils Dropped In;* E. W. D. Beeton; Franklin L. Betz; Bill Bidmead; Rusty Bloxom, Historian, Battleship Texas; Lucille Hoback Boggess; Prudent Boiux; August C. Bolino; Dennis Bowen; Tom Bradley; Eric Broadhead; Stan Bruce; K. D. Budgen; Kazik Budzik KW VM; Les Bulmer; Reginald 'Punch' Burge; Donald Burgett; Chaplain Burkhalter; Lol Buxton; Jan Caesar; R. H. 'Chad' Chadwick; Noel Chaffey; Mrs J. Charlesworth; Chris Clancy; Roy Clark RNVR; Ian 'Nobby' Clark; P. Clough; Johnny Cook DFM; Malcolm Cook; Flight Lieutenant Tony Cooper; Lieutenant-Colonel Eric A. Cooper-Key MC; Cyril Crain; Mike Crooks; Jack Culshaw, Editor, *The Kedge Hook;* Bill Davey; S. Davies; Brenda French, Dawlish Museum Society; John de S. Winser; Abel L. Dolim; Geoffrey Duncan; Sam Earl; *Eighth Air Force News; Eastern Daily Press;* Chris Ellis; Les 'Tubby' Edwards; W. Evans; Frank R. Feduik; Ron Field; Wolfgang Fischer; Robert Fitzgerald; Eugene Fletcher; Captain Dan Flunder; John Foreman; Wilf Fortune; H. Foster; Lieutenant-Commander R. D. Franks DSO; Jim Gadd; Leo Gariepy; Patricia Gent; Lieutenant Commander Joseph H. Gibbons USNR; Larry Goldstein; Bill Goodwin; Franz Goekel; Lieutenant Denis J. M. Glover DSC RNZNVR; John Gough; Peter H. Gould; George 'Jimmy' Green RNVR; Albert Gregory; Nevil Griffin; Edgar Gurney BEM; R. S. Haig-Brown; Leo Hall, Parachute Regt Assoc.; Günter Halm; Roland 'Ginger' A. Hammersley DFM; Madelaine Hardy; Allan Healy; Andre Heintz; Basil Heaton; Mike Henry DFC, author of *Air Gunner;* Vic Hester; Reverend R. M. Hickey MC; Lenny Hickman; Elizabeth Hillmann; Bill Holden; Mary Hoskins; Ena Howes; Pierre Huet; J. A. C. Hugill; Antonia Hunt; Ben C. Isgrig; Jean Irvine; Orv Iverson; George Jackson; Major R. J. L. Jackson; Robert A. Jacobs; G. E. Jacques; Marjorie Jefferson; Bernard M. Job RAFVR; Wing Commander 'Johnnie' Johnson DSO* DFC*; Percy 'Shock' Kendrick MM; the late Jack Krause; Cyril Larkin; Reg Lilley; John Lincoln, author of *Thank God and the Infantry;* Lieutenant Brian Lingwood RNVR; Wing Commander A. H. D. Livock; Leonard Lomell; P. McElhinney; Ken McFarlane; Don McKeage; Hugh R. McLaren; John McLaughlin; Nigel McTeer: Ron Mailey; Sara Marcum; Ronald Major; Walt Marshall; Rudolph May; Ken Mayo; Alban Meccia; Claude V. Meconis; Leon E. Mendel; Harold Merritt; Bill Millin for kindly allowing me to quote from his book, *Invasion;* Bill Mills; John Milton; Alan Mower; Captain Douglas Munroe; *A Corpsman Remembers D-Day Navy Medicine 85,* No.3 (May-June 1994); Major Tom Normanton; General Gordon E. Ockenden; Raymond Paris; Bill Parker, National Newsletter Editor, Normandy Veterans; Simon Parry; Albert Pattison; Helen Pavlovsky; Charles Pearson; Eric 'Phil' Phillips DFC MiD; T. Platt; Franz Rachmann; Robert J. Rankin; Lee Ratel; Percy Reeve; Jean Lancaster-Rennie; Wilbur Richardson; Helmut Romer; George Rosie; The Royal Norfolk Regiment; Ken Russell; A. W. Sadler; Charles Santarsiero; Erwin Sauer; Frank Scott; Ronald Scott; Jerry Scutts; Major Peter Selerie; Alfred Sewell; Bob Shaffer; Reg Shickle; John R. Slaughter; Ben Smith Jr.; *SOLDIER Magazine; Southampton Southern Evening Echo;* Southwick House, HMS *Dryad,* Southwick, Portsmouth; Bill Stafford; Allen W. Stephens; Roy Stevens; Mrs E. Stewart; Henry Tarcza; Henry 'Buck' Taylor; June Telford; E. J. Thompson; Charles Thornton; Robert P. Tibor; Dennis Till; Edward J. Toth; Walt Truax; Jim Tuffell; Russ Tyson; US Combat Art Collection, Navy Yard, Washington DC; Thomas Valence; John Walker; Herbert Walther; Ed Wanner; R. H. G. Weighill; Andrew Whitmarsh, Portsmouth Museum Service; 'Slim' Wileman; Jim Wilkins; E. G. G. Williams; Deryk Wills, author of *Put On Your Boots and Parachutes! The US 82nd Airborne Division;* Jack Woods; Len Woods; Waverly Woodson.

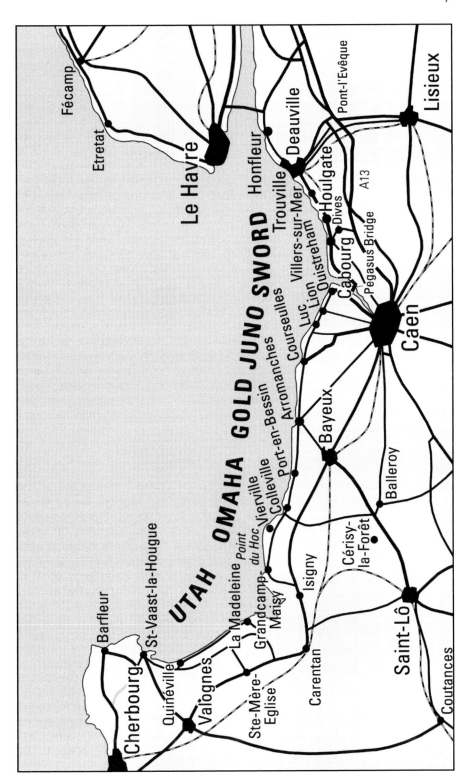

Chapter 1

'Gold'

Twenty-one year old Kanonier Friedrich Würster on sentry duty at Wiederstandnest 33 at La Revière listened to heavy bombers going over, on their way, he imagined, to bomb the towns of Germany; and he was thinking of the air-raid sirens sounding at home and his mother waking and having to get up and go down alone to the shelter again; alone, because his father was stationed as a soldier in the north of Norway and his brother was in the Luftwaffe. The thought of it made him both sad and angry. Würster was the son of a farmer and he had been ten when Hitler came to power. He had joined the Hitler Youth and had now been a soldier for four years. At seventeen, he had marched into France during the Blitzkrieg. At 18, he had marched into Russia. At 19, he had been wounded within a hundred miles of Moscow. Before he was twenty he had been hospitalised and then sent back to the Eastern Front where he had been wounded a second time, so badly that he was only fit enough to man the Atlantic Wall.

At two o'clock he was relieved and he went back to his quarters to turn in; but before he had finished undressing, the alarm bell rang and the battery loudspeakers called everyone to the first state of alert. The naval bombardment just before dawn was the first warning Würster had that anything really serious was happening. It did very little structural damage to the 88mm casement built into the sea wall, which on its seaward side was protected by 17 feet of concrete and was defended by a single platoon. But one of the two machine gun posts was completely destroyed either by a hit from a destroyer or by a bomb and the 50mm anti-tank gun was knocked out probably by fire from an LCG(L).

Suddenly there was silence and Würster stood up and looked out. He had half expected ships, but he had never expected or even dreamed of six hundred ships and at least that number must have been in sight from his battery at dawn. Nor had he ever heard of landing craft; yet there they were, already in the surf and men and tanks were pouring out of them and advancing across the beach to the foot of the hill.

As soon as the battery on the top of the hill had recovered from the bombardment and the shock of seeing the fleet and the landing craft, they started to fire the 88mm gun against the beach; but the firing was interrupted again and again by low-flying aircraft which drove the gunners to shelter with machine-guns and cannon shells. Several men had been killed by the bombing: now the number of casualties grew until the aid post overflowed. It was not very long either until they lost their forward observation post, which was down by the shore. The battery commander was down there and everyone in the battery heard his last call on the communication system.

'They're coming right in the post,' he cried with a frantic note in his voice. And he added 'Lebt wohl, Kamaraden' and the line was silent.[1]

1   Adapted from *Dawn Of D-Day* by David Howarth (The Companion Book Club 1959).

WN 33 was at the eastern end of 'King Red'. The 88mm damaged two Flail tanks and two AVREs of the breaching squadrons and, with the aid of the machine-guns, pinned down D Company of the 5th East Yorks causing 90 casualties, killed or wounded, including six officers. The gun was finally silenced by Captain Roger F. Bell of C Squadron, Westminster Dragoons. He had been twenty when the war began, articled to a chartered accountant in Sheffield and he had joined up immediately, partly because he was afraid he was going to fail his next examination in accountancy. Bell went up to the casement so that he could see the embrasure in the side of the emplacement and the muzzle of the 88 sticking out of it, towards him. At 100 yards he fired two rounds of HE which were in his gun but they seemed to have no effect. The German gun fired but missed and then he fired three more shots with armour-piercing shells. The 88 was dead. Bell and the squadron of flails spent the night in an orchard 200 yards from the casement. At dawn the German gunners saw the tanks and opened fire. The Westminster Dragoons, with two of the flame-throwing tanks of the Royal Engineers, overran the battery at 0830; 45 prisoners, Friedrich Würster among them, were taken.

'On Monday 5th June there was an announcement over the ship's tannoy system that we should be sailing that evening for the coast of France. What had seemed somewhat unreal, almost as though we were only engaged in training manoeuvres, now became a reality. No-one slept much, if at all, that night, many of us being up on the deck watching the flashes from the coast where our bombers were attacking the coastal batteries. I remember thinking that I ought to be frightened and that instead I seemed to be detached and observing myself as though I were watching a film. The feeling of unreality, the sub-conscious thought that this can't really be happening to me, was in some way a calming influence.

'Reveille was sounded at 3.15 am and we hastily went for breakfast. This being an American ship, the galley was equipped with multi-course indented trays which I had not encountered previously. In one indentation was porridge and in another, what must have been surely the most unsuitable of meals that could have been devised. We were served with minced liver (we were to see this for a second time after we had been at sea in the small assault landing craft for a few hours). We were also given a rum ration. For many years after the war I could not bear the smell of rum since, in spite of the thoughtfully provided vomit bags and the fresh sea air, there was a pervading stench of wretched liver and rum in the boats, as we approached our encounter with Jerry.'

Private Tom Tateson, a signaller attached to 'A' Company, 7th Green Howards.

'As we steamed through the night, making for our assigned position as leading ship at zero hour, we passed within hailing distance of the long lines of slower craft which had sailed before us. It was much as if a racehorse was searching for an opening to dash through and win by a short head.

'A story which illustrates well the crowded lines of shipping is one which I was told on the best authority about a Southampton tug. She was a small coal-burning ragamuffin tug that in peacetime had been employed in berthing merchantmen alongside and so had never put her nose outside Southampton water. When the order to sail was given one landing craft could not start its engines. The young captain - desperate at the thought of losing his place in the queue - shouted to this tug to take him in tow. Before he knew what had happened, the old skipper found himself being swept across the Channel with the crowd. Even had the landing craft been able to get going under her own power, he would have been unable to turn round as the congestion of other craft on either side hemmed him in. There was nothing for it but to go on.

'The next morning at dawn this man, who had never given serious thoughts to such minor matters as invasions, found himself off the French coast in the thick of the greatest one in history, with shells falling all around him. But he hung on and got his landing craft ashore. By evening he had got back to Southampton and was safely secured in the old familiar berth. It was a proud moment and called for a couple of drinks to celebrate. A short while later he was approaching his own house, a look of triumph in his eyes. 'You'll never guess where I was last night!' he bragged as his spouse opened the door.

'Oh, yes I can' came the indignant reply. 'It's that big blonde at the 'Red Lion'.' And with that the door slammed in his face. There's no justice in this world!'

'But to return to my own recollections of that long period before zero hour. As the night wore on and there was increasingly less excitement to break the tension, our American Naval liaison officer produced a copy of Life which carried a highly coloured picture of a bunch of New York show girls. Everyone began to stake a claim to their particular choice. It was the sort of scene that would have been considered brilliant understatement in a play or film depicting great heroes covering their true emotions during those grim, moments of suspense before zero hour. In this case it was nothing of the sort. It was a number of bored and doubtless over-sexed men being dogmatic about their particular tastes. I still think I was right about the red-head third from the left!

'As the dawn broke we all crowded on deck to watch our first glimpse of the French coast, the sight we had all been waiting for four years. Yes, there it was, showing up clear over the horizon. There was no turning back now. The greatest event in the history of warfare had commenced. We went down and had another look at Life!

'Admittedly the lack of enemy interference, after all we had been led to expect - there had so far been only occasional bogies on the radar screen and a few flares to break the monotony of the night - produced a very natural feeling of boredom and anti-climax, but apart from that, the tactics employed were not nearly as dramatic in their execution as for instance, those used at Sicily and Salerno. On each of those occasions we had both approached the shore and made the initial assault under cover of darkness. We had left our respective ports in daylight and had had the excitement of seeing our own particular force grouped and formed up in battle array before darkness fell.

'During the night other forces whom we had yet never seen were approaching the same rendezvous. As zero hour approached we had encountered enemy air attacks and the overture of anti-aircraft guns, bombs dropping, tracers tearing through the sky, ships on fire and aircraft spinning down in flames had risen to a crescendo with the pre-assault bombardment by guns and rockets. It had been like sitting in a theatre with the house lights down and the orchestra working up the excitement for the moment when the curtain rose but on an unbelievably grand and thrilling scale. And then, just as the curtain rises in a theatre to reveal some magnificent spectacle, so it had risen with the dawn to reveal that most stirring spectacle of all, the first sight of the whole great invasion fleet grouped off the beaches, with landing craft already hard at work and more and more vessels appearing over the horizon. Ships, ships, as far as the eye could see.

'But at the invasion of Normandy there was none of that. Because of the short sea passage involved, the units of the individual forces formed up under cover of darkness and the heavy minefield ahead necessitated the various forces approaching in line ahead through the Channel swept by the mine-sweepers.

'For various reasons, it had been decided that the assault should take place in daylight and not under cover of darkness as on previous occasions, This again did much to destroy that breath-taking discovery of the invasion fleet as a whole, for all we could see from the leading ship of our force as the dawn broke was the French coastline arid a number of minesweepers hard at work. It was only as one looked astern that one could see the long line of every conceivable kind of landing craft jockeying into position. It was not, in fact, until one made the return trip across the Channel and forced one's way through the never ceasing flow of oncoming traffic, that one was really able to appreciate what was taking place.

'As we came within range, a few shore batteries which had escaped the air bombardment opened up and for a few minutes their shells fell unpleasantly close. But from the moment of their giving away their positions, cruisers steamed past us at full speed, fanned out and took them on.

'Before long only one or two batteries were still in action and their shells always seemed to drop in exactly the same spots. I had the impression that either the gunlayers had been killed and a few braves were still firing on a fixed setting, or that the number of targets were too many and confusing to allow for individual aim.

'As we got closer and the details of the coastline became more distinct, I had a very personal thrill with each particular land-mark I picked out through my binoculars, for by a strange coincidence our force was assaulting Asnelles, where my brother Brian and I had spent so many happy summer holidays as children. The little Hotel des Bains; where, we had always stayed, was our first objective.

'As the assault craft and support craft moved inshore the bombing and bombardment really opened up in earnest. Some hundred Flying Fortresses plastered the defences with great thuds. Cruisers, destroyers, rocket craft and Army guns in the landing craft added to the din. The beaches were soon an inferno of spitting shell-bursts in which no man could hope to live.

'Up till this moment we seemed to have been only fighting the weather. Now at last we were really getting to grips with the enemy.

'The LOCUS - or Landing Obstacle Clearance Units to give them their full title - were amongst the very first ashore. They had been specially trained to clear; the thousands of underwater obstructions which it was known had been laid to wreck our landing craft. They were all youngsters and had been selected as strong swimmers. Over the special silk underclothes, designed to keep them warm in the water, they wore tight-fitting bottle-green rubber suits and helmets. They carried self-contained diving equipment allowing them to stay submerged for considerable periods and their job was to dive into the sea, find the underwater obstacles, attach charges to blow them up and so leave a clear passage for the oncoming landing craft. As they leapt about in the surf, dealing with one obstacle after the other, they looked exactly like little gnomes.

'When I eventually stepped ashore I had to wade through a large pool in the sands where I used to sail my toy boats. A blazing tank occupied most of it. When I found my little room in what was left of the hotel a Hun top-booted leg stuck out from beneath a heap of rubble in one corner.

'At first I found it impossible to associate the past with the present, but as I crept through the bushes skirting the tennis court, the nauseating odours of war were suddenly banished by a long forgotten smell, a mixture of macrocarpa and seaweed, which brought all the childhood memories racing back. As soon as possible I searched for my first love, Adrienne, the Mayor's daughter, but she had departed many years before for Paris. I was luckier with Monsieur Guinod, the chef of the hotel, whom I discovered on the following Sunday coming out of church in a village a few miles inland.

'As we stood on the roadside in the dust thrown up by the tanks roaring by, he threw his arms round my neck and introduced me to all his friends, recalling the most lurid tales of how my brother Brian, Colin Jardine and I had beaten up a number of French boys staying in the hotel. What a change since those happy days! Brian was a. Major-General and Deputy Chief of Staff to Lord Louis Mountbatten. Colin Jardine was a Lieutenant-General and Deputy Governor of Gibraltar. But for the moment, as Monsieur Guinod gesticulated, I was still a boy of ten and they were thirteen and fifteen, wearing shorts and brandishing spades. The passing of an extra-loud tank brought me back to the present.'

The Greatest Invasion of Them All, Half Time by **Anthony Kimmins (William Heinemann Ltd 1947).**

'We were ordered to keep our heads down as we approached the coast to avoid enemy fire. However, our landing craft was disabled by some underwater mine or other obstacle and it became impossible to steer. One of the other boats was brought alongside and although it was already fully loaded with a similar number of men, we had to clamber aboard and abandon our boat. We were now exposed to enemy fire as well as being grossly overloaded. From this position I was able to see more of the action and one image which remains with me is of the rocket ships sending off volleys of rockets, very large numbers on each flight, at an angle of about forty-five degrees. Although there is of course no recoil from a rocket there was to me, an optical illusion of the ships or barges moving backwards, as each flight was fired.

'In the confusion of the hordes of other landing craft of various types and due to the fact that some of the landmarks on which the battalion commander was relying had been destroyed by the bombardment, we landed about four hundred yards to the right of our planned beach position at 0815 hours, forty-five minutes after the leading troops. Without warning, a salvo of gunfire landed right in the middle of the troops to our immediate left, followed by a second shortly afterwards. From messages being passed on the wireless, I learned that no one knew who was responsible, except that it was coming from behind us. When a third salvo descended with the most enormous crack, my signals training deserted me and I sent the unauthorised message, 'Stop this fucking barrage'. By a complete coincidence, but to the flattery of my ego, the firing ceased. We later learned that it came from the Navy off shore, who did not realise we had advanced so far. Unfortunately, 'C' Company had casualties as a result of this mistake.'

Private Tom Tateson, 7th Green Howards, who moved inland to Ver-sur-Mer where two batteries were located. A third was at la-Mare-Fontaine.

'When the guns fired, on the decks below it would shake out half the light bulbs. They'd just snap out of their sockets and break on the deck. They were always replacing light bulbs when the guns were firing.'

Ordinary Seaman Robert Brown, a Canadian, on HMS *Belfast.* **The battery near la-Mare-Fontaine well inland and consisting of four casemates for 100mm howitzers was shelled for two hours by** HMS *Belfast.* **6/AR1716 fired 87 rounds before surrendering to the 7th Green Howards who took fifty prisoners.**

'On the night of 3 June I was sent with a radio operator and two commandos on a reconnaissance mission to the Normandy coast at Arromanches. We crossed the Channel in a small U-class sub and went ashore on a rubber raft. The weather was atrocious - there were heavy gales and 6-feet-high seas. Our job was to find out what obstructions and explosives the Germans had planted on 'Gold' Beach, so they could be dealt with before the troops landed on D-Day. We were noting down the positions of the steel and concrete posts that had been hammered into the sand - they looked like criss-crossing railway lines - when we nearly ran into a sentry having a quiet smoke on the beach. Luckily, he didn't see us. A little later, we were almost by a convoy driving along a coastal road. We all jumped into a ditch by the side of the road and once again we had a narrow escape. We managed to discover the position of several explosives, which were taken care of prior to the invasion. Our sub arrived back at Portsmouth on the 5th. The infantry had been amassing ready for the following morning's invasion. There was such tension on their faces, I felt sorry for them - many of them young lads straight out of training. I got together sweets and cigarettes from the men on the base and threw them to those young soldiers. I was only 20 myself, but I was a veteran by then, which made me feel older.'

20-year old Naval Sub-Lieutenant Walt Marshall.

'The Invasion Armada formed up off Spithead was an incredible sight. The sea was a forest of ships of all shapes and sizes. And not an enemy plane got near us. What a difference from when we left France in 1940. Eventually, after a 24 hour postponement, we set sail at night. It was a fast little ship but the sea was vicious, really vicious, with heavy swells, huge waves, in fact it seemed as if the sea was doing all it could to make our invasion as difficult as possible. No sleep. During the night messages were received of ships in difficulties having to turn back to England. Most of them at the time seemed Tank Landing Craft. 'Here we go again on our own', I remember thinking. Aircraft roared overhead continuously all night. Soon flashes were visible from the Normandy coastline. A cheering sight. Before dawn our signals group from the Battalion were well organised on the small deck which had been allocated to us. Because the sea was so rough and visibility so poor our little ship was ordered to lead the Landing Craft Assault to a point where identification of the coastline was unmistakeable. From just before dawn there was so much activity from our Armada that for a few foolish minutes, I think I believed it would be a walk ashore. Everything was being hurled at the coast-line and beyond. Naval bombardment was fantastic.'

Lieutenant-Colonel C. MacDonald, second-in-command of 6th Green Howards.

'When we landed at Arromanches, I was leading a line of flail tanks, which always headed the set-piece attacks, clearing a path through the enemy minefields. As we went up the breach, my tank hit a mine and there was a hell of a bang. Although the tank was totally disabled, no one was hurt. The tank behind me took up the lead and went over the top of a sand dune directly ahead. What none of us knew and what we couldn't see from our tanks was that beyond the dune was a culvert which the Germans had flooded. The tank drove straight into the culvert and sank. Two of the crew drowned but the rest escaped only to be cut down by mortar fire. There was only one thing I could do. With Doug Arnold the tank captain who had escaped, I built a bridge on top of the submerged tank from rubble, while under continuous mortar fire. There was never any room for fear except perhaps in the quieter moments. That evening I learned that my best friend, John Allen, had been killed. As a joke he had painted a cross on his tank turret saying 'Aim here' – a shell had gone right through the cross. They couldn't even identify which body was which in the tank. That shook me more than anything but I always believed that nothing would ever happen to me.'

Lieutenant (later Colonel) Michael Barrowclough (20) who landed on 'Gold' beach with the 22nd Dragoons Tank Regiment. Many years later the tank was exhumed and has now become a D-Day memorial.

'It became obvious that Jig Green beach was deserted except for four Support tanks under heavy fire. At about this time a 75mm battery on the high ground above Le Hamel opened accurate fire on the LCAs. The CO ordered a turn to port and all craft in some disorder, started running east, parallel to the beach. At least one craft was hit and sunk and it soon became a case of every craft for itself. The beach was crowded with craft and all types of vehicles and equipment, mostly wrecked or swamped. Each craft picked its own landing place. Very few had a dry landing; most grounding off shore, in some cases on obstacles in water so deep that the only way ashore was to dump equipment and swim. One craft at least ran onto a mine and had its bows blown off. Of the fourteen craft, only two returned to the LSI.

'The landing was a shambles. The Commando was spread over a frontage of some 1,500 yards.

'As planned the Commando moved west, in groups of boat-loads, along the road running parallel to the beach towards the RV, the church in Le Hamel. It soon became obvious that Le Hamel was still in enemy hands and 231 Brigade was heavily involved clearing the town.

'The CO, four officers and 73 other ranks were missing; practically all the Bangalores and 3-inch mortar bombs had been sunk. X and B Troops were reasonably dry and equipped, A Troop were complete, but had lost most of their weapons, Q and Y Troop had each lost a craft load, There was only one Vickers and one 3-inch mortar out of four of each and the latter was without a sight. Commando HQ was almost complete, but all the wireless sets were doubtful starters.

Major Paddy Donnell, second-in-command, 47 (Royal Marine) Commando, embarked in fourteen LCAs from two LSIs, which landed on Jig Green beach. They had been ordered to capture the strongly defended Port-en-Bessin and dominated by three hills, six miles west of Arromanches. Port-en-Bessin had been selected as the terminal for Pluto.

'Gold' Beach Timetable

Objectives: To capture Bayeux and the Caen-Bayeux road (enabling the Allies to use the east-west road communications) and to join up with the American troops at 'Omaha' Beach.

0510 hours-0725 hours by Force 'K' conducted by the cruisers HMS *Orion, Ajax, Argonaut* and *Emerald,* the Dutch gunboat HMNS *Flores* and 13 destroyers including the Polish ORP *Krakowiak.* The bombardment on all the British and Canadian beaches is 20 minutes longer than that on the American ones because half-tide, when the landings are scheduled, comes later in the east.

Fifteen minutes before H-Hour (H-Hour is 07:30 hours) Landing Craft (Rocket) open fire on the beaches with ripples of 127mm rockets. 25-pounder Sexton self-propelled guns in landing craft add their fire.

H-Hour minus seven RAF bombers commences their air attacks on the German defences, concentrating principally on the coastal batteries in the area. Five minutes later the USAAF arrives over the beach head to combine their attacks with the shore bombardment.

Five minutes before H-Hour DD tanks were to be launched to swim ashore but with a 15 knot wind whipping waves up to 4 feet) and strong tide it is decided that the DD tanks would be landed directly on the beach.

0725 The first units of 231st and 69th Brigades touch down. DD (swimming) tanks and beach clearance groups, delayed by bad weather, are landed directly on to the beach. British XXX Corps' 50th Infantry Division and 8th Armoured Brigade - hit a defensive wall of 2,500 steel and concrete obstacles with strong German troop emplacements behind on a three mile stretch of coast. They come under heavy artillery fire.

0730 hours Green Howards land on the open beaches between The Dorsets and the town of La Rivière.

As with all the British beaches, success hinges on the speed with which tanks can be put ashore. The tanks of 8th Armoured Brigade are landed by the 15th LCT Flotilla under Lieutenant-Commander Porteous. (They subsequently land the 7th Armoured Division and many hundreds of tanks and armoured vehicle reinforcements until 'Mulberry' is fully operational). Of the six assault regiments on 'Sword', 'Juno' and 'Gold' with DD tanks the weather is considered too rough to launch. However, this is not communicated to two regiments - the Nottinghamshire (Sherwood Rangers) Yeomanry, which launches from 1,000 yards out (and the 13th/18th Hussars, which launches from 4,000 yards out at 'Sword' Beach). The remainder are landed dry on the beaches and cause some delay in supporting the infantry regiments. Four of the first five flail tanks onto the beach at Le Hamel are knocked out, burn furiously and bulbous black clouds of smoke envelop the leading troops and obscure the beach.

0745 Troops make slow progress against raking fire, but three beach exits are cleared within the hour. C and D Companies, Royal Hampshires, having reached the sea wall east of Le Hamel, exploit a gap in the coastal wire and minefield belt and push inland in depth, outflank and capture Asnelles. By **0800** this movement is under way.

0820-0825 Follow-up battalions and 47 Royal Marine Commando land between the 2nd Battalion The Dorsets and Hampshires. With the tide rising, three of the commandos' landing craft founder on underwater obstacles for the loss of 43 men.

0930 Les Roquettes is captured.

0950 Stiff resistance at Le Hamel. Commandos head for Port-en-Bessin to link with American forces.

By mid-morning landings of the follow-up assault bring the 7th Armoured Division - 'The Desert Rats' ashore.

1050 Reserve brigades begin to land; seven beach exits have been secured.

1300 all of the 50th (Northumbrian) Division ashore.

1600 Le Hamel is finally captured. 231st Brigade moves on to Arromanches. About 1600 hours 69 Brigade make contact with a strong German force (a battalion of the 915th Regiment and the 352nd Fusilier Battalion and two anti-tank batteries) in the area between Villiers-le-Sec and Bazenville. After a stiff fight the Germans are driven across the River Seulles.

2030 56th and 151st Brigades reach the outskirts of Bayeux and the Caen-Bayeux road.

By 21.00 hours Hampshire's have cleared the radar station at Ste-Côme-de-Fresné and take Arromanches.

By nightfall British forces hold five square miles and link up with Canadians at 'Juno' Beach. 47 Royal Marine Commando are ready to take Port-en-Bessin on following day. By midnight, 24,970 troops have been landed on 'Gold', for a loss of 413 killed, wounded or missing.

'D-Day 7.30 am. An assault craft heading for 'Gold' Beach with some of my signallers and myself, together with a Naval boatswain. The rule was that, as long as we were at sea, the boatswain was in charge, but that I was in command as soon as we touched shore. We ended up on an underwater obstacle sticking up through the bottom of the boat, which made it spin round like a roulette wheel in the rough sea. There then ensued what seemed to be a lengthy discussion between the boatswain and myself as to whether we were at sea or ashore. Ultimately I won and he let down the ramp. With the famous cry of 'Follow me chaps', I ran off the ramp to find myself up to my neck in water.'

Lieutenant L. E. Anderson, The Border Regiment, Beach Signals Officer, No 1 Beach Group.

'Awakened this morning at 1 a.m. by a distant bombardment, we got dressed thinking we were in for an intense bombing. We heard the big bombers coming in and constantly passing over our heads. We found a corner in one of our rooms where the walls are very thick where we waited. Suddenly the cannon commenced and everything in the house - doors, windows and everything in the loft seem to be dancing. The bombing was intensified and seemed to be coming nearer. We had the impression that all sorts of things were falling in the courtyard. We were not feeling very brave!

'Suddenly a big gun is fired from the sea and the smaller cannon of the Boches were answering. There can be no doubt that a big battle is about to commence. We dare not move and we put cotton-wool in our ears. The noise was terrific and we wondered how it would all end.'

Diary entry kept by Mademoiselle Genget, who was living in the village of Ste-Côme de Fresné.

'With other silly Welsh Buggers (2nd Battalion, South Wales Borderers - the only Welsh regiment to land on D-Day) I landed at Le Hamel on 'Gold' Beach about 3-4 miles up the coast from Arromanches at about 10.30 on the morning, not 12 midday as some reports, on an LCI (Landing Craft Infantry) and ready to hear the 'Go! Go! Go!' as the ram; went down only to see the ramp disappear at right angles to the deck. 'Landing aborted!' was the cry. 'Use the gangway on the side.' The left side as we looked towards the chaos on shore, when the officer shouts, 'You, you, you and you' me being one of the bigger lads preparing to disembark. 'Take one of those ashore with you' pointing to the deck where there were five folding bicycles one on top of another. Not believing what I was seeing, then, 'Come on, snap to it' from the 'Voice'. So off my shoulder came my rifle and bandolier of 50 rounds we began our descent into about 8 feet of water me taking a deep breath in, after seeing little Smithy's pack disappear in front of me, then his helmet went out of sight. My immediate thought was 'he's going to drown', so I let go a guide rope one of the American crew had taken ashore and tied to some object and grabbed Smithy by the back of the collar of his battledress blouse and lifted him up out of the water, until it was my turn to fail to touch the bottom, so a deep breath and I was under. When I let go of Smithy I have no idea Nick and neither have I any idea how I and others, ever made it ashore. Only God above knows as thousands of miracles happened on that day, the 6th June 1944.

'Yes I made it on to the road with the voice shouting 'Up there!' pointing up this road; then 'Evans, give that bike to my batman', thereby denying me of a nice little ride to our rendezvous so I had to footslog it, diving in the ditch as the shells and mortars were still coming over. Took the bridge intact at Vaux-sur-Aure. Nightfall, I lay back in a hollow in the high bank on the left hand side of the road, breaking some over hanging branches down in front of me, as camouflage, hoping to get the first shot in.

'The Château Sully was a few miles short of our objective. Hell let loose, 88mm firing straight down the road at us advancing, on machine gun either side as support. 36 Jones fell to the ground screaming his head off. I ran across to him to see blood oozing from his cheek, ripped open by shrapnel, his cheek bone visible. In my haste I took my own field dressing from my pocket, instead of his and began bandaging his face, to try to stop the bleeding, when 'Evans, leave him for the stretcher bearers; 'Come on, come on!' So it was back into the fray go I. Not far when 'the Voice' shouts 'B' Company. Do a right flanking'. So up the 4-5 feet bank on our right, bulldozed through the hedgerow into a field and then swinging left to another hedgerow towards the rear of the château. As we took a look from a break in the hedge, three tanks on the far side of the River Drome opened fire at us, when 'Withdraw, Withdraw!' was yelled from behind, so it was hell for leather, back the way we had come, the 88mm machine guns had been silenced. We heard long afterwards, Colonel Craddock had been wounded and some German SP or Tiger had attacked HQ, destroyed 3 carriers and radio van. This was hearsay; I was not there.

'The next day I helped search the château, walked up the drive and on a well kept lawn- on our right 8 or 9 of our lads, lying face down dead, as if it had been execution. The lad in front of me stepped on to the lawn and turned the first one over. I then did the same with the second one and recognised him as Private Blackett, now in Bayeaux Cemetery. There is no mention of this in any history I have read about Château Sully, only it was a 'small action', so why the 'BATTLE HONOURS'? On the left hand lawn (well kept) was a 'Spitfire' of ours, a notice on the wall in German we gathered was; 'the 88mm had brought it down'? No mention of that either. Some history says the Yanks were at Sully - Yes, they were 'supposed' to meet us on our right, we being the extreme right flank of the British forces. I NEVER saw a Yank from D-Day till I was hospitalized on 28/29 August on the banks of the River Seine, 2 or 3 days before they crossed, when 14 of 'A' Company got drowned trying to cross when the 'Mascaret' (Big Wave) hit them, like the big wave River Severn bore.

'From Sully next morning, the search of the Château, we were formed up and marched through Bayeaux with rifles at the slope with the people going crazy... lovely. (They still do it with me every year.) Then Ellou, Chouain, Buceels, Tilly-Sur-Suelles, Hottot-les-Bagues, Ste-Germain de Ectot, Villers Bocage, Aunay, Thury-Hacourt, Point d'Ouilly to help close the gap at

Falaise; and onto the Seine before the attack on Le Havre.

'Me, to a Canadian Field Hospital for three days then Blighty, (many wounded and dying coming in, I think). Lucky me to Burton on Trent Infirmary then Derby City Hospital, knee improves, so it is Etwall Convalescent, then Newtown Mid Wales holding battalion and training once more, fully expecting to join our 2nd Battalion. Mount Carmel as an RP not 'Redcap'. Regimental (only) Police. 'See our Boyos behave!' Then over to Cyprus - Makarios & Co, then demob; £68 Demob Pay. I ask the sergeant 'Is that all?' his reply- 'You can start your own business with that, lad.'
Bill Evans, 2nd Battalion, South Wales Borderers.

'Captain Collins' scout car was first down the ramp and it was immediately knocked out by a shell. Collins was unhurt, but Steeles, his driver, was wounded. All the rest of the vehicles, including the ARV, landed safely.

'A number of DD tanks were still on the beach, but I couldn't see whose they were. Dabby, our commander, seemed to know where he was going fairly well and in quite a short time we were off the beach, going up a track with a procession of other vehicles. There were grassy banks on either side and notices bearing skulls and crossbones and the words' Achtung Minen'.

'Before long we were in Ver-sur-Mer. We went straight through the village and out the other end. Quite suddenly, I realised that all the other vehicles had disappeared and we were quite alone, charging up a quiet country lane by ourselves. I knew this was wrong, because I had seen the orchard where we were to rendezvous on the map and knew it was on the edge of the village. I told Dabby this and had a bit of an argument - the first of many that I had with various commanders over similar things - before I managed to convince him. We· turned round in a field about half a mile up the lane.

'On the way back to the village we met Muddy Waters with the leading troop of B Squadron, advancing up the road with their infantry. They had no idea anybody had gone ahead of them. In Ver we found Captain Collins waving us into an orchard opposite the original RV which was mined. Everybody seemed to have arrived safely. One C Squadron crew was there. Their tank had been swamped on landing; they had lost all their kit and been soaked to the skin. They said it had been too rough for a DD landing and the tanks had done a deep wade instead, so all the months of DD training had been wasted.

'Captain Collins announced his intention of travelling on the ARV, until he could get another vehicle of his own. I was rather pleased as he was a decent sort of chap and less likely to get us lost than Dabby.
Trooper Austin Baker, C Squadron 4/7th Royal Dragoon Guards.

'It appeared that the main enemy fire was coming from a large... many storied house. I ordered the Churchill (AVRE) forward to demolish the house with the petard... Maximum covering fire was given by the Sherman tanks. The petard fired and something like a small flying dustbin hit the house just above the front door. It collapsed like a pack of cards, spilling the defenders with their machine guns, anti-tank weapons and an avalanche of bricks into the courtyard.'

Major Peter Selerie, Sherwood Rangers Yeomanry, British 8th Armoured Brigade.

'I was on an American landing ship tank and the skipper took us so far up 'Gold' Beach that sometimes I wonder how he ever got off. But the Germans were shelling the beach and it was early morning, just barely light and the first thing we saw was several rows of dead bodies wrapped in blankets being prepared for burial and then we moved out from the beach area to an assembly area. I was 20 years old.'

George Tuffin.

'Our job was to land on 'Jig' Beach at first light with the advance units to clear away, repair or blow up any shipping hindering landing craft and troops. Because everyone was stacked up we had to wait until late afternoon before we could go in. We passed the time playing cards and my mate Eddie and I cut each other's hair. At first it seemed like a Boy Scout outing to me. I was a bit worried and apprehensive, but I don't think it occurred to me we might get killed. We finally rode in alongside a destroyer with its aft guns blazing - the finest sight I've ever seen. Six shells dropped round our landing craft as we neared the beachhead and underwater obstacles that couldn't be seen because of the high spring tide holed the ballast tanks.

'We immediately came under fire. I will never forget the sheer noise. There was so much going on, with mortar shells banging and guns shooting all round, I went temporarily deaf. It was a warm day and so we stripped everything off. We all had to make do with cheap-looking swimming belts to keep us afloat when we jumped in the water. On the beach we were told by the naval officer in charge to get to work immediately but mortar shells were exploding everywhere.

'I crawled round to safety behind a tank that had had its tracks blown off. To my surprise, I found the tank's two crew crouched there eating tins of pears out of an 'A' Compo Box. They shared the pears with me and told me to keep my head down. Compos were officer's rations and they had the best food. They included tins of soup with heart trips down the middle. In about three or four seconds you had real hot soup. There were Compo Boxes lying about all over the place, left behind by the dead and wounded, so you just took what you found.

'After the shells stopped I joined my mate. He was sheltering against our landing craft. Soon our unit got together and did what we came to do, like digging dead soldiers out of the sand and rolling them in grey army blankets. This was the worst job. We were ordered to cover up our dead soldiers, but to leave the enemy lying, for morale purposes. There were bodies everywhere. At one point I sat down on what I thought was a log with a blanket on it. It was only when a saw a boot sticking out I realised there was a body underneath.'

19-year old commando Bill Davey, Combined Operations Unit.

'They ate 'Compo' (composite) rations: cans of 'M and V (meat and vegetable) stew, 'Soya links' triangular soya bean sausages fried in the grease they came in, fat bacon wrapped in greaseproof paper which could be unrolled like a sheet and naturally, 'bully'. Corned beef was the major component of the 'Compo ration' together with 'Compo tea', a crude ready-mix of sugar, milk and tea. The beef could be eaten cold on 'dog biscuits', the iron-hard Compo issued biscuit (bread being rarely available); it could be fried as fritters, cooked as hash, made into a stew with potatoes and onions 'liberated' from some unsuspecting French farmer's field and even pulped with the 'dog biscuits' to make a kind of crude meatball. Even the available girls were categorised according to the number of tins of 'bully' it took to win their favours. 'Char' was served to wash the meal down and was particularly prized when transformed into 'sarn't-majors char' with the help of a can of evaporated milk; this was a thick, rich, creamy, dark-brown concoction in which a spoon would stand upright and as the name suggests, it was usually reserved for senior NCOs. GS rum, issued, half a mug at a time each day to the men in the line was a great comfort too. It brought tears to the soldier's eyes and in due course removed the lining from his stomach too. Invariably when the 'Compo' ration cases were opened, some wag would crack the same weary old joke: 'Which tin's got the cunt in?'
Charles Whiting.

'We were 50 yards away and saw it all. One man was wounded. Just like a rabbit. Up and down and up they crawled to the sea wall, which had to be stormed like a Middle-Age fortress. Germans on top of the sea wall were chucking hand grenades onto our soldiers below.'
Lieutenant Irwin, Commander of a LCA assault group watching the East Yorks land and rush the beach.

'I was a soldier of the wonderful 69th Brigade; a battalion of East Yorkshire and two battalions of Green Howards - my heroes - who had already defeated the Germans. How could we lose or come to any harm? The struggle across 'Gold' Beach, the casualties, the heat, noise and exhaustion of the fight were absolutely indescribable. I know I should have died of fright alone without the calmness under fire of those wonderful fighters wearing the ribbon of the Africa Star who taught me to survive that day.'
18-year old Private Dennis Brown 5th Battalion, The East Yorkshire Regiment.

'I had been in North Africa with Monty's 8th Army. Within weeks of arriving back in England from the Middle East and in the short period before D-Day, I was to be physically thrown in at the deep end on the very secret Sherman (Duplex Drive) Tank. The DD was capable of 'swimming' ashore from two miles out using its twin propellers and yet within minutes of reaching land, becoming a fighting tank. The regiment moved to Norfolk and to Fritton Lake to prepare for the assault and by May we were in the New Forest for final training. Equipped with our brand new tanks, we loaded on board a LCT in Southampton Harbour on 2 June. I shall always remember our sailing from the Solent; we were on our way. We left in rough seas at midnight on 5 June. Many of us couldn't sleep and were violently sick.

'As dawn broke, we were amongst the vast armada of ships and crafts of all sizes and then the Naval Bombardment started; shells and rockets screaming overhead with the RAF Fighter Bombers adding to the din. The whole coast that lay ahead of us was a pall of smoke and exploding missiles. We approached 'Gold' beach and due to rough seas closed to 1,000 yards to launch at approximately 0720 hours. Action stations were called - all crews were in their places. I had 'netted in' the radio and our supporting canvas superstructure was inflated. The LCT ramp was lowered and we launched into a very choppy sea and then the shells and other incoming fire started to reach towards us but missed. I saw two of the Sherman 'Flail Tanks' brewing up on the beach and wondered about our reception. We finally grounded on the beach, engaged the tracks, deflated the canvas sides and 'hey presto' were ashore.

'The infantry of the 1st Hampshires were taking all possible cover on the beach from the withering fire from the pillboxes and the 88s on the high ground, which knocked out the tank on our right, a terrible sight to see the crew gunned down as they bailed out from the blazing vehicle. We then returned the fire from the pillbox, with success.

'At last the sappers taped off exits from the beach and we all began to move off through the sand dunes. When about 50 yards into our lane there was a loud explosion. We had hit a mine, which damaged our nearside track. We were immobile. This didn't prevent us using our fire power to shell the many targets which presented themselves in support of the advance and to try and winkle out the snipers who were proving a real menace.

'I heard on my radio that our forward units were into Le Hamel and heading for Bayeux. Orders were given for us to sit tight and await the fitters so we closed down and gave what help we could on the beach. There was considerable congestion.

'Late that afternoon, we were standing beside our tank, discussing the damaged track when an armoured bulldozer came towards us widening the beach exit. When within a few feet of us, there was an almighty explosion. All went black and I was flung through the air into a minefield. I crawled towards the shouts of the crew and they bandaged me the best they could and took me to the nearest Field Dressing Station. I spent a very restless night in the open wrapped in a blanket with 'Jerry' strafing the area. Next day it was Hospital Ship to Portsmouth.

'After treatment and leave it was return to the unit and to discover the 'Bocage' and to witness the destruction of Falaise. I was however shaken to hear that the Regiment had already lost nearly a quarter of its Tank Commanders and many crewmen. A terrible sacrifice!'

Ken Mayo, 'B' Squadron, Nottinghamshire (Sherwood Rangers) Yeomanry, 8th Armoured Brigade.

'It was rather a grey morning and I suppose we got into the landing craft at about half past five because we had to get the landing craft lowered into the sea and circle about while we formed up in our flotillas. I didn't sleep much the night before. I was rather apprehensive. I hadn't got back into the rhythm of the war; once you do, you sleep very easily, you're very tired. It was just about first light when suddenly this enormous armada of naval ships opened fire with a terrific noise. I think we passed the cruiser HMS *Ajax*, a six-inch-gun cruiser and she let go just as we were near her. [2] Very heartening if you were going the same way. We bumped around in the landing craft while we formed up for the run-in and I recollect that we'd had tea and rum put in for people to drink as we were going in. But a lot of people were feeling seasick and I think tea and rum was not the best thing.

'We had the advantage of having marvellous models of the part of the coast where we were going to land and so before we ever got on board the ship, we were able to brief everybody from the model. They were very good indeed. They had all the intelligence about the enemy - their positions and anything else that would be relevant. We knew a great deal about the beach on which we were going to land, but going in I suddenly realised that with the bombardment, there was such a lot of dust and smoke from fires, that it was difficult to see exactly where we were supposed to land. We knew where we wanted to land, but we couldn't tell where it was.

'We'd landed a good two or three hundred yards east from where we

---

2   About 3 miles to the west of Arromanches at Longues-sur-Mer was a Kriegsmarine battery of four 15cm (5.9 inch) Torpedobootskanone C/36 guns taken from decommissioned destroyers - a D-Day objective of the 231st Brigade of the 50th (Northumbrian) Division. The guns had been made at the Czechoslovakian armaments plant at Skoda, Pilzen and had a range of 12 miles that covered the approaches to the future 'Omaha', 'Gold' and 'Juno' beaches. The guns were in Type M272 casemates about 1,100 feet from the cliff and were arranged in an arc to maximize their fire zone. As with all naval designs, ammunition was kept in magazines within the casemates. At the cliff edge, a two-storey semi-underground Type M262 Observation and Fire Control bunker had been constructed. It had optical range and direction finding equipment, map room and accommodation. Telephone cables buried 6.5 feet deep ran from the OP to the guns. The battery, manned by 184 sailors, had seven personnel shelters and six bunkers with tobruks. A mortar pit was located behind the No 2 gun casemate. A flak gun was sited to cover the cliffs and as anti-aircraft protection. The whole position was protected by barbed wire and minefields. The battery was bombed on 28 May and 3 June when it received 148 tons of bombs. They did no damage. On the morning of 6 June the guns engaged the USS *Arkansas* and then switched to 'Gold' beach where they straddled the XXX Corps HQ ship HMS *Bulolo*. At 0530 hours the cruiser HMS *Ajax* moved into position and at 7 miles fired 114 shells from her 6 inch guns. Two direct hits knocked out guns No 3 and No 4 and near misses damaged the other two. Within 20 minutes, the battery was silent but half an hour later it returned fire on HMS Bulolo. After a further 20 minutes of bombardment it fell silent but resumed firing soon afterwards on Bulolo which was forced to move. Ajax was joined by HMS *Argonaut* in shelling the battery which was eventually put out of action at 0845 hours. Two of the casemates received direct hits, the shells entering the casemates through their embrasures. It had taken 179 6-inch and 5¼-inch shells from the two cruisers. During the day, the battery crew worked on No 1 gun and during the afternoon opened fire again. The French cruiser FFS *George Leygues* began a duel that lasted until 18:00 hours when the battery was finally silenced. The next day the battery's 120 survivors surrendered to 231st Infantry Brigade advancing from Arromanches-les-Bains. The battery had fired 115 rounds. *D-Day; The First 24 Hours* by Will Fowler (Spellmount 2003)/ *Hitler's Atlantic Wall* by Anthony Saunders (Sutton Publishing 2001).

should have been put down... and the leading assault company which was just ahead of us should have landed right on Le Hamel. They were supposed to have climbed the sea wall and captured the gun position which was important because it was covering the whole beach. It appeared to be some sort of anti-tank gun in a concrete and steel emplacement in an old, reinforced sanatorium.[3] This position was going to cause us a great deal of trouble. It had excellent fields of fire and the Germans in fact did not show much signs of giving up. And because the leading assault company had been swept down the coast, too, they hadn't managed to capture the gun position, so there was a lot of shooting going on and no one could really use the beach.

'We'd hit a runnel - a sand bank - coming in in the landing craft and so we went into four or five feet of water and everyone was carrying a lot of equipment and ammunition which were very heavy, so quite a few of the shorter men drowned and others were hit by small-arms fire.

'The AVREs on the beach all seemed to have been knocked out. We did not find the gaps we expected. Meanwhile the casualties were piling up because the enfilading fire was very strong and it was raking along the top of the beach where people were trying to get. I realized we should have to gap our way through ourselves, using Bangalores which we had with us. While gapping our way off the beach, I saw Brigadier Nelson Smith limping badly. He had been hit in the leg by mortar fragments as he left his LCA. He shouted, 'You'll have to take over the Battalion. I can't go on.' He was put on a stretcher and loaded back into the landing craft he had left moments before. 'A' Company, who should have landed close to Le Hamel, climbed the sea wall and silenced the opposition, had almost ceased to exist as a company. We incorporated all the people we could find into 'C' Company.

'We managed to get over the mines and so on and then I met a tank, an AVRE, a Royal Engineers' assault tank, specially equipped. This particular one had a mortar-like gun on it, called a Petard, which fired a large bomb. So I spoke to the commander of the tank. I told him I wanted him to support this attack on Le Hamel and the tank came forward and it fired the bomb into the buildings and when he did that we assaulted it and went inside and it was silenced. The Germans obviously didn't want to fight. They came out with their hands up... they all came from the 91st Division and most of them were Poles or Czechs or Russians and a few Germans. Although they gave us a pretty rough time in some of our sector, generally speaking they caved in pretty quickly. And that was a great relief to all concerned because there was a lot of landing craft having difficulties on our beach. They could now come ashore; the beach masters could get things organised rather better.

'In the fire plan, Le Hamel east was to receive the bombs of 200 Flying

3   Apart from the main emplacement, which was fitted with a French 75mm gun on a swivel mounting, WN 37 at Le Hamel comprised eight concrete pillboxes for infantry weapons (seven facing seaward and one inland), two concrete shelters and a trench system linked in with the sanatorium. It escaped damage in the bombardment because the 75 tons of bombs planned to be dropped on it by the 8th Air Force fell in fields 3,000 yards south. In addition the navigational and control vessels for the 147th Field Regiment of self-propelled artillery, which was to engage the target on the run-in, fell astern due to weather conditions. *D-Day Then and Now Vol.2* (After the Battle 1995).

Fortresses. We found out later that the bombs had all fallen 700-800 yards inland. Even the effect of 2,000 rockets from the LCT(R) did not seem to have any great impact on the very strong German defences.'

25-year old Major David Warren, commanding 'C' Company, 1st Battalion the Hampshire Regiment.

'Fancy having that lot on your breakfast plate.'

A soldier in the 1st Hampshires during the last mile to the beach, remarking on the roar of the shells and rockets during the bombardment from the ships at sea.

'With the Middle East behind me and aged 20, I felt like an old soldier. I was answering the usual question - 'What's it really like in action?' - from the ones that hadn't been. I tried for the last time to reassure 'Brakey' (18 years old), one of the young reinforcements who had attached himself to me. He was very apprehensive about going on his first op.

'On our craft we had a small keg of naval rum and a couple of bottles of whisky put there by some unknown person or authority - I never found out who - probably with the intention that we might need a little Dutch courage. One drink was enough for me. I hoped it would settle a queasy stomach caused by the flat-bottomed craft tossing about in the swell.

'Things were becoming hot now. 105s or 210s were coming in on us. There was a sharp crackling of machine-gun fire and I quickly got my head down after taking a quick look. The long line of beach lay ahead and immediately behind hung a thick pall of smoke. There were flashes of bursting shells along the whole front. We were in range now of mortar fire, a weapon we had grown to respect in the past.

'The tension was at its peak when we hit bottom. Down goes the ramp, out goes the captain with me close behind. We were in the sea to the tops of our thighs. Floundering ashore we were in the thick of it; to the right and left the other assault platoons were hitting the beach. Mortar bombs and shells erupting the sand and the brrr... br... brrurp of Spandau light machine-guns cutting through the din. There were no shouts: everyone knew his job and was doing it without saying a word. There was only the occasional cry of despair as men were hit and went down.

'To my right I spotted 'Laffy' crawling on his hands and knees with the radio floating in the water behind him. I thought he had been hit; later I learned that he was in the middle of a relapse of malaria - a legacy quite a few of us had from the Middle East.

'The beach was filled with half-bent running figures. We knew that the safest place was as near to Jerry as we could get. A near one blasts sand over me and my set goes dead (during a quiet period later on I find that shrapnel has riddled my set). A sweet rancid smell is everywhere, never forgotten by those who smell it: burnt explosives, torn flesh and ruptured earth.

'High up the beach a flail tank was knocked out. 'B' Company HQ group paused to take cover behind this mass of steel. A shell whipped in, scored a direct hit on them and they were gone in a blast of smoke, out of which cartwheeling through the air came the torn, shrieking body of a stretcher bearer - the red cross on his arm band clearly discernible.'

I. G. Holley, wireless-operator, 'B' Company, 1st Battalion, Royal Hampshire Regiment.

Private George Stunnel [of the 1st Hampshires] saw men going down all about him, but spotted a Bren gun carrier, undamaged, in about three feet of water, its engine still running and its driver 'frozen at the wheel, too terrified to drive the machine on to the shore'. Stunnel pushed the driver to one side and drove the little vehicle ashore, only to be pitched violently to the sand as a German sniper's bullet whacked into the tin of duty-free cigarettes in his blouse pocket. 'Minutes later, he discovered that he was bleeding from wounds in his back and ribs. The same bullet had passed cleanly through his body.'

British Liberation Army 1944-45 **by the late Charles Whiting.** [4]

'There was no doubt in my mind that to launch these crack troops would have even worse results than the charge of the Light Brigade at Balaclava.'

Lieutenant Jim Tuffell, commanding a LCT carrying DD tanks of the 4th/7th Royal Dragoon Guards. 231 Brigade, which was to capture 'Jig' sector to the right (and 69 Brigade 'King' on the left) attacked on a two-battalion front with the 1st Hampshires on the right and the 1st Dorsets on the left. Fire from strongly defended positions at Le Hamel and Asnelles-sur-Mer and a smaller strong point near Les Roquettes covered 'Jig' Sector. Defences at La Rivière and Hable de Heurtot on the coast protected 'King' Section. Higher ground inland had defences at Mont Fleury and Ver-sur-Mer, whose capture was the task of the 6th Green Howards. Le Hamel presented a formidable target for the Hampshires. The beach was flat and sandy, bounded by a belt of low sand dunes. A gentle slope led to the sea wall of German 75-mm guns overlooking the shore. These were to enfilade the entire beach. Machine gunners and riflemen were stationed in every building overlooking the shore.

'What, Bowers, you still alive?' [Lieutenant Colonel Smith] said.

'Just about, sir,' Bowers said; and he told him about the pillbox.

The Colonel, lying in the sand, badly wounded in the arm, listened and then Bowers understood him to say, 'Well, go and see what you can do about it.'

'Very good, sir,' Bowers replied: and he thought, 'Christ, he expects me to take on the whole bloody Jerry army.' [5]

36-year old Company Sergeant-Major H. W. Bowers MM MiD was among the veterans of the Hampshires. A Cornishman, a regular with 17 years' service, the son of a soldier, was not only an old soldier; he was almost an old hand at assault landings, for the landing in Normandy was his fourth. His first had been the invasion of Sicily and the next two were on the Italian coast. All the way over, his stomach had been doing what he called the Butterfly Hop. He had felt the

4   Spellmount Ltd, 2008.
5   Lieutenant Colonel Smith, twice wounded close to the beach, had to be evacuated.

same on his way to the other landings. The trouble was having too much time to think. He knew he would be all right when he got his two feet on dry land... Besides that lurking fear... his British army ammunition boots were killing him; what he meant to win was a nice pair of German boots to give his feet a rest...'

Bowers, armed with a Sten gun, some British hand grenades and a haversack full of Italian grenades, set off for a gap which the tanks had made in the sea wall, to outflank the pill-box from the rear. In the gap he met Paddy and Taffy; two sailors of the RM Commando that had been with him on the landing craft. Glad of their company and of their Tommy guns, the three men worked their way across devastated space behind the seawall, fighting it out with some Germans who threatened to take them in the rear and won a position behind the pillbox, close to the ruins of the sanatorium. A grenade thrown at them rolled along the ground. Bowers shouted 'All right, it's a dud': whereupon it exploded and wounded Paddy in the leg. The others patched him up. Bowers put the two commandos in a position to cover the pillbox with their Tommy guns and under the protection of their continuous fire he climbed into the ruins and through them. He found an empty window above the pillbox and jumped down on to the roof of it. He ran across the roof and lay down on his stomach and leaned over the edge with a grenade in his hand. Through the firing slit below him, somebody was pushing a white sheet of surrender, but he thought 'Hell with you, mate, after all this trouble,' and he dropped his grenade through the slit. After the explosion, the door of the pillbox was opened and the survivors ran out. They had their hands up. Bowers looked down at them with interest, partly because they seemed to be shouting that they were Russian and also because some of them were wearing nice soft German army boots. [6]

'One minute you would be seeing your mate and talking to him; the next you were having to put a field dressing on him, realising it was too late and being thankful it wasn't you.'

Sergeant (later Battery Sergeant-Major) Robert 'Bob' E. Palmer MM who commanded No.1 gun in 'F' Troop, 511 Battery, 147 Field Regiment, Royal Artillery (Essex Yeomanry), which was equipped with Sexton SPs and was part of 8th Armoured Brigade attached to the 50th (Northumbrian) Division, which despite its name, was entirely made up of south coast regiments. During the day Bob was responsible for the destruction at Asnelles-sur-Mer of an 88 mm gun in an enormous and very strong emplacement, an anti tank gun and two heavy machine guns, each in a fortified house. The 88 had already accounted for six British tanks. It held up the advance from the beach until it was destroyed at a range of 300 yards by a 25 pounder SP gun commanded by Sergeant Palmer, who was awarded the Military Medal and was decorated by General Montgomery at a small place called 'Jerusalem'.

'There was quite a shambles on the beach. Out of 'B' Squadron's nineteen

6   *Dawn of D-Day.*

original tanks, only five were still mobile. We paused on the outskirts of Le Hamel and were overtaken by one of the AVRE Churchill tanks armed with a Petard that looked like a short and wicked piece of drainpipe sticking out of the turret. It appeared that the Sergeant commanding it was the sole survivor of his troop. He joined our five tanks and confronted the back of a pillbox that housed an 88-mm gun firing along the beach. The gunner dropped a petard through the back door and blew the place up. We noticed a stream of enemy fire coming from a many-storeyed house. I ordered the AVRE forward to demolish the house with the petard. Maximum covering fire was given by the Sherman tanks. The petard fired and something like a small flying dustbin hit the house just above the front door and it collapsed like a pack of cards, spilling the defenders with their machine guns, anti-tank weapons and an avalanche of bricks into the courtyard.'

Major Peter Selerie, 'B' Squadron, Sherwood Rangers Yeomanry, 8th Armoured Brigade. The AVRE gun was a 290-mm mortar, which fired a 40lb projectile. Only the Sherwood Rangers Yeomanry achieved their D-Day objective in capturing Bayeux on the morning of 7 June, with the assistance of the Commander of the AVRE Sexton tank, which opened the way.

'You had the feeling of what am I doing here? Of all the thousands in uniform, how come I'm right at the front of what we knew was the biggest assault in history. There was another misgiving, which was more or less general that we would not return. This produced a deep calm, something observed in others.'

Canadian, Lieutenant H. Foster, serving with the Dorsets.

'We had to move across the sand at some speed so that the 'Deballiker mines, which were designed to pierce between the legs, only hit one in the fleshy part of the behind. Most of us had seen men shot before but nothing like the damage done by Spandau fire and 88s. Men were blown apart and in the case of machine gun fire, men were hit a dozen times at once - not a chance for them to live. We had been trained in most all aspects and actually pretty well knew what to expect. However, it was not enough to bolster you for this kind of carnage. I took a few minutes on the beach to comprehend, adjust and move forward. Some did not…'

An officer in the Dorsets.

'Blimey! This is where you need you seasick tablets. The little LCA is being tossed about all over the place. We are packed in like sardines, all standing; all thinking that any moment now it will capsize! Except those being sick and I don't imagine they care very much. Off we go. I am rather thrilled and my confidence and spirits are quite high now. About 100 yards from the beach, the bloke in charge of the LCA called out 'Sorry lads, this is the best I can do. Mind how you go off the ramp as it might crush your feet: Well, off we went; bedroll on shoulder, kit on back, rifle slung around neck and fingers crossed!

'The water struck cold at first but I soon forgot that in frantic efforts to keep my feet. The sand was like a quagmire underfoot. As you put one foot down, you had the devil's own job to get it out. And when you did, you kept your balance by a miracle. Although the water probably wasn't more than four foot deep, the shell holes and bomb craters made it eight feet deep in places. The beach itself was a shambles, guns, tanks, landing craft and scores of vehicles either floating around, stuck in the sand or burnt out. Houses and factories just inland bombed or burned, rows of bodies covered with coats or blankets; Jerry prisoners insolent as ever marching down to the beach as we staggered up. It looked just like the main road to Hell!'

Sergeant Mackenzie, Royal Signals.

'Five mighty cruisers were silhouetted against the streaks of light where the sun would soon rise. I don't think I have ever seen anything so impressive; it thrilled me through and through. 'Slowly the vessel nearest us brought its powerful guns round. Then - Boom! Boom! Two resounding crashes. They sounded to me as if they said, 'WE'RE HERE!' for they were the first shots fired in the invasion. Then all the other ships opened fire and it became one series of ear-splitting salvos after another…I think that night was the most dreadful one I have ever been through…In the dawn half light, our task completed, we were free, more or less, to steam up and down, having a good look at everything. There was a terrific bombardment at one end of the bridgehead and when we got there we found two battleships firing away for all they were worth. We were right up close to one - so close we could even hear the sigh of the shells as they left those massive guns. Just before dusk, in the distance, we saw one solid mass of aircraft; wave after wave of troop transports towing gliders - hundreds and hundreds of them. I have never seen so many aircraft all at once. They seemed never-ending and stretched far back into the distance…We sweated blood when we first went in, but it was very exciting too. None of our ships was affected by mines so we knew we had done our job properly.'

Ronald Scott, 20-year old radar operator, on the minesweeper HMS *Ready*, part of the 18th Flotilla which left the Solent on 5 June, in a letter home to his family.

'In the early hours of 6 June, about 0500 hours, on the warning of the invasion we were ordered to Criel, just outside Paris. There in all haste our Dodels were prepared and we took off at about 0930 hours for our first low-level attack on the landing fleet in the English sector of Caen-Bayeux. The landing craft provided excellent targets for the aircraft of our 1 and 3 Staffeln.

'On the evening of the first day we only had three serviceable FW 190s. Hauptmann Huppertz landed at about 2000 with eight FW190s of his III Gruppe. Together with the three aircraft of our I Gruppe, he was going to lead an attack on the beachhead and upon freight-carrying gliders. From our I Gruppe flew Leutnant Eickhoff, Oberfähnrich Bär and myself. We took off shortly after 2030 and approached at low level the great road bridge over Risle, west of Bernay. There we saw twelve Mustangs shooting-up a German supply column. We were too late to help, so Huppertz led us away in a left turn at about 1,200 metres. We headed for a light evening haze. It was then that we saw the other 'Indians'. We dodged away from eight Mustangs and then we caught four more. I got mine in a high reverse turn as he approached the bridge. He fell on fire into a wooded bank on the Risle and set a tree on fire. I then observed Huppertz and his Katchmarek attack another aircraft. The fire was devastating and the Mustang disintegrated. Eickhoff and Bär each scored an Abschuss. Alter landing at Senlis, two reporters sent in confirmation of our victories, for they had seen the whole battle.'

Leutnant Wolfgang Fischer 3/Jagdgeschwader 2. Fischer's combat career ended abruptly on 7 June, when his FW 190 was shot down by AA gunfire while attacking shipping off the British beaches. He survived to become a prisoner. His commander, Herbert Huppertz was credited with five Mustangs destroyed on 6 June.

'At four o'clock this morning we had gone to surface action stations. Those on the flag deck reported that targets inland were getting a very heavy battering from the RAF. We were then moving slowly down the swept channel towards our bombardment position. The Commander reported that the sweepers had made a much wider channel than was expected and we'd have room to manoeuvre (audible sighs of relief!). At 0510 *Orion* was the first cruiser to open fire. Good old *Orion* - always first there! Our shooting was very good and direct hits were soon being recorded. We scored thirteen direct hits on the battery before shifting target. The other cruisers were all ripping away - *Belfast* was firing tracer.'

Ian Michie in the 6-inch cruiser HMS *Orion*. WN 34, the battery near Mont Fleury chateau at Ver-sur-Mer was shelled by *Orion* which hit it twelve times. 3/HKAA 1260 did not return fire. [7]

'Just as it was getting light, a bombing attack was delivered inland of King Sector and fires which appeared to come from Ver-sur-Mer and La Rivière could be clearly seen. Apart from some flak, there was no enemy opposition of any sort, although it was broad daylight and the ships must have been clearly visible from the beaches. It was not until the first flight of assaulting troops were away and the cruiser HMS *Belfast* opened fire that the enemy appeared to realize that something out of the ordinary was afoot. For some

7   Like so many batteries along the Normandy coast, it was still under construction at the time of the invasion. Only two casemates had been completed and only one of these had its 122mm gun installed. The casemates had been constructed using prefabricated concrete blocks to make the inner and outer walls between which concrete was then poured. This speeded up the process but produced weaker structures. *Hitler's Atlantic Wall* by Anthony Saunders (Sutton Publishing 2001). Major Anderson of the Special Observer Party landed on D+6 to assess the damage inflicted by Allied naval and air bombardments. His appraisal of the Mont Fleury site showed that although the casemate housing the battery's only operational gun had been hit by a 500lb bomb the gun was undamaged. He believed that the gun had successfully expended all its ammunition although he conceded that the bombardments had seriously impaired the efficiency of the battery. His assessment of WN 34 at Ver-sur-Mer showed that while the air raids had been on target only one machine-gun was damaged. A 50 mm anti-tank gun in an open emplacement was undamaged despite a 1,000-pounder exploding so close that the rim of the crater was a mere 15 feet away. Few of the bunkers had been damaged and none significantly. *Hitler's Atlantic Wall* by Anthony Saunders (Sutton Publishing 2001).

time after this the anchorage was ineffectually shelled by the enemy coastal battery situated about three-quarters of a mile inland in the centre of King Sector. Shooting was very desultory and inaccurate and the guns of only 6- to 8-inch calibre.

An official observer's report of the pre-assault bombardment, which he described in his official record as 'tremendous'.

'I was the junior officer in a troop of four self-propelled guns. Our role was to bombard the beaches from the sea (the run-in shoot) and then go ashore behind the first wave of infantry. We opened fire at 0650, closing on the shore at the rate of 200 yards per minute and landed at 0805 in support of 69 Infantry Brigade. We landed just below the Ver-sur-Mer lighthouse and in front of the dreaded Mont Fleury Battery. The 6th Green Howards attacked this gun position with great gallantry and CSM Hollis won a VC. On their left the 5th East Yorks took the lighthouse and by 0900 our guns were clear of the beach and deployed in this area. By nightfall the brigade had advanced seven miles to come within sight of the Caen-Bayeux road. We spent the night in Crépon preparing a fire programme for the dawn counter-attack. The beachhead was secure.

'The sun went down three times that day. And we were very young.

Lieutenant Basil Heaton, 86 (Herts Yeomanry) Field Regiment, Royal Artillery. Many outstanding acts of gallantry were performed. Two Victoria Crosses and ten American Medals of Honor were awarded between D-Day and D+12.

'...We had several skirmishes during the day but the talk that night was inevitably of the gallantry of our Sergeant-Major, Stan Hollis, who subsequently was awarded the only D-Day Victoria Cross.'

Lieutenant John Milton, 6th Battalion The Green Howards.

'We had to take a coastal battery at Mont Fleury. I was in charge of a group of two-inch mortars laying down smoke but I noticed that two of our platoons, running up to attack the guns, had gone past a pillbox. This was only about a foot above the ground but I spotted a Spandau machine gun in the firing slit. I went along with my company commander, one of the bravest men I know. They fired at us, but, once we were on top of the box, grenades and Sten guns killed some of them and when I went down inside with my Sten gun I got half a dozen prisoners. It was a big place, two storeys deep and we got all of the equipment intact. So that made things just a little safer for the rest of our company in their attack.

'The fighting all through D-Day was fairly warm and one piece of trouble we ran into was on account of some dogs I noticed at the end of a country lane. There was nobody there but the dogs were wagging their tails. When I went along with the major we found a German field gun supported by machine guns in a farmyard. Elements of 'D' Company attacked from some farm buildings but every time our lads got up to the next wall they were knocked out by machine guns. I tried to get the gun crew with a mortar but they started blazing away with the gun at a hundred yards, open sights and big stones were flying all over. The gun concentrated on one of our Bren groups and things looked bad for them, they couldn't get back, so I tried again with a Bren and this time the German boys got so worried they left our lads alone and we all got back safely.

'Now these don't sound like VC affairs and I don't know if they really are. I do know it was the sort of thing that was happening all over in the first five days in Normandy and jumping into a pillbox full of Germans wasn't so wonderful when you saw your own lads fighting like heroes every side of you. And when you saw lads you knew dropping dead, you wanted to do something to smash the guns that had done it. Just after we were out of the water on D-Day I saw one lad go down wounded; now he saved my life in Sicily and he comes from Middlesbrough too. That sort of thing makes you forget to be scared. I've always been scared when we've gone into action - with the BEF at Dunkirk; Alamein to Sicily - but if your lads see the sergeant-major's got his head down, well, it's a bad do, isn't it? So that's the way it goes and things like snipers' bullets on your cheek and being blown out of trenches and looking into German gun muzzles, they don't count as much as you'd think when you've got men like that round you.

'I'd like them to know that their telegram was the first I'd heard about the VC. I've sometimes heard that chaps who get medals inspire the other men. It wasn't like that in my case. My officers and men, they inspired me.'

CSM Stanley Hollis 6th Battalion, Green Howards.

'During the assault on the beaches and the Mont Fleury battery CSM Hollis's Company Commander noticed that two of the pill-boxes had been by-passed and went with CSM Hollis to see that they were clear. When they were twenty yards from the pill-box a machine-gun opened fire from the slit and CSM Hollis instantly rushed straight at the pill-box recharged his magazine, threw a grenade in through the door and fired his Sten gun into it, killing two Germans and making the remainder prisoner. He then cleared several Germans from a neighbouring trench. By his action he undoubtedly saved his Company from being fired on heavily from the rear and enabled them to open the main beach exit. Later the same day, in the village of Crepon, the Company encountered a field gun and crew, armed with Spandaus, at a hundred yards' range. CSM Hollis was put in command of a party to cover an attack on the gun, but the movement was held up. Seeing this, CSM Hollis pushed right forward to engage the gun with a PIAT [Projector Infantry Anti-tank] from a house at fifty yards' range. He was observed by sniper who fired and grazed his right cheek and at the same moment the gun swung round and bred at point blank range into the house. To avoid the falling masonry CSM Hollis moved his party to an alternative position. Two of the enemy gun crew had by this time been killed and the gun was destroyed shortly afterwards. He later found that two of his men had stayed behind in the house and immediately volunteered to get them out. In full view of the enemy, who were continually firing at him, he went forward alone using a Bren gun to distract their attention from the other men. Under cover of his diversion the two men were able to get back.

Wherever fighting was heaviest CSM Hollis appeared and in the course of a magnificent day's work he displayed the utmost gallantry and on two separate occasions his courage and initiative prevented the enemy from holding up the advance at critical stages. It was largely through his heroism and resource that the Company's objectives were gained and casualties were not heavier and by his own bravery he saved the lives of many of his men.'

Citation, CSM Stan Hollis, Green Howards, the only man to win the VC on D-Day. Stan Hollis died in 1972. When his widow sold his VC at auction it fetched £32,000, a record at the time for this distinguished decoration.

'Monday 5 June passed with an awful tension although somehow we had loads of fun whistling to Wrens on the dockside. At 2100 we were issued with seasickness pills. That was enough. We knew by morning we should be in less peaceful waters. That evening 501 weighed anchor and slid slowly down the river into sailing position. We sat on the decks, looked towards the shore, still calling to any female that could be spied, but behind all these joking habits, much deeper thoughts passed through the minds of everyone aboard.

'As darkness fell, we went below decks and lay on our bunks fully clothed. Outside the wind was howling even more as we turned out to sea. I dozed off before we really turned on full steam, only to be awakened by a horribly sickly feeling inside. 501 was rolling in every imaginable direction, the seasickness pills had failed if ever anything did fail, there was only one thing to do that was to lie still, even that was dreadful and only served to make one feel worse.

'Time passed. I felt more ill than ever before. It was beyond dawn and it was only a few hours before we must engage an enemy of unknown strength. About 0500 I made a supreme effort and crawled on deck. The Yankee sailors manning every gun were dressed in sheepskin clothing and all carried a revolver as only a Yank dare wear it, Hopalong Cassidy style. The lovely fresh air on deck was worth a million pounds. The scene was unforgettable. Over a vast expanse of the Channel there were ships of every type - from small Naval MTBs and Landing Crafts to HMS *Rodney* and her escort. Overhead an array of the immense power of the RAF roared through the skies, each and every plane heading for France. The sea was rolling and in the morning sunlight it was a picture that could not be forgotten. I was on deck less than half-an-hour. Looking at the sea only served to send me back to lie on my bunk.

'The rough sea complicated the landing. Around 0700 we were ordered to dress with all kit. We were below decks wondering what was going on. Heavy naval gunfire could be heard. 501 had landing ramps, which dropped down from her side into the sea, or the beach where it was possible for her to nose far enough in. It was when these ramps dropped we knew the voyage was over. We scrambled up on deck. The kit we had was terrific. Our waterproof jackets came up to one's chest from one's feet. I tore these as I struggled on deck. Only a matter of yards away was the French coast but it was too far to keep dry. As

we scrambled along 501's decks, naval personnel were shouting, 'Get ashore!'
Ships were everywhere like a traffic jam. Down the ramps we went but this
only led into the ship in front, across its decks. Then came ten horrible yards
between ship and shore with water in between. Over the ship's side, still dizzy
from seasickness and into water 4 feet deep, each one let out a gasp as the water
swirled around. We struggled for shore. It was the hardest ten yards I ever did
but we all got ashore, mighty thankful to be off 501 and her terrible motion,
even if the harbour was the beaches of Arromanches. It was a Godsend that all
this took place with nothing more than heavy naval gunfire. It became apparent
that the enemy had been taken by surprise, at least in our particular section of
the attack. One thing was supreme; the water had brought me round like a
footballer's magic sponge. Seasickness was gone. We were ashore. After five
minutes re-grouping as a battalion, I saw a German soldier for the first time.
The lads who beat us ashore were bringing him in as a prisoner. The last few
hours had brought us 80 miles from Southampton to what was to become one
of the greatest beachheads ever.

'The surrounding scenery in Normandy is famous for its narrow country
lanes, small villages and corn fields, which were waving in a sea breeze as we
pushed along a lane leading from the beaches inland, our bikes being very
useful. I'm afraid a lot of us had a cowboy complex as we rode along armed to
the teeth. We reached the high ground without incident and from here one
could see a perfect view of the bay with its vast array of ships of all shapes and
sizes. It was just after this that we came under fire in earnest for the first time.
Strangely enough, it was not enemy fire. We were pushing along done the lane,
all keyed up and expecting almost anything except what happened. Overhead
came a flight of fighter planes, from the Channel and heading over France -
RAF fighters. As they zoomed overhead, they peeled off one by one and
machine-gunned the column. This was far from pleasant and we dived in all
directions, as bits of dirt were flying everywhere. It was over as quick as it
started and we pushed on with nerves that had been somewhat stirred. It was
later that we learned that we hadn't come through without loss. The price of
victory had been paid and a little cross sprang up in Normandy.'

**Eric Broadhead, 9th Battalion, Durham Light Infantry, 151st Brigade
aboard LCI(L) 501.** HMS *Rodney* **a 16 inch gun battleship, part of the
Bombarding Force reserve, left the Solent at 0253 on 7 June and ran down
and sank LCT 427 en route for 'Sword' then 'Juno'. On 11 June** *Rodney* **and
another reserve battleship,** *Nelson* **arrived off the beaches and pounded
targets ashore until 18 June.**

'We sailed from Southampton in the early evening of 5 June and were soon in
very choppy water. I had been many thousands of miles on troop ships, but
had been unable to overcome my sea sickness, so the crossing was a misery for
me personally. We, the officers, tried to persuade the men to get some sleep,
but for the same reasons we could not sleep, neither could they. And the
conversations that went on during the night were many and varied. I don't
remember too much about them, but as we were second flight and not assault
troops, most of the people aboard seemed to be wondering whether the leading

troops would have cleared the beach and established some type of beachhead, because we were not equipped for close combat, bearing only personal arms. In my case, it was a simple .38 Webley pistol. Hopefully, we expected to be able to wade ashore and establish temporary rallying points behind the beach so that our vehicles could be told where to go immediately after driving ashore. I spent some time with the skipper of the LCI on the bridge during the night. Fortunately, the night was warm and fairly quiet. There was also plenty of hot, sweet tea which Private Blair my batman had rustled up somewhere.

'Our voyage was running on schedule. We were due to land at about 0730, so about an hour beforehand we donned oilskin waders tied with tapes under the arm pits. The LCI slowed down but we could see nothing in the direction of the shore. Everyone became edgy because of the unexpected lack of noise. Gradually the coast came into view and there was still no firing, shooting or other action. Suddenly there we were, nosed onto 'Juno' Beach, at a village called La Riviere. The ramps went down on each side of the ship and we were off. As Private Blair stepped off the ramp into the water carrying the front end of the Airborne Motorcycle, he tripped on something under water and stumbled, allowing the bike's engine to dip under water. Fortunately, I was still on the ramp and I was able to cling onto the bike like grim death and eventually between the two of us, we got the bike ashore. Of course the magneto was soaked in salt water and by all the laws of science, the engine should not have started, but start it did at the first kick. I told Blair to stay and keep the engine running for fifteen or twenty minutes until it had dried out. In the meantime I removed my waders which had split in the water. Incidentally, Blair's had not. My boots, socks and clothes below the waist were completely soaked. I had no handy change of clothes so everything had to dry on me. Fortunately, again the day was warm and I did not suffer unduly.

'Time was rolling on, so I established B Echelon in its correct location and found the MTOs [Motor Transport Officers] of 8th and 9th DLI in their proper places and made sure they understood their orders. The MTO of 6th DLI was not to be found although we knew he was ashore somewhere, because he had been seen earlier on. By that time the bike had dried out and so I rode it inland and located Brigade Headquarters about a mile from the beach, reporting to the Brigade Major and Staff Captain that we were ashore. I had to hurry back to the beach because it was about time for our vehicles to start coming ashore. While I was strolling up and down trying to work out what was happening, I met General Montgomery. He spoke to me and asked if I was still doing the same job as when we met on the beach in Sicily, just under a year before. I explained my job and he moved on his way, humming to himself and distributing cigarettes to anyone who wanted to take them.

'Happily, our vehicles started to arrive just then and I satisfied myself that they were being well received and directed by the unit representatives. I noticed with great pleasure that our mess and cooks' truck had arrived. I held them for a few minutes while I made sure everything else was working properly. And, then I went with them back to B Echelon, where Private Blair had some somewhat sad news for me. I had left my rucksack with him and he had begun to unpack it for me, upon which he discovered that the bottle of

Johnny Walker red label scotch whiskey had broken and soaked the towel and ruined the 200 'Gold' Flake cigarettes, staining everything it touched a bright yellow from the cigarette wrapper.

'It was by now early evening and as phone lines had not yet been laid, I went to Brigade HQ for last orders of the day and finally returned to B Echelon quite late at night. I found it to be well organized and I went to sleep in a bivouac put up by Private Blair, who was already asleep somewhere else. That was my D-Day.'

Captain William John Arnold, Durham Light Infantry.

'As I was standing on the top of the ramp, we hit an underground mine that exploded and blew the ramp up and made a hole in the sand. They'd issued us with oilskin trousers, which came right up to your chest, which you tied up with a string. When I got in the water I couldn't touch the bottom and I started to float. The air was trapped in the trousers and the bubble rose up to my chest and I became buoyant and I started turning over. Just then the trousers burst and I sank back into the water.'

Captain Eric Hooper, Motor Transport Officer, 9th Battalion Durham Light Infantry.

'Some of us, including myself, had to carry a folding bicycle, the idea being that we'd rush off down the road as soon as we landed. I also had a spare battery and some extra Bren gun magazines to generally help out so that we'd have sufficient ammunition when we got on the other side. We were given a good supply of condoms with which to waterproof things like grenades; I think all officers had two grenades. Watches, compasses, they all went into condoms. Separate ones. We had a very heavy load to carry and, in addition to that, the final part, they gave us huge waders which went over our boots and up under our armpits, over the equipment, over everything, the idea being to keep us dry going ashore. In common with certainly a number of other officers and probably quite a few of the men, I was in fact wearing my pyjamas under my battledress; the reason being that it prevented chafing.

'…The LCIs started going round in tight circles towards the beach and when they were within striking distance, they peeled off one at a time, rammed their prows into the beach and then the next LCI would come alongside it and ram in there and so on - and it worked like a charm. The prow of our boat went into the shingle and the American sailor lowered the ramp and I knew exactly what I had to do. I was to walk off the gangway and on to the shingle and get off the beach quickly because a lot of shelling was expected. I went down, manfully I hope. I stepped off the ramp into the water. The water rushed over my head and I went straight to the bottom on my hands and knees. The prow was smashing into the shingle next to me and I watched it smashing against my legs and arms whenever it came near me. My waders were full of water and I couldn't get to the surface. I threw away the bicycle that I was carrying. Then I started to tear at the waders and I managed to get them off. I unfastened my webbing and slipped that off and eventually I landed on Hitler's Fortress Europe on my hands and knees, wet through, very frightened and completely unarmed.

'We were intent on just getting through, getting away from the beach, the emphasis being that we must get to Bayeux. Nobody wanted to stay on the beach because we knew that it wouldn't be very long before German artillery ranged on it or German bombers came. We were expecting a real humdinging do and I don't think I was alone in wanting to get away from that particular spot as quickly as possible.'

Lieutenant William Jalland, Platoon Commander, 8th Battalion, Durham Light Infantry.

'I watched these tramp steamers firing bloody great big rockets. They were absolutely blasting the hell out of the beaches. The beaches were cleared really when we got there, the way these things had been going in. It was the first time I'd seen rocket-launchers used.

'Morale was getting pretty low then. People were getting sick and spewing. The smell when you went downstairs, where the men were trying to lie in the bunks with their equipment on - the smell was vile. Chewing gum was supposed to stop you from being seasick - but in fact it made you worse. The handiest things were the spew bags, because you could take them and throw them over the side. I was so nervous, I hadn't eaten anything for two days so there wasn't anything to come up. The orderly corporal came up as I was leaning over the side. I said, 'Good morning. Where's the parade state?' (the book with all the company details).

'He said, 'Here's the bloody parade state/throwing it over the side. He continued, 'This is our fourth bloody do. I wish I was off this bastard.'

'We would have gone into the water, anywhere rather than be sick.

'After a couple of tries, the ship got within 200 yards of the beach and stuck fast. A young American sailor swam ashore with a rope and some of the beach party hung on to it. We stepped in. The water was out of our depth for the first 100 yards. By hooking on to that rope, we got every man ashore. If it hadn't been for the rope we wouldn't have done it, wearing gas trousers and some of us carrying bikes. When we got to the beach the gas trousers were full of water, like balloons. There we were standing like idiots trying to undo the tapes which had shrunk tight. If there had been any opposition on the beach the battalion would have been wiped out.

'When we were finally off the beach, we met up in a 'hide' where we had a self-inflicted wound in 'D' Company. I heard a rifle shot. An old fellow of forty, a bundle of nerves, had shot himself in the hand. I said, 'You've shot yourself, you bastard!' He said, 'I'm sorry, Sergeant-Major. I can't go on.'

'It's all right,' I said. 'Leave your rifle there. Get yourself back. You've been hit in the hand.' I wasn't going to court-martial him. [8] 'From the hide we moved off on our bicycles, trying to keep at the pace of the battalion. We'd used the bikes to

---

8   By the time General Eisenhower made his first tour of inspection of the Normandy front, he was shocked to find that one hospital contained over one thousand cases of self-inflicted wounds. Some rubbed diesel into their chests in order 'to produce an incurable rash which would result in their being sent home. Some shot off their fingers. Some concluded mutual self-mutilation pacts, shooting off each other's toes at a distance to avoid the tell-tale powder burns which revealed that a wound was self-inflicted; others solved the same problem by firing at themselves through a sand-bag or a load of bread. Older men simply 'lost their false teeth - for according to the 'Book' a man who couldn't eat properly couldn't fight. See British Liberation Army 1944-45 by the late Charles Whiting. (Spellmount 2008).

get to the hide and they'd been useful, but cycling at a marching pace was pretty hard work. So when we stopped, I attracted the attention of a passing tank commander. I asked him to do me a favour. 'What do you want?' he asked.

'Run over them bloody bikes. With your track,' I said.

'Run them over?' he said.

'Aye,' I said, so he just ran them over. And then I said to my officer 'The bikes have gone, sir!' 'The bikes have gone?'

'Aye, the bloody tanks have run them over' and he said, 'Oh well, if you haven't got a bike, you haven't got a bike.'

Company Sergeant-Major William 'Bill' Brown, 'D' Company, 8th Battalion, Durham Light Infantry.

Order of Battle 'Gold' Beach
50th British (Northumberland) Division
Major-General Douglas Graham

69th Infantry Brigade
5th Battalion The East Yorkshire Regiment
6th Battalion The Green Howards
7th Battalion The Green Howards

151st Infantry Brigade
6th Battalion The Durham Light Infantry
8th Battalion The Durham Light Infantry
9th Battalion The Durham Light Infantry

231st Infantry Brigade
2nd Battalion The Devonshire Regiment
1st Battalion The Hampshire Regiment
1st Battalion The Dorsetshire Regiment
Divisional Troops
HO 50th Infantry Division
61st Reconnaissance Regiment, RAC
357th, 385th and 465th Batteries, 90th Field Regiment, Royal Artillery
99th and 288th Batteries, 102nd Anti-Tank Regiment, Royal Artillery
233rd, 295th and 505th Field Companies, Royal Engineers
235th Field Park Company, Royal Engineers
2nd Battalion The Cheshire Regiment (MG)

Units under command for assault phase
8th Armoured Brigade
4th/7th Royal Dragoon Guards
Nottinghamshire Yeomanry (Sherwood Rangers)

24th Lancers
56th Infantry Brigade
2nd Battalion The South Wales Borderers
2nd Battalion The Gloucestershire Regiment
2nd Battalion The Essex Regiment
Elements of 79th Armoured Division
2nd County of London Yeomanry (Westminster Dragoons)
2 Troops 141st Regiment, RAC
6th Assault Regiment, Royal Engineers
86th and 147th Field Regiments, Royal Artillery
394th and 395th Batteries, 120th Light Anti-Aircraft Regiment, Royal Artillery
73rd and 280th Field Companies, Royal Engineers
1st Royal Marine Armoured Support Regiment
47 (Royal Marine) Commando
GHQ Liaison Regiment
Beach Groups
2nd Battalion The Hertfordshire Regiment
6th Battalion The Border Regiment
Plus elements of:
Royal Corps of Signals
Royal Army Service Corps
Royal Army Medical Corps
Royal Army Ordnance Corps
Corps of Royal Electrical and Mechanical Engineers
Corps of Military Police
Pioneer Corps

'The regularity with which large formations of our own aircraft of every type flew over reminded one of Clapham Junction during a Bank Holiday week-end'.

Wing Commander A. H. D. Livock, controller on HM LSH (Landing Ship, Headquarters) *Bulolo* **which arrived off 'Gold' Beach at 0556 on 6 June. Originally,** *Bulolo* **was built in 1938 for Burns, Philip as a small luxury liner running between Australia and the South Seas. 'She had the reputation of having cost more per foot than any other merchantman' wrote the author of** *Half Time,* **Anthony Kimmins (William Heinemann Ltd 1947). 'Even now, stripped of all her luxury apartments, she was still very comfortable and made an ideal HQ ship for landing operations' (***Bulolo* **had been as used as the HQ ship in Operation 'Torch'). She was damaged by a bomb near the operations room at 0605 on 7 June and her upperworks were superficially damaged when rammed by** *Empire Pitt* **on 15 June.**

'…It was a bit bumpy in a flat bottom LCT and then the Padre came on board and told us that we were not landing until the morning (6 June), blessed us and left. I sat in the Carrier all night waiting for dawn. At first light I stood up in my seat and looked at all the ships. We seemed to be marking time. The day passed slowly, as we didn't seem to have much to say to each other, another day being tossed about. We all said, 'Roll on morning.'

'As Tuesday dawned there was a flurry of activity. Sitting in a Bren Carrier the field of view was limited but I could see planes overhead. Then at last we started a square run for the beach. Suddenly there was a big bang from the stern and we started to go in at an acute angle and then when the ramp went down, the matting was washed along the beach. The first carrier drove off on the angle and turned turtle. We drifted a few feet then the boat marshal waved me to go out. I stood up on my seat and said that the tank was supposed to go next. He said, 'Bollocks', get out now', so I shut my eyes and eased off the ramp with my heart in my mouth. As the next bit had been practiced so often, I carried on as a drill, over the sand, through the gap, onto the beach road, turn right, forward a few yards and wait for my gun crew to join me. This they did eventually. My sergeant, Lofty Dawson, said, 'Get the waterproofing off.' While I did this he joined the crew in the ditch. I asked Lofty what the puffs of smoke were all over the sky.

'Airbursts', he said.

'What were they for?' I asked. When he said that they were shrapnel shells, I shrank as low as I could to finish the job without being too big a target…My D-Day was a very long day. I had no watch but time just seemed to stand still.'

Private Ken McFarlane, Anti-Tank Platoon, the 1st Battalion Dorset Regiment, 231st Infantry Brigade, 50th Northumbrian Division.

'Prior to D-Day we had done lots of training manoeuvres - we knew exactly what we were going to do. We were all formed up, in and around Fordingbridge, waiting to go. We were crewed up, gunned up and, what's more, sealed up. We had fitted various chutes on the tanks so that they could take what they called a six-foot wave. We had spent weeks and weeks filling each crevice with plastic stuff which was similar to plasticine. Wherever there was a join, it had to be filled and the guns and gun turrets had to be closed and sealed. They called it 'feathering'. In preparation, we had been issued with Rhinos. They were huge platforms fitted with engines to control them. The idea was that we would come off the LST and then get on to the Rhino. This was in case the LST couldn't get close enough to the beach. We had to practise driving up the ramps and on to the middle of the Rhino and stopping there. It wasn't easy, as you can imagine, because these Rhinos would tip up in the water. None of the tanks fell off them, but they nearly did.

'As it happened, we lost the Rhinos on the way over. They broke away from the tow. There they were, floating in the Channel. I've no idea where ours went. Fortunately, we didn't need it; our ship went inshore as far as it could, where the water was just a couple of feet deep.

'We were all ready to go on the 5th, but the weather was bad, so it was cancelled. We were completely fed up. Then the message came across 'Advance' - and it was a wonderful sight. There were ships coming up here, ships going up there, all in arrow-head formations, heading towards specific beaches.

'As we went over, the Navy were running up and down the beaches with their rocket ships, clearing the beaches for us before the landings. I noticed a hospital ship - she looked lovely at night because of all the Red Cross lights. We were under air attack - they would keep nipping in - but they didn't bomb her at all.

'When we got in on the beaches, the Beachmasters shepherded us off the LST and then up the beach. We had a little bit of an explosive charge to unseal the equipment and after that we could operate the guns. The beaches were all mined and we had to follow the white tapes showing where they had been cleared - but the worst thing was the snipers.

'Anyway, I didn't last very long. An 8lb mortar came over and hit the top of the tank and, of course, we all got blown to the bottom of it. It was all down with sympathetic detonation, which means that the power with which we were hit set the ammunition off around the tank. There was a round up the gun and the pressure set that off. I was in the way of the recoil which came back and smashed my arm up. We managed to crawl out and the medical people were soon with us in a half-track. They brought us up forwards of the beach where all the medical tents were.

'They put me in the compound where I was waiting for about a day and a half before they got me on to the hospital ship. There were quite a few young Germans on the ship - two of them refused to be attended to and died.'

Charles Wilmot a Tank Commander with the 24th Lancers who landed with his men at Arromanches beach.

'We knew that we were destined for France when we were issued with French money. Our vehicles were waterproofed, our Bren Gun Carriers had extra sides a metre in height fitted and all were loaded to the hilt. My carrier was filled with .303 ammo, 2 and 3 inch mortar bombs, petrol in jerry cans and a roll of wattle fencing tied to the front. We sailed on 5 June and on the morning of the sixth we approached 'Gold' Beach (Jig sector). The tide was so strong we drifted over towards the Canadian sector and landed broadside against the obstacles which had mines attached to the tops. The ramp was lowered and we could see bodies of the commandos who had gone in ahead of us to clear the mines. On being given the order to disembark I drove off, turned left and reached the beach safely although two carriers were immediately drowned in deep water. We pushed on up the beach amid the chaos and the noise of the naval bombardment and the rocket barrage, which was really terrifying. We were ordered to keep going forward and we made our way down the country roads. As we turned on to the main road we hit a mine on the grass verge which knocked out a front bogie, nobody was injured so we shortened the track and drove on. We pushed on until the evening when we regrouped at Le Hemel with the Battalion Mortar Platoon and the Anti Tank Platoon. On the seventh we pushed on to Port-en-Bessin to help 47 Marine Commando who were having a bad time. By the eleventh we had reached the crossroads at La Belle Epine where I was directed towards an apple orchard. I reached the orchard and on turning into it came face to face with a dug in Tiger tank. That was the lot for me. When I came to I was in hospital in Basingstoke in England.

'I was one of the first in on D-Day and there were bodies all washed up on the beach. How we got on the beach I don't know. It makes me wonder why I am still alive. Why wasn't I one of those who was killed?

Private Reginald 'Punch' Burge, 2nd Battalion, The Devonshire Regiment.

'None of our boats got ashore. They all got shelled or a lot got holed, there were things like railway tracks buried in the sand and when it was high tide, the craft just ran into them. There was water pouring in everywhere... we had a rough time getting on to the beaches... I reckon we lost about a hundred on the beaches... we never got to our full strength again after D-Day. Most of the men were drowned... at least I think they were, but at the time you don't get to look around you. You have your objective to get to and it wasn't until we'd been ashore for some time that we realized that we'd lost our troop commander to start with and a lot of officers. We were being fired on all day long... sniper fire and mortars. I've got to give them their due; the Germans were good mortar men. They'd put their mortar on a sixpence... you couldn't get out of their way. If one of your own soldiers gets shot, they just go down and you think to yourself, 'Well, that's that and there's nothing I can do about it.' It happened many a time: a man next to me would get shot and killed... they are your friends, your mates, but you gotta keep going, you can't stay. When you're shot nobody stops with you. You make them comfortable, you sit them up and give them a cigarette and a drink of water if they want one, but you couldn't stay. There weren't enough men. Nobody would stay with the wounded; that was up to the medical orderlies and the doctor and the padre. When you get shot you're on your own.'

Corporal Gordon Tye, 47 Royal Marine Commando that landed on 'Gold' with the objective of taking Port-en-Bessin by D-Day+3. A link with the Americans on 'Omaha' was made on 8 June (D+2) after 47 Commando had taken Port-en-Bessin, for 200 casualties.

'We beached - I can't remember how far out, but we had to jump into the water, which came up roughly to our waist. As we were wading ashore I became aware that the bombing had left craters in the water, which you couldn't see. Some of my mates walked into these craters and, because of the weight of their packs, were drowned. We got whatever cover we could underneath a wall, because there was still considerable enemy fire-power coming from land. In no way could you possibly advance until these troublesome pillboxes had been destroyed. We lay there in our wet trousers with water oozing out of our boots for what seemed ages. Eventually the pillbox on our right was silenced. That was where I saw my first dead Germans. It was gruesome. I thought really those chaps had probably been called up for service like myself and had no wish to be where they were. They didn't stand a chance, really, not there. What could they do? Nothing, really.'

Sergeant Norman Travett, 2nd Battalion, Devonshire Regiment.

'The Marines, who had been awoken from their slumbers very early, so they could put the final polish to their buttons and check over their equipment, seemed in no hurry to leave us. It soon became clear why. As soon as the way off was clear, the NCO fell them in, dressed them by the right, turned them into line - but instead of then marching them off at the double, as one might have expected, they were stood at ease. At this point, they all took their steel helmets off and replaced them, from their kit, with their normal peaked caps, ignoring our suggestion to, 'Chop, chop!' The right-hand marker then changed his helmet for a top hat and a raised umbrella. Called to attention, they marched off and up the beach to start their job. The inspiring result of this transformation was that large numbers of others, dashing about, paused as they saw the marching Marines. They seemed to be saying to themselves, 'Why am I rushing?' and slowed down. This action by the Marines had a calming effect on all.'

Sub Lieutenant Frank Thomasson RNVR aboard LCT 1192.

'In our tank landing craft, we went about a mile in, opened the bow doors and eight DUKWs went off towards the shore. Then twelve tanks, which had flotation buoys on the side and a propeller on the stern, went off. There was still a little swell and one or two of the tanks went straight to the bottom. Poor sods. Later we unloaded the rest of the tanks and equipment and waited for the ambulances. They brought three or four hundred wounded men straight on board for us to take back to England. It was busy but for me, being a youngster, it was exciting. There was more excitement than fear. You just felt that this scene was amazing. It took your breath away.'

Able Seaman Peter Thompson aboard LST 304.

'The atmosphere in the tank as we hit the beach was a little bit tense because we were battened down and I was the only man that could see. Shells and bullets were coming across the top of us. My co-driver was sitting behind me asking me what was going on and could he have a look. My main concern was the infantry that were lying on the beach. I only had this little visor to look through and I didn't know if they were dead or not, so I had to pick my way through.'

Corporal William Dunn, 26th Assault Squadron, Royal Engineers.

'We cleared the beaches straight after we hit them. Unfortunately, some of the infantry, who'd landed along with us, started to dig in. It seems that was what they'd been taught to do, as part of their training. Well, that wasn't what we'd been taught to do. Our idea was to get the hell out of it as quickly as we could. One of our officers shouted at these chaps, 'For God's sake, don't dig in here. You're going to get shelled and mortared. You're going to be counter-attacked. For God's sake, get clear of the beach.' The infantry chaps didn't know what to do but they followed us - which was probably just as well, because it cleared the beaches for other people to land and bring in supplies. No-one wanted the beaches cluttered up with holes and infantrymen...'

Private Peter Fussell HQ, 1st Special Service Brigade Commando.

'We could hear firing in the distance as we approached the shoreline, which we reached at about 0500. I remember remarking at the time on the absence of an aircraft though one did appear, dropped two bombs and flew off in a hail of anti-aircraft fire from our ships in the vicinity. I asked one of the crew if the plane was a Stuka? In a very broad scouse (Liverpool) accent he said, 'It were and I just shook my fist at him and said, 'You did not get me at Liverpool or London and you ain't going to get me yet and with that the beggar missed!' I remarked that with this sort of spirit we were going to win this war.'

QM Sergeant Robert Fitzgerald aboard a LST.

'I'll never forget the chaos and awfulness of landing craft returning out of control, full to almost sinking with a red mixture of blood, water and oil fuel, with legs and heads sticking out. One or two came alongside. We hauled the wounded out, mostly Canadians and Marines and placed them in their awful suffering along the upper deck, doing what little we could. The wardroom was turned into a ward, so was the entire forehead mess deck - bottles of plasma tied up and hanging over nearly every man - the doctor and his assistants of stewards and stokers doing wonders.'

Sub Lieutenant John Pelly RNVR in the bombarding destroyer, HMS *Eglinton*.

'We grounded and dropped the ramp. We were a hell of a way off the shore and the waves were coming by the side and I thought they were pretty bloody high for shallow water. I said, 'We're not in shallow water, here. We're in deep water, you know!' and this sub-lieutenant said, 'We've grounded!' All sorts were going on all around us but we were in our own little world. We started arguing about the depth of the water and so he called for a stick that he put in the water and said 'Four foot six'.

'I said 'You must be bloody joking! We're in deep water! We're on an obstacle!'

'No we're not!' he said. 'I'm in charge of this ship! I'm the captain!'

'Stupid sod. So I went to my chaps and I said, 'This is going to be a bloody wet landing.'

'One of the crocodiles was first off and went straight down. All you could see was the schnorkel and the top of the turret, so the water must have been about ten feet deep. One recce vehicle was next and turned right. It went straight out to sea. We never saw it again. The next recce vehicle turned left. It got ashore safely. The armoured bulldozer went straight down. One wheel on the trailer caught the chain on the ramp, tipping the trailer over into the water. Men fell off, the trailer floated away. One of my signallers, bomb-happy since Italy, huddled under his gas cape shaking like a jelly. It was not his fault. It's one of the worst wounds there is. The naval officer said he was returning to England for repairs, nothing would persuade him to change his mind.

'I hailed a nearby LCA and he came to the ramp. We loaded our stores, including the Brigade rear link set on its trolley. I left the bomb-happy signaller behind. The LCA pulled in to within six feet of the beach, the ramp went down and a sailor said we are among mines. I told them they would be all right. But they pulled off.

'An LCT was approaching, with her ramp already down and we hailed her. We transferred. Despite the obstacles, up the beach he goes. Down goes the ramp. At last we've made it. On arrival, I found I had the whole of the Battalion communications on my shoulders.

'All along the beach, there were men lying dead and not just in the waves. Some of them still had their tin hats on. A lot of them had been overridden by their landing craft as they came off. The landing craft became lighter as men came off and as it surged up the beach, any man that was in front went straight underneath.'
Signal Sergeant James Bellows, 1st Battalion the Hampshire Regiment.

'The beach was completely deserted as we approached and I remember being puzzled by the comparative silence. At every step we expected to be fired at but were not. The lack of opposition became eerie. Then, after about 200 yards, we must have reached a German fixed line. Suddenly they threw everything at us. The mortars took us first and I was hit badly in the leg. My radio operator and policeman were both killed outright by the same explosion.'
Major R. J. L. Jackson, 6th Battalion the Green Howards.

'A young naval officer addressed us over the Tannoy and told us that the shoreline along 'Gold' Beach was planted with steel girders with mines attached. He added that when he was a few miles from the shore, he intended to 'put his foot down' and get us as close to the beach as possible. 'Meanwhile, gentlemen, get some sleep; I'll let you know when.'

'Hear this! Hear this! 'I realised I must have dozed off. How, I don't know, for the noise was tremendous. It came from the battleships all around us and the shells and rockets that were firing towards the beach. Two hundred yards, 100 yards. Then crash! Our craft came to a shuddering halt amid a loud explosion. A jeep that should have been first off was no more. In its place was a gaping hole in the deck. The ramp went down. With the engine of my Bren carrier roaring, I rammed it into first gear, let off the brakes and shot over the hole into the sea. Its tracks gripped the beach and we moved slowly forward. An eternity then fresh air. On the shore, Hagerty, one of my crew, was looking dumbly down at his leg. His foot had been blown off. This was our first casualty. This was the invasion of Normandy.'
Private Reg Shickle, 2nd Battalion, The Cheshire Regiment.

'What seemed impossible has really happened! The English have landed on the French coast and our little village has become famous in a few hours! Not one civilian killed or wounded. How can we express our surprise after such long hours of waiting in wonderment and fear?

'We got ready in spite of being still very upset and afraid and got to the Villa St Côme. From there what a sight met our eyes! As far as we could see there were ships of all kinds and sizes and above floated big, balloons silvery in the sun. Big bombers were passing and re-passing in the sky.

'Nothing has changed at Arromanches but at Ste Côme up to as far as Courseulles one could see nothing but ships. It is marvellous and an unforgettable sight - a very consoling sight for the sufferings of the last few hours. Whilst we were waiting at the villa we could see tanks and armoured cars passing on the road to Asnelles and coming towards us across the fields we saw a file of soldiers. Going towards the village were the famous DUKWs, a sort of boat which can sail on the seas and travel on land.

'Finally we go back home, leaving the civilians to show the way to the English soldiers through the garden of the villa to Belle Vue on the cliff, as they must see if there are still German soldiers hiding there... the English had thought that all civilians had been evacuated from the coast and were very surprised to find the inhabitants had stayed in their homes in spite of the fierce fighting of the landings.

'Our little church had received a direct hit on the roof and fire broke out, but with the help of the villagers it was soon overcome. Guns were firing on the big blockhouse between Belle Vue and Arromanches and the underground trenches leading to the munition stacks belonging to the Germans. Soon all was wiped out. What a noise everywhere and smell of burning!

'We return to our rooms and from our windows see a file of tanks passing through the fields opposite on their way to Bayeux. Are we dreaming? Is it all really true? We are at last liberated... It is just 7 pm. The weather is lovely - we only hope other villages will soon be liberated and finally the whole of France. We are wondering how Radio Paris will announce this arrival of our Allies. What lies are they going to tell?

'...the enormous strength that all this war material represents is fantastic and the way it has been handled with such precision is marvellous and our Allies say it is not yet the real landing. This will come in about ten days' time! The noise continues overhead and in the surrounding fields where the soldiers are busy exploding the mines. A group of Tommies pass and ask us for water. We fill their bottles, say a few words and, having given chocolate and sweets to the children, they continue on their way. It is very hot...'

Madame Genget's diary records the joy and happiness that she found in that day of liberation.

'I was a soldier of the wonderful 69th Brigade; a battalion of East Yorkshire and two battalions of Green Howards - my heroes - who had already defeated the Germans. How could we lose or come to any harm?

'The struggle across 'Gold' Beach, the casualties, the heat, noise and exhaustion of the fight were absolutely indescribable. I know I should have died of fright alone without the calmness under fire of these wonderful fighters wearing the ribbon of the Africa Star who taught me to survive that day.

18½-year old Private Dennis Bowen, 5th Battalion, The East Yorkshire Regiment, which captured La Rivière.

'As we began unloading the first men, casualties were sustained. Orders were for all wounded to be landed on the beach. There was one soldier being helped by two others, his left foot and boot as one, in a mangle of flesh and leather. I shall never forget the almost apologetic look he gave me as he passed by. A landing craft shot alongside us and on to the beach with its cargo of tanks ablaze and ammunition exploding. The air was alive with bullets and shrapnel. As I ducked back into the wireless offices, we sustained a direct hit. The smell of cordite and the cries of wounded men came from the packed No. 3 troop space, where the shell had exploded, leaving wounded and dying men. As we disembarked the rest of the men, our skipper shouted down the voice-pipe for me to see what was happening in No. 3 troop space, as it had to be cleared. As I was halfway down the ladder, a soldier said, 'Come and help my mate, Jack.' I replied, 'You better get off quick, all the rest have landed.' He replied, 'I can't - my leg has had it - help my mate.' The water was pouring in so the wounded were in danger of drowning. I went to his mate and I saw that his leg was hanging off below the knee, so I opened the tin of morphia ampoules and jabbed one into his thigh with the attached needle. Turning back to the other man who was semi-conscious, I undid his webbing and tried to set him on the seat next to his wounded mate. He was a big chap and his gas mask kept catching under the seat. I said, 'Try and help yourself, mate,' but all I got was a vague, incoherent mumbling. I finally got him seated and saw that both his legs were shattered below the knees, so I jabbed a needle of morphine into each of his thighs.

'By now, some other crew members had arrived in the troop space and the task of getting the dead and wounded up to the deck above began. One soldier looked all right at first, but a closer look revealed a hole of about one inch in diameter behind his ear. He just sat dribbling in a semi-haze. We got him and the rest of the casualties put aboard a destroyer, which carried a medical officer. We had only one wire stretcher, so most of the wounded were carried up the ladder, one man supporting the shoulders with his hands under the arms and one man supporting the legs. Not the most satisfactory way of handling wounded men, as the one supporting the shoulders would be kicking the wounded man in the back as he struggled up the ladder. One of the men I was helping must have had internal injuries, for his face was a leaden colour and he just sighed and gave up the ghost as we reached the top of the ladder. The dead and wounded were placed along a narrow passage on the port side and the wounded were kept as comfortable as was humanly possible.'

Petty Officer Alan Higgins, Telegraphist, Royal Navy.

'On the 5th June we signed for 200 francs and then we knew where we were going. This we received in the transit camp. The marshalling area was behind a Polish fighter aerodrome in a wood, under canvas. We passed the time away playing cards or listening to the wireless. Some of the lads had their hair shaved off to ward off lice. Shaving the head was a good idea but after we had been in action a few weeks some of them got wounded and were flown home, so the first thing they had to buy was a flat cap.

'Orders came to move out and we made our way to Newhaven Dock where we boarded our LCT. We spent four or five hours on board waiting for the tide, then we were away at about 11 pm. The sea was a bit rough and lots were seasick below decks. To put it mildly it was a complete shambles. I spent most of the night up on deck talking to the sailors and eating tins of treacle pudding and rice pudding. Daylight came at last and what a sight. Ships as far as you could see, in front, each side and bringing up the rear, each altering course every three minutes. Everybody was told to stand to on deck. Behind the door at the front, catwalks on the side of the ship were ready to be dropped in the sea for easy access and we were told to disembark as quickly as possible. The ship would then turn round and head back.

'As we neared the beaches we could see buildings in ruins and the harbour wall was breached from recent bombing by the RAF. The place was Ver-sur-Mer, 'Gold' Beach. By now the noise was deafening, mostly from the warships and our tanks, which were landing and exploding the waterproofing which covered them. Machine guns were cracking all the time and ricochets off the ship were like wasps buzzing round. The ship stopped, the beach was 50 yards away, the doors were opened and the catwalks were lowered. Out we went in about 8 feet of water, swimming a bit. I was fully clothed, with a full pack and a Bren gun resting on the pack with pouches full of ammo. We hit the beach and we moved on up the road. Our destination was a field at Coulombes, a small village where we could change our trousers; our dry trousers were round our necks. The whole battalion had their trousers down. Off we went towards Bronay which was in contact with the enemy. We approached Dudy-Ste-Marguerite towards the main railway line from Bayeux to Caen when Jerry opened up on us from outside Audrieu before we crossed the railway line, so we were held up for a while. Then the enemy withdrew and we dug in for the night, or as it turned out, for a couple of days, while the 25 pounders and the RAF softened up Cristot.'

21-year old Lance Corporal Geoff Steer, 'B' Company, 1/4th King's Own Yeomanry Light Infantry. At the end of June Corporal Steer was among those taken prisoner by the Germans in Holland. It was the end of his army career, one he had chosen instead of working in a coal mine. He was incarcerated at Stalag IVB between Leipzig and Dresden.

'Every morning after roll-call we would gather in the recreation part of the hut. Then an officer would come in and guards would be put on the doors to watch out for the Jerries, while he read the news from the day before, from the BBC. One day we were asked if we wanted to go out to work. About twenty five of us said yes, what work was it? They told us it was a jam factory. Well, that sounded OK, so we said yes. The next day, getting our few belongings together, we said goodbye to our mates in the hut and we were marched out of camp. We boarded the train and off we went, once again a very slow journey. This was on a Friday, a day I shall never forget. It was dark when the train slowed down and stopped. We were having a bit of shut eye when the Jerries started shouting for us to get out of the train. When we opened the door we were out in the country. No station. They told us it had been bombed. Out we got and fell in, ready to move off, which we did, across the fields for about three miles till we came to some brick buildings with barbed wire around. We had arrived at our new destination. We asked if it was the jam factory, but they said no, it was a coal mine.'

Chapter 2

'Juno'

ABOARD A BRITISH DESTROYER OFF BERNIERES·SUR·MER, June 6 –
Guns are belching flame from more than 600 Allied warships. Thousands of bombers are roaring overhead, fighters are weaving in and out of the clouds as the invasion of Western Europe begins.

Rolling clouds of dense black and grey smoke cover the beaches southeast of Le Havre as the full fury of the Allied invasion force is unleashed on the German defences. It is the most incredible sight I have ever seen.

We are standing some 8,000 yards off the beaches of Bernières-sur-Mer and from the bridge of this little destroyer I can see vast numbers of naval craft of all types.

The air is filled with the continuous thunder of broadsides and the crash of bombs. Great spurts of flame come up from the benches in long, snake-like ripples as shells ranging from 16 inches to four inches find their mark. In the last ten minutes alone more than 2000 tons of high explosive shells have gone down on the beach-head.

It is now exactly 7.25 am and through my glasses I can see the first wave of assault troops touching down on the water's edge and fanning up the beach. Battleships and cruisers are steaming up and down drenching the beaches ahead of the troops with withering broadsides. The guns flash and great coils of yellow cordite smoke curl into the air. Great assault vessels are standing out to sea in their hundreds and invasion craft are being lowered like beetles from the davits and head toward the shore in long lines. They are crammed with troops, tanks, guns and armoured fighting vehicles of all types.

The tin hatted British and Canadian forces in this sector are cheerful and smiling as they go in. A tank landing craft has just passed with the crew of one tank sitting on top of the open hatch. The tank is named 'Warspite' and the crew give the thumbs up and grin at us.

Conditions are not ideal. A fairly high sea is running and the sky is overcast and dark clouds scurry across the sky. Bombers are passing over in their thousands; we cannot see them, as they are well above cloud level, but the air reverberates with the thunder of Fortress engines. We can see the bombs crashing down on the German gun positions and defences just inland of the first assault troops.

Just ahead of us lies the little town of Berniere-sur-Mer. We can see the spire of Berniere belfry rising out of the swirling smoke. Some German shore batteries are opening up on us but their fire is ineffective and ragged. Away on our port beam a Hunt class destroyer is having a ding-dong duel with one battery and great coils of water plunge up round her as the German gunners try to find their mark.

From the bridge of this destroyer, commanded by Lt-Comdr. Norman B. Muirch of Dawlish, South Devon, I have had a grandstand view of every phase of the operation.

As we plunged through the swirling grey waters of the Channel on the last stages of our trip last night we heard the roar of aeroplane engines as wave after wave of airborne troops passed overhead. Seas were running high and many of the little tank landing craft we were escorting were shipping it green.

It was just after four o'clock when we reached a position some 18 miles off the coast of France. The night bombing was in full swing and from that distance we could see enormous blood-red explosions and hear the rumble of the bursting bombs. One great fire started up with flames shooting high into the air in the vicinity of Pointe de Ver, on the Berniere-sur-Mer beach section.

Events then moved rapidly and I will put on record the diary kept on the bridge. It was cold and wrapped in duffle coat s and thick mufflers we watched the dawn come in and the invasion start in all its intensity.

0507- Lying eight miles from the lowering position for invasion craft.

0518 - Spitfire with cropped wingtips skims low over our deck.

0520 - Grey light of dawn. The great shapes of innumerable assault ships appear smudgily on our starboard beam. A 1ittle M.T.B. follows on our wake, obviously off his course, a young signalman stands on the bridge and flashes, 'We are lost, please direct us to such and such a beach.' We put him on his way with a friendly wave of the hand.

0527- Night bombing has ceased and the great naval bombardment begins. The wind is high and from our position we can hear little sound.

0533 - We move in slowly. Coastline becomes a thin smudge of grey.

0536 - Cruisers open fire on our starboard bow. We can now recognise Belfast and Mauritius. They are firing tracers and we see the shells curving in high trajectory towards the shore.

0545 - The big assault ships start lowering their boats crowded with tin-hatted Tommies. I can pick out Prince Henry, Glenairn and the Queen Emma.

0546 - There are at least one thousand ships of all sizes in our sector alone. Naval bombardment intensifies. Big battleships join in. On our port bow we see Warspite, the 'old lady' of Salerno fame, belching fire from her 14-inch guns. Orion, Mauritius and another cruiser, the Black Prince, are belting away with all they have got. Fleet destroyers are darling round us. Everybody seems to be there. 'What a party,' I hear the captain say. 'I wouldn't miss this for all the tea in China.' I agreed with him. It is something so terrific. So gigantic, that no Hollywood director could possibly equal it on the screen. An unbelievable sight.

0550 - I saw the first flash from a German shore battery. Above us we hear the sweet drone of our fighter cover, sky cloudy, but fairly high ceiling. Four Spitfires pass overhead. So far not one enemy plane has put in an appearance. But it is yet early. We shall see. It appears we have taken the enemy by surprise.

0555 - On our port beam I can see a thin line of stout tank landing craft heading towards the shore. Grey mine-sweepers who have been close inshore sweeping are returning. They have got plenty of guts these fellows.

0600 - The coast is by now clearly visible. Enemy batteries are opening fire spasmodically. Sky is now dull red herring bone. Cruisers continue to belt away, taking on shore targets. One of Britain's brand new Captain Class frigates passes us, her battle silk ensign proudly flying from the after-mast. The bombardment continues and by now big fires are burning ashore. Clouds of black smoke rise hundreds of feet into the air.

0630 - Whole Invasion fleet is now waiting just seven miles off Courseulles.

0650 - The Fleet destroyers now close the shore, bombarding any target they can see. A string of tank landing craft pass us. The Tommies sitting on the turrets of their tanks wave to us as they pass and give the thumbs up. Weather is worsening, sky is turning grey and big clouds are coming up. Spitfires and Airacobras roar overhead.

0700 - First wave of Fortresses come in. Their wings gleam through small patches of clouds. Mostly they are invisible. The roar of the Fortress engines, coupled with the crump of bombs and the crashing of shells, is terrific. The coastline is by now covered with palls of smoke. One pattern of bombs flattens out the beach section opposite our destroyer. An inferno of battleships, cruisers, monitors and destroyers are giving the enemy all they've got.

0720 - It is by now quite light. I can see the spire of the Bernier belfry. We are 9,500 yards from the shore, still closing. The town is covered with smoke. Buildings appear to be smashed and crumpled.

0725 –The first wave of landing craft have reached the shore. I see them touch down. Red tracers from close range enemy weapons are searing across the beach. Men leap out of the craft and move forward. Tanks follow them. By now everything is an inferno. Fortresses have moved their bombing behind the beach-head and continue to plaster the Germans. One little destroyer on our port beam starts a duel with a shore battery. I see splashes from the German shells as they fall wide of the mark.

0735 - We move out on patrol. It is too early to know how the initial landings have gone. But they were made to split second according to time-table. The battle goes on.

Desmond Tighe, Reuters correspondent for the Combined Press, aboard the British destroyer *Beagle* off Bernières-sur-Mer. (No Airacobras were flown on D-Day).

'Knee-deep in water aboard a holed and sinking tank-landing craft, sailors and soldiers feverishly baled with buckets, pans - anything they could get lay their on - in their determination to get the craft, with its precious cargo of tanks, to the French shore, only a few hundred yards away. The story is told by Desmond Tighe, Reuter special correspondent aboard the destroyer Beagle, who watched the landing-craft, towed by a small minesweeper, pass close by.

'I don't know who the young skipper of the landing-craft was' he says 'but if any man had done his job properly in the assault, he certainly had.'

Describing the beach battle as he saw it from the *Beagle* Tighe says:

'Away to the southwest British destroyers are bombarding. Through our glasses we can see German tanks deploying on the beaches just before the sea wall. A stubborn battery on the cliff tops, just to the right, keeps up intermittent fire and the shells are sending up large sprays of water round then destroyers. But the destroyers fight on like greyhounds, darting in and plastering the enemy gun positions. Inland pillars of smoke show where stubborn artillery battles are being fought. We can see lines of Allied tanks and trucks moving slowly over the winding roads across the green fields and hills.

'The climax came when we watched the second wave of glider-borne troops soaring in over the area. They came in hundreds in one endless stream, flying incredibly low. The sky was black with them. As the navigating officer said: 'They look like birds migrating to the Continent.'

'Bales sinking craft to get tanks ashore', *Daily Mirror* Thursday 8 June.

'Captain M. L. Power told the assembled ship's company that our target was some 6-inch shore-based guns, the position of which was known exactly from air reconnaissance. There were some larger guns and possibly some shore-based torpedo tubes, but these would be looked after by the cruisers and battleships and that we must not be distracted from our allocated target. He also told the ship's company that the six destroyers in the flotilla would he anchoring for accurate bombardment about two miles off shore with the anchors on the 'slip' for quick getaway. If after firing a few salvos there was no response from the shore defences we would raise anchors and again anchor accurately closer in. If we were badly hit he would beach the ship and 'whatever happened - if the bridge or gun Control got shot away' we were to keep on firing under local control if necessary.

'HMS *Kempenfelt* led her flotilla in some time before the invasion fleet arrived. Early morning mist was around but it was only shallow, as a steeple and water-tower were all too clearly visible at that range, sticking up through the mist... The First Lieutenant looked up at the gradually clearing shore and said cheerfully 'La Belle France!' The anchored destroyers then fired several salvos without any reaction at all from the shore, so according to plan the anchor cables were connected up and a new position taken up close in shore...Still there was no response. Rocket launchers 'wooshed' off their rows and rows of rocket salvos. Invasion barges passed through and it was not until they were touching the sand that the sparks of rifle fire could be seen coming from all the windows of the buildings along the sea front. We wished we could lower our urns and flatten them, but we continued to fire at our allotted Shore Battery positions - and got not a single shell back. After the experience of Anzio and the build-up we had been given it was quite an anti-climax...'

E. J. Thompson aboard the destroyer HMS *Kempenfelt*, **a gunfire support vessel in Assault Convoy J10 escort.**

'We arrived off Normandy at first light. The Channel was full of ships and we could see lots of puffs of smoke on the coast. We were in touch with twenty-nine planes on D-Day - British, Canadian, Polish, whatever. They found German gun emplacements and we directed fire on to the targets. We were firing beyond the range of the guns. By moving water and fuel from one side to the other, we were able to tilt the ship to give us a higher angle of sight and a longer range. We engaged targets from Courseulles to Ouistreham and were able to reach Carpiquet aerodrome, the airport for Caen. That was quite an effective shoot, I believe.'

Captain Douglas Munroe, Royal Artillery, aboard the Royal Navy's latest cruiser, HMS *Diadem*, **fresh from her Newcastle shipyard and equipped with eight 5.25 electronically controlled guns.** *Diadem* **bombarded the battery at Moulineaux behind 'Juno' Beach and kept her station off the British beaches for three weeks, firing 3,800 rounds from each gun and literally wearing out the barrels.**

'We moved into position in Southampton Water to depart for Normandy with HMS *Isis* as our destroyer escort, at 1230 hours on D-Day. We arrived at anchorage 'Juno' off Ste-Aubin-sur-Mer at 1830 hours. One hour later the ships proceeded to anchorage 'Sword' off Ouistreham to report to Flag Officer, Force 'S' where the LSIs were to marry up with the rest of the naval force for the decision as to which coastal battery was to be assaulted. 'At 2200 hours the order was received that both operations were postponed, the reasons being: 1. Neither battery was harassing our shipping. 2. The weather was considered unfavourable. 'On receipt of this order, the LSIs returned to anchorage 'Juno' for the night.

'At 0600 hours, 7th June, a signal was received that the Unit was to come under the command of I Corps and would be landed at Bernières (The Canadian Division Sector) at all speed. Hasty adjustments and improvisations were made to equipment and personal loads for going ashore at 0900 hours.

'Thus a unit of very angry young men were deprived of the assault on either of the two coastal batteries for which they had trained so hard and the commando was landed on 'Nan White Beach' to join up with our comrades in 4 Special Service Brigade.'

Reg Bettiss, 46 Royal Marine Commando.

'It was nearly six in the morning, time for milking the cows and I had to fetch the milk from the farm where I worked... I had gone about a hundred metres when I saw a bare-headed man crossing M. Emile Poret's meadow. I continued on my way while watching this person. It was definitely a German soldier. He had lost his helmet and his rifle and one of his puttees trailed along the ground (not all Germans were equipped with jack-boots). After cautiously approaching the road, he crossed it a few steps behind me and went through the hedge to disappear in M. Andre Lefevre's pasture. It was just at this moment that a flash of light rose up behind the houses and a cloud of smoke went skywards. For a moment I was shell-shocked and paralysed... The large explosion which caused this was that of a half-track of the Somua type which was full of ammunition for the German 88mm battery. One could still hear some small secondary explosions.

'...my mother came to tell me that some soldiers who did not look like Germans had been seen at the turning by the church. Very quickly I sorted myself out and after making myself presentable joined my father in the street. Three hundred metres away, coming round the church bend, some soldiers were advancing in Indian file. We were in no doubt that these were not German soldiers, who had become very familiar to us since 1940. The soldiers advanced slowly along the length of the stables at M. Andre Lefevre's farm. The first ones, arriving at the bottom of the hill, were hidden by it for the time being. My father and I decided to go towards them. While doing this we listened and looked to the right and the left, but we were sure that there were no more Germans in the vicinity. Since the morning we had seen everything that had gone on.

'I was all eyes looking at and admiring the soldiers. They were sunburnt and their faces were blackened by dust and smoke. I was amused to see them apparently chewing the cud. I was soon to know well and taste for myself what was in fact chewing gum. I also would learn that the little packet they carried under their helmet nets was a personal emergency bandage. At the top of the sleeves of their khaki uniforms was a badge saying: Regina Rifles Regiment. It was a regiment from Saskatchewan, which in Red Indian language means Golden Earth. On average they were tall and solidly built. They didn't tremble apprehensively as the Germans did. Their quiet assurance and the personal strength and resolve which they showed indicated that they were fighting in a just cause which would lead to victory. What a contrast to the Germans! The truth hit us that things had changed and that these Canadian soldiers already carried an air of victory.

'The absence of Germans in the vicinity having been confirmed, the mood became more relaxed and something happened which is difficult to describe but it was very intense all the same. Everyone realized that the great event had happened - we were liberated! Four years of occupation were over and the defeat of 1940 was forgotten. Men's voices were changed by the emotion and their eyes shone while the women came out of the houses with flowers to express their gratitude to the liberating soldiers.

'In return, the Canadians took from their pockets packets of cigarettes, sweets and little bars of chocolate, which they passed among us. I smoked my first 'Sweet Corporal'. They continued to arrive at the cross and sat down on the banks by the road. The soldiers were thirsty. Pierre Heudes and Gabriel Clerambosq went to and fro between the village cross and M. Andre Lefevre's cellar, bringing jugs of cider. I think they must have nearly emptied the barrel.

'Something which added to the emotion was the old-fashioned accent of the French-Canadians, who made up part of the regiment. We had been waiting for the English or Americans but it was the Canadians who had liberated us. We had a sort of feeling that we were discovering distant relations. Our hearts swelled with joy and we lived as if in a dream.'

15-year-old Claude Guillotin.

'The landings on the beach proved to be more difficult than had been expected. Steel posts with mines on top could clearly be seen at the water's edge. At the time of our arrival the water was deeper than had been anticipated - we had been prepared for wading in about four and one half feet - the car exhausts allowed only a few inches more than that. Our craft was the first to land but hit a mine which badly damaged the ramp and by the time that this had been dealt with the water was too deep for wading and we had to wait for the tide to recede. Our sister craft was able to unload... All that we could do was to watch. The Canadian infantrymen... were finding the opposition more than had been anticipated and were having considerable problems with anti-personnel mines which were... scattered in the sand hills either side of the beach exit. The mined areas were well marked... but not the 88mm gun, which scored a direct hit on the first of our Daimler armoured cars to attempt to leave the beach. Here I could only sit and watch the driver, a very good personal friend, Trooper Dixon, burn to death.'

R. Neillands of 'C' Squadron, Inns of Court Regiment, Royal Armoured Corps.

'We climbed down the toggle ropes on the side of the ship and jumped into the assault craft. There were about 38 of us plus our piper, playing a battle tune.

No-one spoke at all. We were tossed about like a cork in the sea and we all felt pretty sick and couldn't have cared less about the Jerries as we headed in towards the beach. Then we hit the sand. The water was over our shoulders as we dashed forward to take cover in the sand dunes. My first night I shared a trench with three dead Germans. Then we were machine gunned and dive bombed by two German planes which had earlier glided in with engines shut off and hit an ammunition ship which blew up, lighting up the whole area. Every anti-aircraft gun then opened up - an unbelievable sight from land and sea.'

Mike Hannon, 8th Battalion, the King's Liverpool Regiment, attached to the 3rd Canadian Division.

'Wait a minute chaps. It's not our turn.'

From the bowels of the craft a voice queried: 'well, just how long do you think it will be, old man? The ruddy hold is filling up with water.'

Lieutenant Michael Aldworth.

'Our landing craft did get in - just! But on our way up to the beach we met an obstacle we had not been told about. They had driven tree-trunks into the shallows with shells fixed to the top. As our ramp was about due to go down, it changed its mind after hitting one - and went up instead. Water poured in the bows and from there we sank. That's where the Marines made a name for themselves. We had a crew of four manning the landing craft - and we looked behind after we heard four splashes - and we had no crew. But one of our lads swam ashore with a rope which he tied to one of the hedgehogs and we used it to get the men ashore including two of our wounded. Bullets were flying everywhere. It was a sandy beach, with dunes and sea grass. But from the water it looked most inhospitable - we could see the barbed wire and pillboxes at the top!'

A British sergeant in charge of a team of sappers.

'LCA 1092. This craft was holed on some stakes about 20 yards from the beach, which held her. The crew were unable to free her and so the order to disembark was given. The first soldier through the door was shot dead and then the craft was lifted clear of the stakes by the surf and thrown on to the beach. All the Military were disembarked safely and without further casualties. This craft managed to clear the beach, but was holed three times in the process. These holes were successfully plugged and the craft was re-hoisted.'

An official report.

'We were up very early on D-Day morning! At 5 o'clock, there was a grey line running along the horizon. Yes, this was the coast of France. We were in the Bay of the Seine and, away in the distance, our planes were carrying out preliminary operations. Now and again, enemy AA batteries would light up the sky, but squadron after squadron came over and we could hear the muffled sound of their bombs exploding. A little later, the naval guns were raring to do their share and battleships and cruisers opened fire. The sea was not too rough. No enemy aircraft in the area. Everything looked unreal. They are bringing in masses of assault troops shouldering their weapons, wearing steel helmets and carrying the strict minimum: their gas masks and 24-hour rations, mess tins, first aid kit. On board several ships, they were greeted with cheers and on another, a Scottish bagpiper - the same one who had given us a rousing send-off as we sailed from England the day before - began blowing into his instrument. The sounds that came out were both plaintive and inspiring. The men had no clarion call to send them into battle.'

Marcel Ouimet, Head of news for Radio Canada's French network, off Bernières-sur-Mer. His father was a journalist and he followed in his footsteps; joining the *Sociéte Radio Canada* on 14 April 1939. Ouimet, who was born in 1915 at Montreal, had taken part in the landings in Sicily and Italy. [9]

'Owing to the fact that we were twenty minutes late and the south-westerly wind which had been blowing for four days had piled up the sea, we very quickly discovered that far from beaching to seaward of the obstacles, we were ploughing right through them. All craft managed to steer between the obstacles and the Canadians quickly disembarked, although as I had observed to the unfortunate Company Command, there was no support on the beaches for them and the Germans were anywhere but with their hands down. They had made a rapid recovery from the very heavy bombardment; and were firing very actively, although the firing to start with was hesitant and spasmodic, but mortars were already ranging and machine-guns were firing concentrated bursts.

'The D.Ds for our sector had not been launched owing to the heavy seas and the LCT carrying them had actually beached not more than one minute before we touched down and in fact three of my Division of Craft beached between two of the LCTs. The first D.D. was on the beach at almost the same time as my Canadians ran out.

'The LCAs carrying the Assault Companies of the North Shore Regiment on the left touched down without trouble at the right place. By this time, however, considerable machine-gun and mortar fire was being experienced on Nan Red. Several LCT (5)s were hit and the Assault Companies suffered some casualties. The LCAs had to beach amongst the hedgehogs. Although no difficulty was experienced in steering the craft in through them, going astern out of them proved more difficult. A high percentage of LCAs of all the three flights set off mines in this way, causing them to founder.

'The assault companies of the Queen's Own Rifles of Canada touched down about 200 yards east of their correct position (i.e. almost opposite to the strongpoint at Bernières). This meant that initial use could not be made of the excellent AVRE bridge. This in turn caused a delay in the troops getting off the beach and therefore more advance of the Brigade inland.'

An assault-craft commander. 'B' Company landed just opposite WN 28, the strongpoint at Bernières on Nan White opposite the village. The Wiederstandnest consisted of four concrete emplacements, one each containing a 5cm KwK gun, a mortar bunker, a machine-gun nest and a tank turret and was protected by an anti-tank ditch to the rear. In just a few minutes 'B' Company lost 65 soldiers - a third of its men - crossing the beach.

9   *Gold' 'Juno' 'Sword'* by Georges Bernage (Heimdal 2003).

Major Oscar Dalton, the CO, requested support from an AA ship, which trained its 40mm Bofors on WN 28 but it still took a grenade attack by five brave men to silence the position. Major Dalton and Lieutenant MacLean were killed. Lieutenant Herbert, Lance-Corporal Tessier and Rifleman Chicosck were decorated for their actions. 'A' Company lost a dozen men to shellfire. At 09:00 hours the Queen's Own cleared and held the village of Bernières, with the help of the tanks which had followed them ashore: Fort Garry Horse tanks, Crab tanks for clearing mines and AVRE tanks (one of them was blown up by a mine, blocking one of the beach exits). [10]

'The first Frenchmen I saw in France were the ones at Bernières, mostly Normans, a few Parisians as well, on a seaside holiday. It was they and their wives and daughters who threw flowers at our troops as they paraded through the streets. However, during the night, they had not slept much and, for many, the landings meant they had lost everything they possessed. But they still seemed happy, they found the strength to smile and shout: 'Long live England! Long live Canada! Long live America!' Some of our soldiers answered: 'Long live France!'... I was to hear an account of these sufferings (endured under the occupation) less than half an hour after landing, from a Norman who will be nameless because he has a son who is a POW in Germany, but it's a typically French name and a typically Canadian name too [actually Paul Martin].

'And what do you think of General de Gaulle, I suddenly asked?' My Norman friend, a man of sixty, stood proudly erect - he had fought with the artillery during the Great War - wearing a beret and his own clothing because he had had to spend the night in a shelter and had lost everything during the bombardment, smiled at me and said: 'General de Gaulle, sir, you are preaching to the converted, I will kiss him on his first visit!' He had answered quite off the cuff and I could only admire this man who had been pretty well off and who was now ruined, but for whom being ruined didn't mean a thing. For four years, he had thought about it a lot and understood that freedom is worth more than that.'

Marcel Ouimet. [11]

'You were just there and you did what you could and when you came to a fellow dying, I'd tell him he was dying. You'd get a nod of the head from him. If he were a Roman Catholic, I'd anoint him. This was all done automatically, with a second for each, you see.'

Captain R. M. Hickey, Catholic Padre, North Shore Regiment, Canadian 3rd Division.

'0530. Not the scene I expected. Grey skies, wind and sea; a black coastline ahead, first shots from the cruiser. One can see the tracers going slowly high up into the air. 0550. Idling along at 5 knots. Cruisers and destroyers inshore but not firing much. Visibility moderate. I doubt if they can see their fall of shot.

10 See 'Gold' 'Juno' 'Sword' by Georges Bernage (Heimdal 2003).
11 'Gold' 'Juno' 'Sword' by Georges Bernage (Heimdal 2003).

Church spires can be identified - nearly. 0600. Sporadic bombardment... streaky pale sky to the east. Rain clouds ahead. Smoke flowing ahead of Hilary. Why? It makes a good screen across the front. 0605. Some aircraft passing towards shore. Wind 280 force 5. No fire from shore yet - hush! 0613 thick cloud of smoke from where the cruiser's shells falling. 0625. An air strike approaching. We are lounging along and nothing much doing. Too rough for the D.D.s. 0638. Signal that S.P. and LCT(R) are ten minutes late. Bombardment hotting up. Can we see water-tower of Courseulles and groynes on the beach by eye. Very dark over land. 0645. It is very difficult to spot targets. No shooting from shore though. What a funny situation!

0701. Force G's LCT(H) firing, or is it bombing? Fog of war or mist over the beaches - dark and grey. 0708. Can see church, the rest is fog of war. Good bombing - black and white smoke. 0714. Good bombing on beach. Can see the obstacles. Cross-wind smoke and dust. 0730. Signal; 'Deliver D.D.s if you wish' (half D.D.s disembarked and half breached). Fishermen's nets alongside. Hope they are not attached to mines. D.D. going out well. 0750. Yellow dingy full of men. Presume a D.D.'s crew. 88 mm? are bursting off beach. Plane down on port beam. One of ours alleged to be hit by a rocket. 0755. Explosion off the mouth of the river. Looks like a controlled minefield; about 50 yards of sea took off just east of the town. Green smoke and flash. 0756. Assaulting infantry on the Mike green. 0805. Machine-gun fire on Mike green. How clear is the air. Well done RAF. About sixteen shells a minute falling in Mike green. Some D.D.s firing.

0815. Empty LCA returning. Wind 280 Force 3. (LCA Hedgerow firing on Nan green. Well placed up on the beach defences.) LCGs on Nan right inshore and knocking hard. 0835. Black clouds over the beaches. Wind Force 4. Many flocks of black duck? Moving out to sea. 0840. A small craft inshore passing out situation messages. Most useful. 0855. The black conical buoy off Mike green is there. I am surprised. 0856. No exits. Beach under shellfire. 0900. Beach under mortar fire. Men bunched inside dunes with D.D. and AVREs - no movement one can see. 0905. Mike red. Slight opposition only. Beach signal station excellent. 0910. Think things looking a bit better. Report of LCAs having been held on beach obstacle mines. LCT passing with a hedgehog stuck on his bow.'

Diary entries, Lieutenant-Commander Thornton commanding LCH 168.

'I don't think any of us realized the danger we were in. Nobody ever went to Normandy to die; they went to fight and win a war. I don't think any man that died thought that it was him that was going to be killed. In my opinion, the reason we stormed Normandy like we did was because the soldiers would rather have fought the whole German Army than go back on the ships and be as seasick ass they were going over. My God! Those soldiers couldn't wait to get on dry land. Nothing would have got in their way... they would have torn tanks to pieces with their bare hands.

'Unfortunately, between us and the battle area, were some of the enemy, so we decided to push our way through and do what we could to mop up the Germans on the way. We soon got bogged down by these 88s and machine-gun nests. The Major called me up as the senior NCO and said, 'Let's put some grenades in there and get rid of them'.

'He said, 'Use your grenades.' But although I had my bomb pouches strapped on, I was not carrying any grenades. 'I've only got shoe-cleaning gear and boot polish in one pouch and my soap and flannel in the other - I'm a sailor and my grenades were in the boxes in the boat.' So I had to take the army grenades. I took the pins out with my teeth and held one in each hand and the other in my pouch. I rushed up to the pillbox although they were firing at me and lobbed these grenades in - and we captured a German pillbox.'
Roger McKinley, a Royal Navy Commando.

'Suddenly, at 7,000 yards, our squadron commander, Major Duncan, asked if we would prefer to risk it. Cheers went up, we were all for it, and the CO, knowing very well what we were facing, agreed and we prepared to launch. The LCT once again took its launching position in the wind, the ramp was lowered and we each, in turn, rolled off. The manoeuvre was difficult owing to the wind and waves. DD tanks had been conceived for a Force 4 wind and we were operating in about a Force 7. All our five tanks were successfully launched and we ploughed into the water, trying to adopt a pre-determined attack formation. (We couldn't fire our guns in the water, because they were hidden behind the huge canvas screen which kept us afloat.) Standing on the command deck at the back of my turret, trying to steer and navigate, that 7,000 yards to the beach was the longest journey of my life. Enemy fire was discernable now. Machine-gun bullets were ripping the water all around me and an occasional mortar shell fell among us. I looked behind to see how the others were faring and noticed that many of the tanks had sunk and the crews were desperately trying to board bright-yellow salvage dinghies.

'More by accident than by design, I found myself the leading tank. On my way in I was surprised to see a friend - a midget submarine who had been waiting for us for forty-eight hours. He waved me right on to my target and then made a half turn to go back. I remember him very, very, distinctly standing up through his conning hatch joining his hands together in a sign of good luck. I answered the old, familiar Army sign - To you too, bud!

'I was the first tank coming ashore and the Germans started opening up with machine-gun bullets. But when we came to a halt on the beach, it was only then that they realized we were a tank when we pulled down our canvas skirt, the flotation gear. Then they saw that we were Shermans. It was quite amazing. I still remember very vividly some of the machine-gunners standing up in their posts looking at us with their mouths wide open. To see tanks coming out of the water shook them rigid.

'My target was on the sea front; a 75 mm, which was in a position of enfilade fire along the beach like all the guns. The houses along the beach were all full of machine-gunners and so were the sand dunes. But the angle of the blockhouse stopped them firing on me. So I took the tank up to the emplacement, very, very, close and destroyed the gun by firing at almost point-blank range.'
Sergeant Leo Gariepy of 'B' Squadron, Canadian 6th Armoured Regiment (1st Hussars) in one of the DD tanks that survived the rough seas and

approached the sea wall just to the left of Courseulles' harbour mouth. Before attacking the emplacement Gariepy stopped, opened and shared a bottle of rum with the crew, then reversed and put seven rounds into the bunker. It stopped firing. By about 1200 hours the Hussars had lost ten tanks including five which never made it to the shore. The Royal Winnipeg Rifles - the 'Little Black Devils' - and the Regina Rifle Regiment who had landed at the port either side of the River Seulles found the support of the DD tanks invaluable. Covered by their fire, were soon storming through gardens into the little town's narrow streets:

'We ended up in a narrow street and there was one of those funny looking trucks with a charcoal burner on the running board. I couldn't get my tank by and I saw two Frenchmen and a French woman standing in a doorway looking at us. So I took my earphones off and told them in good Quebec French, 'Now will you please move that truck out of the way so I can get by?'

'They must have been frightened because they wouldn't budge. So I then called them everything I could think of in the military vocabulary. They were amazed to hear a Tommy - they thought we were Tommies - speak French with the old Norman dialect!'

But it had the desired effect and by mid-morning Gariepy and the Winnipegs and Reginas had pushed two miles inland towards the Caen-Bayeux road. The dash and bravado of the Canadians that carried them through the beaches swept by the machine-gun fire that morning on 'Juno' made a great impression on the British soldiers who were with them. [12]

'We were up in the dunes at the top of the beach, just on the other side of the Seulles River. My task was to deal with the firing pin in this minefield and as we got to the top of a rise I saw my first German. He was alive, but not for very long. These two Canadians who were with me were running up the beach behind me with their rifles. Just as they went up behind me through this opening in the sea wall, the Jerry came up out of the emplacement, with a Schmiesser. I thought - Christ! They haven't seen. I hadn't got a Sten gun; it had gone in the drink. But they just didn't stop running, they just cracked their rifle butt down on the German and that was that.'

An English engineer Sergeant from the sapper squad dealing with the beach minefields.

'As the landing craft approached the beach, it was increasingly clear that the bombardment had failed to destroy any of the enemy strong-points. From a distance of less than 800 yards the enemy opened up with everything they had.

12 In 1970 M. Jean Demota who owned the salvage rights off Courseulles recovered a Canadian Sherman DD from about three miles out at sea. Leo Gariepy had settled in France after the war and he, in conjunction with the Mayor of Courseulles, helped to raise money for the venture. Once on shore Canadian Army Engineers from Germany moved and restored the vehicle and in 1971 it was dedicated in the position it is in today. Leo Gariepy was present, although sadly he died a year later. The road behind the Sherman is named after him (Leo Gariepy, Citoyen d'Honneur de Courseulles sur Mer. 1912-1972.) *Major & Mrs Holt's Battlefield Guide: Normandy Landing Beaches* (Leo Cooper, 1999, 2000, 2002).).

The 1st Hussars' DD tanks had failed to keep ahead of the landing crafts, resulting in the regiment's going in cold. Gripping their weapons tighter, all knew what had to be expected and done once the order 'Open doors' was given. As the doors were lowered, these companies advanced through a hail of bullets. Spandaus and Nazi rifles spat furiously at the invaders. During the run-in some assault crafts were swamped on the reefs which abounded in front of Courseulles.

'Rushing the enemy, 'B' Company encountered heavy enemy fire. Corporal J. Klos, badly shot in the stomach and legs while leaving the assault boat, made his way forward to an enemy machine-gun nest. He managed to kill two Nazis before he was mortally felled, his hands still gripped about the throat of his victim.'

From the official history, the Royal Winnipeg Regiment, who stormed the beach and into the town of Bernières.

'It was very fortunate that we landed that day without getting swamped... but then I was so seasick that I didn't care what happened. I was no sailor. I was real seasick. And when we did land everything seemed so mixed up. The first thing we saw were bodies and parts of bodies, our own people and this country that was strange to us and all these pill boxes everywhere. But I guess you didn't have time to think about anything but your own neck... I can always remember seeing the steeple of this church and there were snipers up there zapping us with lead flying all around. They were there all night on 6th June and the 7th and the 8th too...'

Grant Suche, a twenty-two-year-old rifleman in the Royal Winnipeg Rifles.

'I was having a game of pontoon when the signal arrived for our part in D-Day to begin. Just after mid-day we slipped our moorings and set off for the Normandy coast. On board LCT 770 we had sections of the 9th Canadian Brigade as well as armoured vehicles. A Canadian major asked me, 'Will we need our Wellingtons?' meaning would his troops get their feet wet?

'I said, 'No, we will take you all the way to the beach.'

'The Solent was jammed packed with every type of vessel imaginable; it was as if you could walk across the water, there were so many. I suppose I was a bit nervous when you think I smoked 60 cigarettes that night.

'We were travelling at about 4½ to 5 knots when at about 0130 the bombardment started. I reckoned it was about 40 miles away by the flashes I could see in the sky. I reached my waiting position off 'Mike Green' beach near Courseulles-sur-Mer. There were cruisers, battleships and destroyers all around us. It was daylight by now, the sea had quietened a little and it was quite warm. I reached my waiting position but there was so much congestion in the water we had to put back our beaching from 0950 to 0310. For five minutes before we hit the beach I gave the two 1,000 hp Davey Paxman diesel engines (originally used to power tanks) everything we had and ran full speed for the shore.

'I came up on the starboard quarter of Des Lewis's LCT 632, which went in first. It hit a tetrahedra, a metal triangle with a teller mine attached. The mine exploded but LST 632 carried on. Des, a New Zealander, shouted, 'We've got the bastards, Nobby!' We've got the bastards!' He was of course referring to the Germans. (I didn't see Des again until 1950 when I heard his booming voice in a bar at the Waterloo Hotel in Wellington). There was tremendous German activity, especially from snipers, while we were getting our lads on to 'Mike-Green'. We were stuck there for four hours until high tide refloated us.

'After an hour or so, while we were having lunch, three German aircraft came in from the southeast. For some reason they took a liking to us, probably because we were a sitting target. I went to the bridge in time to see their bomb doors open. Though the bombs missed us by about 25 yards LCT 770, all 360s tons of her, was moved 18 inches, though all the explosions did was to cover us in mud and shingle. I had a very good port gunner and he opened up on one of the bombers with his 20mm Oerlikon cannon. The bomber went down over the hills inshore. Half a dozen other vessels were firing too so we never claimed it. It was like shooting pheasants, when everyone is tempted to claim the downed bird!

'A LCE opened up on a German-held bungalow right on the beach. I was flashed up by Aldis; 'Can you fire into those dummy windows? I can't do any good.' We opened up with the starboard Oerlikon and filled the windows with shells and tracers. A bunch of Germans came out with their hands up. We continued firing and at the same time soldiers in the sand dunes were firing as well.

'Finally, the high tide refloated us and we reached our waiting convoy position to join a convoy heading back to Stokes Bay.

'Three months later, I was sitting in the Oasis restaurant at Arromanches and got talking to a Frenchman andre Andelhof. He asked, 'had I been on D-Day?' I told him that I beached my LCT a mile or so from where I was now sitting but before this a 75mm gun on shore had begun firing at our flotilla and the big shells began exploding around us. Using outstretched hands the Canadian major looked up at me on the bridge and pointed this way and that to indicate where each shell was coming from and I interpreted them. We steered 'port' and a shell exploded where we had been; then 'starboard' and 'ahead'. Each shell missed but they had our range. They were going to sink us. Then suddenly, the firing miraculously stopped.

'Andre listened to my story and said that he was in the Maquis. He asked me what was my craft? I told him LCT 770 with a big 'P' on the side. Andre said that they saw a craft in danger and his resistance group had crept up on the German gun position. It was a hot day and the German gunners had their helmets unstrapped and hanging on the back of their neck. Andre's men twisted the German gunners' helmets and throttled them all.

'I said, 'Andre, I want to shake your hand because you saved my life.'

'The Oasis had very few bottles of wine left that night.'

33-year old Sub-Lieutenant Roy Clark RNVR, Commander, LCT 770, 36th Flotilla.

'We really had been briefed pretty well to know where we should be from the photographs of the coast. But unfortunately when we were out there looking at all those churches and spires they all looked the same. As we closed in we got into a terrible argument. Some said it was this church, some said it was that. To add to the confusion, the heavy seas meant that people who should have been in front were behind and we ourselves were twenty minutes' late.'

A sapper going to 'Juno' Beach.

'Juno' Beach Timetable

Objectives: To advance inland and join up with 'Gold' and 'Sword' Beaches on either side.

Local naval commanders delay H-Hour from 0735 to 0745 until the tide is so high that landing craft can clear the treacherous reefs off shore. However, delayed by a choppy sea, the leading assault craft head in almost 30 minutes later than scheduled and are borne by the tide for several hundred yards through the belt of heavily mined obstacles. 20 of the leading 24 landing craft are lost or damaged. Only six of 40 Centaur tanks mounting 95mm howitzers manned by Royal Marines make the shore.

0750 Canadian 7th Brigade, the Royal Winnipeg Regiment and the Regina Rifles are first ashore on the right flank of 'Juno', west of the River Seulles, followed minutes later opposite a strongpoint in the village of Bernières by the Canadian 8th Brigade and 8-10 DD tanks manned by the Canadian 1st Hussars. On the left, ahead of the armour and running the gauntlet to the sea wall, is the Queen's Own Regiment of Canada, the North Shores and the Canadian 8th Brigade. Losses are significant but the survivors move quickly and are already involved in heavy fighting at Courseulles, Bernières-sur-Mer and Ste-Aubin-sur-Mer as the delayed DDs struggle ashore.

0830 48 Royal Marine Commando lands at Ste-Aubin and heads east. Little beach clearance takes place due to high tides and rough seas. The beaches are congested and under heavy fire.

By 0930 flail tanks open exits on both sides of the Seulles and the worst of the craters has been bridged by fascines and bridging tanks.

0930 onwards 8th Brigade takes Bernières-sur-Mer. Heavy enemy fire in progress.

1040 Five beach exits have now been cleared.

1112 After heavy fighting, 7th Brigade secures the beach exit at Courseulles. The arrival of Canadian 9th Brigade causes further congestion.

1115 Ste-Aubin-sur-Mer falls to Canadians.

1120 Taillerville, Banville and Ste Croix are captured.

1200 Further landings.

1400 The whole of Canadian 3rd Division is now ashore. Rapid advances inland: troops join with 'Gold' Beach to the west. Reserve brigade with four regiments of artillery and a third armoured regiment are able to expand the bridgehead.

1800 Canadian 9th Brigade reaches Bény.

2000 Troops advance to Villons les Buissons, seven miles inland.

By end of day Altogether, 21,400 men, 3,200 vehicles and 2,100 tons of stores are landed on 'Juno'. 12 lanes are clear and Canadian follow-up units - the 7th Brigade on the right, the 9th on the left - are past the assault troops, as planned and heading for Caen. 21,500 men of the 3rd Canadian Division and 2nd Armoured Brigade and British troops' storm 7 miles inland. The Canadians make the most progress of all the beaches and at nightfall are within sight of Caen while 2 battalions are only 3 miles from its NW outskirts. However, the original aim of capturing Carpiquet airfield is not achieved. No link-up has yet been made with 'Sword' beach to the east.

Casualties, 359 killed, 715 wounded.

Order of Battle 'Juno' Beach
3rd Canadian Division
Major-General Rodney Keller

7th Canadian Brigade
The Royal Winnipeg Rifles
The Regina Rifle Regiment
1st Canadian Scottish Regiment

8th Canadian Brigade
The Queen's Own Rifles of Canada
Le Regiment de la Chaudierè
The North Shore (New Brunswick)
Regiment

9th Canadian Brigade
The Highland Light Infantry of Canada
The Stormont, Dundas and Glengarry
Highlanders
The North Nova Scotia Highlanders

Divisional Troops
HO 3rd Canadian Division
12th Canadian Field Regiment SP, RCA
13th Canadian Field Regiment SP, RCA
14th Canadian Field Regiment SP, RCA
32nd Battery, 4th Canadian Light Anti-
Aircraft Regiment, RCA
16th and 18th Canadian Field
Companies, RCE
Cameron Highlanders of Ottawa (MG)

Units under command for assault phase
2nd Canadian Armoured Brigade
6th Armoured Regiment (1st Hussars)
10th Armoured Regiment (Fort Garry
Horse)
27th Armoured Regiment (The
Sherbrooke Fusilier Regiment)

4th (Special Service) Brigade
48 RM Commando
1st Section, RM Engineer Commando
C Squadron, Inns of Court Regiment
19th Canadian Field Regiment SP, RCA
62nd Anti-Tank Regiment, Royal
Artillery
HQ 80 Anti-Aircraft Brigade
372, 375 Batteries, 114 Light Anti-
Aircraft Regiment, Royal Artillery
321 Battery, 93 Light Anti-Aircraft
Regiment, Royal Artillery
5th Canadian Field Company, RCE
26 and 80 Assault Squadrons, Royal
Engineers
72 and 85 Field Companies, Royal
Engineers
3 and 4 Batteries, 2 RM Armoured
Support Regiment

Beach Groups
8 Battalion The King's Regiment
5 Battalion The Royal Berkshire
Regiment

Plus elements of:
Royal Corps of Signals
Royal Army Service Corps
Royal Army Medical Corps
Royal Army Ordnance Corps
Corps of Royal Electrical and
Mechanical Engineers
Corps of Military Police
Pioneer Corps
Royal Canadian Army Medical Corps

'The German machine-gunners in the dunes were absolutely stupefied to see a tank emerge from the sea. Some ran away, some just stood up in their nests and stared, mouths wide open. To see tanks coming out of the water shook them rigid.'

Sergeant Leo Gariepy, Canadian 6th Armoured Regiment.

'We were expecting the invasion; we had signs... we weren't surprised or frightened. All night we went out into garden where we had a dug-out prepared and stayed in the dug-out for the whole night... we emerged from time to time, but there was intense bombing. After the naval bombing the planes came - it was tremendous, we thought the house would fall down and every time we peered out we were amazed to see that the house was still standing. The planes stopped coming over at about six o' clock and it was very quiet and then a little bit later, perhaps about seven o'clock, we began to hear the noise of the guns. They were machine-guns, but to us it was a very sweet noise ...the German Occupation had been very hard, we had been deprived of food, we used to go barefoot, we used to make sugar from beetroots and we got salt from seawater - we'd boil it up in a pail and extract the salt. We could do that as long as we could come to the beach, but after it was mined and all the obstacles were erected we couldn't do that anymore. We were always confident that the invasion would come - we just waited. But the Germans were taking more and more people away from our village, different categories of people. I'm not sure we could have waited much longer ...'

Eleven-year-old Michel Grimaux, who lived with his mother and sisters in the seaside resort of Graye-sur-Mer.

'At the village of Graye-sur-Mer three miles east of La Rivière is a bridge mostly built between eight o'clock and 9.15 on D-Day and it was a masterpiece of improvisation under fire and also a good example of the use of the specialized armour. One who was there when it was built was a coalminer from Sunderland whose real name was William Dunn; but as he was a North Country man in a mainly southern unit, his army friends all called him George or Geordie and most of them never knew he had another name. George was twenty. His 21st birthday was on 9 June and for two or three weeks it had been a matter of argument whether he and his tank crew would celebrate it in an English pub or a Continental cafe.

George Dunn, for his age, was a resourceful, adaptable, well-balanced kind of man; he had been trained to that in a fairly hard school. He had been born and lived all his life in a cottage in a row in a mining village. All the men he knew at home were miners. His father had been a miner; but when George was thirteen, he had been killed by a fall of roof. Naturally, the very day when George left school, when he was fourteen, he went to the mine and asked for a job and got it. He had never thought of being anything but a miner and expected to be a miner all his life. But the job had not lasted long. The mine exported most of its coal to France and when France fell to the Germans in 1940, the mine was simply shut down and almost the whole of the village was suddenly thrown out of work. George was seventeen then. He had to go on the dole, like all his friends and neighbours; and then of course he had to take whatever job was offered him by the labour exchange. They drafted him to an oil refinery far away. It was strange work and a strange place and he was unhappy; and so, although he had never had any dreams of being a soldier, he was not at all sorry when his army call-up came. By D-Day, he was driver of a Churchill tank in the 26th Assault Squadron, Royal Engineers. But he still did not want to do anything when the war was over except to go home and start in the mine again.

The radio operator of George's tank was even younger than he was. His name was Roy Manley. His father had also died when he was young. Roy came from Devonshire. When he left school, he had got a job with a builder's merchant in Exeter; and when he first met George, the two of them could hardly understand each other's language. Roy had more youthful interests: cricket and football and speedway racing and collecting records of Bing Crosby. His ambition was to save enough money to buy a motor bike. He had been miserable on the day his army call-up came; he had dreaded leaving home.

The rest of the crew of the tank were not much older than these two, except the commander, who was a Lance Sergeant called Cecil 'Jim' Ashton. Sergeant Ashton seemed almost middle-aged to his crew: he was nearly thirty. Ashton was always singing and the microphone in the turret seemed to inspire him. His star turns were 'Kiss me, kiss me again,' and a sad Australian ballad with the refrain, 'Why do I weep, why do I cry? My love's asleep, so far away.'

Their tank was a fascine AVRE: it carried a bundle of logs eight feet in diameter. Before D-Day, all the crew had studied the photographs and models of their beach and they had seen the obstacles on the beach and a gap in the sand dunes behind it and the marshy ground two hundred yards wide at the back of the dunes. In the gap, they had seen a tank trap and in the marsh a winding stream and a place where a culvert across it had been destroyed. Sergeant Ashton and George and Roy and the others all understood exactly what they had to do: to follow the flail tanks through the dunes and along the road to the culvert, drop their fascine in the gap where the culvert had been, drive over it and hold a road junction just beyond it while the Canadian infantry followed across the open ground.

Ashton was singing as the landing craft went into the beach and then he stopped singing and opened the turret and put his head out to guide George up the beach, avoiding the corpses as best he could. There was much less shooting than they had expected; and that was because one of the landing craft of their troop had had engine trouble and had made them all late and the Canadian infantry and the DD tanks had already been there for twenty minutes and had crossed the beach as far as the edge of the dunes and decimated the first line of the German defenders. The flails which had landed ahead went up through the gap, churning a track which was easy to see and follow and George went after them till he could see over the marsh to the crossroads and the houses beyond it.

The tank trap barred the way, a ditch fifteen feet wide and nine feet deep. That was not their job and George pulled aside while another fascine tank which should have been in front came past and paused on the edge of the ditch and released its great bundle of logs which fell with a crash in the hole and then immediately crawled on again across its own logs. The flails of the 22nd Dragoons queued up and followed it over the tank trap which, far from trapping the tanks, had hardly delayed them a second.

George drove across the logs and followed the flails which flogged the road to a broken culvert fifty yards beyond; and then they drew aside and let him take the lead, with the tank of the troop commander close behind him. The last twenty or thirty feet of the road surface before the culvert had been destroyed. Beyond the broken end of the road, George saw through the visor a few yards of sand and weeds and then a narrow strip of water where the stream flowed through.

'Crater's filled up,' he said.[13]

'Looks all right,' he heard Ashton say; and on the radio the troop commander told them to carry on.

George eased the tank forward on to the patch of weeds; her nose dipped and he saw the weeds part and water gleaming through and she started to slide. He had stopped the tracks, but she went on sliding and then she fell and the daylight through the visor was cut off and she stopped with a crash. Water fell on top of him and before he could catch his breath it was over his head and with the gasp that he gave it went down in his lungs and choked him. He struggled to get out of his seat and somebody, Ashton or Roy, grabbed him by the back of his neck and hauled him up: and then he was on top of the turret, lying on his stomach being sick and the turret was only just over the surface and it was still sinking. Ashton got him on to the bank and shouted, 'Run for the dunes,' but he hardly had the power to run. The troop commander turned his tank to give cover from the machine-gun fire and the crew made for the dunes and got over the top of the first of them and threw themselves down on the sheltered seaward side; and before they were there, the tank had disappeared except for the top of its fascine.

The crew never saw what happened after that. The weeds on the top of the water had looked so solid-like that nobody who saw them from the tanks had doubted there was dry land underneath. Blown sand had been lying on top of them. But after the tank had fallen in and broken the surface, it was seen that the gap in the road was sixty feet wide. The bridges which the specialized armour carried were only thirty feet long. Perhaps nobody would have thought of sinking a tank in the middle of the gap if George had not already done it by mistake, but that was the only possible way to bridge the gap. A bridge-carrying tank was ordered up and it dropped the far end of its bridge on top of the sunken tank. Captain E. J. Hewitt the troop commander and two other men scrambled out to it, still under fire and stood on the turret which was under water and blew off the wire strop which held the fascine, so that it dropped in the water ahead. There was still a gap beyond it. More fascines were put into place; more tanks were brought up to give covering fire and troops from the beach carried up some logs which the Germans had left there and threw them in as well; and at 9.15, an hour and a quarter after the troop had landed, the first tanks and infantry crossed the bridge and rushed the houses by the crossroads from which the machine-guns and mortars had covered the whole operation.[14]

Jim Ashton and his crew, not knowing the use which was being made of their derelict tank, were lying close together on the back of the dunes, fed up with themselves for having lost the tank when the battle had hardly started and thinking of the eighteen months of training which had culminated in less than eighteen minutes of action. George blamed himself. Ashton reassured him. Roy, from his radio position, had not seen anything at all till the water poured in. Ashton, of course, was the first to get over the shock; he was the only one of them who was really quite grown up, or had been more than a small boy when the war started. He began singing again to cheer them up a bit, not very loudly, against the sound of the machine-guns and mortar bombs:

'Why do I weep, why do I cry?
My love's asleep, so far away.'

He was singing it when he died. A mortar bomb fell right among them.

Roy was lying on top of George. He pushed him off and saw he was dead and glanced and saw Ashton was dead and the others were lying half-buried and still. He stood up and fell and rolled down the steep face of the dune and opened his eyes again in agony and saw a rough board above his head with a skull on it and 'ACHTUNG-MINEN' and he got up again and ran, like a desperately wounded animal can run, till he fell again with his left leg crumpled under him. The doctors would never believe he had run on it, it was so badly shattered, but he knew he had. His other leg was wounded too and he lost his left arm. So he never became a miner, but he got a good job in the mine which a one-armed man can do.

Adapted from Dawn Of D-Day by David Howarth.[15] Roy Manley's fellow sapper, Alf Battson, was killed also. The demolition NCO, Bill Hawkins, survived. Six days' later Winston Churchill landed on 'Juno' Beach and crossed the bridge, now called Pont D'Avre. He was followed in his footsteps by HM King George VI on 16 June. In November 1976 Royal Engineers from the British Army of the Rhine carried out a major operation to dig out the AVRE, which fully restored, has become a memorial. [16]

The Langrune-sur-Mer Strongpoint

48 (Royal Marine) Commando were to land on Nan Red Sector at the extreme easterly end of 'Juno' Beach and from there move eastwards and capture a strongpoint at Langrune, the next village along and link up with 'Sword' Beach. The troops going in were the North Shore Regiment; the New Brunswick Regiment, who were to take the town of Ste-Aubin. Sergeant Joe Stringer in B Troop, 48 Commando had promised his fiancée Peggy that they would be married on 3 June. At Warsash waiting for the off he had asked both the padre and his CO, 38-year old Lieutenant Colonel James Moulton if he could contact Peggy and explain. He was met with a blanket refusal; the camp had been sealed and no communication with the outside world was allowed. Six LCI(S) s from the 202nd Flotilla would transport the Commando; each carry 96 fully laden troops below deck and 18 bicycles on the upper deck. The wooden

---

15   The Companion Book Club 1959.
16   See *D-Day Then and Now Vol.2* (After the Battle 1995).

craft were very light and wallowed and rolled incessantly, even in moderate sea.

'Our final briefing included an address by the CO of the Canadian North Shore Regiment whose men were to carry out the initial assault and clear the beach before we landed. He finished with the phrase: 'Come Hell or high water, we will get you ashore.' We had every confidence that they would.

'When we moved off on the evening of 5 June we passed through the rest of the craft lined up in Southampton harbour and on the Solent and we were told by our CO 'Get on deck with your green berets on. Let them see you. Give them encouragement.' We sailed through to cheers and what have you. 'I was the leading man on the left-hand side of the craft going in on the left-hand ramp. Lieutenant Curtis and Sergeant Bill Blyth were leading No. 1 Section on the right-hand ramp, immediately exposed to the machine-gun nest at the far end of the beach. Most of my demolition section were carrying a lot of explosives in addition to our normal service equipment so we were heavily laden. As we came in we could see that the Canadians were in difficulties and the beach was not completely taken. We could see a lot of fire on the shoreline, most of it coming from the left, whipping down the length of the beach. The pre-landing bombing looked as though it had not been successful for there were still many active German pillboxes and other defences. The North Shore Regiment had obviously not cleared the beach. There were lots of casualties lying about. We were all immediately exposed to the machine-gun nest at the far end of the beach. Two of our craft were sunk on the approach to the beach and we lost a lot of men trying to swim ashore. As we approached the beach, our CO had had the good sense to get our mortars stationed in the bows of the craft so that they did lay down a smoke-screen, which did enable us to get on to the beach once we were clear of the water. Our progress down the ramp was very slow, not like the popular image of a landing, where a flat-bottom boat dropped its ramp and the troops came running off and up the beach. Our craft had light wooden ramps which floated about in the heavy surf, lurching with every wave. Some matelots from the boat tried to hold them down in the water, but they were too heavy and difficult to control. As each man stepped from the craft on to the ramp he became very exposed. He then had to struggle down the near-vertical boards that were shaking and tossing about beneath him. Immediately behind me two of my men were hit by machine-gun fire. We lost a lot of men this way. When we came off of the craft it was into at least four feet of water, about chest high. We stormed across the beach to the far side, avoiding the wall where the poor Canadians had bought it, but moved more to the left towards the dunes trying to get away from the worst of the machine-gun fire.

'The beach was covered with casualties, some Canadian, some ours. The surf was incredible, with beached and half-sunken craft wallowing about in it. Offshore, other craft came steadily on. Some tanks struggled ashore and some bogged in the shingle.' **Captain Dan Flunder, Adjutant, 48 Commando, who tried in vain to stop a Sherman tank driven by its panicked driver, crushing a line or crouching Canadians of the 8th Infantry Brigade on the beach. He yelled at the top of his voice 'They're my men!' but the tank man did not react. Flunder then beat the hatch with his swagger stick and when that did no good he pulled out a grenade and blew off the Sherman's left track. Only then did it finally end the slaughter.**

There was a lot of chaos on the beach, lots of wounded lying about. The Fort Garry Horse in their Sherman tanks were coming in at this time with their hatches down, landing from LCTs quite close to us and a lot of wounded were being badly mauled by the tracks. It was very, very chaotic and this is where Colonel Moulton really shone. He called us together, what was left of his commando.'

Harry Timmins saw the colonel 'walking steadily and steadfastly, bolt upright, despite the shells and mortars dropping all around and the ping, ping, ping of the bullets whizzing by. He stopped, looked around and at the top of his voice cried out, 'Four-Eight Royal Marine Commando - this way,' pointing along the Beach. Everyone within earshot got up and followed him.'

'Of the five hundred who had left the previous evening from Warsash' continues Stringer 'I think he assembled about 223 of us and we hadn't even started the job that we had been allocated, so it was a pretty rotten situation to be in. But we finally did leave the beach under the direction of Colonel Moulton, under his reassurance and pulled together. We left our wounded on the beach being tended by our padre, the Reverend Armstrong, who himself was very badly wounded and we moved off to our allotted task, which was a strongpoint at Langrune, another seaside village.

'As soon as we moved out along the road that ran parallel to the beach, we came under fire. Lieutenant Geoff Curtis, second-in-command of B Troop, was fatally wounded immediately by Oerlikon fire coming from one of the warships off the beach. I think one of their lookouts had seen our advance and had assumed that we were Germans. The bullets had ripped through the lieutenant's stomach leaving him in a bad way. We had to leave him by the side of the road. The gunfire had also killed another marine and wounded a couple of others. But eventually after clearing a few houses we found ourselves in the rear of Langrune. We had more street-clearing to do, more houses to negotiate along this street, which we eventually did and we got within striking range of the strongpoint.

'Captain Perry then called an O group in one of the last houses at the end of the street we had cleared, which all senior NCOs attended, giving us his plans for attacking the strongpoint. After briefing us on the situation, he stepped outside to take a last look at the opposition before we put in our attack and he was immediately hit by a sniper's bullet and killed. At the same time they mortared us and another two of the sergeants were hit. That left Sergeant Bill Blythe and myself as the only two sergeants and now our commander of B Troop was 19-year old Second Lieutenant Anthony

Rubinstein, [17] who'd only joined us just prior to D-Day. So we were very badly hit.

'By this time, because of the shortage of officers, we had started getting directions from Colonel Moulton himself. One of these was directed to me and my section. He told me to gather as much explosive together as I could and make a pole charge, then have a go at blowing the six-foot concrete wall which barred our way into the strongpoint. Langrune had been constructed of a dozen houses, a terraced run of houses, linked together with trenches and barbed wire round them and minefields in the gardens. My section and I retreated to a railway line we'd come over and scrounged some timber. We made a sort of a builder's hod and put the explosives and gun cotton slabs in that and we made our way down to the wall, under some considerable fire but fortunately not very accurate. We got right up to the wall, placed our charge, withdrew slightly and fired it. There was an almighty bang, but the demolition wasn't very successful. I didn't have much hope as we couldn't bring enough pressure on it to make any impact on the wall, which was very solid. But we were now immediately under the wall, my section and I and the Jerries behind the wall were slinging over stick grenades. They were not very effective for they seemed to be made of thin metal more like cocoa tins. They were, however, tying them in bunches to make them more deadly. One bunch landed behind me and one of my section yelled out, 'Look out Joe!' I turned my back to it in a natural reaction and it went off, spattering me and one of my men with shrapnel. The amount of blood on my tunic led me to believe that I had a bad wound.

'Colonel Moulton was concerned about us, so he called for us to withdraw. When I got back to our side of the road I called for a medic to have a look at me. He looked very hard to find any external wounds and the only major thing he could discover was that the lobe of my ear had been badly serrated and that was where the large amount of blood was coming from. So if wasn't a 'Blighty' wound! A few bits had gone into my rear end and thighs, which I carried for a number of years. They used to fester up occasionally and cause me some discomfort and would then work themselves out.

'It was now getting late in the afternoon and things were getting very desperate. Apparently the Colonel had received instructions from the Brigadier that we were to hold what we'd got at all costs and make preparations for what was expected to be a counter-attack from a Panzer division that was approaching our way. So we were told to dig in, make

17   Rubinstein was the son of a distinguished family of lawyers and his childhood in England in the 1930s had been carefree and comfortable and sheltered. When the war began, he was in his second year at Cheltenham College. For three more years he had the cloistered life of an English public school and when he was 17 had gone straight from the sixth form to the army, because it was the accepted thing to do. On 5 June he sailed as a second lieutenant in command of a section of 30 men, nearly all of them older than he was and most of them had more experience, not only of war but also of life in general. But...during their training on Scotland and in the bombed streets of south-east London, he had found then very easy to get on with. He liked them and enjoyed their company. Dawn Of D-Day by David Howarth (The Companion Book Club 1959).

some sort of fortification to assist us. This we did; but the counter-attack didn't take place.

'On the second day we got some help from tanks and managed to blow the wall and get into strongpoint. Once inside the Germans gave up easily, they were not of high calibre. One was a bit slow in putting up his hands and I gave him a jab in the stomach with my Tommy gun. Colonel Moulton didn't like that sort of behaviour and snapped: 'There's no need for that, Sergeant!'

'I saw Moulton at various times throughout the day. He was with us virtually all the time, wounded though he was. Both his hands were wounded. There were lots of our officers who were wounded but they stayed with the troops. I think every troop commander was killed or wounded and most of the subalterns. Our officers took a hell of a pasting. Sergeant Bill Blythe had unfortunately stepped on a mine and received bad wounds which had him evacuated back to England. Sergeant Kemp had a very serious wound and lost a lot of blood from his head before we got him to the RAP. He survived and came back to join us later in the campaign. By the end of this second day, B Troop was down from 50 marines, six sergeants and three officers to just 15 men, myself and Second Lieutenant Rubinstein. Of course not all of the men we lost were killed, a lot were wounded and a lot had been drowned on the beach trying to swim ashore with heavy loads. Altogether it was very, very sad day for 48 RM Commando for it had been a tragic introduction to the war. I think Colonel Moulton said that that was the day we finished our training. The youngest commando had come of age.'

'After the final pre-D-Day exercise in Bracklesham Bay, we learnt that six of our craft were to embark 48 RM Commando and land them on Nan Red beach on the left of the Canadians in Area 'Juno'. My own craft 526 (Sub Division leader) and 536 (Laidlaw) were to carry HQ Group 4th RM Commando Brigade. Our two craft were to land ten to fifteen minutes after the main group at a point, as we should see fit, some 300 yards to the west. 'On D-1 the whole flotilla sailed under the command of our Flotilla Officer, Lieutenant Commander Georges C. C. Timmermans DSC RNVR (later C-in-C of the Belgian Navy). Our group also included some LCT. The next morning on arrival off the Normandy coast, our LCT (s) detached and circled the headquarters ship HMS *Hilary* until zero hour. Commander Timmermans six craft sailed and headed for the beach and at the appointed tine my sub-division turned away to make our final run in to 'Juno' beach. On watching our FO's approach to Nan Red beach, I soon realised that his group was in serious trouble.

'540 could he identified bows down offshore and as we drew closer, we could see 513 and 539 both sinking. Underwater mines and obstructions were causing most of the craft casualties, whilst a strongpoint along and just behind the seawall was causing casualties to both the Royal Marine commandos and the crews aboard these craft. In 526, I signalled 536 of my intention to pick a spot where the curve in the seawall afforded some protection from the strongpoint and to land close by an abandoned LCT(v) 2283 on our port side. The CO of the LCT, (Lieutenant Collins) was the only survivor on board his craft and the LCOCU (Landing Craft Obstacle Clearance Unit) he was landing had apparently all perished with his crew. Most of the men of the LCOCU could be seen lying at the water's edge, together with their scattered equipment. Through the carnage Churchill AVRE tanks with the aid of bridging material were struggling to get over the seawall, at the same time leaving a white taped mine free path.

'The beach was now in confusion and it was poignant to see the ashen faces of the more seriously wounded, packed so close together, seeking every vestige of shelter under the sea facing walls of the houses, with their accompanying medics holding plasma drips, magnificently ignoring the mayhem around them. The upper floors of the houses under which they were sheltering were still occupied by the enemy, since from this direction, short menacing bursts of automatic fire prompted us to keep our heads down. Not so fortunate in my craft was the leading commando Marine Casson; the poor fellow was shot in the neck and died instantly before reaching the port ramp.

'AB Keen DSM, a member of the ramp crew, was hit in the leg in several places but steadfastly stayed by the port ramp to assist its retrieval on our withdrawal from the beach. Matters were now being made worse by mortaring and some of these were falling uncomfortably close. One in particular fell between 526 and 536 and this helped to hasten the departure of the remaining group of wireless carrying commandos, who left behind two portable motorcycles and a quantity of PIAT ammunition. We received an encouraging wave from Laidlaw (CO 536) but it was noticed that his first lieutenant, Sub Lieutenant Cobbe was supervising the ramp crew with the upper part of his uniform turning crimson. He had been shot in the upper arm and had declined to get attention until forced to do so by his own weakness.

'AB Dixon, the port Oerlikon gunner, was firing into the upper storeys of the houses on the sea front and he concentrated on one room in particular, where he had noticed movement. When later on Major Peter Wood RM visited us, he told us that his troop had discovered several dead in this room together with an assortment of weapons. He was convinced that one of the dead was in fact, a female.

'We now concentrated on unbeaching but discovered that we were taking in water in No.2 troop space. I gave the order for our engines to be put half and then full astern but we were seemingly stuck. Just to help matters, at that point the port engine intake manifold blew. The crew worked magnificently to stem the leak and despite only having one engine, we got off. We proceeded slowly seaward and managed to reach the LSI *Prince Henry* and with the aid of a Neil Robertson stretcher, we were able to get AB Keen, now in much pain, transferred to obtain medical attention. *Prince Henry's* priority was to disembark troops and for this reason, they would not accept the body of Marine Casson and we gave him a rather impromptu burial at sea the next day.

'We were ordered to embark fresh troops and we were inclined to feel sorry for them as they descended the scrambling nets down the aide of the ship, for they were weighed down with equipment and weapons. The first soldier to step on board our craft with his metal studded boots promptly slipped on our steel deck and fractured his ankle. He was just as promptly re-transferred on board his ship and that presumably ended his D-Day.

'We were to land these troops in 'Gold' sector but the prospect caused us some disquiet, since water was coming through our makeshift repair and the craft was becoming unmanageable allied to the fact that only one engine was operational. Having accomplished our task, I decided to dry out on the beach, pump and bail out the water and attempt further repairs. That afternoon while we were stranded on the beach, we were straddled by four bombs from a German bomber, a bomb splinter hitting the side of the bridge, fortunately without other mishap. However, two soldiers jumping from a Rhino ferry that had just landed were killed outright, their bodies lying on the beach until they were covered by the sea…'

Lieutenant Brian Lingwood RNVR, **LCI(s) 526. 202nd Flotilla suffered 87% casualties.**

'…Under a rather overcast sky with patches of blue here and there, we are looking out on an absolutely fantastic scene to the accompaniment of incredible sounds. Overhead the thunderous roar of Fortresses and Liberators going in to blast the coast. On the horizon flash after flash from the guns of bombarding ships. The destroyers fairly close in-shore, the cruisers right on the horizon astern of us some seven miles out or so and we know that beyond them too are battleships firing their fifteen- and sixteen-inch guns against shore targets.

'Five minutes before H-Hour the assault craft are bouncing on the waves. There are white horses on deep green sea now and it's been a pretty uncomfortable journey for them into shore. And the moment they touch down they've got to leap out and go into the assault. And we on board this ship… we standing here wish those boys who've gone in all the luck in the world.'

§Michael Standing of the BBC on board HMS *Hilary.*

'Most of us preferred to sit on the deck despite the cold wind and rain. The hyscene tablets issued did little to prevent sickness, which affected the majority of the commandos. The beach was clearly recognizable from the air photos. We passed close to the beach control ship and continued inshore. We had been told the tide would be low enough for the craft to beach below the beach obstacles. Actually the beach obstacles were under water and only a narrow strip of beach remained visible; consequently several craft hit obstacles which were sunk. There was a heavy swell and a vicious tidal stream, which carried away and drowned men. Mortar and shell fire became intense. MG fire started from the beach. Some commandos were killed by small arms fire on the craft before landing. The enemy had held his fire until we were beached and had us cold.

'The landing craft ramps failed because of the underwater obstacles. Many officers and men attempted to swim ashore, a high proportion of these were lost through drowning. I got ashore. After running up the beach with two of my mates we stopped near the sea I looked my left and saw many dead and wounded men. Another commando came running towards me but he didn't quite make it; he was killed with small arms fire. Another commando was running behind him, stopped and seeing he was dead picked up his rifle, which was a sniper's rifle. He got down on one knee and started firing at the strong point. He fired two rounds but was killed by small arms fire. His name was Lance Corporal Appleyard MM. He was awarded the MM in the Sicily landing. The commando who was standing on my right was also killed. I think his bullet saved my life. I moved along the sea wall and tripped over a wounded Canadian. I thought he was dead. Another Canadian threatened to shoot me. I never had time to say I was sorry. My troop commander had been shot in both arms and was unable to carry on. One of the men gave him a cigarette and lit it for him.

'A quick reconnaissance showed that the beach exit to the right was free from aimed (SA) fire except for occasional shots, as this was the quickest way to the assembly area. On the way to the assembly area a commando was sitting on a bank. He beckoned me. I ran over to him seeing he had a field dressing on his neck. As I asked him if he could walk a shot came from a house which killed him. A tank was there; a Canadian stood beside it crying. He said all his crew in it were dead, blown up by a mine.

'Passing a small house, which had a shell hole in the roof, I saw an old man inside. I went inside to look around. There was an old man and old woman crying. A young woman who was also crying offered me a piece of brown bread. As I walked from the house she followed me to the gate. Two German prisoners were being marched past with hands on head; one of them saw the young woman. He stopped and said something to her as he was being marched down to the beach. He kept looking round at her. I think they were sweethearts.

'The assembly area was much quieter. It was found possible to reorganize. We advanced to Langrune according to plan where we started working on the beach defences between Ste-Aubin and Langrune. We cleared the houses up to the strongpoint; we rushed the crossroads and gained the houses on the far side. By the end of this action 48 Commando strength had been reduced to 223 men, the total casualties being 217 men. Seventy per cent of all casualties occurred on the beach and in the landing craft. On D+2 one troop was sent to bury the dead in the garden of a house near Nan Red beach. A year later this cemetery was moved by War Graves Commission to Bayeux.'

Sam Earl, 48 (Royal Marine) Commando. It was not until 7 June after bitter hand to hand fighting that 31 prisoners emerged from the strongpoint.

'I felt that the briefing officer that came to give us our objective on landing was very cavalier in the outcome. He said we were going in under the protection of the RAF and many battleships, cruisers, destroyers, monitors and rocket ships that would bombard the coast so heavily that any Germans left alive would be too dazed to fight back. I felt that this gave the Canadians a false sense of security. I had been in action before and I knew what the enemy was capable of having served in the retreat to Dunkirk from 10 May to 1 June 1940 coming out on HMS *Worcester*. I resolved to keep my head down under the protection of the armoured bulldozer.

'Our instructions were that the bulldozer operators had to start the machines up around 0060 so the engines were warm when we entered the water. Mine would not start but when the ramp went down and the Centaur in front of me pulled off I was able to use the manual start. The bulldozer to my left started to approach the ramp. We were under heavy fire from those who were supposed to be too dazed to fight back, when the operator misjudged his alignment going down into the sea and slid sideways blocking the exit. I was called on to get in position to tow the beleaguered machine back up the ramp in a straight line.

'Because of the noise and the poor visibility I had sitting down in the turret looking through the bullet proof visors I had to stand up and expose my head like a coconut on the stand. A Canadian engineer crouched behind perched on the Hyster winch gave me instructions to get the towrope in place. I had just managed to right the machine in front and off it went when I was hit in the face with such force it let me slumped into bottom of the turret dazed and bleeding. A voice called out to me, 'Are you OK?' 'Would you like a spare operator to take over?' My answer was 'No'. I was not being brave but climbing out of the turret would make me a sitting duck.

'Whatever the missile was that hit me had been fired from the pillbox directly in front of us. I examined my wound. It had slit my left cheek and I had small abrasions above my left eye and right cheek. I took my field dressing out and tied it round my face in the manner of one suffering with a toothache, tying the knot on the top of my head. I then went down the ramp into the water making for a place to give cover to my Canadian ground crew so that we could regroup and try and make out how best to tackle the job we sent to do. Of the four bulldozers that landed from my craft two operators were badly wounded by mortars. One was the one who had blocked the exit. Another had struck a mine. (It was a few days before I had time to go into a field dressing station to have my wounds seen to, they were not life threatening).

'We were being pinned down by the fortification that was directly above us. The Canadian captain got in touch with the two Centaurs and they made their way up behind the Germans and put the fortification out of action. My crew and I started to dismantle the obstacles and mines that we could get at the telegraph pole devices. I was able to flatten them but we were unable to explode the explosive heads because they had too much pitch blend around the nose caps to protect them from the seawater.

'On D+1 we moved inland where I was being used to remove German and our own damaged vehicles and remove other debris cluttering the road to

Caen. Then we got the message that a Panzer group was trying to cut us off so we had to fall back to the beach.'

Jim Gadd

'I was woken before dawn on what was to be one of the most significant days of my life. After having slept but fitfully with violent motions of the boat adding to my inner strain, I went through all the automatic preparations for any ordinary day. I tidied myself up, checking my few possessions and stowed away my supply of just two ounces of tobacco. It was an absurdly small amount, but I felt I might be tempting fate if I took a sensible supply!

'I stepped out on to the spray-blown, wind-swept tank deck. In the half light of near dawn, the tanks stood up in the dark silhouette, straining against their rasping chains. One of my lads was lying on the water-swept deck, being too sick to care. I hoisted him to his feet and bundled him into the mess deck. I then climbed up to the wheel house and, circling round it to the narrow after deck, I paused to look at the vague shapes of the vessels which were following us. Our wake carried a quite brilliant display of multicoloured phosphorescent lights which seemed singularly inappropriate in a setting and on a day when beauty was the last thing one might expect. It was there, completely alone, that I found I had to fight down a feeling of near panic which made me want to dive overboard and swim home. I just could not accept the situation I had made for myself.

'I made my way into the Mess Deck where the Colour Sergeant had already assembled the men, washed, dressed and in all respects ready to face the day. We lined them up and the Sergeant issued the grog. It is a strange thing that when troops are facing a particularly perilous situation, they become noisy, tell outrageous jokes - at which they roar with laughter and generally behave as if life was one big party. On this occasion, when we could not even guess our chances of survival, everyone - including me - was unbelievably cheerful.

'We were now close enough for those fearsome rocket-launching craft which operated from not far astern of us to send their warheads over our heads towards the beach. Each of these vessels carried 1,000 rockets which were-released in a series of volleys. To have released them all at one time would have threatened the fabric of the vessel itself. We had always disliked these rockets; they passed all too close above our heads in an erratic cloud. We feared a mid-air collision over our heads or a drop-out in our direction. On this, the only 'for real' occasion, a swarm of these things was flying towards an area also the target of one of our diving aircraft. I foresaw the tragedy ten seconds before it happened. The aircraft exploded in a ball of fire.

'Before we too went into the water, the tank jarred violently. I knew we had been hit. I checked that nothing untoward had happened in the driver's compartment, so assumed that nothing too serious had happened. Later I found a scar on the turret about a foot long and one inch deep in the middle. Had the anti-tank solid shot which had bitten so deeply into the steel of the turret struck us at a slightly less acute angle, it would have been curtains for us. The plan had been for the first wave to land below the first of the obstacles so that the Royal Engineers could tackle their clearance problems before the rising tide put later arrivals at risk from obstacles which would then be under water and capable of doing considerable damage. It occurred to me that had there been an experienced yachts-man on the planning committee, he would have recognised that with the heavy westerly winds which had been storming up the Channel for some days, tides would have been earlier than stated in the tide tables and have brought H-Hour forward.

'Still dodging these obstructions, I was concerned to hear some erratic noises from our engines. At the same time, the driver reported that he was up to his ankles in water - but somehow we made the water line to join the two Centaurs and I ordered the drain cocks to be opened. A glance back showed me what I suspected. Our air and exhaust extensions were pitted with bullet holes.

'We were now in our required position and were joined by the other two Centaurs which landed only shortly after we did. We could now settle down to keeping as many German heads down as possible to ease the lot of the Queens Own Rifles of Canada, who were now beginning to come ashore. We had no more open sight targets in view. We could only wait for indirect fire instructions from the advancing troops, or await our orders to move off the beach to our first normal gun position. With devastation all about us I could scarcely believe that my five tanks were largely undamaged and we had no casualties.

'During the lull, I ordered all tank crews to dismount to clear the bodies which had been washed up against our tracks. I could not move the tanks further up the beach while they were still there, in case any were still alive.'

John Leopard, who commanded a troop of four 95 mm howitzers, mounted in Centaur tanks - part of a 100-strong tank unit, formed specially to give close support for the assaulting infantry. The Royal Artillery and tank boys had bowed out - this job fell to the Royal Marine Armoured Support Group. Only half a dozen of the 2nd RM Armoured Support Group's forty tanks made it safely ashore. One was commanded by Colour Sergeant Jim Tuff:
'On the run-in we fired our 95mm and then the LCT broached-to [slewed broadside-on to the incoming waves]. By the time our Centaur went off it was pointing back almost to England! We went right under. A couple of waves came right over us. We were all waterproofed, except the top hatch just above my head, so the water was running down my neck. And I was ordering the driver 'Drive left... drive left... drive left...!' He said all he could see was seaweed.

'Originally a ramp was going to be put on the front of an LCT and two Centaurs side by side [would] fire over the bows during the run-in to the beach. But then they decided that was a complete waste of a landing craft so they let us go ashore. The boffins came up with some good ideas, like tins of soup with heating elements in the centre. In the middle of the night, sitting there on watch, you'd have hot soup in seconds. They were wonderful. Sometimes their ideas weren't so good. For example, because you could only carry so much ammunition inside the tank, they decided to attach a steel sledge, sealed and waterproof and packed with ammunition, to be towed behind each tank by two massive chains. When you were on the ramp on the LCT the sledge slid underneath. And as you moved off the chains tightened and you pulled it after you. So in Normandy we started off, dragging these things behind us. It was all right on the sand, but then we got on the road and you should've seen the sparks! These things were absolutely hot! So we just took as much into the tank as we could and then dumped them. We were only supposed to help form a beachhead and then go home but in fact we were there much longer than planned.

'We'd been shown photographs of what was where - 'that's a fortified house, over there's a pillbox, that sort of thing'. They said, 'But they won't be there, because with the Air Forces and the shelling from the warships, they'll probably all be obliterated'. Well, they were still there, all right. Then the main thing was to get off the beach. Once you got off that beach you weren't too bad. Those Beachmasters were terrific. Naval officers, shouting their lungs out. The organisation was just absolutely unbelievable. The stuff they had to think of. That's why it succeeded. We surprised them and all the stuff kept coming in - the kit, the troops.'

There were some things Jim Tuff wished he could just wipe out from my memory. 'Friendly tanks ran over some of our own people because you had to get off that beach. Never mind anything else, get off the beach. That'd been drummed into us. It was the only thing that mattered. Get us off the beach so they could pile the stuff in behind us.' [18]

'We had set off on the Sunday morning for invasion only to get well out from the Nab tower and get a recall and wait 24 hours to set off again on the fifth of June. The troops had been on board since the Saturday and the Mark V LCT had no provision for troop space. As well as tanks, we carried armoured bulldozers and the Command Centaur tanks mounting a 95mm howitzer on a special ramp at the forward end of the tank deck. Their job was to give fire support to the troops on the beach, an idea that evolved from the disaster at Dieppe when initial troop landings were decimated by enemy fire. It was intended that the Canadians would take the beach and secure it. Then the RN commandos would arrive to mop up and take further enemy strong points.

'As we passed the battleships the bombardment was going on and great belches of smoke were coming from their guns. The LCT(R)s were firing their salvoes of rockets and again there were great clouds of black smoke. A flight of Spitfires got caught in the salvo and one burst into flames and fell away to our port side. We passed the LCA carrier ships lowering their craft full of infantry and some were already heading for the beach. We had gone to action stations and would soon be at beaching stations. The noise was ear splitting and expectations were at high pitch. The troops were prepared and alert.

'We were approaching the shore and Bernières-sur-Mer was on our port side. Because of the German machine gun and sniper fire it was suicidal to expose any part of oneself so that my account is really a series of snapshots obtained by lightning peeps through the slits in the wheelhouse, keeping well to port away from any chance of fire from the immediate front.

'I saw shot hitting the church spire. To starboard was open land with a farmhouse in the distance. Bofors fire and tracer was going in to the farmhouse.

18 Adapted from *Invaders: British and American Experience of Seaborne landings 1939-1945* by Colin John Bruce (Chatham Publishing 1999).

The craft was lodged on the obstacles and as the waves came along it would lift the bow and then it would drop down on to the obstacles puncturing the hull. The rear of the craft was slewed to port and the props were also fouling the obstacles and stalling. The stokers were desperately trying to restart the engines. You could hear the 'thunk' as they engaged. (In fact the propeller blades were being torn off, of the three shafts there was only one blade out of 12 which survived).

'There looked to be a very bad situation on shore. The Canadians virtually ran into a wall of enfilading steel which decimated them. God knows how they found the courage to press on in such terrible circumstances. A large number of men could be seen under the shelter of the sea wall. They were without arms or helmets and looked in a critical position. These men were survivors from damaged LC(A)s, which had sunk attempting to navigate through the obstacles. One of the army officers on board tried to swim ashore to see if he could help but he was washed back and dragged onboard exhausted. As the LC(A)s went in the Germans opened up and one to starboard lost many men. Perhaps twenty or more men fell in an arrowhead. One or two struggled to get up and then fell back. When the commandos arrived in their LCI(S)s the beach was still being defended by the Germans.

'We were in a bad situation sinking slowly on to the beach. Then there was an almighty explosion on the port side and the craft heeled over to starboard. We had hit a mine. The engine room was flooding and we were going down on to the beach. The skipper gave the order to abandon ship'. Then realising we were on the bottom he belayed the order and we watched the water come up the tank deck and up to the mess deck door. But it came no higher. Someone said to come and help a chap in the water. They said the firing had stopped. He was an LC(A) coxswain, a Royal Marine. His craft had sunk and he was swimming for dear life. We had to lower a man down to grab hold of him and then dragged him up the side, got him down below with a blanket and a tin of self-heating soup. He was saying, 'You saved my life. You saved my life.'

'The Canadians had secured the beach and we had a look round. Everywhere there were dead men lying in all sorts of positions. Mostly Canadians, you could see the darker green uniforms. Damaged craft and debris, what a spectacle of despair and sadness.

'We stayed on board with our tins of self heating soup and air raids at night for three days, the dead all around us. We then were taken out to the 'Gooseberry' (a ring of sunken merchant ships) and then sent ashore as a working party at Courseulles where we stayed for six weeks before returning to Cowes roads and Southampton.'
19-year old Malcolm Cook, Wireman LCT(A) 2306, 103rd Flotilla, Second Support Squadron.

'It still amazes me how we got that big Landing Craft, Tank (Rocket) up the Beaulieu River that night; and with two right-turning screws, as well. Because in order to get LCTs into mass production they'd given them two identical 500bhp Paxman Ricardo diesels, 12 cylinder jobs. That meant two right-turning screws, which made manoeuvring very difficult. When you started up, for example, there was an immediate kick out to starboard by the stern. Going astern it moved to port. At least with out-turning or in-turning screws you're balanced. Incidentally, all LCT(R)s, with their very high profile, not only rolled like 'flat bottomed cows' but also made 3 to 4 knots broadside-on downwind if the engines were stopped. The engines themselves were pretty good, but they had to have a major service after every 1,000 hours. Whoever heard of a marine engine having to be serviced every 1,000 hours?

'Everybody thought that this new type of rocket craft was pretty hot stuff. In particular, its reputation from Salerno was such that the Army said they wanted rocket craft for Normandy and that was that. I think for the morale of the invading troops, as much as anything. The chaps in these little LCAs were enormously cheered seeing these rockets going over their heads and the entire beach disappearing under friendly explosions. However good your training, it's still very hard when you know that you're going to be the first man ashore. The fact that there may be another thousand following on behind you isn't really very relevant.

'The rockets were in racks. You manhandled them into the launchers and slid them down in. The forecast was we were going to lose a lot of these craft, 50 per cent losses on D-Day, so we were told to carry just one load. Then if we survived we'd come back and they'd put Royal Marines on to take the donkey work off the crew and we'd be rearmed and turned around in twelve hours. Each rocket had to be lowered down with a sort of hooked stick. You were watching all the time, in case it hit the bottom and came straight out at you again. One did! Landed in the Mayor of Southampton's garden, I think. The rockets themselves weighed 56lbs. Half of that was cordite propellant, which was deemed to be pretty safe and half of it was high explosive. You had a fuse on the front, which when it accelerated would arm itself. But before that you had to pull out the locking pin, so off the coast of Normandy you had to lug each rocket back up again, with your hooked stick and take this arming pin out and lower it gently back down again.

'The firing procedure was to go down below, everybody except the CO and the signalman. The radar operator would be calling the range - LCT(R)s were the only landing craft fitted with radar from the outset. The rockets fired a fixed distance ahead of us, because all 1,080 of them were set at 45 degrees to the deck. when your radar picked up the beach you had to calculate the mean point of range - perhaps you were trying to hit a gun emplacement 100yds inland, so you had to run on that distance - then add corrections for wind, corrections for temperature and so on. All done at the last moment.

'I would be down in the wheelhouse with the helmsman. We had beautiful big gyro compass So the helmsman could judge it perfectly, because of course the only way of aiming was to aim the whole craft. I'd watch the helmsman and make sure the radar operator was getting the right ranges in. He'd start off in 100yd steps and then down to 50 yard steps and then when he reached the appropriate one - we'd tell him which one to emphasise - he would sing out.

'By that time the CO would've instructed the signalman to get below. He'd disappear and join us. That would leave only the CO up top. Since the bridge was untenable while the rockets were being fired, there was an armoured box built there, with a voice pipe down to the radar operator, so the CO could hear the radar operator's voice. The CO would duck in at the last minute and slam the hatch and when the radar operator said 'Fire!' he'd close the master switch. Until the CO's master switch went over, he had the power to arrest the firing. The Navy does cling to this idea that the Captain's the only one who knows what's going on.

'After that we just fired blind, for however long it took - thirty salvoes of 36 rockets each. About three minutes. During which time our speed would decrease steadily - we'd be slowed down from 6 knots to about 1 or 2, by the efflux from all the rockets blasting away. We reckoned on 5 per cent of the rockets not firing. I think on D-Day our particular count was fourteen misfires.

'Everybody stayed below deck for half an hour to let the deck cool down, because it got red hot. Only the CO and the signalman were allowed back on the bridge. After the half hour was up you could go on deck and have a look and after an hour you could remove the misfires and chuck them over the side. And then, of course, there's a sudden feeling of emptiness. Wondering what the hell to do next. The instructions were to turn round and make for a position out of the way. I'll never forget turning round and looking back out to sea again, at this mass of ships. We retreated over to a corner of 'Juno' and then we threaded our way back, so we were in the Beaulieu River that night and maybe a day, or two days later we were sent down to Portsmouth to reload. I remember complaining to this Royal Navy captain that I'd yet to see any evidence that the Germans existed. 'Oh, don't worry about that', he said, '1 was in the Great War. I was at sea the whole time and I only ever saw the enemy for eleven seconds!'

Temporary Sub-Lieutenant Dudley Roessler RNVR. [19]

'At 0300 I awoke and after a few minutes I remembered that this was D-Day and that maybe I'd better get up and see what was cooking. After a wash, shave and bit of food I went on deck. What a sight! The sun sparkled on the pale green water, here and there were patches of deepest blue, where the shadow of a fluffy white cloud passed. Everywhere I looked I saw ships and craft of all sizes and shapes. Our five LCIs were travelling line ahead and listing gracefully to port and starboard as they ploughed their zigzag way toward the invasion coast. on our port side were seven big LSTs also line ahead, pushing their way through the rollers with set determination, while on the starboard side, some LCTs were spanking the waves in a noble but losing effort to keep up with the band. On the horizon on either side were the cruisers and destroyers with an occasional huge form of a capital ship. Bombers and Fighters passed over us in continuous waves, all with their bright new black and white stripes. The steady throbbing roar of their motors dispelled any doubt in my mind as to the outcome of the whole affair. Now and then a fast escort vessel would break out of formation and go scudding off in a contrary direction. The skipper would grunt and say, 'The bastards are trying to get in on our starboard, 'E'll get a

19   Adapted from *Invaders: British and American Experience of Seaborne landings 1939-1945* by Colin John Bruce (Chatham Publishing 1999).

penny's worth if he tries that'.

'At about 0715 we could see the long low line of white cliffs. Already great columns of smoke were rising. The Air Force was doing its job with a vengeance. The battleships were throwing in their share of stuff. Things were beginning to liven up. At about 0800 our craft formed line and we were going in. I was on the verge of descending from the bridge when a shell tore through our rigging and another burst in the water a few yards away. It had no restraining influence on me. I almost jumped from the bridge and I had on my 'light assault jacket' which weighed at least a hundredweight.

'Most of the fellows were ready to go in, their Mae-Wests giving them all an outlandish shape. I was very interested in the expression on their faces. Some looked like a wounded spaniel; some were quite nonchalant about it. Others made a feeble effort at gaiety. What amused me most was a fat boy trying to whistle but the best he could do was blow air with a squeak now and then. Just between ourselves I was pretty scared myself about that time. Those last few moments were pretty awful. It was the waiting that was hard. We were coming under pretty intense small arms fire by this time and everyone was down as much as possible.

'At last the gangways were run down and it was a case of get up, get in and get down. I manoeuvred into position to be as near as possible to the front. I wanted to be one of the first to land; not because of any heroics, but waiting your turn on the exposed ramp was much worse than going in. A sergeant and a corporal started down. I was third. The sergeant couldn't touch bottom but pushed away and swam in towards shore. The corporal started to follow and I plunged in but the weight of my 'light' jacket, filled with enough canned goods to start a grocery store, pulled me under, in spite of my Mae West. I got back onto the ramp and the skipper, very sensibly, decided to pull off and try and come in a bit better. A couple of sharp cracks in the water near me made me jump onto that ramp in a hurry. While I was floundering about in the water, the corporal got into trouble. There was a terrific back wash and only quick action by a brave merchant navy lad saved him from drowning.

'The next run at the shore put me in about 3 feet 6 inches of water. A naval fellow with a life belt went in with a rope and I followed. I must have been a ridiculous sight, holding onto my pistol in one hand and a bag of my valuables (mostly cigs) in the other, as well as trying to hold on to the rope. Some of the men had great difficulty ashore, particularly the short ones. One poor chap was crushed to death when the ramp broke away in the heavy seas and slammed him between it and the side of the ship.

'I didn't lose much time getting to the back of the beach where there was a bit of protection and wriggled out of my assault jacket. I swore then and there never to wear that thing again. Many of the assault troops had already crossed the beach and were fighting forward towards their objective, a ridge a few hundred yards back from the beach. The houses along the waterfront were well stocked with snipers, having been bypassed by our forward troops. If, as the radio announced later, that it was an unopposed landing, God forbid that anyone should ever have to go in on an opposed one! Our beach was littered with those who had been a jump ahead of us. A captured blockhouse being used as a dressing station was literally surrounded by piles of bodies. Many of the lads on our LCI never got ashore. A Spandau opened up just when the water was full of men struggling to get ashore.

'I crawled and ran to the place where I was to meet the rest of our little organization. This was accomplished without mishap except that a tin hat, much too small for me, which I had borrowed from a poor chap, was knocked from my head by something or other, which I neither saw nor heard.

'The afternoon and evening of D-Day was devoted to 'delousing' the houses behind our beach and quite a job it was. We were a bit clumsy at first and lost quite a few because of it, but soon it became more or less a drill. We found ourselves in little groups, nothing intentional or premeditated on anyone's part. I had a small group of two sergeants and six sappers. They had plenty of guts and were simply eager when we formed a plan to 'do' a certain house. By dark most of the houses in our immediate vicinity were clean. My loot up to that point was a swastika flag, which I had torn from the wall of a sort of HQ or Mess. Some of the houses just refused to be deloused so we burned them. We set one on fire, which had caused us a lot of grief and when it really started to brew one young Jerry made an effort to escape through a window. He got partly out when a gunner on a LCT saw him. A streak of about fifty Oerlikon rounds hit him. He hung there for a couple of days until a burial party found him…'

A Canadian Officer on board a LCI.

'On Monday the long wait ended. The engines of our American LST at anchor in the Thames Estuary came alive, the rumble of the anchor chain, the engine room telegraph and we were off. (The LST was fitted out as a hospital ship (of sorts) for the return journey, with rows of folding bunks on each side of the tank space and an operating table in the Ward Room (Officers Mess). It is impossible to describe the feeling of relief. It was strangely exhilarating. The sense of brooding suddenly evaporated and gave way to smiling faces, jokes, light heartedness and rudery. Out to sea we went, past North Foreland, Ramsgate, the Goodwins, much too far out in the Channel for my liking. There was France on our left with all its heavy coastal artillery. They must presently blow us to pieces but strangely not a shot was fired. Two destroyers passed at speed laying a welcome smoke screen. On and on we went in this ever-growing, awe-inspiring fleet heading for 'Piccadilly Circus', the area South of the Isle of Wight where the ships from the East met those from the West and were joined by a monumental armada from Portsmouth, Southampton and the Solent. This was something the world had never seen before, the biggest invasion in history - 4,000 ships. The Spanish Armada had 130!

'Night came and another day - D-Day.

'Looking from the bridge we saw men moving about, some sitting on top of the covered wagons, one playing a banjo, one having a haircut, gunners swivelling their weapons - a spirit of nonchalance. Then came the voice of the BBC Home Service at full volume throughout the ship: 'Under the command of General Eisenhower, allied Naval Forces began landing allied armies this morning on the Northern coast of France'. The already high spirits went even higher - Jubilation! But this was short-lived for we were approaching a large curious looking object in the water and passed close by it. It was the underside of an upturned landing craft. It had a sobering effect and your imagination is as good as mine.

'Soon we were at our appointed landing place and were ordered to anchor offshore until the beach-head was secure as we were carrying highly secret equipment which must not fall into enemy hands. My church pennant was now hoisted. Canadian and British troops had stormed the defences and we listened to the battle further along the beach and just behind the rising ground in front of us. A signal came from ashore, 'Send in your chaplain'. Three US sailors delivered me ashore in one of our assault craft, on grounding they dropped the ramp and I was about to step into the water when I was suddenly swept off my feet by two large sailors and planted dry-shod on the sand. Then they began to dance about with boyish delight at being on 'Juno' Beach on D-Day. I thought, 'I wish to God they would do it somewhere else?'

'I went on my way up the beach walking (like that Old Testament character Agag who 'walked delicately'.) There was a Sherman flail tank going to and fro exploding mines. I was astounded at the number of them, mostly small but occasionally a big one when the tank would immediately stop (and the chains hang limply down) whilst the driver had time to recover from the blinding blast and concussion right in front of his face. Things were relatively quiet apart from sniping. Of course there were artillery shells, mines and booby traps and occasional hit-and-run raids by enemy aircraft. It was no place for German pilots that day for we had 11,000 aircraft in the sky.

'My first encounter was with three Canadian soldiers who had been in a slit trench, five of them, when a bomb landed in one end. When it exploded so did a petrol bowser across the road. These three men had no hair on their faces, no eyelashes, no eyebrows and no hair below the line of their helmets. Their faces were scorched scarlet. They were in a sorry state scarcely knowing where they were. I asked about the other two. Couldn't find a trace of the first. Of the second all we could find of him was in a sack on the ground. You could pick it up with one hand.

'Having stayed with them for a time I moved on to the wounded on stretchers, (the majority of them were Germans as they had suffered a fearful bombardment from sea and air before our landing) and then on to the burial of the dead. (These casualties were later exhumed and moved to war cemeteries.)

'There was much work to be done that day: 'The Longest Day'. The briefest survey must include my admiration for the doctors and sick bay attendants.

'I had at least 16 Channel crossings in the ensuing weeks. I vividly remember the rows of dead German soldiers all carefully laid out on the ground by our orderlies with the contents of their pockets and identity discs in bags attached to their uniforms, subsequently to be sent to their next of kin. They looked so young compared with our more mature soldiers. I remember the farmyards and paddocks near Courseulles, where horses and cattle lay dead in the fields, pigs with their feet in the air and groups of cows still alive crying out pitifully to be milked.

'There were two exciting days and infernally noisy nights with vehicles, tanks, armoured cars, pouring ashore past our high and dry landing craft in a constant

stream, everybody blazing away with their guns at the sound of aircraft passing over. It is impossible to describe 'the volume of noise and flak going up like a firework display to end all - and of course our own shrapnel coming down like rain. We were all in danger of being killed by our own gunfire.'
Chaplain Mike Crooks RN.

'With our LST now a hundred yards off the Normandy shore, Crusader tanks fitted with 20mm anti-aircraft guns unlashed and all ready to go, the front doors were opened. The ramp lowered and down into the sea went the tanks; long since carefully water-proofed and tested as well they needed to be, for the water was all of five feet deep. To the left and right were other LSTs, some disabled having hit mines, but we managed our dash to the shore without any problems, weaving our way on the sea-bed between steel spikes, sticking up at all angles and put there by the Germans to deter us. Like hounds at a hedgerow, looking for a way through, we were soon up on dry land, stationary with guns at the ready to beat off the German air force which never came and the drivers - pulling savagely at the waterproofing so that the engines could once again run as their makers had intended. Suppose that in all that movement, on something never before tried in world history, to have been only half an hour late was something of a triumph for the masterly organisation which we saw throughout.

'My first real shock was to see not one but perhaps a hundred of our men dead, lying at the water's edge, their bodies rolling unnaturally on the sand as the tide washed around them. Devastation was everywhere. Nothing was in one piece. Tree trunks snapped off by shells were strewn across the road. Every building was wrecked by the earlier bombardment of the Navy. Cows lay awkwardly, legs in the air, dead or dying from bullets and shrapnel which had ripped through the air not half an hour before. Overhead was the fierce crack of the Navy's 21 shells on their way inland to stop the Germans from coming forward at us. The noise was unbelievable, made worse, if possible, by Frenchmen in berets worn like skull caps, running here, there and everywhere, too bewildered to know what they were doing.

'Bill Lean, my troop commander, met up with me and together we walked down the village street, now in ruins, the road so jammed with debris that we could not see the tar, to get to the church and spy out the land for the best gun positions. A shell had hit the church steeple and now there was a gaping hole six feet across. Up there was a German sniper. Before long we heard the familiar crack of rifle fire over our heads but we were seemed immune because of our training with live firing and the sound was not so unusual. 'Do you know something kid?' said Bill beaming all over, 'I think someone's firing at us.' But we just walked on and to this day I have no idea why we did not bother to take cover. It never occurred to either of us. However a few minutes later a well-aimed Bofors round put a stop to that little nuisance and I heard no more shots.

'Our job was to reach two bridges, one over the Orne canal at Bénouville and the other 100 yards to the east, over the Orne river. We were to protect them from air attack as they were the only road link between the beach and the 6th Airborne Division who had landed to the east of the river. As it turned out we did not see a German aircraft for at least a week. The bridges lay on the other side of a minefield. As I had been on the course I was told to organise a way through for the tanks. In their methodical way the Germans had every minefield marked with barbed wire and on the top strand hung a notice saying, Achtung Minen. If the writing sloped to the left it was a dummy. To the right it was an anti-personnel field. Upright meant an anti-tank one. The way I wanted to go was through an area with upright lettering so I knew I was looking for buried mines and not those showing on the surface. I knew exactly what to do until I came across the first mine. I had never seen one like it before. Even if I knew all about German mines I was not prepared for this and all the others to be British; captured at Dunkirk in 1940 and used against us now. I had no idea how to handle any of them.

'When eventually I did clear a way through no one would volunteer to drive the first tank down my taped path. 'You cleared the way, sir,' said the troop sergeant-major, 'and if you don't mind', he added with a huge grin, 'perhaps you would prove it is all right by taking No.1 down there yourself?'

'On my first run down the lane and at the end of it, it was necessary to turn sharp left; in doing so on sandy ground, a track broke under the strain of the earth which built up against the tank' side. It could not be easily mended where it was, so I hunted round for a Royal Engineer's road-laying tank and asked the Major with it if he would pull my helpless tank to better ground. To do so meant going down my cleared lane, but the tracks of a Churchill tank differ from those of a Crusader and although I had manage it successfully, the wider tank ran over a mine I had managed to miss, wrecking it and killing the driver.'

22-year old R. S. Haig-Brown, 93rd Light AA Regiment, Royal Artillery.

'A feature of 'Juno' was a concrete wall, which provided good cover for assault troops who reached it. But the wall was fifty yards from the water's edge and many perished on the open sands in between. The beach was sprayed from all angles by enemy machine guns and now their mortars and heavy guns began hitting us. The noise was deafening. All the while enemy shells came screaming in faster and faster. As we crawled along we could hear bullets and shrapnel cutting into the sand around us. When a shell came screaming over you dug into the sand and held your breath, waited for the blast and the shower of stones and debris that followed.'

'Hickey crawled along the sand towards a group of three badly wounded men. He had just reached them when a shell landed among them, killing the three wounded but sparing the padre. He reached many others before they died and identified their religion from a disc worn around the neck. Whether Catholic or Protestant, I would tell the man he was dying and to be sorry for his sins and often I was rewarded by the dying man opening his eyes and nodding to me knowingly. I will never forget the courage of the stretcher bearers and first aid men that morning,'

'Hickey helped to put the wounded on stretchers and carry them to the shelter of the sea wall.'

Reverend R. M. Hickey, chaplain to Canada's North Shore Regiment whose work on D-Day resulted in the award of the Military Cross.

'Our job was to breach the walls and make a roadway up so we could get our tanks through. We landed in the water sitting in the truck. We were under heavy fire at the time although it did cool down a bit in the afternoon. There were bodies everywhere and soldiers running around getting dug in. D-Day was when I first had the shock of seeing our fellows killed.'

'People were placing bets on who in my company would be seasick first. I was the reluctant favourite and did not disappoint my backers. We had a Scotsman with us who used to get us out of bed in the morning by playing the Reveille on bagpipes. We said he wasn't going to take them to Normandy and on the way over someone got into his cabin and threw them in the sea. The Scot was not a happy piper but he did live to enjoy the last laugh. In the wee small hours of D-Day plus one, as the exhausted sappers snoozed away their first night in Normandy, they were suddenly woken by the Sound of bagpipes played by Scottish Canadians camped next door!'
Sapper Ron Field, Royal Engineers.

'…We watched one salvo go high over the beach just as a Spitfire came along. He flew right into it and blew up. That pilot never had a chance and was probably the first casualty on 'Juno' Beach. Overhead we can hear the roar of large shells from battleships, cruisers and destroyers. Beside us is a boat with pom-poms (anti-aircraft) guns shooting away at church steeples and other high buildings, which had observers who were spotting for the German ground troops.

'Soon we were only 500 yards from the beach and were ordered to get down. Minutes later the boat stops and begins to toss in the waves. The ramp goes down and without hesitation my section leader, Corporal John Gibson, jumps out well over his waist in water. He only makes a few yards and is killed. We have landed dead on into a pillbox with a machine gun blazing away at us. We didn't hesitate and jumped into the water one after the other - I was last of the first row. Where was everybody? My section are only half there - some were just floating on their Mae Wests.

'My Bren gun team of Tommy Dalrymple and Kenny Scott are just in front of me when something hit my left magazine pouch and stops me up short for a moment. The round had gone right through two magazines, entered my left side and came out my back. Kenny keeps yelling Come on. Come on!

'I'm coming, I'm coming I yell to him. We are now up to our knees in water and you can hear a kind of buzzing sound all around as well as the sound of the machine gun itself. All of a sudden something slapped the side of my right leg and then a round caught me dead centre up high on my right leg causing a compound fracture. By this time I was flat on my face in the water - I've lost my rifle, my helmet is gone and Kenny is still yelling at me to come on. He is also shot in the upper leg but has no broken bones. I yell back, I can't, my leg is broken - get the hell out of here. Away he goes and catches up to Tommy. Poor Tom, I've got ten of his Bren gun magazines and they're pulling me under. I soon get rid of them and flop over onto my back and start to float to shore where I meet five other riflemen all in very bad shape. The man beside me is dead within minutes. All the while we are looking up at the machine gun firing just over our heads at the rest of our platoon and company and then our platoon Sergeant and friend of mine, who had given up a commission to be with us was killed right in front of me.

'Finally I decided that this is not a good place to be and managed to slip off my pack and webbing and start to crawl backward on my back at an angle away from the gun towards the wall about 150 feet away. I finally made it and lay my back against it. In front of me I can see bodies washing back and forth in the surf. Soon, one of my friends, Willis Gambrel, a walking wounded, showed up and we each had one of my cigarettes, which surprisingly were fairly dry. Then he left to find a first aid centre. A medic came along and put a bandage on my leg. I had forgotten all about the hole in my side. Then two English beach party soldiers came along carrying a 5-gallon pot of tea. 'Cup of tea Canada?'

'Yes sir - and they gave me tea in a tin mug. It was hot and mixed 50/50 with rum. It was really good.

'Okay? he said and as darkness fell on 6 June. I was soon asleep.

'By this time all that was left of my platoon of 35 men was one Lance Sergeant, one wounded Lance Corporal and six riflemen. All the rest were dead or wounded. Field Marshal Erwin Rommel had been right - it had been and will always be the longest day. Altogether The Queen's Own Rifles lost 143 men killed or wounded.

'Lest we forget.'

Private Jim Wilkins, The Queen's Own Rifles, 3rd Canadian Infantry Division.

'It was around midnight on June 5 when we became aware that we were moving. One could sense tension rising. At last the order came for us to don our equipment and prepare to move down to the vehicle deck. Nothing could be heard except the drone of the ship's engines and it was 6 am when we sensed that we had stopped.

'Once outside, we found we were at least two miles out from the coast, which we could just see from our low position. The sea was full of ships of all shapes and sizes. Naval destroyers were firing over our heads towards the coast. All this time we were plodding forward, so slowly it seemed at times we were not moving. A DUKW's normal speed is about 4 knots in calm water, but loaded and in a heavy swell, our speed was more like 2 knots.

'I suppose one could describe the scene on the beach as organised chaos. A boat had been sent out to guide us in and the engineers had done a fantastic job in clearing areas of the beach enforcements, which were all piled in huge heaps. I can't say how many landing craft were on the beach at that time - a number of them were burning and had obviously been struck by shells. But apart from the spasmodic shell coming over on to the beach, there didn't appear at that time to be very much danger. We understood that the Canadians had moved inland some half, three quarters of a mile. One was still conscious of a lot of gunfire - in other words, ships were still firing inland to various points, but basically we were very tensed up about it and one could say it was organised confusion.

'The beach itself was cluttered with debris; a number of landing craft were burning on the water's edge. My first shock was spotting the first dead body. I'd never seen a dead body in my life before. This particular chap was so immaculate - just as though he had been stood to attention, with his small pack and his webbing all beautifully blancoed. There he was and we had to stop for a moment right beside him. It was if he had been standing then just gone flat down on his face. It absolutely shattered me - I couldn't take my eyes off him. We saw quite a lot of other bodies lying around, but what the Medical Corps had done was to set about treating the wounded and get them away and then take care of the bodies afterwards.

'There was a sniper in the church tower and we had to wait for them to be cleared. We passed into the centre of this small town - not even a square - then we turned into an open field.

'Looking over the fence, the best part of a herd of cows had been slaughtered by the shell fire and were lying around with their feet in the air - which rather upset me, coming as I did from the country.

'After that we dismounted and unloaded the ammunition into heaps and were escorted back down through Courseulles, along the causeway, to the outskirts of Bernières-sur-Mer. We turned into a fantastic driveway of a château which had hardly been damaged at all. We drew round the back where orchards were laid out and were told to disperse around the perimeter there. There was a lot of noise going on there, but one felt quite remote from it. We were very delighted to have got there in one piece.

'We got together and dug one hell of a big trench then constructed a ledge half way down so we could sit and covered the top with apple branches which had been knocked down by the shells. We covered over with groundsheets and had a hot meal of stew - we did nothing else but smoke and talk about the events of that day.'

Bill Williams RASC, **seconded to the 3rd Canadian Division for supplies.**

'June 5 1944 was my 24th birthday, celebrated aboard an American-crewed landing ship. I was the driver of an ambulance jeep. But as I was about to drive from the ship on to a landing craft a naval officer attached a trailer full of ammunition to my tow-bar. What about the red crosses on my vehicle? What about the Geneva Convention? But at such a moment how can you start an argument with a superior officer? About 30 minutes later we were on 'Juno' beach behind Canadian infantry and armour. Flame-throwers had been directed against German pillboxes and blinded soldiers in them. Many of them were doomed. They were treated by medics and seated in deckchairs. There was nothing else that could be done for them.'

A. W. Sadler.

'Waiting off Normandy beaches I was to go ashore 10.30 am, D-Day, having been briefed early on that the first 48 hours, was crucial, due to German Panzers splitting into three groups and would take 48 hours for them to assemble into an attack force and that 50 per cent casualties were expected on landing. On our section, 'Juno', we had before leaving the UK, been attached to the Canadians and they were due to land at 6.30 am. Taking Caen was the main objective due to crossroad and also that our beaches would be out of range of the German 88's. We had been told that, no soldier under 19½-years old would be sent into the invasion. I was now just over that age, being called up on 4 March 1943 at 18.

'Damage I saw: Caen, badly damaged by massive air strikes. Cologne was the same, but the strange part was the bridge which we travelled over and cathedral was still standing among this destruction. This is where I felt sorry for the German people, what it must have been; the nights all those bombs and incendiaries came raining down.

'Back home whilst on my first leave since going to Normandy, there were some prisoners of war, who had just walked past. Then an oldish lady rushed over to me and shouted 'Them are better than you lot, bugger off back to Germany!' The lads had been lambasted by the press because they were speaking to the Germans, when they had been told not to. I spent most of my leave in bed under my parent's roof. It was nice to be home, after spending each day as if it was a bonus. My mate and I went to a local dance at the village hall, while on this leave and you know what, we spent the evening talking to German prisoners of war that were camped nearby, as if we were all comrades in arms.'

Tom Whitehouse, driver, Royal Army Service Corps.

'…The night of D-Day was a weird fantastic thing. The wind had died down. Several buildings were burning viciously. Others were just smouldering. An ammunition DUKW hit in the early evening burned brightly and crackled with the detonations of exploding ammo. All night we 'stood to' as we fully expected a counter attack or German paratroops and with the sea at our backs we had no alternative positions. I got terribly cold but there we all were. Jerry bombers were constantly overhead and dropping everything that would drop. Our AA was magnificent both from the ships and the shore and more than one Jerry plane came down in blazing pieces. Big guns helped to make the night a veritable bell, particularly those across the mouth of the Arne. It was the longest night I ever knew but at last day began to break and D-Day was a thing of the past. So much for D-Day, D+1 and up to D+10. Every day had its full quota of incidents. The shelling of our beach continued non-stop day and night for 70 days, but it was remarkable how flew casualties there were for so much shelling.'

A Canadian Officer.

'When we dropped anchor off the Normandy beaches we were at last allowed out of the hold onto the deck. The fresh air did us all good. What we were then to see I will never forget. It was unbelievable. There were hundreds of landing craft, large transporters, large and small warships. I have never seen so many. The landing craft were buzzing around like hornets carrying troops and supplies to the beach. The warships, including HMS *Warspite,* were sending salvo after salvo of shells in land. All of a sudden it was our turn to go over the side. First our half tracks and Bren gun carriers were lowered into the landing, craft followed by their crews. The scramble nets were then slung over the side then we had to go down the nets with all our gear on our back and our rifle around our neck. The little landing craft were rising and falling with the swell and I remember thinking, 'one slip old son and its goodbye life', but I'm glad to say we all made it. Once we were all into the landing craft we were away towards the beach which was about six hundred yards away. Once we hit the bottom the ramps went down and we were away onto the beach as fast as possible. We had landed on 'Juno' beach.

'The first thing we did was to remove the water proofing from the engines and then to make contact with the rest of our Battalion. I remember the terrible smell. The stench of cordite burning buildings but most of all was the stench of dead animals. There were hundreds of them lying dead on their backs. It was a hot day and the smell was terrible, never have I seen such terrible slaughter of animals. It made you feel sick. We pulled into an orchard for a rest for a few hours and have a meal. We hadn't eaten since we left Tilbury. We had a chance to write home and we were able to have a church service. I remember that the apples on the trees looked really inviting so I tried one, Ugh, they were cider apples; should have known.'
Rifleman Eric Patience.

'About a mile or so from Berniéres-sur-Mer I and my DUKW was unceremoniously slung over the side of the supply ship and into the sea and I had to drive that distance onto the beach to rendezvous with the rest of my platoon and to discharge the load of stretchers that I was carrying. All hell had broken out; the noise from all types of gunfire, shells and bombs exploding was everywhere. What I was about to witness in the next few hours and months, no training or teaching in the world could prepare you. Death and destruction was all around me; they were unbelievable scenes and ones that I will never EVER forget, but for all that I had a job to do and had to get on with it if I wanted to survive. We made our HQ in a small Chateau about a mile from the beach and by midday the Canadian infantry had got about 3-4 miles inland and were able to set up a supply dump this meant that we could start our work of getting supplies ashore from the supply ships as quickly as possible. We worked from dusk till dawn every day, seven days a week. I sat in my DUKW at four thirty in the morning, waiting to go down to the beach to start work when Cleckner, our Provo corporal, climbed up the side of my vehicle and said 'caught you Smithy': Smoking on a WD vehicle and he put me on a charge. I went before the CO next morning and got stopped two weeks pay; and this was in the first week of the invasion! How's that for discipline? It didn't end there. Two weeks later the very same corporal did me for being improperly dressed, i.e., not wearing my hat, that cost me another two weeks pay, so in five weeks I lost four weeks' pay but what the hell; there was nowhere to spend it anyway.'
Leonard Smith RASC. 'Because the Germans had us bogged down we worked the beaches with our DUKWs, for about five weeks till the fall of Caen. We then changed the DUKWs for three ton Ford Wat Six's; they turned out to be really good, reliable workhorses.'

'We had been in North Africa, Sicily and Italy and I suppose we were veterans, having taken part in two landings. We knew when we were all told to man our tanks and prepare to start engines that the time to land was close. The ship slowed to a halt, the bows opened and there before us in the morning light was the beach. Fighting was going on just off the beach. Sitting in the driver's seat, I began to move our Sherman fitted with its new 17-pounder gun (the first we had ever had, up until then we had the 75mm gun) down the ramp. I moved the tank very slowly down the ramp and began to ease her off the end, waiting for the drop into what we had expected to be about 6 feet of water. We were all battened down and well waterproofed, which as it turned out was just as well, because instead of 6 feet there was 10 or 12 feet of water we fell into. Unknown to the ship's captain, we had pulled in right onto a shell hole and there we were, well under water. Before I could decide what to do, voices were reaching US over our radio telling us not to try to move. The water as it turned out was almost to the top of our air intake and if we had tried to pull out, the rear of the tank would have gone down and perhaps we would have all been drowned. I was told to cut the engine and wait for instructions. We sat there waiting for the tide to go out for almost two hours. We were able to follow what was going on, on the radio, but seeing nothing except water through our periscopes, until at last as the water went down, we could see and finally with the better part of our Regiment well off the beaches we were able to rejoin them. We had not enjoyed our forced stay in the water but who knows, because of it perhaps I am alive today.'

Trooper M. G. Gale, the driver of a Sherman tank in 44th Royal Tank Regiment, 4th Armoured Brigade, who landed on 'Juno' on D+1. Gale and his crew were saved by the extension on the air intake which was designed to keep the engine dry while the tank was in the water. It was to be blown away by a small pre-set charge once the tank was on dry land.

'Next day [7 June] saw us in action amongst the villages and farm houses around the big air base just outside Caen. There were quite a few machine gun nests to deal with. If anyone had told me years earlier that I would be taking part in the greatest invasion this world had seen I would have laughed. Still here I was, just goes to show that you can never foresee the future. We were in action all along the front line and sadly we were slowly losing our men sometimes having to bury some of our mates just where they fell. The Germans fought hard and gave us a hard time. I often wonder what would have happened if we had been defeated in that bridgehead and been driven back into the sea. We had a very bad storm one day which did a lot of damage to our harbour but things turned out OK.

'On or about 3 weeks after D-Day we, that is the 11th Armoured Division, plus two infantry divisions were given orders to capture bridges across the Oder and Oden rivers. There was to be a heavy artillery barrage of over a thousand guns, this was Monty's trademark just like El Alamein a couple of years before. The noise was very loud and we had no ear protection like today. The guns started in the early morning and the noise was shattering, it went on and on, it seemed like hours. As we waited for the order to move forward, please don't ask how I felt because I could not tell you. All I did know was that I was glad I was not on the receiving end of this barrage. As we moved forward so did the shells, this is called a creeping barrage. The infantry divisions went first and the barrage stopped at last. As it did out came the Germans from the cellars in the villages and from their holes in the ground. They were shaken but still full of fight. We managed to capture the bridges across the rivers but with heavy loss. The Germans lost more and the prisoners we took were all ages. Some of them were only 15 or 16 years old but they were the worse. We soon learnt not to trust them or turn our back on them.

'More and more animals were being killed, towns and villages were being destroyed and hundreds of men were being killed or wounded but we still had to carry on. We had to eat and sleep when we could, washing was a thing of the past and eating was rare. Every section, which consisted of nine men, had their own rations which we had to cook and eat when we could. By now I had been in action for about three weeks and at no time had any of us taken our clothes off or had a decent meal. You slept when and where you could. We lost a lot of our tanks by anti-tank guns, one being the 88mm. The Shermans we had were called 'Tommy cookers' because after being hit they would blow up. Sometimes the crew were able to get out and sometimes they were killed or wounded but the very worse was when a crew member was wounded and couldn't get out their screams were terrible and it was terrible to listen to, knowing we couldn't do anything to help. I remember when one of our carriers hit a mine the driver lost both his legs and it was terrible but thankfully over quick. We buried him in his carrier which was a wreck. He was only 21. We had two brothers in our company. The elder one was badly wounded and sent back via the mobile hospital. He was put on a landing craft which was to carry him and the other wounded soldiers to the hospital ship lying off shore. We later heard that the landing craft hit a mine and no one survived. The younger brother was devastated but he had to go on.

'The city of Caen was being bombed and shelled all the time but the Germans still fought on. We came across Hill 112 (this later became famous). We had to take this hill and we did twice but lost it both times. The third time we held it and the villages below it. It was hell in one village; Gavrus. We took it but there were machine gun nests at one end which we had to capture. We lost one officer by the name of Lane. His family was a well known jockey family from Newmarket. We lost our platoon Sergeant and plenty of others were wounded. My section under Corporal Peter Bisset was told to attack across a field. We got within about a hundred yards when we were spotted. The Spandau - it could fire about a thousand rounds a minute - opened up and Peter who was next to me but about six yards away, just dropped down on his face. We knew he was dead. I hit the ground and lay there for a few minutes. I looked around and realized that I was alone apart from Peter. I knew if I moved they would get me but I knew I couldn't stay there. There was a ditch either side of me about 25 yards away that's where the other lads had gone. I remember choosing the ditch on my left. I gathered my thoughts and moved as fast as I could. I got up and ran. The machine guns were behind me and to my right. I was, as far as I can recall, about halfway when they opened fire on me. The bullets went over my shoulders one went through the side of my beret and then there was a burst about the size of a tennis ball which hit the hedge in front of me. I landed in the ditch and lay still for a while. Someone then spoke to me; it was Butch our Lance Corporal. He asked if I was all right and I was, but just a few seconds later there was a huge explosion on the edge of the ditch and just above my head. It was a mortar bomb. Three times I had been close to death in a very short time and to this day I still believe that I should have died in that field near the village of Gavrus.

'After the bomb went off I turned around to see if Butch was OK and all I saw was Butch staring at me with his mouth wide open. I think he thought I'd had it. My back was killing me and I had a piece of shrapnel about two inches long in my neck and I had to get back to the medical tent. Next thing I knew I was being flown back to England with some other lads who had also been injured. We landed at Swindon's Air Force Base and after we had been given a meal we were put on a hospital train. It was the early hours of the morning but what day or date it was I had no idea. We soon found ourselves in the Midlands. Half of us went to a hospital in Birmingham and the other half to a hospital in Wolverhampton. I remember being put to bed by some lovely nurses and Red Cross workers. I had nothing only the dirty clothes I was in and I hadn't washed for days, I must have looked a right sight and I know I felt it. I woke up, which seemed like hours later, to find two nurses giving me a blanket bath. I had never had one of those before. When they saw I was awake they said 'Hello how are you feeling'?

'All I could say was that I was so sorry for the trouble I was putting them to and I was sorry that I was so dirty. They didn't mind one bit they just smiled and said that they were only too pleased to help me. They were wonderful. I will always remember Staff Nurse White but I used to call her Chalky. She was usually our Staff Nurse on nights and if I couldn't sleep and she saw me she would always come and talk to me. Lovely Chalky, she was only about my age. The first visitors I had were from the Salvation Army. They asked us if there was anything we needed and within hours we had cigarettes, matches, writing paper and stamps. They also brought us fruit and sweets. Lovely people.

'We also had young girls from the WVS come in to see us to see if they could help us and to talk to us to make sure we were OK. They used to bring our newspapers and books. A couple of the girls took to me and my mate from the Middlesex Regiment. I would really love to meet them again just to say thank you for everything they did but we were discharged before we had a chance to say our farewells. My sister in law, Mary and her sister came to see us three or four times. I had written to Mary and to my family at home. They were the first letters I wrote since leaving England. It was lovely to see Mary and her sister, Kate. Mary also told my ex girlfriend where I was and what had happened and it was a nice surprise when she came to visit. I had X-rays on my back and they had to remove small fragments of metal and also the shrapnel from my neck. We went out into town one day and what a welcome we got. We didn't have to pay for anything, not even the haircuts that we went out for. There is one thing that I will always remember. We were walking along the road looking for the barber shop when all of a sudden this middle aged lady came across the road and gave us a two shilling coin. All she said was God Bless and she was gone before we could even say thank you. Lovely people in that part of the country.

'We were both discharged after a month in hospital and my mate returned to his Regiment and I had to report to the training battalion in Nottingham. When

I arrived I met about six of my mates and one of my platoon sergeants. We were given all new gear and had orders to report to a transit camp near Southampton.

Rifleman Eric Patience. He returned to the front line and went on to see action in France, Belgium, Holland, the Ardennes and Germany and participated in the liberation of Belsen. He was demobbed in September 1946.

'We didn't feel much like sleeping that night. In any case, even if anyone had wanted any sleep on my boat they could not have got it. It was full of French Canadians, the Chauderie and the Winnipeg Rifles. All they did all night was sharpen up their knives!

'In one respect, I don't think anyone wanted to miss anything. After months and months of training we were suddenly aware that everything was fitting into place. Naturally, there· was tension. Everybody was really frightened of letting the other bloke know that underneath it all you were really afraid. The sum total of this was that nobody appeared to be afraid. Yet, if we were honest, we were all terribly afraid.

'It was easier on deck because it was all so impressive to us to see these hundreds of ships with destroyers and minesweepers on either side. The whole thing going across in one steady pattern - just steaming across to France. Then, late at night, there were the waves and waves of planes going across overhead. It really was impressive, very impressive.'

Major Smith, who was on the deck of his troopship.

'Breakfast on the *Clan Lamont* was really first class. We had pork chops and a choice of stewed prunes, apricots of fresh fruit. A lot of the men couldn't face it but one had to be sensible about this - you didn't know when you were going to eat again.

'We were lucky. We were able to get into our landing craft on the davits. The little assault craft were on davits and were lowered like lifeboats. But it was a big bump when they hit the water. We were supposed to be going down a Jacob's ladder, but it was so rough that one moment the craft was 10 feet above you and the next right down below so we went down a scramble net. It was dangerous, you had to watch it. You had to catch the craft as it was going down and drop into it. One of our chaps didn't and the boat caught him and the force broke both his ankles. There was nothing we could do about it. We had to take him in to the beach even though he was wounded.'

Sergeant Reg Cole.

'Our mission was to land with the 3rd Canadian Infantry Division and recce for a site to receive and store bridging equipment for the Caen Canals and any other engineer equipment which would be landing later the next day by DUKWs. I had been detailed off to be Major 'Charlie' Wade (his name was Cyril really), the OC's bodyguard and runner for the landing. We arrived at the beaches on board the *Clan Lamont*, a cargo ship that had been quickly converted to a trooper with landing craft in the davits instead of lifeboats. We had been on board for two days, having been called back to Southampton waters on the night of the 4th of June because of bad weather. The *Clan Lamont* was commanded by a Canadian Navy Captain Angus Campbell OBE and it was crammed full of French Canadian troops. They spent most of their time on board queuing up to sharpen their commando knives on the 'one and only' grindstone in the galley and playing 'Crown and Anchor' on the mess deck; using the invasion money we had been paid. I befriended a corporal of the North Shore (New Brunswick) Regiment who was running the 'Crown and Anchor' board and became his cashier, collecting all the cash and paying out the winnings. I stuffed all the cash in my battledress blouse for safe keeping. I still had the full blouse of money when I landed, as he said on leaving for the landing, which was before ours, that it was no good to him. A great set of guys.

'The time 0930 hours. Our landing craft was now speeding through the black cloud of acrid smoke. Plumes of waterspouts were shooting up left; right and centre as the mortars and shells came down. I felt a sharp veer to the right probably to avoid an underwater obstacle and for the first time we heard the bark of small arms fire overhead as we came into shore very fast. The OC and I had now positioned ourselves to observe the beach coming into view to identify the coloured beach marker flag. Beachmasters had landed with the first wave assault carrying their colour standards. These were small flags on poles that were implanted in the sandy beach to signify its colour code (i.e. 'Nan Red', 'Queen White', 'Mike Green' etc.)

'It was very difficult to see anything now for all the sea spray and smoke. There was a terrific jarring, grating sound underneath, as though the whole bottom of the craft was being torn out. We all lurched forward with the impact. I gripped my rifle hard. The stench of spilled diesel oil and cordite stung my nose and made my eyes water. Two explosions occurred just about fifty yards to our left and water spurted up and showered down onto our craft in an absolute deluge. The assault craft surged back a bit from the beach then moved forward again, dug in and held, 'bottomed'. Crash! Down went the armoured plated front and we had our first, but very brief, view of the beach. The OC yelled 'Clarke, look for the marker flag what's its colour?' It was green! We had landed on Mike Green, right off our target; we were supposed to be on Nan Red. I ran up the beach and dived for cover behind a sand dune, to my right were some of the first wave troops in the same location, I saw the corporal I had befriended laying in the prone position if to fire his weapon, called to him but there was no response, he was dead.

'An assault craft, broadside onto the beach, lay on its side next to us. It was shattered; not a single Canadian soldier or the crew had made it. It was a bloody mess two bodies were actually hanging from the side, where they had been blown by the force of the explosion. The clothing on the lower parts of their bodies, which were badly mutilated, were missing and large streaks of red ran down the side of the assault craft to the sea where their life blood had drained away.

'Obstacles were everywhere; one vicious looking pronged object with heavy explosive devices hung around the prongs was to our right. Quite a number of damaged assault craft, some on fire, were beached. There were armoured assault vehicles damaged and shattered by gunfire were lying inert, not clear of the water as the tide was still coming in.

'At the uppermost part of the beach I saw firing coming from a bombed house, just beyond the formidable sea wall of concrete. A nasty wire fence just in front of the concrete wall was decorated with the sprawled bodies of about twenty Canadians; one was headless, God only knows what had hit him. But the most ironic was one young infantryman being supported by the fence in a kneeling and praying position!

'The only thing in my mind now was to GO! And get to the beach. I was so tense, like a coiled spring ready to move like mad when I was told. I felt a bit numb and scared and not ashamed to admit it. A Beachmaster Major was standing right out on the open beach at the water's edge bellowing his instructions to the incoming assault through a megaphone held to his mouth. He was a very brave man ignoring his dangerous surroundings. Short, sharp, blasts on infantry whistles. No time to think now. Out at the double into about four feet of water, just about up to my chest. I touched bottom and forced myself forward. The water seemed to be holding me back, but at last I was on the beach and running like hell for cover. The OC and I, being first out, were well ahead with the troop fanning out close behind. There was a large number of dead on the beach staining it red with their blood. I hurled myself down behind a sand dune by the side of a Canadian soldier, who I had met on 'Clan Lamont'. He appeared to me to have taken up a firing position, I spoke to him, but there was no reply, he was dead. Looking round quickly; I saw that we were a bit spread out now but I was glad to see we had suffered no casualties. All my mates were with me and my confidence returned somewhat although I was out of breath and my heart was thumping.

'There was an enormous crash behind us as I felt the blast in my back. The assault craft, which had brought us in, had caught a packet even before she had had a chance to back off. Mortars had straddled her, even though she had cleared the beach, was listing badly and on fire. Peering through all the black smoke I could see that only some of the crew had survived.

'Another LCI (Landing Craft Infantry) came tearing in at that moment and it had its underbelly ripped right open by an obstacle and was almost upended. It had a huge gash underneath and the troops aboard had to leave from the rear and swim for it. They must have been glad of their life jackets. There were a number of dead bodies floating at the water's edge they were being pushed out of the way by the swimmers coming in.

'The heavy naval shells continued to pass overhead and further waves of Tiffies (Typhoons) roared in letting off rockets into the defences over the sea wall out of our sight. Two things are stamped on my mind forever. The first was the sound of those sixteen-inch naval shells passing overhead continuously. But the most important and overpowering other thing, was the obnoxious stench of spilled diesel oil from the damaged armoured vehicles. The beaches, as far as the eye could see, were littered with these vehicles all with diesel in their tanks. The whole atmosphere absolutely reeked of it and to this day memories come flooding back to my mind when my nostrils detect the smell of diesel oil.

'The OC looked concerned and well he may be. We were slightly right of our target; this was apparently when our craft had veered sharply to the right to avoid a hedgehog obstacle when approaching the shore. This was Nan Green beach, but glancing to my left along the beach, in the distance the blood red flag of Nan Red was flying at its standard.

'The first waves in had been very gallant, storming up the beaches by sheer brute force; it had been costly to them. They had been delayed by ten minutes to allow the tide to come in further to allow their assault craft more water free board and the delay had helped the Germans no end, giving them time to cover the beaches with cross fire. Many of the casualties lying everywhere were caused by the mines sown on this stretch of beach.

'The Queen's own Rifles of Canada had landed to our right with no DD tank support and that one company of the battalion had lost half its men, cut down in the cross fire, in only a few minutes. But they had now come to grips with the enemy and were advancing off the beach. They also landed in the wrong position; 200 yards east of, near to the strong point of Bernières and for a while were in a lot of trouble that delayed them considerably. The toughest and hardest fighting however took place on Nan Red where the naval and air strikes were devastating and effective. The North Shores were even now fighting on the esplanade and advancing inland. However, they were not having it all their own way; the Germans were not giving an inch.

'The OC and I, after seeing all were under reasonable cover, left the party, going along the beach towards Nan Red our nominated landing beach. As we scrambled along the beach we both kept a wary eye open for both anti-tank and anti-personnel mines or other obstacles. When, any of these were located I would mark them with the small triangular white mine markers carried by sapper NCOs. The first waves had caught a packet, I felt dismayed and thoroughly dejected as I shifted my position to take a good look around. The beach was carnage with the dead soaking the sand red with fine Canadian blood. They had been mown down by German defensive machine gun fire as they left their assault craft. Some had managed, by the grace of God, to get over that concrete bastion in front of us and were fighting in the houses just beyond it.

'Four Typhoons screamed in low letting off their rockets into the enemy positions. This gave us a lot of assurance when glancing towards the sky; we could see hundreds of our aircraft completely in control for the time being. They were easily recognisable by their white stripes on the fuselage and wing.

'Our navy was now really giving the enemy grief; the capital ships were bombarding the coast with shells. The mortaring of the beach seemed to be getting a lot worse as the Germans hit back and we became a little uncomfortable about making a move to get off this beach.

'The OC and I had scouted along the beach for a suitable breach in the wall and a route inland and had found one on 'Nan Red'. It was about half a mile east of our position and we would have to proceed along the beach, which at that time had not been effectively cleared of mines and was still under constant mortar and sniper fire.

'The OC sent me back down the beach to bring the section up to the breach in the wall, the party was assembled in file and we moved off hurriedly going east along the beach, with Fred Page and Ted Mills (both ex Boys) bringing up the rear with the LMG. The Beachmaster, still out in the open, I'm sure he was glad to see us go as he was continuously urging the troops, through his loud hailer, to keep moving to make way for more troops, tanks and equipment still coming in.

'Having brought them to a position near the breach in the wall and taken cover behind the sea wall an 'O' group was held whilst Sergeant Dixon, the admin Sergeant, collected our 'parcel label' nametags before we left. It may seem odd, but the Army's administration must carry on, even under battle conditions. It was his task, when possible, to return these labels of the twenty-one personnel of HQ Troop, which formed the advance party, to GHQ 2nd Echelon, London, to show we had all disembarked with the British Liberation Army (BLA).

'We saw our first French civilian shortly after this. He was standing on the western wall, quite a way from us out in the open ignoring all the missiles whizzing around him. He was mighty pleased to see us! However, between us was a most comprehensive set of obstacles thought up by the Germans, the same that had hampered the first assault waves who had been forced, like us, to move east along the beach to penetrate its defences. The Frenchman looked typical with his black beret and light blue overalls. He was gesticulating and shouting, I presumed, greetings to all of us and we waved back. He certainly looked elated - I wish we felt the same.

The OC quickly issued his orders and once more we left to try and locate the CRE (Commander Royal Engineers) and look for a suitable site near to the village of Tailleville to use as a collection depot for the RE stores.

'We climbed through breach in the sea wall and had to dive for cover as soon as we hit the road above, there were snipers about and we were told they were firing from the Church Tower in Ste-Aubin-sur-Mer. We looked around and saw many more people doing the same thing, taking cover and a number of Sappers of an Armoured Assault Squadron who had been responsible for making the breach in the wall.

'We were told that if we went to our right, we could avoid the sniper fire by advancing along a single railway line link between Courseulles and Ste-Aubin-sur-Mer that was shielded from the field of fire by houses. We checked it on the map and then we went that way, but we still experienced small arms fire. Diving into a ditch at the side of the railway line for cover when the fire became too hot, we found it occupied by a dead German officer and some French people also dead; I admired the binoculars and Mauser pistol attached to the officer's belt and was about to take them when Charlie ordered me to leave them alone, 'they might be booby trapped'. I remember that I was leading and Charlie Wade the OC was about 10 yards behind, urging me to keep an eye open for mines on the track, at every crack of rifle shot he dived to the ground and yelled at me to take cover. I also remembered that I had been told that if you hear a rifle crack then it's 'missed', so I did not keep diving to the ground. Eventually the OC did the same so we advanced at a much faster pace.

'Our objective, I was told, was to find the CRE who was supposed to have landed before us and locate a spot for digging in for the night.

'Seeing a Bren-gun carrier in the middle of the field behind a haystack we approached it with caution, there were three Canadians one a young Lieutenant who was screaming and he had tears in his eyes, his men were firing a mortar to the front and towards Tailleville, 'our objective for that day'. Charlie reluctantly approached the Lieutenant and asked him if he knew where the CRE was, he exploded and turned on Charlie 'who the Bloody Hell is that' and many other choice words. We took cover with them behind the carrier and found out that the Lieutenant had lost 15 of his troop and they were the only ones left. As they were getting some return fire we left them to it and proceeded back along the hedgerow towards Tailleville. Still in the lead I had to pass a gap in the hedge and was fired on as I crossed the gap. Fortunately they missed. Charlie also traversed the gap whilst I kept cover on the other side, again a shot rang out as he crossed the gap, but this time I saw the flash in a tree about fifty yards ahead. I responded instantly, firing back at the tree from behind cover, Charlie said 'again Clarke'. This time I took a little longer over my aim and a body fell out of the tree, whether it was fright or he was actually hit, I do not know, but it did clear the way for us to proceed. That was my first shot in anger and I didn't even think about it, it came naturally, so all the training must have paid off.

'We arrived in a copse (small wooded area) near to the Château Tailleville, which had not been cleared of Germans and we started looking for a clearing where the troop could dig in for the night. Having found a suitable site the OC told me to get off down to the beach to bring the others up to the place we had selected, whilst he made a more detailed recce. This wasn't as easy as it sounds. After crouching and crawling back down the road towards the landing beach, I had to stop and take cover in the ditch by the side of the road, as it was being mortared. I jumped in alongside two Canadians from the North Shore Regiment who were organising some German prisoners on the road. They all seemed very young and were lined up on the road with their hands on their heads. I was invited to help get them down to the pen on the beach; as I had to go that way I said 'OK'. We moved them out of cover into the centre of the road. The mortaring stopped and we then marched them down to the beach and handed them over to Military Police at the pen. Interesting, one of the prisoners at the rear and near to me turned and smiled. He said in good English, 'I go to England to drink your beer and you stay here and fight the battle'.

'Having got down to the beach I now had to find the rest of the advanced party to lead them back the way I had just come. Remember, I wasn't travelling light. I had full pack and rolled blanket bound to the pack with ammunition, rifle and packed rations also on my back. I was sweating somewhat. I eventually found the rest, more or less where we had left them but dug in a little more deeply. After a de-brief by Lieutenant Hingley and the Sergeant-Major, they were eager to get away from the beach.

'I was once more on the move, in the lead, on the road to Tailleville. 'Follow me men!' Thank god the sniper in the church had been disposed of and we could use the road through Ste-Aubin-sur-Mer rather than going along the railway line again. The advance along the road was uneventful, most of the resistance had been silenced and it was now just after midday. We arrived at the wood where the OC had been lying in cover waiting for us, he immediately ordered everyone to take cover and start digging, sentries were posted at the perimeter of the site and we started to feel a little surer of the situation and the usual banter started. We suffered a few emergencies with incoming fire, from where, we never found out, but we suspected that it was friendly fire from 48 Commando who had to clear the Château Tailleville 120 yards up the road.

'Having settled in to rest, eat some battle rations and await the arrival of stores from the beach ready for the ongoing assault, 'some wishful thinking', a dispatch rider arrived with urgent message for us to return to the beach area as an assault by panzers was imminent from the East, the part of the beach assault where we had landed, 'Juno', had not joined with 'Sword' beach so there was a undefended path to the beach for the Germans.

'So I was up once again to retrace my steps back to Ste-Aubin for the second time in a day, this time I was accompanied by the whole of the advance party, it was more comforting to have some company, I could rest from the high alertness of guiding the troop, thank God someone else was ordered to scout ahead. We were once again in the front defending the beach against Panzers, what we were going to do when they arrived I will never know, thankfully they did not arrive at our part of the beach.

'When we arrived back at the beach we were ordered to dig in once again and standby. After lookouts had been positioned in front of our position from where we expected the Germans to come, I was so shattered; I decided to flop down under the nearest hedgerow, I pulled my gas cape over my head and tried to sleep. I had travelled that road to Tailleville four times that D-Day, in full kit, weapons with extras strapped to my pack; no way could I face the prospect of having to wield a shovel to dig in again. And I was supposed to be battle fit! After all the training we had had. I was thankful for some good mates they did all the work whilst I rested.

'I managed to get some fitful sleep but it was more like rest from exhaustion, often being disturbed by gunfire from the Navy and exploding shells from an ammunition dump, which was on fire nearby. I survived the night, at the breaking of dawn I was prodded awake by the Sergeant-Major giving me a kick in the backside and a bollocking for not having dug in as ordered, he did however tell me to get my mess tin out and he filled it with steaming hot tea. Within ten minutes we were once again on the move up the same bloody road to Tailleville that I had traversed many times before.

'I had survived D-Day and vowed that I would never again march on my feet with all my gear on my back. This is not what Sappers do. the very next day Freddie Page, another ex-boy and I relieved a group of German soldiers of their Opel car as they were trying to retreat (get away) and it became our transport for the next few weeks.'

Lance Corporal Reg A. Clarke with the advance party of 176 Workshop and Park Company, Royal Engineers.

'We actually mounted up and got ready about 2 or 3 miles from shore, as we knew we'd be in action directly the LCT beached and that our lives depended very much on each other, however ill we felt. When we grounded the first flail got off and started up the beach OK, but as the second one commenced to land, the third vehicle - one of our AVREs with a Bangalore torpedo on the turret; that's like a long drainage tube packed with explosive - took a direct hit from German artillery. The AVRE commander was killed, as was the commander of the flail in front of him and many from both crews were wounded. The rest of us were badly shaken. I should've said that this was about 7.55am and the Bangalore torpedo was to clear barbed wire entanglements that we expected to meet.

'Because of the damaged vehicles we were completely unable to get off the LCT and as others were waiting to come in behind us, we had to pull out and return to England again.

'That night we were allowed out to the local pubs to celebrate being alive. While we were waiting to board at Portsmouth we'd been issued with condoms and as we were all anticipating that we might have to swim for it, we'd used these to wrap up our watches and the new French francs that we'd also been issued. When we got to the pub and searched our battledress pockets for English money, the landlord, seeing the French letters, said 'I thought you went over there to fight the Germans!'

'As soon as the locals learned where we'd been we all had several pints lined up in front of us, but we never got to finish them, because our Pay Corporal came and said anyone who wanted a seventy-two hour pass should get back to barracks, so that's where we went.

'On arriving home, my dear old mum said, 'Thank the Lord you weren't in those landings, son...'

Mick Goldsmith, a turret gunner in an AVRE in the 80th Assault Squadron, Royal Engineers, who had served in a General Construction Company, Royal Engineers in France in 1940[20]

---

20 *Invaders: British and American Experience of Seaborne landings 1939-1945* by Colin John Bruce (Chatham Publishing 1999).

An ARVE Carpet-Laying Churchill tank.

These tanks unrolled the carpet under fire, which once laid, provided a firm track for vehicles in soft sand and boggy ground.

A British A4M3 Sherman Crab flail tank. The mine flail consisted of a number of heavy chains, ending in fist-sized steel balls, (flails) that were attached to a horizontal, rapidly rotating rotor mounted on two arms in front of the vehicle. The rotor's rotation made the flails spin wildly and violently pound the ground, causing the mine to explode without causing any damage.

Preparations to Invade

British Sherman tank crews carry out last minute maintenance in a transit area prior to embarking on landing craft for Normandy.

Shipping off Lee-on-Solent looking towards the Isle of Wight on 5 June photographed from a passing Sunderland. In the foreground is the tug anchorage and the large vessel off the left wingtip is *Aorangi*, a converted Canadian Australasian liner. Just discernible in the middle distance are tank landing ships and the minelayer turned LSE (Emergency Repair) ship HMS *Adventure* and the cruiser HMS *Despatch*, an HQ base and AA defence ship (in the centre) with (top left) LSI(S) *Prinses Astrid* and LSI(H) *Maid of Orléans*. In the background are some of the roadway sections waiting to be towed to Mulberry harbours.

BEACH OBSTACLES

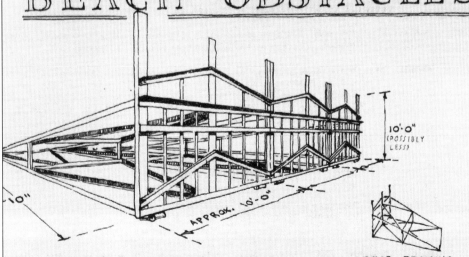

10'-0"
(POSSIBLY LESS)

10"

APPROX. 10'-0"

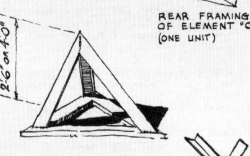

REAR FRAMING
OF ELEMENT "C"
(ONE UNIT)

ELEMENT "C" (3 UNITS)
CONSTRUCTED OF STEEL
ANGLES AND PLATES.

2'-6" or 4'-0"

TETRAHEDRON
USUALLY CONSTRUCTED OF
STEEL RAILS — CHANNELS
AND ANGLES MAY BE USED.

HEDGEHOG
CONSTRUCTED OF
STEEL ANGLES OR
RAILS.

5'-7"

NOTE:
THESE OBSTACLES MAY HAVE WELDED,
BOLTED, OR RIVETED JOINTS, AND/OR
CONCRETE ANCHORS.

VI - ENEMY DEFENSES

A wave of Canadian infantry await their turn to run into the beach.

Commandos on a LCI(S) during their run-in to Sword beach.

An LCT(R) fires a salvo of rockets
in support of the landings.

HMS *Fury* left the Solent on 5 June as the escort for Convoy J-1. She arrived at the beachhead and
took up her bombardment position on 6 June where along with HMS *Venus* she carried out a
preliminary support bombardment of the area west of Courseulles. She was then deployed with the
Eastern Task Force after the initial assault. From the 7 June to 20 June she was engaged in support
duties and convoy escort in the Eastern Task Force Area, returning to Portsmouth to refuel and
replenish as required. On 21 June *Fury* struck a mine off the beachhead and was driven ashore in a
gale. She was subsequently salvaged and towed back to the UK and later scrapped.

Three men of the 1st Battalion, the Royal Norfolks wade ashore on 6 June.

The *Tomsk* beached following the Normandy landings.

A British Army vehicle drives to the shore along one of the two floating roadways at the Mulberry' 'B' Harbour at Arromanches.

Men coming ashore on Gold beach

Cunningly disguised defences on the beachfront somewhere in France, with steps and handrails painted on this bunker.

Captured Germans and wounded Canadians are seen in front of two 50mm anti-tank gun bunkers built into the sea wall at Berniéres-sur-Mer, part of the Juno beach landing area.

Men of the Green Howards of British XXX Corps are welcomed by French locals after landing on Gold beach.

Maxted who reported the Normandy landings for the BBC.

Captain Class frigate HMS *Stayner,* an anti-E-boat warship which helped patrol the D-Day beaches on and after D-Day.

About to touch down on Nan White Beach, Bernières-sur-Mer on D-Day at 12 noon. (John Cooke via Gordon Cooke)

Satan's Chariot, a British Army Cromwell tank stuck in the sands on Omaha beach. It was transported to the Normandy coast by the Mark 6 Landing Craft (Tank) LCT-542 in the background..

Amphibious Sherman DD tanks. Although this picture was taken later during the crossing of the Rhine, the same vehicles were used in excactly the same manner during the Normandy landings.

HMS Scylla was at the French North Africa landings (Operation 'Torch') as part of Force 'O' with the Eastern Task Force, in November 1942 and in September 1943 was part of the Support Carrier Force at the Salerno landings (Operation 'Avalanche'), but came home to refit for duty as an Escort Carrier Flagship in October, which lasted until April 1944. She was present at the Normandy landings as Flagship of the Eastern Task Force. On 23 June 1944 she was badly damaged by a mine and declared a Constructive Total Loss. Although towed to Portsmouth, she was not disposed of until 1950, after use as a target between 1948 to 1950.

GIs inspect the Type 683 casemate at the Ste-Marcouf battery which held out for two days before its capture by the Americans. The casemate, which contained a 210mm Skoda, was later partially demolished by US engineers.

Unloading on Nan White Beach, Bernières-sur-Mer after sustaining damage from a beach mine. (John Cooke via Gordon Cooke)

An aerial view of the 'Mulberry' 'B' Harbour at Arromanches with surrounding 'Gooseberries';
a ring of sunken merchant ships towed from Scotland and sunk alongside the 'Mulberrys' to
act as breakwaters.

Chapter 3

'Sword'

The bombardment fleet for the eastern beaches which sailed on 2 June included the battleships Warspite and Ramillies, the old monitor Roberts, the cruisers Mauritius - the flagship of the eastern bombardment fleet - Arethusa, Danae, Dragon and Frobisher and was led, in the latter part of the crossing by two Norwegian destroyers, Stord and Svenner. Lieutenant-Commander Tore Holthe from Trondheim, the 30-year-old captain of the Svenner had a particular reason to be proud of the place which his ship had been given, for she was straight out of the builder's yard. When the Germans invaded Norway in 1940, Holthe was captain of a coal-fired torpedo boat built before the First World War. The Svenner was a fleet destroyer of 1,800 tons, four 4.7-inch guns, eight torpedo tubes and a complement of over 200 men.

At 11 pm they entered the easternmost channel, between the lines of lighted buoys which the minesweeper flotillas had laid like street-lamps across to France. Mauritius was in the van with Svenner 30 degrees on her port bow at a range of 1,000 yards. At midnight, Holthe ordered his crew to action stations. A little after midnight, the force moved into line ahead, with Stord leading and Svenner second. Towards dawn Holthe and his look-outs saw the flashes of bombs on the coast ahead and the flicker of fires reflected by the clouds. At 5.30 in the grey of dawn, the battleships and cruisers anchored in range of the shore ahead and also of heavy batteries at Le Havre, about eight miles to the east. To protect the ships from that direction, aircraft began to lay a smoke screen. Svenner and the other destroyers stopped to the west of the capital ships, to wait for the minesweepers to open a channel even closer towards the shore. It was in that moment that Holthe saw, 300 yards away, the unmistakable track of a torpedo.

Three 1,400 ton German torpedo boats - each one the size of a small destroyer - had emerged from the smoke screen on the far side of the fleet after having left the harbour at Le Havre, where Korvettenkapitän Heinrich Hoffmann commanding 5 Torpedobootsflotille had kept them in port not because of the roughness of the sea, but because of the moon. When he first saw the smoke screen, Hoffmann thought it was a natural bank of fog; but then he saw an aircraft dropping smoke floats confirmed his belief that a major operation was under way. He headed for the ships at 28 knots in line ahead. When he came through the smoke he was amazed to see straight ahead of him, in the early light of dawn, six battleships or heavy cruisers and fifty more minor warships that he had no time to count them. To his further surprise, not one of them opened fire. He signalled his base that he was going to attack, set course to present the smallest silhouette and had time to manoeuvre his ships into a text-book approach. Between them, they fired seventeen torpedoes.

At the moment when Hoffmann fired his torpedoes, the first British salvo of shells fell in front of his bows, so close that his ship, still moving at 28 knots, steamed into the spouts of water before they fell. The concussion put out all lights on board and cut off the radio. He altered course abruptly to avoid the fire and returned it impudently with his four-inch guns. By vigorous evasive tactics, all three of his ships got back into the smoke screen and not one of them was hit.

From Hoffmann's point of view, it was bad luck that Svenner was the only ship his flotilla's torpedoes hit. They went right through the close-packed British fleet. Two of them passed between the battleships Warspite and Ramillies. A third headed straight for Largs, the headquarters ship of the area, which only avoided it by going full speed astern. The destroyer Virago reported a near miss. The torpedo which hit Svenner had already gone through the fleet from one side to the other. After half an hour, the stern of Svenner rolled over and disappeared, but the bow stood there for a long time and thousands of troops on their way to the beach saw it projecting above the surface, like a tombstone. Holthe was picked up, while the bombardment in which he had hoped to take his part roared overhead towards the beach and the town of Ouistreham.

One officer and 32 crew and two of the British liaison men were lost on the *Svenner*. [21] Hoffmann was awarded the Knight's Cross for his exploit.

As HMS *Largs* (the former French passenger liner *Charles Plumier* and the flagship of Rear Admiral Arthur Talbot, commanding Force 'S' ('Sword') brought the tail of the LSI convoy up to lowering position, Bombarding Force 'D' was already at anchor at the end of Channel 10, where it had been bombarding the German artillery batteries since 05:40, HMS *Warspite* opening up from 17 miles against the Villerville coastal battery (1./HKAA 1255) about 3 miles west of Vasouy. This battery consisted of six 155 mm guns in open emplacements which, with a range in excess of 13 miles, were capable of firing on the Allied invasion fleet.[22] At the start of the bombardment the battery on Mont Canisy, just south-west of Deauville, known to the Allies as the Bénerville battery (Heeresküstenbatterie 2./1255), was engaged by the 15-inch guns of HMS *Ramillies*. When completed this battery should have comprised six former French 155 mm guns in casemates but just one was in a casement and three other 155 mm guns were in front of the six original open emplacements. [23] The two casemates at Houlgate on the Tournebride plateau which also consisted of six 155 mm guns (3./HKM 1255)

21 Adapted from *Dawn Of D-Day* by David Howarth (1959)
22   Their original purpose was the protection of the approaches to the Seine. *Hitler's Atlantic Wall* by Anthony Saunders (Sutton Publishing 2001).
23   Only one of these was occupied by another gun of the same calibre at the time of the invasion. The position was protected by a ring of minefields and a number of machine-gun tobruk as well as several 50mm anti-tank guns in open emplacements. The front of the site was guarded by an emplaced Renault R35 turret. A variety of other bunkers for personnel were dotted about the heart-shaped site, including two fire-control posts. The battery was silenced by *Ramillies* but it later came back to life and fired on *Warspite* who had to move to avoid the salvoes from Mont Canisy. This battery continued to shell the ships off 'Sword' and the beach itself until the end of August. As a result of shelling from the Mont Canisy and Houlgate batteries, the use of 'Sword' to unload supplies was stopped on 25 June. Several times, these batteries were temporarily shelled into silence by battleships and cruisers but they were never destroyed despite more than 1,000 heavy and medium shells being fired at them. They damaged a number of landing ships along with HMS *Locust,* a HQ ship, and a number of other vessels including a coaster loaded with ammunition which was set ablaze. *Hitler's Atlantic Wall* by Anthony Saunders (Sutton Publishing 2001).

was shelled by the 15-inch guns of the monitor HMS *Roberts*.[24] HMS *Arethusa* was to bombard the Merville battery (1./AR 1716) if the cruiser did not receive a signal from the 9th Parachute Battalion to indicate that the battery had been taken.[25] Arethusa also used its guns against the Le Mont battery. At Riva-Bella at the front of Ouistreham there were six open emplacements for 15.5 cm guns at the eastern end of a strongpoint that extended for 1,200 metres westwards and was 200 metres in depth.[26] Within the eastern half, there were numerous bunkers and tobruks along with a 17-metre high command post. Southwest of Ouistreham near a water-tower was a battery (WN 12/4./AR 1716) consisting of four 15.5 cm howitzers with the Allied codename 'Daimler'. A third battery (WN 16) - 'Morris' - of four 105 mm guns in casements, one of which was still under construction (2./AR 1716), was nearby, located west of Colleville-sur-Orne. The Riva-Bella battery was shelled by the 7½-inch cruiser HMS *Frobisher*, 'Daimler' by the 6-inch cruiser HMS *Danae* and 'Morris' by the Polish 6-inch cruiser ORP *Dragon*. [27]

'I recall that first week in June 1944 so well. There were flags and bunting all the way, with cheering crowds yelling 'Good luck, Boys!' and giving us cups of tea to help us along. Once at London docks we were sealed off from the outside world. No letters, no phoning, for we had now been officially told our destination was France. Work consisted of waterproofing vehicles and checking equipment. Once aboard, we rendezvoused with a naval escort and put our vomiting bags to good use. I wrote to my mother: 'Here I am en route to Normandy by courtesy of the Royal Navy - Not a Jerry plane in sight, the RAF rules the skies.'

'Luckily our landing was dry. I clearly remember driving across the beach between white ribbons - the sign that it had been cleared of land mines. The few houses were just ruins. British bombers had gone in before us, the Germans had retreated and the fighting was going on way ahead of us. But British troops and vehicles were everywhere. We headed a few miles inland to a deserted farm house. Our first task was to unload the camouflage nets and remove sticky

24   It was last shelled towards the end of August by HMS *Erebus* before it was finally captured. *Hitler's Atlantic Wall* by Anthony Saunders (Sutton Publishing 2001).

25   The battery was taken and the paras left before the allotted time. But this allowed the remainder of the garrison and the battery commander, Leutnant Steiner, who had been in the battery's fire-control post in one of the Franceville strong points in front of Merville east of the River Orne when the assault began, to re-occupy the battery. (Two strong points, with machine-gun bunkers, tobruks and anti-tank gun bunkers at Franceville Plâge were sited to protect the Merville battery about half a mile inland). During the assault, Steiner had called in fire from the Houlgate battery on to his own initiative. When the Merville battery attempted to fire on the ships Arethusa returned fire. The battery was bombed on three more occasions and was again shelled by Arethusa to support the Commandos trying to retake the battery the next day. The explosions of naval shells and RAF bombs removed the earth that once covered the casemates. No. 1 casemate is now a museum. No. 3 has a defused 4,000-pounder underneath it. See *Hitler's Atlantic Wall* by Anthony Saunders (Sutton Publishing 2001).

26   a result of air raids in May the guns were removed and emplaced to the south of Ouistreham at Ste-Aubin-d'Arquenay.

27   These batteries and the strongpoint were taken by ground assault on D-Day, 'Daimler' by the 2nd East Yorkshires with tank support from the 13th/18th Hussars (it held out until 1800 hours), 'Morris' (and 'Hillman') by the Suffolks.

waterproofing from our hot engines and then to dig in. That first night we were ordered to sleep under our lorries but I found a stretcher and had a comfortable night's sleep in the back of mine...

'The most memorable thing about that first day in France was the smell; the stench of death. Not human flesh, but cattle. Scores of them all lying on their sides - pot bellied and dead. The sun didn't help much.

'...The organization and planning of the D-Day operation was brilliant - absolutely nothing was forgotten... On landing, each man was given a pre-printed field postcard on which to write home. It consisted of sentences such as 'I am well' or 'I have been wounded' which could be struck out. We all had tin rations plus a portable cooker with tiny solid fuel tablets. I can still recall the delicious steak and kidney puddings... Special praise, too for the Army Laundry Ablution Units. Dirty shirts and underwear were just exchanged for clean ones and if they fitted you were lucky! Every day was an uncertain one, but the comradeship and spirit has never been equalled.'

John Frost, an army driver.

'It was like driving to a race meeting with the AA controlling the traffic.'
Lieutenant-Commander A. J. R. White RN **on convoy S-7 shepherding the LSLs.**

'On June 4 Portsmouth Dockyard was alive with military vehicles of every description, tanks, armoured cars and trucks... When we set sail, landing craft were everywhere, filled with soldiers, their faces blackened ready for combat. We anchored with the rest of the great armada off the Isle of Wight and then learned that the invasion was postponed for 24 hours because of rough weather.

'The evening of June 5 came; the seas were still very rough. But, the invasion was on despite the rough seas. We were taking part at dawn the next day, June 6, in the D-Day landings, three weeks after my 18th birthday. The invasion began at 06:30. Our target was the town of Ouistreham. Our instructions were to bombard the town with our main guns, to soften up the German garrison. On our way across, we all had to make a will. The Captain spoke to us over the address system telling us that they didn't know what to expect from the German defence and 'that by this time tomorrow we could all be in Kingdom Come'.

'...When we arrived off Normandy the bombardment began. It was like all Hell had been let loose. Ships of all the Allied navies, large and small, were shelling the coast. The noise was incredible. The sky was full of aircraft towing gliders filled with paratroopers that would be landing in enemy occupied territory. As we fired salvo after salvo our ship vibrated to the extent that everything had to be battened down. The air was filled with cordite fumes. Orders were barked down voice pipes from the bridge as we went about our tasks like clockwork.

'As the day wore on we were allowed to return to the mess-deck, two men at a time, for a drink of cocoa and a sandwich. Whilst I was in the mess-desk I heard a violent explosion. All the men not on watch were ordered to the port side. A ship had been sunk and survivors were in the water. We threw a scrambling net over the side and our ship stopped to allow them to climb

aboard. The men were covered in oil, some wounded, others obviously
stunned. We reached down to haul them aboard; the deck was a mixture of
water, oil and blood ...'

**Wilfred Foulds RN on the cruiser HMS *Scylla*, the flagship of Rear Admiral
Sir Philip Vian who commanded the Eastern Task Force on D-Day. *Scylla* struck
a mine on 23 June while sailing from 'Juno' to 'Sword' which caused extensive
damage. She was towed back to Britain and in 1950 was scrapped.**

'I thought that the air bombardment was placed rather too far to the westward,
but it was difficult to judge through the smoke and dust. Approaching craft
reported that they could not recognise the beaches from a distance once the
bombardment started. The early waves, however, saw all they needed and all
spoke highly of the value of the models and photographs which they were
shown in the commercial Buildings, Portsmouth, prior to sailing. I was
surprised to see several houses in the front in 'Queen' Sector undamaged and
with windows still intact in spite of the bombardment.'

**Official report of the pre-assault bombardment by the 22 ships of
Bombarding Force 'D' led by HMS *Warspite*.**

'Approaching the Cherbourg Peninsula, the shore ['Omaha' beach] seemed to be
congested with vehicles, craft and men with no sign of penetration beyond the sea
wall. Fire could be seen within 500 yards of the beach. There was a direct hit on a
house near the harbour mouth of Port-en-Bessin; spouts of water where shells were
falling near some of the ships; one or two fires a short distance inland; a damaged
landing craft, half awash; a most majestic sight, HMS *Warspite* bombarding at anchor
with her attendant small craft laying a smoke screen round her; but above all, the
figures of men, the morning light upon their bayonets, moving slowly,
remorselessly, forward. The air was very bumpy and since the cloud base was
below 2,000 feet, the sky was congested with aircraft because the top cover, the low
cover and the naval spotting aircraft were all working at the same approximate
height. From time to time pilots could be heard on the Very High Frequency
telephone, saying 'Going down to investigate'.'

**Air Commodore Geddes, Deputy Senior Air Staff Officer of the 2nd
Tactical Air Force, who traversed the beaches from end to end in a Mustang
fitted with an 8-inch lens camera. He photographed the scene from a height
of between 800 and 1,000 feet and thus provided the Commander-in-Chief
with a valuable panorama.**

'I arrived over the beachhead at H-Hour for the first of five sorties on D-Day.
We were flying Spitfires Mk 5 in pairs and speaking by R/T directly with the
gunnery officers aboard the ships. The fireworks display which ensued as every
craft opened up, viewed from 10,000 feet in the dawn light, is something I shall
never forget. The battleships, with armaments ranging from 14- to 16-inch guns,
were lying about twenty miles off-shore so the shells had quite a high trajectory
and a 15- to 20-second time of flight. On one occasion when firing with HMS
Warspite (15-inch guns) and flying midway between the ship and the beachhead
at between 9,000 and 10,000 feet, I gave the order 'fire' and turned slowly

broadside on to the shore to wait for the fall of shot. Suddenly, in the clear sky my aircraft experienced a most violent bump which practically shook me out of my wits. At the same moment, I saw two enormous objects moving rapidly away from me towards the shore and immediately realized that I had flown at right angles through the slipstream of Warspite's two ranging 15-inch 'bricks'. Awestruck, I followed the shells down quite easily with my eyes during the rest of their curved flight and saw one of them actually hit the gun emplacement we were engaging! Not only that, the German gun was blasted out of the rear of the emplacement.

'I think my report of the fall of shot to Warspite was a little incoherent but I did manage to assure them that no further 'fire for effect' was needed and after congratulations all round, we switched to another target... we had one or two inexplicable losses during those weeks which we finally had to attribute to pilots being hit by their 'own' shells.

Wing Commander Leslie C. Glover, a fighter reconnaissance pilot on 26 Squadron RAF who directed the ship's gunfire on to the targets. *Warspite* **was fitted with eight 15-inch guns and eight 6-inch guns, which were directed against the Villerville battery. The battery was neutralized with three direct hits accurately spotted by the aircraft.**

'No communication could be established with the spotting aircraft. A most regrettable thing in which the bombarding force were not alone. However, we had the great advantage of being able to see our target and fire was opened upon it at 0547.

'Up to this hour there had been no sign of life from Ouistreham One Battery nor, as far as I am aware, did it ever open fire. Whether there was any life left in it after its aerial bombardment or whether it was playing possum and waiting for H-Hour and whether the ship's fire thwarted that purpose we shall never know.'

Official report from the cruiser HMS *Frobisher* **off 'Sword' beach.** *Frobisher's* **target was the Riva Bella battery but 1./HKAA 1260's guns had been moved to south of Ste-Aubin-d'Arquenay.**

'Once more unto the breach dear friends...'

Major 'Banger' King of the 2nd East Yorkshires who would be killed in action before the campaign was over, who read Shakespeare's famous eve of Agincourt speech from 'Henry V' over the loud hailer as his craft went in.

'We'd expected casualties' one private recalled, 'but nothing like this. The lads were going down on all sides. Hardly out of the boats and they were scuppered. By hell, it was something! ... Corporal Fred Mears, following the East Yorks in, charged up the beach, determined to make 'Jesse Owens look like a turtle'. He too was shocked to see that the East Yorks had failed to spread out and had consequently been slaughtered by the hundred. But as he told himself, somewhat unfeelingly, 'they would know better the next time.'

Charles Whiting.

'Day and night there was some kind of shit flying at you. If it wasn't these machine guns it was tank guns, if it wasn't tank guns it was artillery, if it wasn't artillery it was some bugger in an aeroplane dropping bombs on you... I think what war teaches you is how fantastic human hate can be. Because it's clearly insane, really, this spectacle of men and machines trying to destroy one another. It's really quite hideously insane. And one wonders whether there is any future for an animal that can do this.'

21-year old 2nd Lieutenant David Holbrook, East Yorkshire Yeomanry.

'I do not recall any mention of fear on the way to France, although many like me must have felt a little worried at what the next 24 hours would hold in store. There was plenty of apprehension and some tension amongst the crew, but most of all there was an overriding excitement and pride that we were playing a leading role in the greatest sea- borne invasion the world had ever known. We all wondered how long it would take the Germans to spot us and how well we would be able to defend the armada against mass dive-bomber attacks.

'Before passing through the minefield we became aware of a heavy drone above us that distracted us from the awesome spell of mine spotting. There was an endless line of shadows in the sky, which we realized to be a strong airborne force of men in gliders and 'tugs' or tow planes. In the half moonlight of that summer night we imagined - or did we really see - the force that was destined to make the first assault on the British sectors of the Normandy coast.

'At 5.30am we closed to some two miles from the coast off Ouistreham and took up our bombarding position. As the light of dawn increased, the enormity of the invasion fleet became more apparent - the vast number of ships and craft of every description becoming visible, stretching as far as the eye could see. It was quite unbelievable. Someone said: 'What will the Germans on shore think when they see this lot?'

Petty Officer James R. B. Hinton RN aboard HMS *Scourge*, part of the 23rd Destroyer Flotilla.

'I remember my motor launch was out amongst this immense throng of craft plunging through heavy seas to the beaches. On one of the landing craft it looked as though something had gone wrong with the rudder because one of the seamen was hanging over the stern in the water steering it with his feet.'

Lieutenant-Commander Stanbury. When a heavy sea wrenched away the steering wheel on LCA786, the coxswain, Corporal George Tandy, a 19-year old Royal Marine acted for four-and-a-half hours as a human rudder, slipping over the stern to stand with one foot on the rudder guard, guising the rudder with the other. On the seven-mile run-in from the LSI the surging waves first landed him high in the air and then plunged him breast-deep in water, but he hung on until 35 men were delivered off the shore. Then Tandy fought the LCA back to the LSI, this time with the wind and sea against him.

'At 0635 I was lowered in LCA 796 from LSI SS *Empire Broadsword* with thirty men and a captain of the Suffolk Regiment. We formed up and left the lowering position at approximately 0645, commencing the run in to White beach to touch down at H plus 60. The sea was fairly rough but the soldiers, with one or two exceptions, enjoyed the run in. At just over 1,000 yards, I signalled all craft to increase to maximum revolutions and, regardless of our own barrage, some of which fell in our midst, the flotilla hit the beach at full speed, LCT 947 touching down at 0726. Just after the first tank had got ashore from LCT 947, we were hit forward by mortar fire, which exploded the Bangalore torpedoes. The second tank (flail) was put out of action, also the tank astern of it. Three Army personnel were killed, including the Colonel and seven others wounded.'

Coxswain, LCT 947 heading for White Beach with soldiers of the Suffolk Regiment.

'When I first saw the beaches and what lay ahead I thought to myself: 'Gosh, I'm 25. I'll never be 26 and I'll never see my wife.' But somehow I did survive. So many of my friends didn't and others thought I was dead because my helmet came back before I did.'

'All my life I have been called Jumbo. People called Jarvis were. I always loved the sea and I joined the Norwich Sea Scouts. I'm jolly glad I did. After leaving school I got a job at a shoe factory and then went into the building trade as a painter and decorator. I proposed to my girlfriend Gladys and I remember sitting in church to hear our wedding banns read out and the vicar interrupted the service to announce that war had been declared. From then on everything changed. A month after we married I was on my way to war. I had asked to join the Royal Navy but they said they had enough sailors, so I went into the Royal Marines. I ended up in the Royal Marine Brigade. On the train I met Fred Palgrave who I had been to School with. I was No 1002 and he was No 1003 - a small world.

'After training at various places we ended up on the coast of West Africa, where we saw our first action. We managed to get home in one piece. We ended up doing more training in Scotland where I met Jack Martin, also from Norwich. Because both of us had worked in the shoe trade we were told to repair boots and shoes. We both got bored by this so I volunteered to be a commando and went off to Wales for more training, this time in seamanship. Because of my time with Norwich Sea Scouts I passed with flying colours - 98 per cent. I was proud of that and it was suggested I apply for an officers' training course, but when I was interviewed by the Colonel he asked if I had a private income. I told him the only income I had was the one they gave me and I had to hand most of that to my wife. He said if I hadn't got a private income I could forget about becoming an officer as I couldn't afford to pay the mess bill. I then became a coxswain on a landing craft and by June we were at Southampton, in terrible weather, waiting to go over.

'We knew the invasion was on but none of us realised how large it would be. I was in charge of a landing craft which had a crew of four. We could carry 150 men. When we left for Normandy on the morning of June 6 we were all amazed to see the size of the armada. No one had ever seen so many ships. 'It's difficult to describe what met us as we arrived at 'Sword' and I tried to get in as near to the beach as possible. All hell was let loose. Everyone was frightened and anyone who tells you he wasn't isn't telling the truth. I was 25. My crew were aged 18 and 19 so I was a man. It was my duty not to be scared, to look after them and the troops on my boat, which I did to the best of my ability.

'I chain smoked and tried to concentrate on the job and get my troops as near to the beach as possible so they didn't get dropped in the sea. I saw some that were killed before they even reached the beach. We went back and forwards from Southampton to France again and again. We didn't stop to sleep. On one occasion a bigger ship carrying more than 2,000 troops received a direct hit. We had to pick the wounded out of the sea and take them to another ship for treatment. And on one occasion we had to take limbs and bodies out of another boat that had been hit and put them into bags. Six men had been sitting around a table. They had all been blown up. It was terrible. My deck-hand was killed and my stoker had a breakdown. He couldn't go back to the beaches anymore. He'd had enough. It was so upsetting to see him. They were still in their teens. They looked up to me as a man because I was 25 and I had to act like one. Inside I was scared stiff.

'I was hit once. A piece of shrapnel flew past my head and knocked my tin helmet off. It was a good job I never used my chin-strap otherwise my head may have gone with it.

'A few weeks later back in England, a mate of mine said he thought I was dead because my helmet had been found on the beaches and had been sent back home. It must have been blown more than 300 yards. If I had been a cat then I would have used up most of' my nine lives in June 1944.

'After that we travelled up the coast, bringing in more equipment and men as the fighting moved inland - we were finally winning the war.'

Arthur 'Jumbo' Jarvis.

'I was commanding 3 Commando on this occasion. I was on the bridge of a landing craft talking to Lieutenant P Whitworth who commanded our division. The sea ran high, the weather was dull and gloomy, but the sight of HMS *Ramillies* belching 15-inch shells at the Benerville battery was almost as good as a rum ration. A shell landed in the water 100 yards away and to port we could see a tank landing craft blazing; the crew were going over the side as the ammunition exploded. Battered houses along the shore looked vaguely familiar from the photographs we had been shown. Tanks were creeping about on the beach, but from in front of Ouistreham a German gun was firing at us every few seconds. This did not seem to be the time or the place to slow down. I asked Lieutenant Whitworth 'What are you waiting for?'

'There are still five minutes to go before H plus 90' the captain, a young RNVR officer replies.

'I don't think anyone will mind if we're five minutes early on D-Day.'

'Then in we go.'

'We set off in a beautiful line and not a moment too soon. Another shell burst almost overhead; the bits that reached us had lost all force. This time a splinter hits the front of my jacket. Someone ducks and his helmet clangs on the deck. Another flash from in front of Ouistreham. This time the next craft to starboard is the target - a near miss, or a hit, maybe. The craft shies like a horse. Our craft is to port of the rest, which somehow makes us feel more exposed. As we beached the gun at Ouistreham hit us and many of my men were up to their necks in water before they could struggle out of the hold.

'The 4th division got all its five craft ashore, though three were hit and two completely wrecked. Such was the spirit of the RNVR, who put us ashore on D-Day. The commando lost about 30 men, mostly from the explosion of our own mortar bombs in one of the stricken craft. The first man ashore was Major J. E. Martin, our veteran administrative officer, who, as a trooper in the 9th Lancers, had had his baptism of fire on the Western Front in the year that I was born. He went right through - from Normandy to the Baltic.

'There were quite a lot of infantry sitting about on the beach and one cried out 'Don't touch the bloody wire, it's mined.'

'We sorted ourselves out among the houses on the dunes, undisturbed except for a little indiscriminate mortar fire. Ahead lay 1,000 yards of flat marshy meadow without a vestige of cover. This, the first stage of our journey to the Benouville bridges, was covered by a German quick-firing gun, but we survived its attentions more or less unscathed and pushed on to our forming-up place. Nearby we found a company commander of the assault brigade. He had his CSM (Company Sergeant-Major) and two men with him. The rest, 1 rather thought, might be the men we had seen sitting on the beach.

'Another shell.'

Storm from the Sea, **Lieutenant Colonel (later Brigadier) Peter Young.**

'I found a disorganized group of engineers crouching in a deserted pill-box and as I passed to see if I could not break through the wire at that point, an enemy sniper put a bullet clean through the skull of a man lying at length and, as he imagined, in safety, on the sand. We began to run through the gap I had seen on the right. The men floundered in the loose sand under their top-heavy loads of ammunition and I ran up and down the line yelling them on with every curse I remembered... Other troops with the stupidity of sheep were digging in along the length of the wire; they had not sense enough to realize that the enemy would blast it as conscientiously as a drill routine. One man, sitting upright as if he was alone on the sands, clutched his knee and wept over the bloody mess...'

Lieutenant Douglas Grant, who came in with the first wave. 28

'Up on the tiny flag deck a senior naval officer stands beside the Skipper, a microphone in his hand. Behind him is the trumpet of his loud-hailer. By swinging it in the right direction he can make himself heard across hundreds of yards of water. It's coming up to time. Not zero hour yet, but zero hour minus. The moment when the assault craft are to set off from their assembly area for the beaches. The convoy has come to a standstill. Engines are ticking over. The mother ships - the troopships - have been lowering their assault craft into the water. A mine-sweeper comes sliding alongside us out of the blackness. A voice calls from her, thin and strained. Our loud-hailer comes aloud with a click. 'Hello there', it says, 'Glad to see you. Everything all right? What do you make of our exact position? ... Good, that checks with our own calculations. We're OK thanks.' And off goes the shape into the darkness.

'Astern of us the assault craft are now assembled. You know that they are

28 Douglas Grant, *The Fuel of the Fire* (Cresset).

neatly marshalled there in formation, but you can only make out the leaders. The loud hailer checks them over. Voices reply faintly out of the darkness. The naval commander is looking at his watch. He puts the microphone to his mouth. 'Off you go' and then 'and good luck to you.' Engines rev up and those small dark shapes come abreast of you, row after row of them and shoot ahead like so many dark beetles on the surface of the water. You feel you want to give them a cheer as they pass.'

Frank Gillard of the BBC, recorded on the control ship off the French coast on D-Day morning watching the assault craft get under way.

'This is the day and this is the hour. The sky is lightening, lightening over the coast of Europe as we go in... the whole sea is a glittering expanse of green with white crests everywhere.

'The sun is blazing down brightly now. It's almost like an omen the way it's suddenly come out just as we were going in. The whole sky is bright. The sea is a glittering mass of silver with all these craft of every kind, moving across it and the great battleships in the background blazing away... You can't imagine anything like this march of ships, just marching in line like soldiers marching in line, a purpose shared by many hundreds of thousands of fighting men, who are going to the coast of Europe to the biggest job they've ever had to do.

'I can't record any more now. The time has come for me to get my kit on my back and get ready to step off on that shore - AND IT'S A GREAT DAY.'

Colin Wills, BBC Correspondent. Canadian Stanley Maxted of the BBC on board a minesweeper spearheading the vast armada, described 'a night of second by second vigilance. The faces of those men were streaked and taut with weariness. As we neared the end of the sweep, tension crept up a notch higher. Would we be spotted from the shore? Would a searchlight suddenly glare out-and fasten on us? And the shore batteries? Would this... ? Supposing that... ? I began to wish I could yell and jump up and down, or break something to cut that silent, taut wire of strain.'

'It was barely light, but we could see that we were among war ships of all sorts. As we got closer to the coast of Normandy we could see smoke on the shoreline, from the long range battleship assault. We were all looking at this incredible sight when we were ordered to go below decks. By now it was about 9am and the first brigade was already ashore and fighting. I went onto the deck to have a look at what was going on and we were about 400 metres off shore. We could hear the sandbanks on the bottom of the boat and we were very nervous about mines. About 100 metres off shore we were ordered back on deck. On the front of the LCA there was a gangplank on each side of the bow, up on deck. When you get inshore they shoot these forward on pulleys and you walk down. As the gangplanks went forward the chaps were nearly on them - it was no good hanging around because there was already shellfire coming at us. The boat on our right took a direct hit, making us very anxious. The right hand ramp turned over with a whole lot of chaps on it, so everyone had to go down the left ramp. I think I was in the fifth section to go down. One of the naval chaps had tied a rope to the end of the gang plank and had run onto the beach with it, so that we could all hold onto the rope to guide us onto the beach. Chaps were disappearing under the waves. You could just see their hands holding on to the rope. It was very comforting to finally get onto the sand, much better than being at sea. We had been issued with waterproof waders that can keep you dry up to the chest, a bit like the ones fishermen wear. In theory this was great, but in practice it only worked if the water came up to your waist. Chaps were going under water and trying to wade out with these waterproofs absolutely filled to bursting. I got out a knife and started slicing the waterproofs of the chaps that were struggling to walk on shore wearing these things. I did this for about seven or eight blokes, the men in my group. Then I looked around and saw a sea wall, about two or three foot high and I sheltered behind it on my own, My sergeant came up to me and said, 'You're not going to win this war on your own, get your men.'

'I could see smoke and smouldering tanks that had been blown up earlier. The seafront area had already been taken, but there was still some resistance and we were still being fired on.'

Bob Littlar, 2nd Battalion King's Shropshire Light Infantry.

'0800 hours, 4 June at Langstone Harbour-Hayling Harbour. A dozen 12 LCMs (Landing Craft Mechanised) of 602 Flotilla were gently lapping water at anchor. The weather over the past few days had been atrocious with storms and high seas. We knew something big was coming off due to the build up of stores, ammunition, tanks and vehicles of all descriptions that were piling up all along the south coast. Our craft was fully stored and fuelled, ready for any eventuality.

'At about 0900 hours all the crews were told that landings were to be undertaken along the coast of Normandy. Various areas had been allocated to American, Canadian and British forces - ours being 'Sword' Beach. Following the briefings, the landings were postponed for a further 24 hours. Now we had been briefed, we were all restricted to our rooms and could not contact anyone. You can imagine what the tension was like and we were all relieved when we were told to rejoin our craft and make ready. The time was 1700 hours on 5 June when we raised anchor and slipped slowly out of harbour. As we came out of harbour, we had a clear view of both Portsmouth and Southsea. Landing craft were emerging from every creek and inlet. We were to follow a private yacht that had been bought into commission and would navigate for us across the Channel. As the first strains of light began to break, we gradually became aware of the immense build-up behind us. There were craft of all descriptions, including old Thames barges being towed as they had previously been converted to kitchens. From a bigger vessel we could faintly hear the sound of Glenn Miller as it drifted across the water. Everything seemed so peaceful and yet on everyone's mind was the fear of the unknown.

'When we were about five miles off the French coast, we became aware of a darkening in the sky behind us and a noise which increased until it became deafening. Gradually, as it came nearer, we could make out planes towing gliders, hundreds of them. This was the airborne and glider troops going to their targets. All was quiet until we were about 400 yards from the coastline.

Then all hell opened up. The Royal Navy was bombarding with their heavy guns and there was quite a bit of return fire. An LCI (Landing Craft Infantry), which was loaded with troops and sailing to my right, just disappeared in a ball of flame. Many landing craft were hit and sustained considerable casualties. We could feel and hear the shells exploding under our craft but kept going to the beach.

'As we hit the beach we would see a naval officer [Colin Maud, immortalized in the film The Longest Day by Kenneth Moore] with a flaming red beard and a voice like a foghorn. He had a dog on a lead and they both seemed to have a charmed life, dodging bullets and shouting obscenities to all and sundry. He became known as 'Ginger'.

'We unloaded in the beach just in time as two German planes came down the shoreline, shooting at anything that was there. At this point, the men I had trained with, No. 1 Commando Brigade, was going ashore, headed by a piper with Lord Lovat. All the commandos were loaded down with equipment and personal kit. The disciplined courage of those men, with all of their lives in front of them, facing the merciless fire of the machine guns was something I will never forget. But the piper went through the hail of bullets and I imagine the sound of the pipes, wailing above the noise of battle, made many a German's blood run cold.

'A coaster full of 500lb block-buster bombs was set on fire. It went up with an almighty bang and a pall of thick black smoke drifted across the beach. It was scattered with flaming debris which in turn set off ammunition dumps. 'The stokers and mechanics that came out with the flotilla were now on the beach, scavenging the numerous wrecks looking for spare parts.

'Back to 'Ginger'. A Bren-gun carrier had come down the ramp of a landing craft and had stalled when partly submerged. 'What's up laddie?' barked 'Ginger'.

'It won't go, sir!' said the driver.

'My old Granny used to say, if things won't go, give them a whack with a stick,' shouted 'Ginger'. This he promptly did with the big cudgel he carried and then said to the driver, 'Try it now.'

'The engine burst into life.

'For a week we lived on hard tack biscuits and dry rations and had little sleep. We had not washed or shaved and our once proud Royal Marine uniforms were in tatters. We were then invited onto a cruiser for fish and chips. It was a feast.

'By now the sea was getting rough again and it was a job to keep upright on the decks. Unloading heavy equipment was a real struggle. Shell fire from German guns was exploding on hitting the water and sending out fragments. These underwater explosions increased so much our bilge pumps couldn't cope. The oil got in our eyes, making it painful and difficult to see and eventually we were pulled on board another boat. We took over a landing craft that had lost its crews and then carried on ferrying troops from the bigger ships onto the beach. On the return of our fourth trip, we took a number of German prisoners on board with orders to find a destroyer to take them back to England. They were on board all night. Many wore the armband of Rommel's

Afrika Korps and sang German songs. It was a long night. We carried on for about three weeks and by then the 'Mulberry' harbour at Arromanches had come into use.

'It was then decided to withdraw the landing craft from 'Sword', owing to the number of casualties. The Germans still had mobile 88mm guns where they could pick off our craft as they came on the beach. They would fire a few shots and then vanish, so it was difficult to spot and destroy them. We went to work the beach at Arromanches, but history repeated itself. The bottom of our craft was like a pepper-pot and we found ourselves in the drink for a second time. This time we were not so lucky in finding another craft. The beaches were littered with wrecked landing craft. Having lost all our gear, we were put on a destroyer and taken to Southampton. When landing, all I had was a boiler suit with a towel around my neck and a pair of naval sea boots. As we were going through some form of customs check, an official asked if I had anything to declare - my response was unprintable. Then they looked at us and saw we could not walk in a straight line. They said if we 'did not pick ourselves up' we would be arrested for being drunk. We had to convince them we were suffering from 'landing craft fever'. The military police then escorted us the rest of the way to shore to make sure we didn't fall off the jetty. We were kept in camp for a week, fed well and re-kitted, before being given a 14-day pass.'

Royal Marine Commando Corporal William 'Bill' Kurn. The only Luftwaffe presence over the invasion beaches that morning were two Focke Wulf FW 190s flown by Oberstleutnant Josef 'Pips' Priller, Kommodore, Jagdgeschwader 26 'Schlageter' and his regular Kacmarek (wingman), Unteroffizier Heinz Wodarczyk of the Stab flight at Priller's Lille-Nord command post. The pair took off into grey skies at 0800. Priller, in his usual FW 190A-8 'Black 13' Jutta. His only orders to Wodarczyk were to stick close. They headed west at low altitude, spotting Spitfires above them as far east as Abbeville. [29] Near Le Havre they climbed into the solid cloudbank and emerged to see the invasion fleet spread out before them. Priller and Wodarczyk each made a full-throttle (400 mph) 50 feet low level strafing run over 'Sword' beach with cannons and machine guns before landing at Creil. [30] The three Gruppen of JG 26 reached the battle zone that afternoon and contributed to the 172 total combat sorties flown by Fliegerkorps II and the 5th Jagdivision (121 combat sorties) on D-Day. [31] Priller claimed his 97th and

---

29   Probably 12 Typhoon IBs of 440 Squadron RCAF who during the initial assault were the only aircraft allowed below the cloud base. Flying Officer James Beatty reported that the only aircraft they saw at their elevation were two Focke Wulfs as they climbed into the cloud base.

30   Earlier that day Priller was told that JG 26 was now under the command of the 5th Jagdivision and that he should begin transferring his Gruppen at Nancy-Essey, Mont de Marsan and Biarritz to bases nearer to the beachhead area, to the JG 2 airfields at Creil and Cormeilles. Priller went to see Major Bühligen Kommodore of the Richthofen Geschwader (JG2). Bühligen had no more fighters than did Priller. Only one of his Gruppen was immediately available; another was en route from Brittany and the third was in Germany for rebuilding and had not yet been released to return to France. *The JG26 War Diary, Vol Two 1943-1945* by Donald Caldwell (Grub Street 1998).

31   'Major Bühligen scored the first victory for JG 2, a P-47 over the Orne Estuary, at 1157. II/JG 2 was active over Caen from noon and III/JG 2 joined in after it arrived at Cormeilles from Brittany. For the day, the Richthofen Geschwader claimed three P-47s, five P-51s and nine Typhoons, for the loss of nine

98th victories, a P-47 and a P-51, on 7 June and his 100th victory came on 15 June when he shot down a B-24 Liberator of the 492nd Bomb Group. Wodarczyk was KIA on 1 January 1945. Oberst Priller survived the war with 101 victories.

'Just before dawn, those of us on the bridge of HMS *Danae* had a tot of the most superb 1812 brandy from a bottle laid down by my great-grandfather in 1821 - sent to me by my father with the comment, 'You may find this of some use in the near future.' We then commenced the operations for which we had been trained, namely engaging and knocking out three enemy batteries. At about 10 am we closed the beaches to knock out the opposition to the landing forces in the Ouistreham area. Our open 6-inch and twin 4-inch guns went into independent fire - the guns being laid, trained and fired by the crews stripped to the waist. This was real 'Nelson Stuff'. We knocked up a fantastic rate of fire. X and Y guns were firing at least 19 rounds per minute on occasion. We all joined in, jumping in to relieve the exhausted crew members where we could. It was exhilarating beyond description and even my thirteen-year-old boy bugler fired Y Gun with the lanyard while the captain of the gun, a corporal, leapt to get more charges into the breech. Then it all came to a halt and we sailed to Portsmouth for re-ammunition.'

Captain J. H. B. Hughes, Royal Marines, aboard HMS *Danae*.

FW 190s. The P-51s included an entire flight of four 4th Fighter Group aircraft, bounced while strafing a convoy near Rouen... By late afternoon, the JG 2 armourers had fitted some of the Focke-Wulfs with launchers for 21 cm rockets and Leutnant Heinz Kemethmüller led his 4th Staffel in the first rocket attack by the Geschwader on land targets; they had been trained for this at Cazaux. The 2nd Staffel leader, Oberleutnant Franz Kunz, scored the day's only air victory for the Geschwader, downing a Mustang southeast of Caen at 2055. This was probably a 4th Fighter Group P-51 that had aborted from a mission to Dreux with a bad magneto and was attempting to reach the Allied lines to force-land. [In JG 26] Unteroffizier Hans-Werner Winter of the 3rd Staffel either got lost or was chased east by Allied fighters and was shot down and killed by the Abbeville flak. Führer Gerhard Schulwitz was missing for a day after being shot down by naval gunfire, but returned with slight injuries. Fhj-Unteroffizier Friedrich Schneider of the 2nd Staffel was also hit by naval gunners and belly-landed on Beaumont-le-Roger.' *The JG26 War Diary, Vol Two 1943-1945* by Donald Caldwell (Grub Street 1998). 8th AF fighter units, operating mainly in the Chartres and Rouen areas, took their own toll of the few German fighters that appeared. P-47 and P-51 pilots claimed 13:0:1, including five FW 190s claimed by the 4th Fighter Group, which caught nine Focke-Wulfs in the circuit at Evreux airfield. However, of the 25 8th Air Force fighters reported missing, no less than ten came from this Group, including a complete section of four bounced by German fighters from JG 26 near Rouen in the early evening. Two hours later, Mustangs from the 339th and 355th Fighter Groups swept the area near Orleans and surprised a large formation of Ju 87 Stukas, claiming 11:1:6 for the loss of three P-51s. In addition to the fighter sweeps, the 8th Air Force fighters also carried out fighter-bomber missions. 9th Air Force squadrons, flying close support over the 'Omaha' and 'Juno' beach areas, lost nine fighters, but F-6 pilots of the 15th Tactical Reconnaissance Squadron, flying Tactical Reconnaissance sorties in the areas of Dreux and Laval, engaged FW 190s claiming 3:0:1 without loss. The 9th Air Force...sustained seven losses, two Marauders and five A-20 Havocs, but a FW190 was claimed shot down over Argentan by a Marauder crew. 1944: *The Air War Over Europe June 1st-30th Over The Beaches by* John Foreman (ARP 1994). Shortly after dawn on 7 June a Focke Wulf 190 which before it hit the sea, dropped a 250lb phosphorous bomb on the deck of the *Bulolo,* killing three officers (two RAF and one RN) and blowing a 5-foot hole in the foremost bulkhead of the operations room.

'Early in the evening of 5 June the entire ship's company who could be spared from duty mustered on deck and our captain briefly put us in the picture as to the part we were assigned to play in the events planned for the next day. To close the proceedings he removed his cap, lowered his head and spoke the opening words of the prayer Lord Nelson had confessed in his cabin before Trafalgar. 'May the Great God whom I worship grant to my country and for the benefit of Europe in general a great and glorious victory and may no misconduct in anyone tarnish it and may humanity after victory be the predominant feature in the British Fleet'. Those words were as relevant as they had been in way back in October 1805.

'Within half-an-hour or so we shipped anchor and headed into the Channel to catch up and overtake the grey columns of troop transports and landing craft which for several hours had been leaving the Solent and now stretched to the horizon and beyond. We had our own rendezvous with the pages of history when next day we would, in company with many other naval vessels lead them, to the beaches of Normandy. D-Day dawned and 'Sword' beach came into view. Ahead of us were a group of minesweepers and astern a mighty fleet of transports and Landing craft filling the scene as far as the eye could see. Overhead the sky was filled with an aerial armada of bombers. The din was tremendous and added to it was the roar of the big guns of the heavier ships bombarding the shore. Before long the bombardment ceased and the first of the assault craft began ferrying the army ashore from the big transports.

'From our viewpoint a mile or so off the beach it was evident that the operation was going well. There was sporadic opposition from hidden German guns, which had escaped the initial bombardment and here and there landing craft were hit but the majority were reaching the beach unscathed. At 0800 I had to return to the wireless office to take my turn on watch and so far the rest of the morning had to rely on a running commentary provided by off-watch staff. That night we returned to Portsmouth carrying twenty wounded Canadians who had been transferred to us by an assault craft.'

John Gough, radio-operator aboard a destroyer at Harwich.

'We, together with another LCT of the 43rd LCT Flotilla, LCT 1018 (Lieutenant W. Peacock RNVR) each carried several hundred tons of ammunition and had to 'dry out' on 'Queen' 'Sword' Beach for unloading. We had rehearsed the 'profile' of the beach and it was uncannily reassuring to find that it looked exactly like the model prepared in England. On beaching we holed ourselves on one of the 'hedgehogs', so puncturing several of our double-bottoms, but not in the upshot causing serious damage. In a quiet spell after beaching I remember sharing a tin of peaches or apricots with Sub Lieutenant Anthony Rowland and sitting beside the binnacle on the bridge, reading Livingstone's *'Selections from Plato'*. I remember that we had some difficulty in unloading our cargo, as the troops we took over with it failed to return after beaching. Some of the material was unloaded on to the beach, but later that day, in the evening, was set on fire and began exploding. Luckily the tide had returned and we pulled off the beach, with a slight list and anchored off the beach until the following morning, when we came back to complete our unloading.'

A Sub Lieutenant RNVR in command of a Mark IV LCT 1013.

'It was a fantastic sight. Ships everywhere. I couldn't really take it in. It was a bit like a traffic jam by the time I arrived. One feels very proud to have taken part. I also feel very lucky to be alive.'

Bluey Arthurs, a watch keeping officer on a LST carrying around 20 tanks and heaps of lorries. They left Portsmouth at midnight and reached 'Sword' beach in the morning. His operation went without a hitch but he recognises just how lucky he was to land at that time and at that beach and is only too aware of how many others lost their lives. His tour of duty pretty much came to an end afterwards and three trips later he was aware again how lucky he was - his former boat was sunk with almost all on board losing their lives.'

'I remember very well it had been a difficult passage down. The final approach to our bombarding position was hair-raising; in a narrow swept channel, with a strong cross tide, we were almost constantly under helm, dodging myriads of landing-craft whom we had to overtake in order to open fire on prearranged targets well before the small landing-craft carrying the soldiers in went into touchdown. At about 0530 we were one of the first warships to fire on our target battery. Just before 09.00 I left the bridge and went into the charthouse. In the charthouse was a loudspeaker connected to the BBC. As I came in on this, perhaps the most momentous day in the annals of the British Empire, a voice said: 'Now girls; are we all ready? Then stretch the arms; stretch the legs.' It was May Brown conducting morning exercises for the ladies.'

Frederick Parham, captain of the 6-inch cruiser HMS *Belfast*.

'I thought we were going to tear up and down at high speed blasting everything in sight but quite the opposite. We just stopped. And then it started. Bang! Bang-bang-bang! A crash and a bang and a shudder. A crash and a bang and a shudder and a crash and a bang and a shudder. Not quite as fast as this, but monotonous. There's a crash and a bang and a shudder. It's exactly the same sensation as a near miss: if someone is shooting at you there's a crash and a bang and a shudder and the ship shakes. And you get used to this till eventually it fades into the commonplace, if I can use the word.

'Much more significant to our way of thinking were the horrendous outpourings of rockets from the rocket ships. We had landing craft fitted with a hundred rockets and when these went off with a 'Woosh! Woosh! Woosh! Woosh! Woosh! Woosh! Woosh!' they would all stream inland and there would be a vast series of explosions on shore. You couldn't help thinking that there would be nothing left surviving underneath.'

Engine Room Artificer Ronald Jesse on HMS *Belfast* off 'Sword' Beach.

'Rommel had placed beach obstacles all along the Western defences. These were in the form of tetrahedrals, steel posts, which had shells and mines attached to them. Our landing craft were fitted with twenty-four 60lb spigot bombs and the object was to blow up the beach obstacles at half-tide, clearing a passage for the LCTs that were carrying tanks with flails. The flails would clear any mines that were left and then the troops could go in. As we arrived thirty yards off the beach to do our job, destroyers were bombarding inland, but at precisely H minus one minute the bombardment lifted. We let go our spigot-bombs and there were tremendous explosions. I went to port and then along came this LCT that beached and out of it came the flail tank. And the most incredible thing was that there wasn't a shot fired. It was absolute peace, probably for a minute or two minutes. Then this tank waddled up the beach, the flails started off, there was an explosion as the waterproofing was blown up and then there was black smoke from the tank as it received a direct hit. There weren't any flames for a moment but they were obviously all killed inside.'

Lieutenant-Commander Hugh Irwin, Commanding 591 LCA (HR) Flotilla.

'A Force 9 gale was blowing and I think it was one of the worst tows that we ever had. I mean, you think of towing, you think of the tug being ahead but there were times when the block was abeam - it was really close. When we got over there, we shortened the tow and went to this long row of ships that had been sunk as a marker for us. Small tugs tied up alongside and guided her in and then they opened the seacocks and sunk them and that was more or less the start of the 'Mulberry' Harbour. There was a Royal Navy commander with a ginger beard who called us all sorts of names, but we did it in the end.'

Chief Petty Officer Albert Barnes, Quartermaster, aboard a Royal Naval tug, towing a 'Mulberry' Harbour caisson.

'We went through and under the battleship fire and passed the Svenner which had been struck amidships and went down like a V... we actually passed her when the men were still jumping off. We had no loss going in - a number of ships were damaged, but on the whole minor damage, the sea was roughly half-tide when we went in but we had a gap and we went through that gap so that our first tank was the first ashore. She went up shortly after that on a mine, the next tank managed to wriggle round her and went up right across the beach and got over the sea wall. I think we then landed two Bangalore torpedo tanks and two armoured bulldozers... and that was our load.'

David Divine, a naval war correspondent in an LCT carrying AVREs.

'I served on LCT 1094, commanded by Sub Lieutenant Harry Surtees RNVR with the 45th Flotilla of Force S. Our Flotilla Officer was Lieutenant R. S. James RNVR (later Lieutenant Commander DSC) at Portsmouth. I well remember postponing my security briefing for a last run ashore to Kimbells Dance Hall in Southsea before embarking tanks of AVRE (Assault Vehicles Royal Engineers) and sailing overnight on 5 June to beach at 'H Hour' on the 6th. As we were due to beach first, we were among the last Landing Craft to leave Spithead and threaded our way through the impressive avenue of assault ships and craft en-route to the 'Sword' sector beaches to the west of Ouistreham, towing an LCA, commanded by Lieutenant Fortescue RN, which, sadly foundered in heavy weather, her crew transferring to 1094. On the run in to the beach, we grounded on a drowned DD tank (duplex-drive), but managed to pull clear and beach on time, unloading the AVRE: whose task was to clear Beach obstacles for the follow-up assault. I remember seeing the Norwegian destroyer *Svenner* torpedoed off the mouth of the River Orne, with her bows and stern high in the air, forming a spectacular 'V for Victory'.

'Having successfully off loaded the AVRE, we hauled off but were hit and our Paxman engines failed. However, a passing LCT took us in tow back to Portsmouth, where, much to my surprise, I found myself at Kimbells Dance Hall on the evening of June 7th! Repairs completed, we sailed for the beaches again, this time, to Arromanches and the shelter of the breakwater formed by old ships and the 'Mulberry' Harbour, where we were kept very busy ferrying vehicles, troops 'and supplies from ships lying off to the beaches, subject to the state of the tide. We sometimes 'dried-out' on a beach and actually 'set foot' in France! Several incidents come to mind - one such was when our Cox'n, A. B. Tinman, staggered aboard with a massive Gilded Cockerel (weather-vane), which he had 'acquired' and of his chagrin when we said we didn't want it: Another was when all LCT's, were ordered to secure alongside HMS *Rodney* to form a protective skirt (three thick) in response to a threat of an attack by frogmen/midget subs. Nothing came about, however, but we acquired much needed fresh bread and provisions and I could truthfully claim 'I was on the *Rodney*'!

'On another occasion, we took a 'deck-cargo' of German PoWs back to Portsmouth. They far out-numbered our crew of twelve and our lone rifle and revolver hardly seemed adequate to police them, especially as our Oerlikons wouldn't depress to cover-the 'tank deck! Fortunately, they were quite docile although curious to look around our 'un-ship-like' craft with its flat bottom and 'drawbridge' bow and the non-return valves along the tank deck, which would drench the unwary in any sort of sea.'

'This is how I spent June, July and August in 1944, proud to have been part of the historic invasion, thankful not to have time ashore with the assault troops and even more thankful to have survived to meet and marry my lovely Wren and to enjoy our children and grand-children.'

Dennis Till.

'We had to do this DD training in Yarmouth and then right to the north in Scotland to Fort George. We did practice landings in these DD tanks. The problem was... it was a bit of a hairy scary thing. We were sometimes under the submarine command... we had to have Davis escape apparatus... if the tank sunk we had to put on the Davis escape apparatus, a bottle on our front, we had the bag on our chest; we had a nose-clip where we took the oxygen in. The submarine lieutenant there said, 'It's only to give you a bit of buoyancy, if you sink in these things, you'll go down so fast you'll get the bends.' I think it was in Yarmouth that they stuck us in a big tank, a big pit and the water just flowed in and the water came up your body that quick... you had to put the Davis escape apparatus on. The water went all the way over you and went up about twenty or thirty feet and you had to get out. If you couldn't swim you were a bit panicky.

'DD tanks were compulsory. The regiment I was in did the charge of the Light Brigade and that was it, the Charge of the Light Brigade came all again -

officers with big moustaches and they all thought they were charging at Balaclava... DD tanks were a bit weird. All it was was a canvas screen and that kept the tank afloat. There were about thirty-two air pillows. The canvas screen came up - there was a mesh that kept it up. So all there was between you and the bottom of the sea was this canvas screen. The drive from the engine was transferred from two propellers at the back. You pulled a lever and it turned these two propellers and you went around 5 knots an hour and when you got heavy seas you really rocked... In training we lost about three crews up in Scotland, they went down in about three hundred feet of water and we never saw them again. It was a bit weird when you thought what might happen on D-Day, but we took it philosophically...

'On D-Day there was a hell of a swell on... we launched three miles out and the waves came up that high that we had to get out of the tanks and hold the canvas screen up, what a way to land... We were awash with water, we were sea-sick, we had the Davis escape apparatus on, we had the ear phones on, you'd got a mike, you'd got a Mae West on, you didn't know which to pull next.

'The real panic came when the other stuff started to back up on us. We were supposed to be ahead of it but we were going that slow that the other stuff was catching up on us. If we got too close the landing craft just ploughed into you and sunk you. They didn't worry. Their idea was to get to the shore and if you were in the way that was just your hard luck. Being outside the tank instead of inside we could see these landing craft coming closer and the stuff was going over from the battleships, the fifteen inch shells, sixteen inch shells. The air force was flying around at about five hundred feet. You didn't know what to do and you were sick and you'd got all this gear on. People say, 'Were you panicky?' There was that much confusion you hadn't got time to feel frightened.'

Sergeant Howard Ray (John) Clewlow, 13th/18th Hussars, turret gunner, DD tank.

'Towards the end of May my Regiment had been briefed that in a few days we would be heading for the shores of France to spearhead the invasion. We were shown maps with no names and aerial photographs which showed a line of white houses along the beach-line and we were told that those were our targets; that they were enemy gun emplacements and there would be firing coming from there. Once we were on board ship we were called for our final briefing and shown maps with names on so that we knew that we were land on a beach code-named 'Sword', at the little town of Lion-sur-Mer. We were to be the left flank of the assault in amphibious tanks (DD) swimming in from 5,000 yards.

'The journey over was absolutely horrible. The LCT is a flat-bottomed ship with not much to it apart from a large deck which was the tank deck. There were five Sherman tanks on each LCT and they weren't built to accommodate so many men and tanks so there was nowhere to sleep and we bedded down on the hard iron tank deck... we had been issued with hammocks, but very few soldiers knew how to swing a hammock... It was very exciting for the first hour or so whilst we watched the armada assemble, but gradually the sea got rougher and in the next hour or so we began to get very seasick and this went on for several days. Hardly a man aboard wasn't very sick. We had sea-sickness pills and a certain amount of rum went round, but it didn't really help.

'When we got about 5,000 yards from shore, our flotilla stopped and we mounted the tanks, put up the screens [on the DD tanks] and got everything ready. And one by one we launched off through the doors and out into the sea and a force eight wind was blowing and it was very rough indeed and we could feel what that was doing to an LCT that weighed hundreds of tons, so what was it going to do to a poor little DD Tank with a screen round it? But it was a matter of drill: once the ramp was lowered there was only one way to go and that was out. The door went down and the ramp leading into the sea went down and I was second tank off. Our troop sergeant went off first, he went down the ramp, nosed into the sea, straightened up, got out of the way and then off we went down the ramp into the sea and finally we straightened up too. The waves must have been five or six feet and we went right up and then right down into the trough of a wave, but I gave the order to drop the propellers and the propellers came down and engaged and we could feel them bite in the water and we started on our way following the sergeant's tank in front. You could see the shoreline briefly now and then from that low angle. As a trough appeared in the waves, so the tank slid into the trough; and with the engines racing, it managed to climb up to the crest of the next wave, where you could see what was going on, then down into the next trough. The wind was behind us and very strong and this was a bit of a help, I suppose, because it helped us toward the beach. It took us well over an hour to cover the four miles to the beach and a couple of tanks were lost. The screen tore on one and it went down and one was run over by its own LCT which should have stayed back because of sea conditions, but it was moving forward. All the crew went down, except the captain - he managed to get free. Disaster struck one DD tank as he went off from another LCT. As he was going through the large doorway the ship rolled and as it rolled the tank lurched to one 'side and the canvas screen brushed the iron side of the entrance and slashed it. There was nothing they could do. They couldn't go back because there were other tanks to come off. They had to go forward. Nobody was sitting in the turret and as it hit the water the water gushed in through the screen and that tank sank. Luckily the crew got out. They had their rubber dinghy, which they jumped into and they were saved.

'The rest of us were still ploughing on through the water. We had three miles to go and it was very tough going. The only one who was inside on my particular tank was the driver and he had to sit there keeping the engines running because if the engines stopped we were in deep trouble, so he was down there in the bowels of the tank. I had the rest of the crew on deck and we were making sure those struts stayed put. Water came in over the top of the screen from time to time from these large waves. We had a manual-operated bilge pump - we'd thought it was a piece of Meccano, but it worked - and the co-driver was kept very busy with this bilge pump and we were bailing all the way to the shore with our tin helmets and everything to keep the water down inside the tank.

'The opposition started before we got ashore, they must have woken up with the naval bombardment and the aerial bombardment and they started to retaliate, so we were under fire for the best part of 1,000 yards coming in. But from the German point of view there was very little to see... all you could see from the shore of the DD Tank afloat is a little piece of canvas floating on the water, so if our security had worked, they weren't even aware that these were tanks until we came out of the water and dropped the canvas screen. Within a minute of landing the first shot had gone off. The plan was that the tanks would get to the water-line, stop and start firing while the assault engineers who'd come in right behind us would go ahead and clear the minefields and then we'd follow the engineers and start making paths through the mines and we'd hoist a windsock which was our signal that there was a path to drive inland avoiding the mines.

'The Royal Engineers had a certain amount of trouble in their voyage across the Channel and so they were late and there we were, at low tide, sitting on the beach, firing away. The infantry were now coming past us ashore in their little landing craft and under cover of our fire they were going up the beach. But we had landed on a fast incoming tide. We'd landed at low tide, so the longer we stood still and waited for the mines to be cleared on the beach, the deeper the water became. It wasn't long before the driver started complaining bitterly that, because we'd dropped our screen and the water was getting deeper, it was now coming in over the top of his hatch and he was sitting in a pool of water. He said, 'For God's sake, let's move on up the beach!' This was a failure on my part: I should've used my initiative and said, 'Go for it!' but I didn't. And as we sat there, wondering what to do, the problem was solved for us because a particularly large wave hit the stem of the tank and swamped the engine compartment and the engine spluttered to a halt and was drowned. Well, now we had a thirty-two ton tank and no power so we couldn't move even if we'd wanted to.

'So we sat there and fired and continued firing until such time as the tank became swamped. The water level inside the tank was rising and when the water got to the gun breach inside the turret we couldn't carry on. So we inflated the rubber dingy, took out the Browning machine gun and some ammunition and we got in the rubber dinghy and we had to abandon the tank and start paddling for the shore. By now, of course, the tide had come in so fast and so far that it was several hundred yards to the shoreline and it seemed a long way and the water was quite deep and it was being speckled with bullets. We were under fire all the time from the shore now and we used the map boards as paddles and there were five of us sitting in this little dinghy, trying to get ashore. We hadn't gone very far when we were suddenly hit by a burst of machine-gun fire. This punctured the rubber dingy which collapsed and threw us into the sea and we lost our machine gun and ammunition and one bullet hit Gallagher the co-driver in the ankle so we now had a wounded man on our hands.

'We were obliged to swim for the shore, now 300 yards away. Halfway there I clung to a post sticking up out of the water and glancing up I saw a large black Teller Mine attached to the top of it which exploded if you happened to touch it in the wrong place so there wasn't much chance of stopping for a breather - I swam on. We were floundering around in the water and we started to splash our way into the beach and were trying to get the wounded man there at the same time. We were all five of us pretty exhausted when we reached dry land. In the meantime the infantry had come ashore and there was a battle going on all around with the Germans retaliating with mortar and shellfire and altogether it was a pretty unhealthy place to be.

'One of our tanks came up beside us and the commander shouted out: 'Can't stop I'm afraid' and he threw us a tin of self-heating soup, which we gratefully shared between the five of us. We lay there on the beach, swigging down hot soup and wondering what to do next and I remember being suddenly approached by a captain in the Royal Engineers and he was very angry and he came up and said, 'Get up, corporal. That's no way to win the Second Front.' Then he pushed off on his business. Of course he was quite right and I felt a little bit ashamed about this.

'I finally found the Beachmaster, a Royal Naval lieutenant commander, who was a very busy man trying to organise things. I reported to him and said, 'Here we are, what can I do to help?' And he said 'You want to help me?' I said 'Yes, sir.' He said, 'Well, get off my bloody beach.'

'The beach was now an inferno of machine-gun, shell and mortar fire, but we reached the promenade behind it and met up with some other unhorsed tank crews. Later we were directed to make for the village of Hermanville where we found the survivors of 'A' Squadron and our five remaining serviceable tanks.'

Lance Corporal Patrick L. M. Hennessey, DD tank commander, 4 Troop, 'A' Squadron, 13th/18th Royal Hussars. The DD tanks of 'A' and 'B' Squadrons of the 13th/18th Hussars landed at H-Hour at 07:25 hours. HQ and C Squadron 13th/18th Hussars landed at 0810 hours. Two DD tanks were hit and sunk but the 21 DDs that made it ashore, together with specialised armour that enabled nine beach exits to be cleared from 'Queen Red' and 'Queen White' Sectors within two hours, by 1130. Fifty per cent casualties were suffered by the armoured vehicles. In Hermanville the well of 'Mare Saint Pierre' supplied the British forces with 1.5 million gallons of water between 6 June and 1 July.

'The guns have been finally checked and the ship's clocks on board synchronised. Everything is now ready for the signal to hoist anchor and sail with our cargo of men, ammunition, petrol and mines. Months of preparation have ended. This is invasion eve.

Imagine the biggest lake you know plastered with bobbing autumn leaves and you have a picture of what I can see from the salt-sprayed bridge of our ships. Everywhere on the sea are steel ships. You can't get away from them, can't look anywhere without seeing long lines of troopships, supply vessels, assault craft and warships - stretching away to faint blobs on the horizon.

Within sight of green fields and houses that draw their black6y5-outs at dusk, one of the great Allied invasion fleets is assembled - just one of several along Britain's coast.

Swarming over every ship are khaki-men and dungareed seamen. At the docksides are thousands more troops, loaded with their kits and in rare good humour. Dozens of soldiers swarm over the decks of this coaster. They live in a huge canvas tent on the deck. Brown tents are to be seen everywhere. Sleek warships are alongside us and minesweepers stretch out on the port side.

How have the soldiers and seamen spent their last leisure hours without newspapers, or the privilege of writing to the women and children from whom they have disappeared? They have turned the ship into a fun fair. John Fuller of Aniaby Road, Hull, a big husky seaman of 20, has skippered a comic football team on the battened forward hold. I asked Fuller, the Tommy Trinder of the crew, how he felt about setting sail in a couple of hours.

'Me? Bloody champion I feel. I can't get there soon enough.'

For Jack Upperton of South View Road, Southwick, Essex, the invasion will satisfy a curiosity born off the beaches of Dunkirk, when he brought back 1,560 men and was machine-gunned by German E-boats.

Neatly all the soldiers have shaved.

'Damn it, we must make ourselves presentable when we call on Jerry' explained one.

Midships I found a corporal painting a girl's name on the back of the leather jerkin of Private Kenneth Linley. It was the name of Linley's wife. They were married a few weeks ago.

The soldiers are singing... 'O God our help in ages past.' Quietly at first, then louder.

That was invasion eve on board one of 4,000 ships which yesterday ferried a great army to strike at Hitler in France. The soldiers who played comic football on her decks are now in the greatest game of all.

Great Armada Stretched Over Horizon; John Hogan, *Daily Mirror* correspondent with the Merchant Navy who cabled this picture of the immense convoy fleet on the eve of the historic D-Day.

'On going on deck as we approached the Normandy coast the first thing I saw was a destroyer which had been mined going down by the stern - and at that moment a Sten gun was let off accidently on the mess deck and three men were unfortunately killed. Not an auspicious beginning.'

Major C. H. Giddings, Troop Leader in the 629th Field Squadron.

'The whole sky was filled with friendly aircraft of all types - Stirlings, Halifaxes and Dakotas. Inevitably some were hit. A Stirling, which was well ablaze, seemed to be heading for our ship. But suddenly the plane banked to her right and dived into the sea. It was our belief that the pilot deliberately ditched in order to avoid our ship, thus saving many lives.'

Les 'Tubby' Edwards signalman, HMS *Locust*, a gunboat in LSH Force S1, which was escorting landing craft.

'As we crossed the bar, I said, 'I suppose I better open my bag' - my sandbag with the maps in it. And while I was going down to the cabin to get it, I passed the exhaust from the motors of the engines of the ship - and I began to feel queasy. Up to that point, I'd enjoyed the smell of diesel smoke - but from that point onwards in my life, I didn't. I got them opened - I got the relevant maps to the other tank crews on the ship and that was it - I was sick. As the landing craft headed into the rollers, there was a thud and it slipped sideways and upwards and downwards and all ways. Water splashed on to the deck and began sloshing from one end of the ship to the other, carrying with it sandwiches, oil and vomit. This went on all night as we were going pretty slowly. It was the worst journey I have ever taken in my life ... words fail me. Everyone was sick except the skipper. All I wanted was dry land. I didn't care two hoots about the Germans.

'When I opened the sandbag, I found a map, which showed where we were landing and showed all the defence information - the height of the seawall, the kind of beach, the kind of guns in the DUKW houses - the minefields, the telephone lines, the wire - everything. But in addition to that, there were several photographs. There were photographs of families sitting on the beach, building sandcastles - with the seawall in the background. These had been collected during the previous two years and it must have been a tremendous job, sorting out thousands of holiday snapshots, because the government had asked for snapshots of beaches from Spain to Norway. In addition to these photos, there were aerial photographs taken a couple of weeks before from a low-flying Mosquito, showing the Germans working on the sea defences on the beach - and running as the plane approached. The only thing all these photos didn't tell us was how the enemy were going to react.

'...There was this ripping sound, like calico being ripped apart and a flight of rockets went up. You could hear it even above the radio and I saw a Spitfire flying along the beach and that suddenly disappeared in a puff of flaming smoke. [32] It must have flown into the flight of rockets. You could see them landing on the shore, not on the beach but the land behind the beach and the fire burning and the smoke, a tremendous amount of smoke.

'We'd worked out roughly where we were going. I drew my tank to the foot of the ramp and shot, sighting the gun through the barrel as they were so close to the target. That was successful so the tanks started up the ramp but by that time the tide was rising and we were forced to abandon our tanks and try to get ashore. It was very difficult because the undertow was very strong and there were several dead bodies and wounded men and we had great difficulty in pulling ourselves out... but we were under strict instructions that under no circumstances were we to stop and help the wounded men. The essential thing for us to do was to make an exit for the follow-up troops who were coming ashore. We were not to stop for anyone, which was rather hard - but necessary. There was a concrete ramp up from the beach to the top of the sea wall and on top of that was a huge gate built of railway lines welded together.

'Two flails flailed up to the sea wall and backed away as per the plan. A bridging tank came forward but the commander was killed by a shell which landed on the turret; it also cut the cable and the bridge dropped. So we then had to make use of the existing stone ramp off the beach which was sealed with

---

32 A 'spotting' Spitfire was attacked and shot down by Spitfires on beachhead patrol and a Tactical Reconnaissance Mustang was believed to have been shot down by a naval shell. Two Spitfire squadrons, Nos. 349 and 485; operated over the beachhead in the early afternoon and found the first Luftwaffe bombers to be seen in that area. Twelve Ju 88s were chased to the Caen area, pilots claimed 4:0:4 for the loss of a Spitfire and pilot. ADGB units operated throughout the day in small numbers, losing three Spitfires during the early morning operations, all to engine failure. Their sole success came in the evening, when 165 Squadron, flying a Rodeo near Baud, engaged and destroyed a Ju 88, but lost two of their number. 1944: *The Air War Over Europe June 1st-30th Over The Beaches* by John Foreman (ARP 1994).

Element C and barbed wire. That meant I had to drive up to the end of this ramp, which by now was underwater and I had to fire at the Element C.

'Now, in order to fire the gun, I had to blow the waterproofing off so I could rotate the turret a little, I was clear of the water level by this time but the business of firing at Element C is a lengthy one - it meant the commander sighting the gun through the barrel at every joint of the welding. You peer down the bore of the gun: we called it posting letters. Some fired HE and broke up the Element C. I then had to drag it out of the way because the other Churchill AVRE, he went up, he pushed the Element C to one side and drove to one side and blew up on a mine. But the Element C was still blocking the top so I had to attach a towrope to it and tow it down the ramp back out to sea. By this time the tide was much higher and just as I'd said, 'Right, that'll do,' the driver said, 'I've got water coming in and it's coming up to my neck. What shall I do?' I said, 'Bail out.'

'We dismounted our machine gun from the top and got the tripod and boxes of ammo and grenades and dropped off into about five feet of water, which was very cold, right up to our necks. But the most difficult thing of all was climbing out of the water on to the ramp, The pull of the tide and the fact that our clothing was full of water and we were loaded down with grenades and things made it very difficult to get out and there were various bodies floating about which didn't help either. But we did get out and we set up the machine gun on the top.

'While walking along the sea wall I saw a wounded Canadian with most of his face blown away and a padre was trying to comfort him and the chap wanted a cigarette, but there was nowhere to put it .. .it wrings you seeing things like that and not being able to do anything to help. The next thing I remember seeing was half a dozen Germans with their hands up and a big Alsatian dog waiting to surrender and that pleased me enormously ... when I got back to the tanks, there were two Frenchmen coming towards us and they said. 'Bonjour ... vous etes bienvenus en France.' But I'm afraid I wasn't in a very sociable mood at the time, I was too busy, but I shook hands and that was it ...'

Major Ian Hammerton, Sherman Crab flail tank commander, 1st Troop, 'B' Squadron, 22nd Dragoons. Eight Royal Engineer (77th and 79th Assault Squadrons) obstacle-gapping teams, each one made up of two flail tanks of 22nd Dragoons, three AVTREs and one bulldozer, had landed after the 13th/18th Hussars who landed at H-Hour at 07:25 hours.

'As I was to follow the flails through the gap I asked my gunner to lay the log carpet in the gap, but this and the turret had jammed and I had to cut it loose - the log carpet fell in a heap and formed more of an obstacle than a road. While I was doing this there was a bang, flash, red lights, blue lights etc and I found myself lying on the sand, having been hit by a hand grenade thrown from the house alongside the tank. I was assured later by the flail commander that the thrower had a 90mm shell all to himself in return.'

Major W. Carruthers, Troop Leader, 3rd Troop, 77th Assault Squadron. For their work on D-Day 77th and 79th Assault Squadrons between them were awarded two DSOs, four MCs, two DCMs and three MMs.

'My father was a colonel in the Royal Marines and I loved life in the Wrens as Third Officer Marion Salter. I was 22 and was assistant secretary to Rear-Admiral Cyril Sedgwick at HMS *Collingwood* at Fareham, near Portsmouth. Though I worked from an office I had to take my turn on parade, which was quite terrifying because the ritual in a training establishment had to be just right. Towards D-Day, the Portsmouth area was sealed off. At my home in Purbrook near the city the lanes were full of troops. Some sat waiting in their tanks for days. Communications had been cut and you couldn't make a phone call. The one thing the troops wanted to do was 'phone home. The men had baths in our house and my mother was feeding them what she could. They all wanted the lavatory too, so it was good that we had an outside loo.

'On the night of 5 June I was duty officer at the base. It was my job to see that: the Wrens went to the shelters if there was an air raid. But that night I clearly remember there was no alert at all, which was unusual. It was just as well. Every ship was on the move. The activity was phenomenal. If German bombers had come over the troops would have been sitting ducks and we all knew it. The invasion had been scheduled for the fourth, but the weather changed and they didn't go. But some men were out there in their boats riding at anchor. They were terribly seasick for hours. The Germans can't have known what was happening. There were a lot of decoy tactics to mislead them - false tanks were scattered all over the place.

'We were amazed when we heard that the invasion had been launched. June 6 is also my birthday so after work I went out for a meal with my mother and my best friend. There was a roadhouse called the Bastion and when we were walking in, I saw the gliders going over on their way to France. It was a beautiful sight. We all felt elated. I did not know it for days afterwards but I had lost my fiancé on that day.

'Alec Aldis and I were secretly engaged. The plan was to go to his home at Christmas and tell his parents. I didn't expect a message or a birthday card from him because personal correspondence was strictly controlled. We hadn't seen one another for quite a time. Those of us in the Armed Forces accepted that. He had been on Southampton Common waiting with his troop under canvas. It wasn't very far away but it had been impossible for us to see each other. However, it was the same for everyone and you couldn't expect any favours.

'What I didn't know as I enjoyed my birthday dinner was that Alec was already dead. He was the signal officer of 41 Royal Marine Commando. He was shot to pieces as he landed on 'Sword' beach. Other than the sea he has no known grave. Someone saw him disembarking from the landing craft but nothing after that. A career soldier, he was very ambitious and at the age of 24 had won the Military Medal in the battle of Crete. I never got to meet his family at the time and I felt I couldn't intrude on their grief.'

Third Officer Marion Salter.

'On the evening prior to the D-Day landings, the senior arms officer gave us a briefing and I will always remember his final words. 'Don't worry if all the first wave of you are killed,' he said. 'We shall simply pass over your bodies with more and more men.' What a confident thought to go to bed on.'

Able Seaman Ken Oakley Royal Navy, Beachmaster's bodyguard, 'F' Commando.

'Reveille was early; approximately 03.30 and the Beachmaster, Lieutenant John Church RNVR and I boarded the LCA to run for our target: Lion-sur-Mer/Hermanville (codename 'Queen Red', 'Sword' Sector) which was about five miles away. The sea was rough and several of the soldiers were sick, but as we ploughed along I could see that all around us were landing craft and warships of all shapes and sizes. Off to our port side an LCT (R) discharged a salvo of rockets in the direction of the Merville battery we had been briefed about. We evaded all the small-arms fire, but suddenly the dreaded steel stakes with mines or 56lb shells attached loomed ahead of us. All around the sea was one mass of craft, landing craft of all kinds, shapes and sizes. A lot in our immediate area were LCAs because we were going for the initial assault. There was a good feeling as we went forward - except that most of the army was seasick. I wasn't very happy myself. However when we got within sight of the shore we were getting spattered with light gunfire; nothing very heavy at this moment. Finally we got within sight of the stakes, the dreaded stakes, with the shells and mines on, which protected the beaches. Our coxswain did a marvellous job. We were headed straight for this stake and I could see the 56lb shell lashed to it. In just the last second, he missed it. He got it just right. He steered us in between the stakes and got us ashore without touching one of those shells. At the order 'Down ramp,' we were all surging ashore. We were in a few inches of water. All around were craft beaching and chaos and more gunfire was pouring down on us. We ran, under fire, up to the top of the beach where we went to ground, about a hundred yards from high water. People were going down and screaming and crying all around us. As we hit the sand at the top of the beach we took stock of our bearings and realised we had landed almost exactly in our correct positions. We landed on 'Queen Red One', 'Sword' Sector, Colleville-sur-Orne.

'We were now left with the business of organising the beach, getting everything moved off the beach and getting the signs laid. The beachmaster's responsibility was to get that beach cleared - get it organised - and he was the senior officer on the beach, irrespective of rank, whether the army guy was a general or whatever. He was the man in charge of the beach. He sent his various teams to do the clearing, get the stakes out, get the roads laid down for the heavy vehicles. After some time, one of our chaps came up to me and said, 'Oh, Ken, can you help me? Sid is down there, very badly wounded.' Sid Compston was an old friend. I went and found that he was severely wounded. Sid Willis the assistant beachmaster said, 'He caught it across the back. His kidneys were hanging out. I've pushed them back in and shoved on this dressing. Can you get him to the first-aid-post?' We had to half carry, half drag him but we got him to the first-aid-post and left him there under a bit of canvas. I had to go back to my duties on the shoreline. More and more craft were coming in continuously and I was directing them. The trouble was, when the soldiers came ashore, their first reaction was, 'Let's group up and have a little check and then we'll have a cup of tea.' We had learned on exercises that you must not allow this to happen. You must keep the beaches clear and the momentum going. If the beach is clogged up, the whole impetus is lost. You have to keep it moving. There is no other way. This is what we were doing - chasing them, telling them to get off the beach. That is your exit. That is your exit, over there, over there.'

'To our left the patterning of mortar fire seemed very intense, but we seemed to be just under the arch of fire so that we were relatively safe. The main part of the mortar fire seemed to be to our left, further down, which suited us fine, but for the people that were under that, it must have been awful. A commando was screaming, 'Help me, help me,' and I looked at the beachmaster as if to say, 'Should we go to help him?' but we couldn't. My duty was to stay with the beachmaster - he was my prime responsibility. The commando had a huge pack on his back anyway which would protect him from various splinters and shrapnel. It didn't look good at all, but he wasn't the only person who was in dire straits all around us. The mortar- fire was very intense. Some people were filtering through, only some, not many. Then behind us came the roar of a tank. A duplex-drive tank had managed to get ashore. He pulled up behind us, opened his hatch and fired and that was the end of the mortar-fire. One shot, honest, no more than that one shot screamed over our heads, whoosh and it must have gone straight down into the bunkers. Fantastic, I thought - a great job.

'A great deal of my time was spent at the Beachmaster's HQ and on third day he asked me if I would attend the burial service of all those men who were killed in the Beach Area. I said, 'Yes,' I would go as a representative of Fox Royal Naval Beach Commando. We travelled a short distance from the beach to a large apple orchard. Here, the bulldozers had dug out wide trenches in which the wrapped bodies were laid side by side. The smell of rotting flesh was appalling and I will never forget it. The burial service was attended by three padres, one of each of the main denominations. Whilst we stood silent, among the laden apple trees, I reflected how lucky I was to have survived this one, especially after the experience of Sicily.'

Able Seaman Ken Oakley Royal Navy, Beachmaster's bodyguard, 'F' Commando.

'On the army side of high water mark, each beach had its beach commander and under him a beach control group had been assigned to each exit. Each group had a radio and beach control had its own net, so that if one exit was blocked or came under heavy fire, the beach commander could be told and could divert the traffic to the others. The job was only expected to last until D+1 and so most of the officers and men who were to do it were chosen from regiments which were not scheduled to land in the first week or so. When the beaches were well organized and no longer under fire, the beach control units were to hitch-hike back to England to rejoin their regiments and prepare to go over again.

'On 'Sword' Beach, the 3rd Reconnaissance Regiment provided the men for this unpromising assignment; and among them were Major Neville Gill and Captain Ivor Stevens. Gill was thirty-one, a solicitor from Newcastle with the learned interests of his profession: Stevens was twenty-five, the son of the landlord of a pub in Bradford-on-Avon and he had joined the Grenadier Guards as a guardsman before the war. Gill had no interest in sport and preferred a quiet sedentary life: Stevens, on the other hand, was an enormous athletic man, as strong as an ox, who rowed and played football and cricket. Both, it was true, were alike in being bachelors, but whereas Gill was destined to remain one. Stevens, on D-Day, was in the middle of a whirlwind courtship of a Scottish girl called Connie Bowes. He had only met her five times; but the fourth time they met, she had promised to marry him, so that to him the Normandy campaign was merely a job he had to get done before he could attend to much more interesting prospects. Both of them had been at Dunkirk and had been in Britain ever since, endlessly training.

'Gill and his group were due to land 19 minutes after the first wave of infantry. Gill took his command very seriously. It was a very small command for a major, it was true, only about a dozen men all told; but it was an unusually independent command, because his only link to any senior officer was by radio. The craft was commanded by a subaltern of the Royal Marines. He had a photograph of the beach and so had Gill. As they drove on, they could see the row of seaside villas which were shown on their photographs, but by then they had been badly knocked about and through the fog of the bombardment it was difficult to tell which villa was which. Gill was sure they were heading for the wrong beach. The marine was sure he was right. But while they were afloat, the marine was in charge, so Gill had to let him have his way.

'The dropping of the ramp gave each man in the boat, before he plunged into the sea, a momentary photographic glimpse of the scene he had imagined for so long: the few yards of breaking waves, lapping the shore in a thin line of foam, the almost level sand, two tanks burning, the stakes with mines on top of them, the swirling smoke and far away, the line of the dunes and the ruins of the villas. Gill found he was chest-deep and he waded forward with only one thought in his head: to find out where they were, which side of the place where they ought to have come ashore. There seemed to be nobody moving on the beach ahead. He supposed the first wave of the infantry were across it and in the dunes: they should have been by then. Stevens and the others came splashing through the waves behind him. 'Steve,' he shouted above the din, 'we're in the wrong place. Get the men under cover. I'm going to find out where we are.' And he walked up the beach alone.

'Stevens had soon lost sight of Gill. Staying in the water gave a feeling of being under cover, but he knew quite well it was no protection against the stray shots which were flying around and that he ought to get the men somewhere safer till Gill came back. He made up his mind to make for the nearest derelict tank ahead. And then, before they could move, the corporal on the other end of the radio was shot. He fell in the water. One of the others picked up the radio and Stevens shouted to them all to follow him. Dragging the dying man, the group ran forward to the tank. As they dropped down in this momentary shelter, one of the men called to Stevens: 'There's the major.' And Stevens looked and saw Gill all alone on the open beach: and in the same second, he saw him fall down and lie still.

'Stevens left the lee of a burnt-out tank and ran alone across the open beach to where Gill had been shot. 'Steve, I can't move,' Gill said. 'Where did it get me?'

Stevens could not see a wound, so he turned him over. There was blood on the back of his battledress. He rolled up the tunic and found a jagged wound below the shoulder blades. He got out a field dressing and started to put it on. Then Stevens went and roused the medical orderlies behind their tank and made them come out with a stretcher. And there the two men parted: Stevens to find the beach exit which Gill had been looking for and Gill to lie all day under morphia on the beach, to learn that a bullet had gone right through his chest from front to back and broken his spine, to spend a year in a plaster cast and a lifetime of pain. Fourteen years later, he died as a consequence of his wound.'

Dawn Of D-Day. [33]

'I had to land immediately behind the assault infantry and carry out a reconnaissance of the brigade area for anti-tank purposes. One troop of self-propelled M10s had landed immediately behind the infantry and the remaining eight guns would be going ashore as soon as possible after mid-day. I stepped into three feet of water on 'Queen Red' beach. The area was under intense shell and small arms fire, with casualties drowning and floundering around.

'Dead ahead was a low beach wall at La Brêche. Fortunately, my inelegant scramble exposed a Teller mine (a booby-trapped anti-tank mine) linked to several others. I gingerly pushed the sand back to further expose the trap and got out on to the lateral road in front of strong-point 'Cod'[34,] which was under assault by the East Yorks.[35] I hared off to catch up with the South Lancs entering Hermanville. There was a deal of sniping by a scattered enemy. My reconnaissance took me south to the open country near Mathieu and then back seawards to Colleville.

'In a wooded clearing not far away I came across a railway wagon surrounded by dozens of Tellermines and other booby traps in various stages of assembly in what was obviously a workshop. As Wellington said; 'A close run thing.'

'From an anti-tank point of view the fields with barbed wire aprons and festooned with 'Achtung Minen' signs raised doubts. Which were ruses de guerre?'

Troop Sergeant Chris Clancy, 67 Anti-Tank Battery, 20th Anti-Tank Regiment, Royal Artillery.

'It was in the late afternoon of 5th June we learned landing would take place early next morning. We were woken at about 4 am for a very early breakfast and the first echelon was ordered into craft just after 6 am. The assault landing craft were suspended in fixed heavy steel davits on either side of the ship in two layers. Being the first to land we got into the lower position and were lowered away into a heaving sea. As soon as we were free of the lowering tackle we moved out from the ship and awaited other craft to join us in procession towards the distant shore. The lowering position of the vessel was six miles off the coast, which with a craft speed of 4 knots meant an approximate run-in of

---

33 By David Howarth (The Companion Book Club 1959).
34 Wiederstandnesten (WN) 20, Hermanville-la-Brêche (Colleville) on 'Queen Red Beach'.
35 With precious little shelter from the 88mm gun fire and machine guns enfilading the beach, the A and B Companies of the 2nd East Yorkshire Regiment lost 200 men on the beach in the space of a few minutes. In all, the Regiment lost 72 killed and 141 wounded on D-Day.

90 minutes to reach the beach.

'We could see nothing beyond a horizon of water. Many of us found ourselves mentally checking that the sky was lightening on the port side, showing that we were indeed running south and not back on to an English beach on yet another exercise. The run in was long and gradually, in the dispersing gloom, we found ourselves joined by more and more craft, whilst from the shore started a crescendo of explosions as the air bombardment carpeted the defences.

'As the dawn light increased, we were surprised at the number of ships we could see on the horizon. An unexpected sight was our passing close by the midget submarine X23. At this time we had no knowledge of how long she had been there, awaiting our arrival, to guide us with precision to the shore. Closing to the shore, we gradually made out a line of smoke haze caused by the naval bombardment, supplemented by the sudden roar of the rocket-carrying landing craft as they loosed their rockets. We were now approaching the shoreline, but in the misty weather conditions and with the smoke and flame from houses hit by supporting gunfire, it was difficult to recognise our exact position from the maps with which we had been issued. Stabbing orange flames showed the strike of both artillery and the naval bombardment that had now joined in and then suddenly the air was torn with an ear-splitting roar as the rocket-ships loosed their projectiles.

'It was at about this time that our 4 Royal Marine Commando dropped over the side to start dealing with underwater obstacles and we shortly ran in to a defending line of steel uprights topped with mines or shells, 500 metres from the shore high water mark. It was now half tide, a compromise between personnel having to land and traverse a completely exposed stretch of sand and the feasibility of succeeding waves of incoming craft touching down in conditions of a rising tide-that would still allow them to reverse off and make way for others. We weaved our way through these steel stakes and it was with a lurching bump that our craft touched down in about 2 feet of water: Immediately the front ramp was dropped and the inner steel doors flung open. As we neared the waterline we heard the crack of bullets overhead and cursed those following us for their enthusiasm for giving us covering fire.

'However; it was only when some of these shots thudded into the front of our craft that we appreciated that the opposition on the beach was very much alive and well.

'Then we saw the first setback: a returning LCT with her ramp seemingly jammed in the half-lowered position. These craft, four to each beach, carried the specially equipped AVRE tanks that were to work in groups of three, the centre tank being armed with a 'snake', a 60-foot long heavy tube of explosive to be pushed through the beach defences and detonated.

'Not only would this breach the wire but the explosion was calculated to set off any mines in the near vicinity. It would then be the job of the Exit Teams to clear and widen the corridors by hand and then to signal in following craft as the exits became operative. That one of these AVRE carrying craft had been unable to land its tanks meant that at least one of the Beach Teams would have to make its exit the hard way.

'Steadily the flotilla of LCAs pressed onwards towards the beach. Four hundred yards from the shoreline and the Royal Marine frogmen slipped over the side to start the job of clearing underwater obstacles. This would be sufficiently hazardous at the best of times, but add to it the risk from all those churning propellers - with many more following - and their task became most unenviable.

'Closing to the shore rapidly, eyes scanned the clearing haze for familiar landmarks. There were none. A burst of machine-gun fire uncomfortably close overhead brought curses upon those in following craft for their enthusiastic 'covering fire'. Suddenly a burst ricocheted off the front of the craft, telling us that this was no covering fire. The opposition was very much alive and well.

'We had still been unable to identify our position but we were by now right on top of the beach. The protective steel doors in the bows were opened and everyone waited, tensed for the soft lurching bump. 'Ramp down!' - and out into knee-deep water. I was in the front of the craft and led the way jumping out into shallow water: However; there was a stationary tank nosed up against the small strip of dunes at the head of the beach and a line of prone figures just above the water's edge halfway up the sand. I assumed that the tank belonged to the assault engineers, who might still be placing charges amongst the defences and that the line of prone figures ahead of us, following the same instructions as given to the Beach Exit Teams, were hanging back as ordered until the assault engineers had finished their tasks. In order not to crowd the beach and provide an obvious target for enemy machine gunners, I ordered everyone to crouch in the water and wait until the demolition teams from No. 5 Assault Engineers Regiment had completed their tasks. I was just ahead of the ramp of the craft. It was then that a wave lifted the craft a little and I was struck by the edge of the ramp and pushed flat into the edge of the water as enemy fire opened up upon anything that moved.

'To the west I could see troops crossing the beach unhindered and with enemy fire being reduced I assumed that this was an opportunity to make a dash for the beach. Hampered by the weight of my now waterlogged assault jerkin I made a dash for the top. I had been able to make out the outline of reinforced concrete defences, on the centre of which was an ominous embrasure, which we anticipated could erupt into flames at any minute with the discharge of a coastal artillery piece. There seemed to be a lull in the firing and I took the opportunity to make a run for the top of the beach. I had not gone far when I was tripped by some underwater wire and with no hope of retaining balance with the heavy Assault Jerkin pack that had been issued to us, went flat on my face. Attempting to rise, I was struck a heavy blow on the back which flattened me again. Then suddenly the machine-gun opened up on us once again. The fire came from dead ahead and we could now make out the shape of a heavy embrasure in the low silhouette of some concrete fortifications at the top of the beach. We then realized that, by the narrowest of margins, we had landed immediately in front of Strongpoint 0880, code word 'CoD'.

'Both mortar and light artillery defensive fire being brought down by the enemy in front of the strongpoint now intensified and the still unspotted machine-gun made an instant target of anything that moved. The prone figures that had first been seen just above the water's edge, we found to be casualties from the leading craft but on White beach to our right, troops could be seen crossing the beach and reaching the top.

'There was a brief lull in the firing and we immediately took this opportunity to make a dash for the top of the beach. Briefly seeking cover behind the motionless tank to count heads, it was found that only the signalman of our group had managed to come through unscathed. As I neared the gun emplacement I came upon the prostrate body of Lieutenant Colonel Richard Burbury, [36] killed by a sniper as he crossed the beach. With him, lying wounded in the arm was the Battalion medical officer to whom I offered my help. This was politely and possibly wisely declined and I pressed on to the tank. It was only the night before that Colonel Burbury had shown me the pennant that he proposed to carry ashore, at the same time showing me how clever he had been in waterproofing his watch with an item of medical protective gear.

'I ran up to the tank above my head on the edge of the promenade, which was immobile and silent. I ran around to the back of the tank where I knew that the army should have a telephone for contacting the tank commander, but there was none. I returned to the small cluster of men who had followed me up the beach. Just then, the trenches above our heads sprang to life and German grenades came somersaulting through the air. As they exploded, I was amazed to note that the grenades, landing in soft sand, caused no apparent injury to men standing quite close by. I quickly asked those around me if anyone had grenades that we could return, but none was to hand. Then, suddenly, the tank above our heads sprang to life and moved off, bearing our colourful good wishes.

'We had hardly jettisoned our heavy equipment when the strongpoint above our heads sprang to life once more. German stick-grenades somersaulted through the air, their effects being greatly reduced in the soft sand, whilst we in turn desperately sought grenades from amongst the remnants of other detachments now grouping with us. However, further action was promptly eclipsed by the sudden arrival of Lieutenant Tony Milne who had just landed at H+40 with his machine-gun platoon of the 2nd Battalion Middlesex Regiment. The platoon was equipped with Bren-gun carriers, having the heavy Vickers mounted above the engine casing and were the first infantry fighting vehicles to land. I told him that Germans were entrenched just above our heads, lobbing grenades at us and we had none to throw back. Immediately he called for his platoon sergeant to get the Vickers MG carriers that had just arrived off the tank landing craft and without a moment's hesitation, waterproofing shields were ripped away, thereby exposing the guns. On the command to free the travelling clamps that held the machine-gun fixed, the four carriers advanced firing and the leading carrier drove straight at the trench line above our heads with a long swinging traverse from the Vickers, depressing into the trench as they closed. A brief pause - silence - and then 16 German soldiers emerged from the end of the trench system with arms held high. Strongpoint

---

36 Commanding 1st Battalion, The South Lancashire (Prince of Wales Volunteers) Regiment, the assault infantry on 'Queen White'. The 2nd East Yorkshire Regiment was the assault infantry on 'Queen Red'. The South Lancs lost 288 officers and men on D-Day and in the subsequent campaign.

'Cod' had been taken.

'A first-aid post was quickly established in the concrete emplacement of the strongpoint and then every hand was turned to helping vehicles through the soft sand above the high-water mark. The self-propelled guns of the 76th and 23rd Field Regiments, together with the Royal Marine Artillery, would be coming in at about 0900 hours - and were indeed to establish their first gun line on the water's edge. Already it seemed that we had been there all day.

'However we were to have one more surprise just before the next echelons were due; the sudden appearance over the top of the low dunes of a gleaming brass fireman's helmet, surmounting the figure of the Mayor of Colleville. He was accompanied by a young French girl who quickly made her way to render help in the first-aid post. These were the first French people to greet us and all were deeply impressed at the courage of these two who had obviously taken such astonishing risks in exposing themselves to make their way to the beach at such a time.

'The task now was to create a gap in the defences and it was then that I discovered that from our assault craft of 30 men, only myself and Private Skelton, the signaller, had survived to reach the top of the beach. It was Private Skelton who drew my attention to the fact that we had lost Corporal Roulier our wireless operator, who had been hit on leaving our craft and assumed that he was still in the water. I therefore called upon nearby individual soldiers to help recover the wounded from the fast incoming tide before setting off with Skelton to search for Roulier. We eventually found him sitting up, with his head above the rising tide. Together we lifted Roulier and took him up the beach to the concrete gun emplacement of strongpoint 'Cod'. This was being turned into a first aid point and we were able to hand Roulier into their care.

'To return to our duties, the next task was to be the opening of an exit. Not having the assault engineers, the possibilities seemed limited. However, when looking at the beach and shoreline it came to my mind that there must have been a safe access way through the mines. Suddenly, there it was. We had our exit and I raised the green flag in identification to incoming craft that there was an open exit in this position. I had signal flags, one red, one green, strapped on to the back of my assault jerkin and it was only at this time that I discovered the damage that had been done to them by a shell fragment. Both flags had holes in them: these were not made by the moths.

'It was now coming up to 9 am (8 am French time) and the tide was coming in very quickly. Landing Craft Tanks (LCTs) were discharging more and more vehicles and congestion on the beach was building up. Only later did we appreciate that altogether some eight exits off the beach were delivering vehicles on to one solitary lateral road. Further landings were suspended for one hour while attempts were made to clear the blockage. It was unfortunate that this impeded the discharge of the tanks of the Staffordshire Yeomanry that were to carry the men of the King's Shropshire Light Infantry to Caen.

'Gradually the congestion eased and the beach, now reduced to a width of 10 metres, was relatively clear once more and traffic was flowing easily. It was early afternoon and the sun came out just as small arms fire broke out towards the centre of the beach to our right. German snipers of 21 Panzer Division had somehow infiltrated to the beach area and were firing upon beach personnel. One of the first casualties was the Royal Naval beach commander, an obvious target as he had been striding the length of the beach with a large map board tucked under his arm.

'By now a number of beached LCTs were returning sniper fire with the Oerlikon (20mm) mounted in their bows. The Army beach commander ordered me to collect some men and do a house-clearing exercise; I replied that I could only start that when he got the Royal Navy to stop firing their Oerlikons, which were systematically tearing to pieces the fronts of the homes. (In the event this was not easily done. They had brought all the ammo from England and they weren't going to take it back.)

'A small German fighter aircraft on a. reconnaissance mission swept the length of the beach. It bore wide identification stripes in white paint on the wings and body, the same as Allied aircraft.

'It was now well into the afternoon and the tide was receding quickly. The one remaining member of my team and I walked down and out across the sand to see if there were any obstacles yet to be cleared. We were approached by a group carrying a stretcher on which lay Major Neville Gill, suffering from severe wounds and being evacuated. I was puzzled at the urgent but deferential enquiries being made by the Sergeant concerning a letter that Neville had in his pocket. It was only later that I came to learn that this was an official authorisation allowing the four assault teams to return to their units still in the UK.

'Congestion on the beach had now been largely cleared and the tide was running out fast. Evening was approaching and it was then that we witnessed the enormous flyover of aircraft carrying reinforcements for the 6th Airborne Division that had landed east of the River Orne, to secure bridges over the Caen Canal.'
Lieutenant K. P. Baxter, 2nd Battalion of the Middlesex Regiment.

'It had just broken daylight when we arrived - and the shambles! I was the third man out and when I saw the things going on in the beach I thought, 'How the hell are we going to get through that?' We waded ashore and all I remember next is a blinding flash and a smell of cordite and my mate Charlie Orrell lying down on the deck, the blood was pumping out of his neck. I lay down next to him, then in a matter of seconds a voice said, 'Get going. You're not supposed to stop. Get going.' So I went and just before I got to the wire, a captain shouted at me, 'Give me a hand here!' and he was trying to get the waterproofing off the Bren-gun carrier. When we got it open, it had had a direct hit inside it and it was all just a mess. But that's the shambles that an organised beach landing becomes, I suppose.'
Sergeant James Kelly, 41 (Royal Marine) Commando.

'Woke up at 0600 hours and found we had arrived off the coast during the night. The Chief Engineer was feeling sad as this ship had to die. For after we had been off-loaded she was due to be sunk to form a harbour together with other old cargo ships. The sea was very rough and I felt rough too. The air was rent with the thunder of the heavy guns of the warships firing shorewards. The salvoes of the rocket ships were impressive. At 2pm I went down the rope ladder onto the landing craft that was to take us ashore. The sea all around was being peppered with shell bursts and I was really nervous as I could not swim. We had a dry shod landing, driving ashore in the CO's car. On French soil again for the first time since June 1 1940. Shells bursting on the beach, a very excited Camp Commandant giving orders, dead bodies everywhere and prisoners being herded in batches. We drove to the assembly area to find out what was to be done next. The village was Ouistreham, the sector 'Sword', the beach section 'Queen'. The French civilians we met were delighted to see us and pinned roses on our battledress, offering us glasses of wine. I don't know how these people managed to survive all the shelling. We drove inland and headed for Caen but were stopped by a Military Policeman at a crossroads and directed to Colleville, where Divisional HQ had been set up. At 8.30pm we unloaded the car and set up our office in a wooden hut filled with wheelbarrows. There was a lot of sniping and I was feeling nervy. Managed to get a German steel helmet as a trophy before having something to eat from my pack and then sleeping out under a tree. Continuous firing from tanks and field guns. It was the noisiest night of my life.'

Corporal Ernest Bayley, 3rd British Infantry Divisional Signals.

'Forget those bristling stakes…the mines on them look as big as planets. How do you feel Middy? Myself, I wouldn't be elsewhere for a thousand quid. Well not for a hundred anyway…Cox'n, you're a lucky man. Not everyone gets paid for taking a trip to the Continent. Why must I give way to the affectation of flippancy? To forget we were running on a timetable towards terror.

'Now eyes for everything, eyes for nothing. The beach looms close, maybe a mile. There are people running up and down it. There are fires and the bursting of shells. Yes and wrecked landing craft everywhere, a flurry of propellers in the savage surf among the wicked obstructions. Beach clearance parties I expect, bloody heroes, everyone. The special craft stooging quietly in, some of them on fire though. Diesel fuel burns black. That vicious destroyer is irritating me, but the Colonel doesn't seem to mind. He's cool, but I'll bet he's worried. Curious how all these soldiers dislike assault by water. I'd hate to dash out of foxholes at machine-guns. Damn him, I can pretend I'm cool too. It's the noisiest gun - Starboard ten! - it's the noisiest gun in the Navy that 4.7 - Midships Cox'n.

'What a cool disinterested reply he makes. Colonel, you make me grin. I like your nerve.

'We are on those bristling stakes. They stretch before us in rows. The mines on them look as big as planets. And those grey nose shells pointing towards us on some of them look like beer bottles. Oh God, I would be blown up on a mine like a beer bottle.

'Whang - here it comes - those whizzing ones will be mortars - and the stuff is falling all round us. Can't avoid them, but the mines and collisions I can avoid.

'Speed, more speed. Put them off by speed, weave in and out of those bloody spikes, avoid the mines, avoid our friends, avoid wrecked craft and vehicles in the rising water and GET THOSE TROOPS ASHORE...

'Everything is working as we've exercised it for so long. Oh hell, this new tin hat is far too big for me - I'll shake it off my head with fright, if I'm nor careful.

'Slow ahead together.' Slow down to steady the ship, point her as you want her, then half ahead together and on to the beach with gathering rush. Put her ashore and be damned! She's touched down. One more good shove ahead to wedge her firm. Smooth work! 'Now off you go! Good luck, Commandos, go like hell! Next meeting - Brighton!' How efficiently, how quickly they run down the accustomed ramps, not a man hit that I can see and there they go, slashing through a hundred yards of water, up over more of the fiat beach than that and out of sight among the deadly dunes. The Colonel turns to wave and is gone with them. They ignore the beach fire. They have their objective and they are going for it.'

Lieutenant Denis J. M. Glover DSC RNZNVR, Commanding Officer, HM LCI(S) 516. This was part of the landing of 6 Commando; their objective Ouistreham. Glover's and Lieutenant J. F. Ingham RNZNVR's handling of their landing craft, LCI(S) 516 and LCI(L) 110, respectively, under heavy fire while negotiating mines and underwater obstacles in order to put commandos ashore at Ouistreham resulted in both being awarded the Distinguished Service Cross. On the beach Lieutenant R. Crammond RNZNR's work as naval liaison officer with the commandos earned him a mention in dispatches and a Croix de Guerre. Lieutenant N. Watson, commanding MTB 453 and Lieutenant C. J. Wright, commanding MTB 454, engaged E-boats in six separate night engagements and both were awarded the DSC. 4 Commando had landed earlier than the rest of the brigade, its vital mission being to push inland rapidly and link up with the hard-pressed men of the 6th Airborne Division holding the bridges over the River Orne: The rest of the brigade had the difficult task of prizing the Germans put of their heavily fortified positions at Riva Bella and Ouistreham. The port marked the entrance to the Orne and the locks to the Caen ship canal. In a twist of history the local inhabitants had set up a monument to their successful repulse of a British landing attempted on 12 July I792.

'We were on top of the world. We were all looking forward to it like mad. We were all picked men, the commandos and we'd been training and training in the UK and getting absolutely fed up with it and now we wanted to see if all this hard work and training would really work. We'd obviously learned lessons from the Dieppe raid and the various Combined Ops in North Africa and Italy and Sicily and we had the whole thing sewn up as far as it possibly could be.
'As we were lowered from the parent ship, we took a large wave into the craft and we found that the bilge pump wasn't working, so we had to start baling water out with our tin hats which wasn't very easy in a confined space on a choppy sea with men being seasick all around you. Approaching the beach all hell going on but anything preferable to this horrible boat. As the front ramps went down, she finally sank in four feet of water, so we were able to scramble ashore. There was another landing craft coming in on our left. One of the subalterns stood up to get out and he was absolutely bowled over by machine gun fire and he was cut to ribbons. It was very frightening.
'We started crossing the beach. I was carrying a heavy load - about 90lb - and was soaking wet. I reached down to unzip the map pocket on my leg and out came a great sodden mess of paper, quite useless. A flail tank just in front

of us to my right, with its flail going looking for mines, got a direct hit by an anti-tank shell or something and blew up. There was machine-gun fire all around and there were bodies washing about in the engine oil at the water's edge and men kneeling in the water trying to fire and then they'd get hit.

"I ordered all my chaps to throw their smoke grenades which created a big belt of smoke down our left-hand side and protected us from a pillbox. A little while later a subaltern from my unit managed to creep up to it and put a grenade into the firing slit; he won an MC.

'Anyway, we got across the beach and into some sand dunes, where we organised a bit, although a lot of my chaps had been wounded. At that point I think I had lost about a quarter of my troop, either killed or wounded. Our job was to make our way to a coastal battery on the outskirts of Ouistreham, about a mile and a half away and destroy the guns with special charges made of plastic explosive. We moved straight away and found a château with a sort of walled garden, where we cleaned our weapons and dumped our rucksacks and then set off towards the battery.

'We had to cross a big anti-tank ditch and when we got there we found someone had left a plank across it, which was just as well because one of the blokes who was carrying a specially made collapsible bridge had been killed on the beach and the bridge had been smashed to pieces.

'On the way we passed a small house and a frantic Frenchman came running out and said that his wife had been wounded and asked if we had a doctor. At that very moment I heard a mortar bomb approaching and threw myself flat on the ground. The Frenchman was a little slow on the uptake, presumably he had never been mortared before, because there was an explosion and as I looked up I saw his head rolling down the road. It was very sad, kind of off-putting.

'When we got to the battery, we found that the guns were dummies, just telegraph poles lashed on to wagons and we learned afterwards from a Frenchman that the battery had been withdrawn some three or four days previously and had been re-sited a couple of miles back. In the centre of the position was a huge concrete observation tower, an enormous thing with walls about ten feet and some Germans who were at the top of it started firing at us. My signaller, who was just beside me, was shot and killed and one of my subalterns, who had got up close to the tower, was killed when they dropped a grenade on him. He was a great friend of mine; I'd been best man at his wedding only two months before. He was trying to see if we could smoke them out, but the only access was up a single staircase in the middle and so the men inside were as safe as houses.

'The best thing that we could do was to get the hell out of there as fast as we could and fulfil our secondary objective which was to link up with the 6th Airborne on the other side of the Orne and hold the left flank.'

26-year-old Major Pat Porteous VC of 4 Commando whose Victoria Cross award was for action at Dieppe.

'4 Commando had to dash along the coast road, a distance of about a mile, to destroy and blow up a battery of big guns at Ouistreham on the mouth of the River Orne. Then we had to speed with the utmost alacrity to rejoin the brigade at the bridges a few miles inland. We had about 500 men, which included 60 French commandos attached to us for this little episode. I never reached Ouistreham. I was shot on the way; I believe by an automatic weapon. I can't say what type because I never saw it. However, a couple of bullets made a mess of my left arm, shattering the bone in four places. I didn't realize how fortunate I had been until back in England some days later, when they took off my Mae West and found three more bullet lines running along the Mae West and completely missing me. Strange as it may seem, I didn't feel a thing when the bullets hit me and had no pain at all, but I was knocked to the ground. I did feel most annoyed because I was out of action. One of the lads picked up my Bren gun and off he went. You see, in circumstances like those there was no stopping to help the wounded. This we all knew. Luckily, I was able to get behind a sand dune and gradually made my way to the landing area, though not before I had nearly been run over by one of our tanks. The driver didn't see me and I had to roll out of the way a bit sharpish. I must have fainted because when I came to there were a couple of Medics beside me. They helped me back to a dressing-station by a pillbox. They couldn't do much except strap my arm across my body. I had the comfort of a stretcher and was lifted on to a DUKW and ferried out to a hospital ship which sailed next day to Tilbury. I had some injections, but no other treatment until reaching England. They soon got me to hospital and started the repair business. Six months later, I left hospital, almost new.'

Private Farnborough, 4 Commando, 1st Special Service Brigade.

'We watched them going ashore. From the bridge of my ship, they looked like little models - moving forward, stopping, firing and moving forward again. Coming in from the big ships were the flotillas of the landing craft and as we watched, the guns still blazing away, they formed in line abreast and were rushing for the surf line of the beach. I found myself banging the bridge with my clenched fist, 'By God, we're ashore in France, we've done it, we're back in France again.'

Lieutenant-Commander Roger Hill aboard HMS *Jarvis*.

'Where we landed we found 'Rommel's Asparagus', as we called it. It was four triple bars and triple wooden stakes and on the end of every one was an 88mm percussion cap shell, strapped to blow the bottom out of you. But the Royal Navy Beach commandos had gone in first and cleared pathways. We could see men getting shot down. Not everyone got hit - some of them made it right up the beach. As callous as it seems, we didn't bother, although we saw some terrible sights, because it was nothing to do with us. I saw some of my mates die. We saw the hospital ships lifting them up on the stretchers, on to the decks to tend them - but you don't bother. You just get on with your job. This is what you're trained for.'

Corporal Bernard Slack, Royal Marines.

'We held our position in the trenches for more than an hour. It was the most terrible time of my life. We were continually shelled and under fire from snipers. One of our bazookas hit a Canadian tank. We saw the flap opening and a soldier was half-way out when there was another explosion and it burst into flames with the soldier still hanging from the turret, I said to Ferdie, 'I hope we have a better death than that. I'd rather have a bullet.'

'After about an hour we were ordered into a bunker, which was a command post almost entirely underground with a small observation hatch on the top. It was already full of wounded men. There were about thirty of them lying on straw blankets, absolutely terrified and crying out all the time. There was hardly any air inside and a man in the observation hole shouted that the Canadians were starting to pile earth up against the ventilators. It started to get very hot and difficult to breathe.

'The company commander told us to breathe together: 'Breathe in when I say IN and out when I say OUT.' The battalion commander was firing a machine gun through a small aperture by the door. I will never forget the smell and the heat and noise inside that bunker, the cries of the wounded, the stink of exploding bullets and gases from the machine gun and the company commander yelling, 'IN, OUT, IN, OUT .. .'

'Finally the company commander said to the battalion commander: 'Sir, we can't carry on. The wounded are suffocating.' The battalion commander said it was out of the question. 'We'll fight our way out of here if we have to. Count the weapons and the men preparatory to getting out.'

'At that point there was almost a mutiny and some men started pulling the bolts out of their rifles in defiance. They knew that the door out of the bunker led to a trench and that on the other side of the trench the Canadians would be waiting for them.

'Ferdie said to me: 'You're the only one beside the battalion commander who's got a machine gun. You'll be the first out of here, believe me.' I said: 'No, I'm not going to do it,' and I pulled out the locking pin that held the machine together. Just then the man in the observation post shouted: 'My God, they're bringing up a flame-thrower!'

'We heard the 'woof' of the flame-thrower, but the flames couldn't get through the staggered sections of the ventilation shaft, although it turned red hot before our eyes. Now there was near panic. One German could speak two words of English and he kept shouting, 'Hello boys, hello boys, hello boys ...' The wounded were shouting their heads off and a radio operator in the corner was shouting to try and establish contact with headquarters. The battalion commander seemed oblivious to what was going on and kept firing his machine gun out of the aperture without once looking round.

'People were shouting, 'We've got to do something, we've got to do something,' and eventually we took one of the dirty white sheets from one of the wounded and with the help of a broomstick pushed it out through the observation hatch. A voice from outside shouted, 'All right then, come on out.'

'We dropped our weapons and made for the door, more scared of what the battalion commander would do than of the Canadians outside. Suddenly he turned round and asked the radio operator if he'd made contact. The operator shook his head. The battalion commander went very white, stepped back and then dropped his machine gun.

'One of the soldiers opened the door and went out carrying the broom-stick with the white sheet. Through the opening, we could see Canadian troops standing on either side of the trench. They started to shout, 'Oucha come, oucha come.'

'We were made to lie down on the grass at the end of the trench, take off our equipment, boots and tunics. I said to Ferdie, 'Well, it's all over for us now.'
19-year old Joseph Haeger of the 736th Infantry Regiment.

'On that rainy evening [5 June], my adjutant and I were waiting for a report from No. II Battalion that the night exercise had ended. This battalion was in the area Troarn-Escoville, hence fairly near the coast, while No. I Battalion, equipped with armoured personnel carriers and armoured half-track vehicles, had taken up waiting positions further to the rear. I had given the more basic order that in the event of possible landings by Allied commando troops, the battalions and companies concerned were to attack immediately and independently; and to do so, moreover, without regard to the prohibition from the highest authority on engaging action except after clearance by High Command West. But in view of the weather report that we had been given, I had no thought of such an engagement that night.

'About midnight, I heard the growing roar of aircraft, which passed over us. I wondered whether the attack was destined once again for traffic routes inland or for Germany herself. The machines appeared to be flying very low - because of the weather? I looked out of the window and was wide awake; flares were hanging in the sky. At the same moment, my adjutant was on the telephone, 'Major, paratroops are dropping. Gliders are landing in our section. I'm trying to make contact with No. II Battalion. I'll come along to you at once.'

'I gave orders without hesitation. 'All units are to be put on alert immediately and the division informed. No. II Battalion is to go into action wherever necessary. Prisoners are to be taken if possible and brought to me.'

'I then went to the command post with my adjutant. The 5th Company of No. II Battalion, which had gone out with blank cartridges, was not back yet from the night exercise - a dangerous situation. First reports indicated that British paratroops had dropped over Troarn. The commander of No. II Battalion had already started a counterattack with uninvolved elements and had succeeded in penetrating as far as Troarn, to which elements of the 5th Company had already withdrawn under their own steam.

'We telephoned the company commander, who was in a cellar. 'Brandenburg, hold on. The battalion is already attacking and is bound to reach you in a few moments.'

'Okay,' he replied, 'I have the first prisoner here, a British medical officer of the 6th Airborne Division.'

'Send him along as soon as the position is clear.'

'In the meantime, my adjutant telephoned the division. Generalmajor Feuchtinger and his general-staff officer had not come back yet. We gave the orderly officer, Leutnant Messmer, a brief situation report and asked him to obtain clearance for us for a concentrated night attack the moment the divisional commander returned.

'By now, we had a slightly better idea of and grip on the situation. Prisoners who had misjudged their jumps and fallen into our hands in the course of our limited counterattack were brought in to me. Before I had them escorted away to division, in accordance with orders, we learned during our 'small talk' that the 6th Airborne Division was supposed to jump during the night in order to take the bridges over the Orne at Ranville intact and form a bridgehead east of the Orne for the landing by sea planned for the morning of 6 June.

'Gradually we were becoming filled with anger. The clearance for an immediate night attack, so as to take advantage of the initial confusion among our opponents, had still not come, although our reports via division to the core and to Army Group B (Rommel) must have long since been on hand. We made a thorough calculation of our chances of successfully pushing through to the coast and preventing the formation of a bridgehead, or at least making it more difficult.

'I remember the British medical officer who was brought to me as the first prisoner. In his parachute equipment he looked like any other soldier. As a good Briton, he kept his composure, but seemed deeply disappointed and unnerved, at being taken prisoner immediately on his first mission. Since he too would only give his name and number, I began, as always with a British prisoner, to make small talk. I spoke about my last visit to London in March 1939, about Piccadilly Circus and my British friends. At that he thawed and I learned more about British intentions and the task of the 6th Airborne Division.

'The hours passed. We had set up a defensive front where we had been condemned to inactivity. The rest of the division, with the panzer regiment and Panzer Grenadier Regiment 192, was equally immobilised, though in the highest state of alert. My adjutant telephoned once more to division. Major Forster, IC and responsible for the reception of prisoners, came to the phone. He too was unable to alter the established orders. Army Group B merely informed us that it was a matter of a diversionary manoeuvre: the British had thrown out straw dummies on parachutes.

'At daybreak, I sent my adjutant to ask divisional command post to secure us immediate clearance for a counterattack. On his arrival, Liebeskind witnessed a heated telephone conversation which Feuchtinger was evidently having with the army: 'General, I have just come back from Paris and I've seen a gigantic armada off the west coast of Cabourg, warships, supply ships and landing craft. I want to attack at once with the entire division east of the Orne in order to push through to the coast.' But clearance was strictly denied.

'Hitler, who used to work far into the night, was still asleep that early morning.

'At the command post I paced up and down and clenched my fists at the indecision of the Supreme Command in the face of the obvious facts. If Rommel had been with us instead of in Germany, he would have disregarded all orders and taken action - of that we were convinced.

'We felt completely fit physically and able to cope with the situation. I concealed my anger and remained calm and matter-of-fact. My experience in previous theatres of war had taught me that the more critical a situation, or the more alarming the reports, the more calmly every experienced leader should react.

'The best way to calm an excited orderly officer, or a dispatch rider coming straight from an apparently desperate situation, is to sit him down, give him a cigarette and say, 'Now tell me what has actually happened.'

'So the tragedy took its course. After only a few hours, the brave fighting units in the coastal fortifications could no longer withstand the enemy pressure, or else they were smashed by the Allied naval guns; while a German panzer division, ready to engage, lay motionless behind the front and powerful Allied bomber formations, thanks to complete air superiority, covered the coastal divisions and Caen with concentrated attacks. In the early hours of the morning, from the hills east of Caen, we saw the gigantic Allied armada, the fields littered with transport gliders and the numerous observation balloons over the landing fleet, with the help of which the heavy naval guns subjected us to precision fire.

'The situation forced us to regroup. Strong combat units were formed on either side of the Orne, east and west. We continued to wait for clearance for a counterattack. In view of this superiority, I thought, on seeing the landing fleet, there was no longer much chance of throwing the Allies back into the sea. Bringing up reserves was even now extremely difficult for us. The 'second front' had been established. The enemy in the east pressing with superior strength, the ceaseless bombing of our most important industrial centres and railway communications - even the bravest and most experienced troops could no longer win this war. A successful invasion, I thought, was the beginning of the end.'

Oberstleutnant Hans von Luck, 125th Panzergrenadier Regiment. Generalmajor Edgar Feuchtinger, the commander of the 21st Panzer Division, was a Kanonier (artilleryman) with no experience of tank warfare, was a convinced Nazi who had helped organise the Berlin Olympics of 1936. On the night of the invasion he was with his mistress - the Black Actress' - in Paris. His staff officer in charge of operations, Oberstleutnant von Berlichingen, was also away in the French capital. While Feuchtinger was at Divisional HQ in Paris, at around 0200 Hauptmann Wagemann, on detachment with the division as a staff officer training course tried to deputize for von Berlichingen. By this time Wagemann was convinced that the invasion was under way and so he put the division on Alarmstufe II (level II alert), ordering the motorized units to be ready to move in an hour and a half. [37] Wagemann managed to get in touch with Feuchtinger who, when told that parachutists were landing in the Troarn area, announced his 'immediate' return. Feuchtinger called Oberst Hermann von Oppeln-Bronikowski his Battalion tank Commander (Panzer-Regiment 22) with orders to take up action stations. [38] 'Imagine' Feuchtinger said, 'they have landed.'

'Sword' Beach was potentially the most vulnerable of all the beaches with 12th SS Panzer to the east and 21st Panzer on the outskirts of Caen

---

37 21st Panzer was composed of: Panzer Aufklarung Abteilung 21 (reconnaissance); Panzer Regiment 22 (two battalions) Panzer grenadier Regiment 125 (two battalions) Panzergrenadier Regiment 192 (two battalions) Panzer Artillerie Regiment 155 (three battalions) Panzerjager Abteilung 200 (anti tank); Panzer Pionier Battalion 220 (engineers).

38 *'Gold' 'Juno' 'Sword'* by Georges Bernage (Heimdal 2003).

at Ste-Pierre-sur-Dives, 15 miles from the coast; the one Panzer division close enough to intervene in the early stages of the assault.[39] On paper 21st Panzer had a strength of 170 armoured vehicles and tanks but much of the Division relied on captured French armoured vehicles and tanks captured in 1940 and obsolete weapons.[40] Of the ten Panzer and Panzer Grenadier divisions in the West it was the only one considered unfit for service on the Eastern Front. [41] In an interview given to Milton Shulman, then a major in the Canadian Army, in August 1945, Feuchtinger claimed: 'I first knew that the invasion had begun with a report that parachutists had been dropped near Troarn a little after midnight on 6 June. Since I had been told that I was to make no move until I heard from Rommel's Headquarters, I could do nothing immediately but warn my men to be ready. I waited impatiently all that night for instructions. But not a single order from higher formation was received by me.[42] Realizing that my armoured division was closest to the scene of operations, I finally decided at 0630 in the morning that

39 Of five divisions in von Rundstedt's strategic reserve, only the 12th Waffen-SS-Panzer Division 'Hitler Jugend' near Evreux and Panzer Lehr in the Chartres-Le Mans area were readily available. At 0230 hours on 6 June Generalleutnant Fritz Bayerlein's Panther Battalion was being loaded on to railway flats in preparation for a move to Poland when news of the invasion fleet was received! He was ordered to begin moving north that afternoon at 1700 hours but he wanted to wait until dark to reduce the threat from Allied fighter-bombers. This was refused. By the end of the day he had lost forty trucks carrying fuel and 90 others, five of his tanks were knocked out and 84 half-tracks, prime-movers and self-propelled guns. 17th SS, south of the Loire, was 200 miles from Bayeaux and, anyway it had no tanks; 1st SS commanded by Obergruppenführer 'Sepp' Dietrich, whose HQ was at Rouen, was at Turnhout in Belgium close to Antwerp still refitting after combat on the Eastern Front; and 2nd SS faced a 600-mile journey from Toulouse through country infested with Maquis. The Panzer Lehr Division consisted of two armoured infantry regiments, the 901st and 902nd Panzer Grenadier Lehr with an armoured regiment, the 130th Panzer Lehr Regiment. The division also had its anti-tank, signals, engineer and reconnaissance units. [It was at full strength and had 196 tanks including eight Tigers, 58 anti-tank guns and 53 artillery pieces]. Panzer Lehr had not begun to move until 1700 hours on D-Day and could not be expected before 8 June since they were making the 130-mile journey from Châteaudun on their own tracks. When Generaloberst Friedrich Dollmann, Commander of the Seventh Army ordered the Panzer Lehr and 12th SS Panzer Divisions to move to the front he instructed them to do so in daylight, but to maintain radio silence. These orders led to chaos in the Panzer Lehr. Allied ground attack fighters destroyed 40 loaded fuel trucks and 84 half-tracks and self-propelled guns and numerous other vehicles. Even by moving at night the only additional force which could reach the Caen area by the morning of D+1 was the 12th SS Panzer group which was ordered to 'join forces with 21st Panzer Division and wipe out enemy forces which had penetrated west of the Orne' but his motorised and armoured columns were so repeatedly strafed from the air that they averaged barely 4 mph. See 'The Struggle For Europe' by Chester Wilmot and D-Day; The First 24 Hours by Will Fowler (Spellmount 2003) and Steel Inferno: 1st SS Panzer Corps in Normandy by Michael Reynolds (Spellmount, 1997, 2007).

40 Self-propelled anti-tank and artillery vehicles were produced using the chassis of captured Hotchkiss and Lorraine tanks and armoured vehicles. These included the 7.5cm Pak 40 auf GW 39h(f), a self-propelled anti-tank gun on the Hotchkiss H39 tank and the FH 18 auf GW Lorraine Schlepper, which mounted a 10.5cm howitzer.

41 Feuchtinger said that 'Another great difficulty in the training of the 21st, as in many other divisions, was that 15 percent of the replacements were so-called Volksdeutchen (German nationals from abroad), many of whom did not even have a proper control of the German language.'

42 The Nazi command structure was such that orders were being issued to the two to three Panzer Divisions by no less than six headquarters.

I had to take some action. I ordered my tanks to attack the 6th Airborne Division which had entrenched itself in a bridgehead over the Orne. To me this constituted the most immediate threat to the German position.

'Hardly had I made this decision when at 0700 hours I received my first intimation that a higher command did still exist. I was told by Army Group B that I was now under command of the Seventh Army. But I received no further orders as to my role. At 0900 I was informed that I would receive any future orders from LXXXIV Infantry Corps and finally at 1000 I was given my first operational instructions. I was ordered to stop the move of my tanks against the Allied airborne troops and to turn west and aid the forces protecting Caen.'

The two tank battalions of Panzer-Regiment 22 had finally received their marching orders at 0800 hours by which time six vital hours had elapsed when the Panzers might have been decisive. More time was wasted back-tracking and re-crossing, tank by tank, the one surviving bridge over the Orne at Caen after being ordered to drive west of the river towards 'Sword' Beach. They were harassed along the route by navy shellfire and attacks by fighter-bombers.

Near Caen six Panzers (including five command tanks) were destroyed by eight Typhoons. By late afternoon the British and Canadians were within sight of Caen and the British thrust had reached Blainville. Then, on the outskirts of the village, in Lebisey Wood, just two and a half miles from Caen, three troops of the Staffordshire Yeomanry and their 'Firefly' Shermans armed with the 17-pounder gun, met forty of the Mk IV Panzers. They were led into action by Colonel Jim Eadie, a Territorial officer and a director of Bass breweries in Burton-on-Trent, who had served under Montgomery at Alamein. The Germans lost thirteen tanks broadside on in the ambush and brief encounter that followed.

A small force of Panzers led by Oppeln-Bronikowski, short of infantry, managed to slip through and headed for the coast where a four-mile salient divided the British and Canadian beaches. [43] The tanks of the 21st Panzer that remained behind were the only armour that stood between the

---

43 This gap had opened up as a result of the late arrival of the British 9th Infantry Brigade because of congestion on the beach and the failure of the Royal Marines in breaking through at Ste-Aubin and Lion-sur-Mer. A correspondent who was there wrote: 'the landing of the 9th Brigade began amid such chaos...The roads were blocked by eager soldiers wanting to press on quickly ahead. Fortunately, the Germans did not bombard the area'. The plan was for the 9th to pass through the 8th Brigade (which would capture Bernières and cover the landing of the 9th Brigade) and secure the left half of the divisional objective while the 7th Brigade was to capture the port of Courseulles and secure the high ground south of the Seulles. The 9th Brigade would then continue its advance on the right. A mortar bomb which wounded the Brigade Commander during his first 'O' Group ashore made the quick deployment of this reserve Brigade impossible and by the time Brigade was ready for rapid movement inland late in the afternoon it was urgently needed to cover the 3rd British Infantry Division's western flank where the Royal Marines had been checked in their attempt to clear the area between the British and Canadian beach heads. Another factor which contributed to the opening of the gap between the Canadians and the British occurred on the afternoon of D-Day when the British I Corps commander, Lieutenant General John Crocker, fearful of a major counter-attack east of the Orne, ordered the 9th Infantry Brigade to cease its attack between Caen and Carpiquet airfield to support the airborne division.

British and Caen. [44] Once over the Orne River, Feuchtinger drove north towards the coast:

'By this time the enemy, consisting of three British and three Canadian Infantry Divisions, had made astonishing progress and had already occupied a strip of high ground about ten kilometres from the sea. From here, the excellent anti-tank gunfire of the Allies knocked out eleven of my tanks before I had barely started. However, one battle group did manage to bypass these guns and actually reached the coast at Lion-sur-Mer, at about seven in the evening.

Near Périers-sur-le-Dan General Marcks, the commander of the LXXXIV Corps joined Feuchtinger, as the Allied invasion force could be seen in the distance. Red faced with anger Marcks blamed Feuchtinger for the delays and then took charge. Only six tanks of the 21st Panzer-Division accompanied by some of 21st Panzer's armoured infantry - the panzer grenadiers of 192nd Regiment - led by Marcks, standing erect in his staff car - reached Luc-sur-Mer on the Côte de Nacre, between 'Sword' and 'Juno' Beaches. Before Oppeln-Bronikowski attacked, Marcks personally told the Prussian aristocrat and Olympic 'Gold' Medal equestrian: 'Oppeln, the future of Germany may very well rest on your shoulders. If you don't push the British back we've lost the war.'

According to Generaloberst Alfred Jodl (Chief of Operations Staff, OKW)'s orders in a telephone call late that afternoon to Generalmajor Max Pemsel, Chief of Staff, Seventh Army, 'all available forces must be diverted to the point of penetration... The bridgehead there must be cleaned up not later than tonight.' Pemsel replied that this was 'impossible' but the 21st Panzer Division was ordered to 'attack immediately with or without reinforcements'. OKW ordered that the bad weather conditions must be utilised to the full for bringing up reserves during the night of 6/7 June. [45] At 2000 hours Feuchtinger was ready to commit Oppeln's Panzers into a

---

44 The 2nd Battalion, King's Shropshire Light Infantry led by Lieutenant Colonel F. J. Maurice got within 3 miles of the centre of Caen and 1 mile short of its northern suburbs but was halted by the 192nd Panzer-Grenadier Regiment concealed in Lebisey Wood. Feuchtinger's anti-tank battalion, which had been stationed with its two dozen 88mm's on Périers Ridge providing a formidable barrier between the coast and Caen, had come under the command of the 716th Division before dawn and was ordered westward. Concentrated, these guns might have halted 3rd British close to the beaches but of the original 24, only three were still in position on Périers Ridge when Maurice's battalion and one squadron of tanks of the Staffordshire Yeomanry began its thrust for Caen soon after 1 o'clock. They came under heavy fire from 88mm's and a company had to be diverted to put the guns out of action. By 1600 hours the KSLI and tanks were advancing from Bieville but they encountered 24 Panzer tanks from the west. The Yeomanry and some self-propelled anti-tank guns knocked out five enemy tanks and the rest were driven off but when the leading company came under intense fire from Lebisey Wood the company commander was killed and the advance petered out. (KSLI's casualties so far were 113 killed, wounded or missing). Maurice realised that nothing less than an attack in some strength could rout the enemy but he could ill-afford to do so for as long as there was the possibly of renewed action by 21st Panzer and while the Norfolks were held up by the failure of the Suffolks to take 'Hillman'. At Bieville that evening Maurice consolidated his position while the enemy strengthened its hold on Lebisey Wood. It would be five weeks before Caen finally fell to the Canadians.

45 12th SS Panzer reached Feuchtinger's HQ at Ste-Pierre-sur-Dives south-west of Caen soon after midnight but their fuel tanks had been almost drained by repeated diversions, slow running and frequent stops. 12th SS Panzer had been expecting to draw fuel from a dump near Evrecy, but Allied aircraft had already destroyed it. *'The Struggle For Europe'* by Chester Wilmot.

concerted attack but the arrival overhead of 250 gliders on their supply drop panicked Feuchtinger, who for some reason feared that it was an attempt to cut his Division off from Caen.

'I now expected that some reinforcements would be forthcoming to help me hold my position, but nothing came. Another Allied parachute landing on both sides of the Orne, together with a sharp attack by English tanks, forced me to give up my hold on the coast. I retired to take up a line just north of Caen. By the end of the first day my division had lost almost 25 per cent of its tanks.'

Feuchtinger ordered a rapid withdrawal and the chance to surround and isolate two beach-heads was lost.

Although Caen could not be taken on D-Day, had the panzers not barred the way and if 21st Panzer and 12th SS Panzer could have counter-attacked when the British and Canadians had limited numbers of tanks ashore, the situation on the beaches could have been disastrous for the Allies. As it turned out' wrote Chester Wilmot 'it was fortunate that the indecision of the German High Command more than counter-balanced the delays and difficulties on the beaches.' If 'Sepp' Dietrich of 1st SS Panzer Corps had been able to rely on these divisions and Panzer Lehr and what little remained of the 716th Infanterie-Division, which comprised many Russian and Polish conscripts, to commence an attack on the British around Caen at dawn on 7 June as ordered, this force might have driven the invasion forces back into the sea altogether. But continual Allied air attacks, lack of fuel and the delayed start of 12th SS Panzer and Panzer Lehr resulted in the counter-attack being postponed. Major General Fritz Witt, commander, 12th Waffen-SS-Panzer Division 'Hitler Jugend' Division[46] sent Standartenführer Kurt Meyer commander, 25th SS Panzer-Grenadier Regiment to see Generalleutnant Wilhelm Richter commanding 716th Division at his HQ. A devoted Nazi and a ruthless fighter, Meyer's men called him 'Panzer Meyer'. It took him 'about eight hours' to reach the HQ in a tunnel in a quarry at la Folie 3km north of Caen and he had spent 'more than four hours in road ditches because of air attacks'. Meyer's columns suffered heavy losses too, from the Jabos or 'meat-flies', as 12th SS Panzer called the Allied fighter-bombers. Feuchtinger and a liaison group from the Panzer Lehr Division were also waiting for Meyer and a discussion took place on the possibilities of a coordinated attack by the three Panzer Divisions on 7 June. The officers from Panzer Lehr made it clear that there was no chance of their Division arriving in time and Feuchtinger was pessimistic about the chances of success with anything less than three divisions. The fact that he could not communicate with his own HQ at Ste-Pierre-sur-Dives could not have helped matters.

'About midnight, Kurt Meyer arrived at my Headquarters. He was to take over on my left and we were to carry out a combined operation the next morning. I explained the situation to Meyer and warned him about the strength of the

46 (Hitler Youth, or HJ) recruited from volunteers in the leadership schools of Nazi youth movement and men from the veteran Waffen-SS Division Leibstandarte 'Adolf Hitler'.

enemy. Meyer studied the map, turned to me with a confident air and said, 'Little fish! We'll throw them back into the sea in the morning.' We decided to drive towards Douvres and 12 SS was to take up assembly positions during the night.'

Between them Meyer and Feuchtinger had about 160 tanks and five battalions of Panzer-Grenadiers available for the counter-attack and with a large gap between the British and Canadian 3rd Divisions in the Douvres area, there was every chance of success if only these forces could be refuelled and coordinated in time. Meyer's own Tactical HQ was located in a café about 4km to the west of Caen at Ste-Germain-la-Blanche-Herbe. Liaison officers had instructed his unit commanders to report to him there as soon as possible. But as Meyer was about to leave Richter's HQ he received a telephone call from Witt calling from Feuchtinger's HQ at Ste-Pierre-sur-Dives. He asked for a situation report and then said:

'The situation necessitates speedy action. First of all, the enemy has to be denied Caen and the Carpiquet airfield. It can be assumed that the enemy has already brought his units to order and that they have been readied for defence in so far as they have not deployed for further attacks. Therefore it would be wrong to throw our Divisional units into battle as soon as they arrive. We can only consider a coordinated attack with the 21st Panzer Division. So the Division is to attack the enemy with the 21st Panzer Division and throw them into the sea. H-Hour for the attack is 7th June at mid-day.'

Meyer briefed Feuchtinger and both men left to join their respective Headquarters. Witt had been unable to tell Meyer when additional forces could take up their positions on Meyer's left flank. Until then there could be no Divisional attack.[47] It was necessary therefore for Meyer to adopt temporary defensive positions. West of the railway line from Caen to Ste-Luc-sur-Mer (the boundary between 21st Panzer and 12th SS Panzer) his 1st Panzer Grenadier Battalion and 16th SS Panzer Pionier Company took up positions around Epron and la Folie north of Caen; 2nd SS Panzer Grenadier Battalion was at Ste-Contest and Bitot. When SS Oberstleutnant Karl-Heinz Millius' 3rd SS Panzer Grenadier Battalion arrived, it would occupy positions south-east of Franqueville, astride the Caen-Bayeaux road.

---

47 Witt had grouped the 2nd SS Panzer Battalion of SS Major Karl-Heinz Prinz and the 3rd SS Artillery Battalion with Panzer Meyer's 25th SS Panzer-Grenadier Regiment and SS Major Arnold Jürgensen's 1st SS Panzer Battalion, the 12th SS Panzer Pionier Battalion and the two other SS artillery Battalions with Wilhelm Mohnke's 26th SS Panzer-Grenadier Regiment. Early on 7 June Witt confirmed the telephone orders he had given to Meyer during the night. The 12th Waffen-SS-Panzer Division 'Hitler Jugend' would 'attack the disembarked enemy together with 21st Panzer Division and throw him back into the sea'. However, H-Hour was delayed because many of the essential elements for this counter-attack had not yet arrived - in particular the tanks. It was 1000 hours before about 50 Mk IV tanks of 2nd SS Panzer Battalion arrived; the other 40 or so were not expected until later in the day or even after dark. The 48 combat-ready Panthers of 1st SS Panzer Battalion [requiring 8,000 gallons of fuel], were stranded east of the Orne and 26th SS and the SS Pionier and other artillery battalions had still to cross the Odon. *Steel Inferno: 1st SS Panzer Corps in Normandy* by Michael Reynolds (Spellmount, 1997, 2007). Witt would be killed by shell fire on 14 June and his replacement would be Standartenfüuhrer Kurt Meyer, the commander of 25th SS Panzer Grenadier.

'It seems incredible that German intelligence once noticed nothing of the vast preparations for the invasion and that individual precise reports from the German command posts were ignored. On the other hand, it's not that surprising because the Deutsche Nachrichtefl Dienst (intelligence service) was riddled with spies putting out duff information.

'I volunteered for the Waffen SS in 1940 because I wanted to join the best. And they were the finest there has ever been. We're often compared to the Royal Marines but we were better than they were.

'I was asleep when the Invasion began, when the Allied paratroopers were landing, even before midnight. The masses of troops that landed in the early morning can be said to have decided the war. They came with an armada whose size far exceeded all German fears.

'The HJ had been alerted during the night of June 4/5 for manoeuvres on 6 June The night before there was unusual aircraft activity and towards morning it was certain. We knew they were coming. We were marched towards Lisieux at first but were later switched to the west towards Caen. We soldiers in the battle units knew nothing of the confusion over higher staff but confusion there certainly was. We didn't reach Caen until deep in the night and some units didn't arrive until early next morning. We had been on the move for many hours. There were the usual technical problems and the drivers were falling asleep in their seats every time we stopped. When we arrived, the tanks were arranged in a great semicircular defensive line north of the Caen-Bayeux road to prevent the enemy from taking the important Carpiquet airfield and penetrating the city of Caen. What did it feel like? There was no time to feel only time to do. The enemy attack was expected and it happened as expected. Our battle group leader, Standartenführer Kurt Meyer, known as 'Panzer Meyer', had set up our command post at Ardenne Abbey. Its strong arches offered protection and cover and we had a good view to the coast from the towers and a gallery running all around the roof. Under cover of the gallery, we could observe the enemy tanks and infantry advancing closer to our Panzer IV tanks standing in ambush positions. To me, it was like watching a piece of theatre from a balcony seat with running commentary from the radio.

'The drama became a tragedy for the British [sic] when, on the command 'Fire at will!' our tanks fired as one. Numerous enemy tanks immediately burst into flames. Others drove away in surprise and confusion, going every which way all over the battlefield.'

22 year-old Leutnant Herbert Walther, 12th Waffen-SS-Panzer Division 'Hitler Jugend'. Meyer's forces inflicted heavy casualties on the Canadian Sherman tanks of the Sherbrooke Fusiliers and the North Nova Scotia Highlanders 48 trying to outflank Caen and capture Carpiquet airfield, but the gap on the Channel coast had been closed and the British and Canadian

---

48 On 7 June in Authie, north-west of Caen the North Nova Scotia Highlanders of the Canadian 9th Infantry Brigade experienced their first baptism of fire. Its advanced guard was caught off balance and 84 North Novas and seven citizens of Authie were killed. The village marked the furthest point reached by the Canadians during the first six days after D-Day. *A Guide to the Beaches and Battlefields of Normandy* by David Evans (Michael Joseph, 1995 and Amberley 2010).

beach heads were firmly linked.

There were rumours that Canadian prisoners-of-war had been shot by 12th SS Panzer on 7 June when the village of Buron was first liberated after fierce house-to-house fighting involving the North Nova Scotia Highlanders and the 27th Armoured Regiment (Sherbrooke Fusiliers). That afternoon the Germans counter-attacked and retook the village. British and Canadian troops re-took the village again on 9 July, the Highland Light Infantry suffering heavy casualties. In December 1945 Kurt Meyer was found guilty by a Canadian Military Court of charges relating to the murder of 19 Canadians of the Royal Winnipeg Rifles - seven at Meyer's regimental HQ at the Abbaye d'Ardenne on 8 June and 11 more over the next two days - and he was sentenced to be shot. His sentence was commuted to life imprisonment but he was released after nine years. He died in 1961.

'We were going to take Caen! We had now reached the high ground on the left hand rout into the City of Caen, this dusty road that looked down on the Colombelles' industrial area on the outskirts of Caen, with the high building of the ironworks far below, all rusty and gaunt. From our vantage point it was possible to see for miles down below and the ground spread out all round in a wide panoramic view. Blissfully unaware that the area was still in German hands and that he was watching our every move, (we had been told that the 51st Highland Division had taken it) After having a long look at the ground down below we the carried on sweeping and clearing our way forward, to ensure that the way was free from the Enemy and from mines. The enemy soon put a stop to this, we had just entered and cleared a farm house when all hell was let loose, from the tall rusty looking steel works down below, came a tremendous barrage of shell fire. Point blank shell fire, where one does not hear the shells coming until the last split second, when the incoming fire sounds like an express train with the scream of shells, with violent explosions and tearing shrapnel, the farm house exploded in a great shower of splintered wood and then came down about my shoulders, the flying debris, the continuing scream and flashing fire, the rippling explosion of the shells, an intense barrage, the swirling smoke and pandemonium and ones whole being gripped with fear.

'It is not only images and scenes that remain with one through the years, but also sounds, sounds that can remind one of times long past. The moans and cries of mortally wounded men, my mouth dry and choked with dust. After the fire died down I started to extricate myself, covered in dirt and dust and splintered wood, the bitter stench of cordite. When in the distance, I heard the sound of the bagpipes, above all that noise, I could hear the skirl of the Scots pipes, when I got out of the rubble I looked down the dusty track and there he was, nonchalantly marching slowly towards us, this piper, khaki kilt swaying from side to side, as he made his way forward concentrating on his playing. Sounds of war! Whenever I hear the pipes I must admit to having a great big lump in my throat, I have been into battle with the sound of the pipes and I cannot hear them without being deeply moved.

Brian Guy, 246 Field Company, Royal Engineers - 3rd British Infantry Division.

'The big question was whether we should have got to Caen. The bombing of the Brigade headquarters [caused by a chance mortar bomb, which wounded the Brigadier and made a 'shambles' of his first operational conference] certainly held it all up because it had to be reconstituted and the battalion had to be re-coordinated. By then the Germans had reinforced very rapidly and there were two German top-quality divisions around Caen within a matter of a few days. It's interesting, whether or not, if we had captured Caen, we would have, quite frankly, managed to hold it. I like to think we would have done, but...'

Captain (later major general) G. C. A. Gilbert, 'C' Company, 2nd Battalion, the Royal Lincolnshire Regiment, which landed on 'Sword' Beach.

'They haven't come any too soon. There'll be a very unpleasant surprise for the enemy... You can hear the aircraft roaring over me I expect as I still speak. I can still see the signs of a typical Panzer battle being raged on the slightly high ground just about three or four miles ahead of me and these paratroops are coming down just between where I'm speaking which is just about above the sand dunes. Down they come. They're being attacked pretty harshly as you'll hear, but they're landing in great force between the sand dunes between the beach area and the battle and they may have a very decisive effect on that battle.'

Alan Melville, BBC correspondent, at Ouistreham.

'Sword' Beach Timeline

Objectives: To advance inland towards the city of Caen; to link up with the airborne troops, who had landed by parachute and glider and were protecting the eastern flank of landings against German counter-attack.

H-Hour (0530) Shore bombardment is delivered by two battleships, HMS *Warspite* and *Ramilles*, the monitor HMS *Roberts*, cruisers HMS *Mauritius* (Rear Admiral Arthur Talbot's Flagship), *Arethusa, Frobisher* and *Danae* and the Polish ORP *Dragon* and 13 destroyers including two from the Polish Navy (plus two more as part of the covering force) and the Norwegian HMNS *Svenner;* naval support having been increased because of the many German batteries in this sector.

0537 While the smaller vessels head towards their bombarding stations, the *Svenner* is hit amidships by German torpedo boats on patrol from Le Havre with the loss of one officer and 33 crew.

0650 the self-propelled guns of the 3rd Infantry Division open fire from their landing craft at a range of 10,000 yards.

0725 British 3rd Infantry Division commanded by Major General Thomas Rennie and 27th Armoured Brigade, 18 minutes later than scheduled, go ashore with 40 DD tanks (six, including two which are rammed by landing craft out of control, are lost) and flame-throwers and come under mortar fire. The first wave of infantry, the 8th Infantry Brigade Group, the 1st Battalion the South Lancashire Regiment and the 2nd East Yorkshires, arrive to find that the first of the 13th/18th Royal Hussars' DD tanks are already ashore and firing at strong-points.

0750 Nos. 4 and 10 (Free French) Commando land. Heavy fighting on the beach.

0821 Flail tanks from the 22nd Dragoons and the Westminster Dragoons clear paths through minefields and exits from the beach are opened more quickly than on any other beach.

0835 Three beach exits cleared of the enemy.

0930 Hermanville taken. Riva Bella casino strongpoint captured by the Free French. Heavy German opposition halts the advance. With a fast incoming tide, the beach becomes congested; the reserve brigades are held up.

1000-1200 German strong points inland are gradually overcome.

1215 Panzer tanks reported north of Caen. 21st Panzer Group - 20,000 men - commanded by Generalmajor Edgar Feuchtinger, disobeys orders and attacks between Caen and Bayeux.

1100 185 Brigade, whose mission is to capture Caen, ashore and formed up but traffic jams keep them from advancing until 12.30.

1230 British 185th Brigade move inland from 'Sword'.

1330 Brigadier Lord Lovat's 1st Special Service Brigade, composed of four Army and one Royal Marines Commando, reach Pegasus Bridge en route to help other units of the Airborne Division.

1400 Fighting on Périers Ridge overlooking 'Sword' which is cleared by the 2nd King's Shropshire Light Infantry even though their tank support fails to turn up.

1600 9th Brigade moves inland. 185th Brigade repulses attack of the German 21st Panzer Division at Périers Ridge and destroys 16 tanks but the British advance pauses.

1800 British advance on Caen halted.

1900 With a battle group of tanks and a battalion of infantry 21st Panzer Division mounts massive counter-attack. Drive fails just short of the cliffs at Luc-sur-Mer, with the loss of 13 tanks.

2000 Bénouville is captured. A German counter-attack is made towards the sea between 'Sword' and 'Juno' Beaches. The 'Hillman' strongpoint is secured, after a long battle.

2100 A group of 250+ Allied gliders fly in and deter the German attack. 185th Brigade halts at Biéville, three miles short of Caen.

2400 Six square miles of beach is under British control. 29,000 landed. Casualties, fewer than 1,000. The troops have reached six miles inland.

'We carried metal-detectors ashore but we found them quite useless for the simple reason that there was so much shrapnel around, that as soon as you switched on your detector, you picked up noise. So we had to do it the old-fashioned way - we prodded for the mines with a bayonet. Once you got the pattern of a minefield, it was quite easy. The Germans were very methodical and laid them in very regular patterns. You just went forward in lines, carrying white tapes and cleared and marked an area about three or four foot wide. We had Pioneer Corps people with us and after we'd disarmed the mines, they would take them back along the beach and blew them up twenty at a time. These explosions were going on all the time, which was reassuring.'

Corporal Thomas Finigan, Mine Clearance, 85th Field Company, Royal Engineers.

'On 1 June we embarked onto a LST at Gosport. On board were men from various regiments but from the 53rd there were just seven with a 15 cwt truck. We were the Survey and Recce party. We laid in the Solent in the most appalling weather until 1930 on 5 June when we set sail, arriving off 'Sword' beach at 1000 on 6 June. A Reuters newsman who was on board sent the first bulletin back to the UK by pigeon, as there was strict radio silence. The LST had a top and bottom deck. The lower deck was first to unload and then a lift brought the vehicles from the upper deck to the lower deck for their turn. We unloaded by driving onto pontoon rafts, which then ferried us to the beach. After the lower deck had been cleared a German plane (remember there were only supposed to be two German planes over the whole beachhead) machine-gunned our ship and dropped a bomb, which exploded under the bow doors. This distorted the bow doors and wrecked the lift. In order to finish unloading we had to pull away from the beach and tie up alongside another LST that had already unloaded and run our vehicles across from one ship to the other by means of wooden planks. It was a quirk of fate that with the thousands of ships in the area, one of the two German planes in the air managed to hit us.

'I arrived in France on D-Day, travelled through Belgium, Holland and Germany and yet remained unscathed. My brother-in-law landed in Normandy two weeks later and was killed within days of his arrival.'

Gunner Len Woods, 53rd Medium Regiment Royal Artillery.

My dear Sally,

As you have probably gathered I have been unable to write, however this is just a brief note to say cheerio for now and I'll hope to be seeing you shortly. At present everybody is in good spirits. I am well. So don't worry at all. I'll be back soon.

My love to you, John.

Lieutenant John Blower, a soldier on 6 June, the day he landed in Normandy. Four days later he was killed.

'It was teatime on Monday 5 June, when noticing the minesweepers beginning to creep out, I realised the show was on. I had been offering heavy odds that it would be cancelled again at lunchtime. I felt rather appalled, when I looked at the sea. It was blowing half a gale from the SW and banking up black and beastly for what promised to be a thoroughly dirty night.

'We were issued with real maps and real place names. Our job was to land on the left-hand edge of ['Queen'] Red Beach, that is to say the extreme left of the whole Invasion; at the western part of Ouistreham, the mouths of the River Orne and Caen Canal.

'The East Yorks were going in at H-Hour to clear the beach defences and to make gaps in the wire and minefields for us. We were to go in 30 minutes later, pass through the East Yorks, dump our rucksacks and crash into Ouistreham, taking the beach defences up to the canal mouth from the rear and clearing the strong point round the Casino and the six-gun battery at the eastern end of town. The French troops were given the Casino job. The rest of the Brigade, numbers 3, 6 and 45 (RM) Commandos were to come in at about H plus 2 Hours and make straight for the Orne and Caen Canal bridges and link up with

6th Airborne Division. In the event of the Orne and Caen Canal bridges being blown we would have to cross the river and canal in rubber boats. We were to follow the rest of the brigade into the Orne bridgehead with all speed as soon as we had cleaned up the Ouistreham defences. It was not our job to mop up Ouistreham. This fact gave me a considerable headache on D-Day as it turned out, as no one seemed quite clear who was to do the mopping up.

'Now all the shipping was quietly and slowly filing out through the booms, the LCTs with their camouflaged loads of tanks and ammunition, the big LSTs packed with vehicles, the LSIs, all slung around with their LCAs and the little LCIs with their troops sardined aboard. All the rest of the Brigade was in LCIs and our French troops ranged up alongside us in theirs to give us a hail.

'Besides all these hundreds of craft, were countless corvettes and frigates, rows of destroyers, cruisers and the monitor Roberts. It was wonderful to watch the quiet steady stream of craft slipping out past the Portsmouth forts, so silent and orderly, with no sirens or fuss, their balloons marking those already hidden by swarms of intervening craft.

'Feeling rather small and chicken-hearted, I set about my final packing. I spliced my identity discs on string and gloomily hung them round my neck. I dished out anti-sea sickness tablets and morphine and talked to all the troops about my final medical plans. I had a heated tussle with the Brigade Major on the subject of the rum issue, finally settling that the troops could only have it 30 minutes before landing. To issue it as intended, before embarking in the LCAs, with two hours of cold and sea-sickness ahead would have been folly.

'I had a bath. 'Washing off the B. Coli in case you stop one', as the Naval doctor said. [49]

'The wind howled and it rained in vicious scuds. As the skipper said in his speech to ship's company: The High Command must be counting heavily on surprise, for the Germans must surely think that not even Englishmen could be such fools as to start an invasion on a night like this.'

'Breakfast was at 0400 hours and I only slept a little, rather fitfully. The wind howled, the ship rolled and the adjutant who was in my cabin was sick in the basin. It was grey dawn when I emerged and I could just see the shapes of the ships. There was some ack-ack in the distance and the occasional red flare. I went in to breakfast on porridge, bacon and egg, toast and marmalade, which went down very well, though some of the poorer sailors did not make much of it. As I was finishing, there was a distant metallic thump. I went out on deck in time to see a Norwegian Hunt Class destroyer [the Svenner] on our port beam roll over with a broken back and heave her stern and bows out of the sea. It seemed as if no craft took the slightest notice and like chaff on a stream the swarms of ships drifted on. However, before long, a little tug or trawler was alongside picking up survivors.

'The thunder of the big guns now began as the battleships got on to their targets. The coast of France was a low grey strip to the southward, with a cold-looking tossing expanse of sea in between. The anchor went down with a shuddering rattle,

---

49 Bacteria carried in the colon, which spreads to the skin via the anal passage; is a possible source of infection if wounded.

as the Princess Astrid anchored in her appointed place seven miles out. 'Troops to parade, troops to parade', came over the loud hailer and we collected for the last time in the mess decks. There seemed to be much less room than usual, as everyone really had everything with him, probably for the first time.

'We stepped gingerly over the gap with our heavy loads and began to pack ourselves in. As always the last man couldn't sit down. Soon 'lower away, lower away', sent the LCAs down in turn to bump and wrench on their davits as the swell took them. Quickly the shackles were cast off and we rode free in that sea.

'We were rolling heavily in a big south-westerly swell which broke continually over us, drenching us and chilling us to the marrow. My hands grew numb and dead and my teeth were chattering with cold and fright. My batman looked awful, but he gave me a big grin through his green. It was H-Hour, 07.00 and the first infantry were going in. We passed round the rum and those who were not too seasick took a good swig. The sea was well dotted with 'bags vomit' and I could see the boys on the LCIs rushing to the rail.

'The chaps in the other boats were passing round the rum. I could hear snatches of song through the hellish din. Hutch Burt's boat went in singing 'Jerusalem'. We didn't sing in ours. My mouth was as dry as a bone, I was shaking all over and I doubt if I could have produced a note. The shore was still obscured by smoke, but I began to make out the fountains of shell bursts and the rattle of small-arms fire cut through the roar and scream of heavy shells. Something was hit on our starboard bow and a huge cloud of black smoke went up with orange flame flickering against the murk of battle. It was now 07.30 and with 400 yards to go we were a little late. We began to struggle with our rucksacks, an almost impossible feat. I gave it up until we grounded.

'Bullets began to rattle on the side of the craft and splinters whined overhead. 'Ready on the ramp,' we cowered down. The explosions were very near now and one threw spray over us. 'Going in to land.' We touched, bumped, slewed round. 'Ramp down,' the boat began to empty. At the stern, my men and I were the last to leave. I heaved on my rucksack and seized a stretcher. No one seemed ready to take the other one, so I picked it up too, staggered to the bows, cautiously down the ramp and flopped into the water. It came up about mid thigh. I struggled desperately for the shore. There was a thick fog of smoke all over the beach. The tide was flooding. There were many bodies in the water. One was hanging on the wire round one of the tripod obstacles. As I got nearer the shore, I saw wounded among the dead, pinned down by the weight of their equipment. The first I came to was little Sapper Mullen, submerged to the chin and helpless. I got my scissors out, with numb hands which felt weak and useless I began to cut away his rucksack and equipment. Hindmarch appeared beside me worked on the other side. He was a bit rattled, but soon steadied when I spoke to him and told him what to do.

'As I was bending over, I felt a smack across my bottom as if someone had hit me with a big stick. It was a shell splinter I found out later, but it hit nothing important; I just swore and carried on. We dragged Mullen to the water's edge at last and he was able to shuffle himself up the beach, so we let him carry on. I looked round to take stock. The Commando were up at the wire and clearly having trouble getting through. As there was no point in standing about,

Hindmarch and I went back to the wounded in the water. I noticed how fast the tide was rising and the wounded men began to shout and scream as they saw they must soon drown. Woe worked desperately. I don't know how many we pulled clear, not more than two or three.

'I saw Donald Glass at the water's edge, badly hit in the back. I went to him and started to cut away his equipment. As I was doing so, I was conscious of a machine-gun enfilading us from the left front. In a minute I was knocked over by a smack in the right knee and fell on Donald, who protested violently. I tried my leg and found it still worked though not very well. I got Hindmarch to open a stretcher and put Donald on it. I looked round for help, but the only other standing figure anywhere was my batman, who was working on his own with drowning wounded in the water. He smiled and waved to me. I tried my leg again and took one end of the stretcher. Hindmarch is a big strong fellow, between us we began to carry Donald up towards the wire. At the finish I was beat and just lay and gasped. We took the stretcher from Donald, we knew we would be needing it later and left him in a hollow in the sand. The troops had by now got through the wire and recognising where I was, I stumbled after them, across the minefield, to the demolished buildings, our assembly area, which the air photograph had showed so clearly.

'...I found the unit assembling in some confusion among the buildings. Someone gave me a swig of rum, which did me good. Lance-Corporal Cunningham put a dressing on my leg. It turned out to be a lucky wound through the muscles and tendons behind the knee joint, which had missed the popliteal artery very narrowly. The little bit of shell in my buttock made me very stiff, but it was not worth bothering about. Soon we moved off through the minefield and wire to the main east-west road leading straight into Ouistreham. The road was under heavy mortar fire and I came on six of our men lying dead only about 100 yards along the road at the corner of a copse. We hurried on at the end of the column. I was very lame, but a Marine carried my rucksack and gave me an arm. The gaps between the houses were my trouble; it was unwise to linger there. About 200 yards further on, we passed two more of our chaps, one dead, the other almost gone with his head smashed. I pushed his helmet over his face and went on. A mortar bomb had severely wounded another of our men in the shoulder. I nearly gave up on him, as his shoulder was practically severed and blood was gushing from it. With some trouble we got the bleeding under control with finger pressure in the neck and holding on to this point, we put him on a stretcher, carrying him to where the assaulting troops had left their rucksacks about 300 yards further on.

'Here I set up my RAP on a patch of grass between some villas and under some pine trees. The attack on the battery and the casino was soon well under way. I was very preoccupied with my badly wounded man. I packed the wound as best I could, before giving him a pint of plasma, which brought his pulse round, although I thought it was going to be too late. By this time casualties were pouring in and I was hard at it until late afternoon.

'The battle died down at about 11.00 hours and the troops began to reassemble for the move to the Orne bridges. The Troop leaders reported the numbers missing. We had suffered heavily, about 150 all ranks killed or wounded. The French doctor was among the dead, killed by a burst of fire from the Casino as he was tying up someone.

'I remained in Ouistreham for the rest of D-Day. I drove around the town in a jeep collecting the wounded, becoming increasingly cautious when it became clear that the only troops in town were the Germans. Eventually the Germans became very frisky, shooting from the direction of the Casino, the lock gates and the battery area. I went to the beachhead with a plea for troop to clear them. Soon a column of AVREs came down the road and following my directions, discouraged the Germans, most of whom surrendered, except for about fifty in the Casino area. [50]

These were rounded up in the morning. As soon as it was dark, the Boche began air attacks on the beach. I dozed rather fitfully in a shell hole on the edge of the road, deriving slight comfort from the fact that the drivers of the tanks rumbling past my head had not yet learnt the continental rule of the road and still drove on the left. I was so exhausted, my wounds were so stiff and sore, that I preferred to stay in my little shell hole, with tracks grinding within a few feet of my head, than attempt moving to somewhere off the road.'
Captain Joe Patterson, 4 Commando.

'Now was the moment - we clutched our weapons and wireless sets, all carefully waterproofed. A shallow beach we had been told, wet up to our knees or a little over and then a long stretch of sand and obstacles. Suddenly there was a jarring bump on the left, looking up we saw some of the beach obstacles about two feet above our left gunwale, with a large mine on top of it; just as the photographs had shown us; the mine the same as we had practised disarming. For a few brief moments there was just the music of the guns, whang of occasional bullets overhead, the explosions of mortar bombs and the background noise of our own fire. The doors opened as we grounded; the Colonel was out. The boat swung, as one by one we followed him. Several fell and got soaked. I stopped for a few seconds to help my men with their heavy wireless sets to ensure they kept them dry. I began to recognise men of the assault companies. Some were dead; others struggling to crawl out of the water, the tide was rising very rapidly. We could not help them; our job was to push on. I saw one of my signals corporals with a wound in his leg and I took his codes with me, promising to send a man back for his set before he was evacuated.

'Just off the beach, among some ruined buildings, we began to collect the HQ. The other boat party was mostly missing, also three-quarters of my sets. The Colonel was getting a grip on the battle and I was sent back to the beach to collect the rest of us. I did not feel afraid, but rather elated and full of beans. There were some horrible sights there and not a few men calling out for help. I had no time or duty there, the beach medical people would gradually get round to them all. Under the sides of a tank that had been hit, I saw a bunch of my people. I bawled at them to get up and start moving, since they were doing no good there and could safely

50 Elements of 4 Commando mopping up the Riva-Bella strongpoint omitted to check the concrete tower at the range-finding station, where 53 Germans remained completely cut off until the evening of 9 June without anyone knowing. *'Gold' 'Juno' 'Sword'* by Georges Bernage (Heimdal 2003).

get along to HQ. I felt a little callous when I found nearly all of them had been hit and some were dead. But sorting them out, I made up half a wireless team and went in search of more.

'Further on were the Adjutant and the Padre with their party, also taking cover. I took them back with me. By persuading a couple of blokes with shrapnel in their legs and feet they were good for a few more hours yet, I got my wireless lifted and we returned to HQ, which was just moving off further inland. Later I discovered that numerous others had been killed on the beach landing at the same time as myself. The move inland was not much fun. Although we had cleared the beach defences, Jerry was mortaring us pretty badly from positions in his rear. Besides we had to cross a marsh, in places up to our armpits in muddy water and slime. The mortars had our range. As I helped my wireless people through the deep parts (why are all Yorkshire signallers only 5 foot 2 inches?), the bombs were bursting only 50 yards behind us.'

Lieutenant Hugh Bone, signals officer, 2nd East Yorks with Battalion Headquarters and the follow-up companies.

'About 20 of us were told the Grenadier Guards were forming an independent tank brigade to be called the 4th Tank Battalion. You had to be no less than 5 feet 10 inches - I just got in by one inch. Lucky me! Training continued, our uniform changed and after four weeks we began to look like Grenadiers - and we were proud of it. Our commander, Corporal Vic Garner from Walthamstow chose me as gunner and radio operator. 'Nobby' Clarke was co-driver and Stan Bradford as driver. We all got on well together.

'D-Day was fast approaching, although at the time we didn't know it. We travelled to a wooded area near Gosport and spent our time waterproofing and protecting the tanks. It didn't stop raining. We were wet through and covered in mud. It wasn't much fun sitting in a tank, wet through with no means of getting dry, but no one bothered. We could be killed soon anyway.

'On June 5 we got orders to go to a small street in Gosport, not far from the harbour. It was getting dark. There was a lot of heavy traffic on the move. We were all getting a little nervous and apprehensive. We didn't know what was in store for us. At 2200 we got orders to go on board a landing craft. It was still very wet and windy. Our tanks were loaded into the hold. I went on deck and watched the searchlights on the coast. I wondered if I would ever see my family or girlfriend again. The sea was rough. I was no sailor. The only boat I had ever been on was a rowing boat around the common with my girlfriend.

'At last the ship dropped anchor about two miles off the beach. All hell was let loose ahead of us. Heavy gunfire could be heard, explosions. Fires were burning on land and on the sea. The sea was too deep to unload the tanks. We were lucky we didn't get blown out of the water as some German shells came close to us. At last the captain managed to get his ship nearer to the shore. It was getting light. I looked over the side of the ship. It was a sight I shall never forget. Dead British soldiers floating in the water. Some with no arms or legs. At times the sea looked red with their blood. Vehicles with their cabs just showing above the water; wrecked landing craft, some still on fire. If my man said he had not been frightened then I would call him a liar. We managed to get our tank ashore under heavy fire from German artillery and machine guns and we made our way to the sand dunes. Dead soldiers everywhere.

'We kept on going. If we had stopped we would have been a sitting target, but we had a good driver. We had to use our guns to fire at any opposition we came up against. Eventually we drove down a country lane not knowing what was round the next corner and stopped in an orchard under heavy mortar fire. It was hot and dusty. The smell of death was everywhere. Dead British and German soldiers. Lying under the trees were dead horses, cows and sheep. Corporal Vic Garner got wounded. A piece of shrapnel had taken the muscle off his right arm. I bandaged it with field dressings and he was taken back to England. He was in great pain. After heavy fighting, our tank was eventually put out of action. We had to bail out but it didn't catch fire. We had to hide in a wood for two days and defended ourselves with revolvers. When our new tank arrived we had some hard driving to do to catch up with the rest of our troop, meeting pockets of enemy resistance on the way.

'Sitting in a tank for two or three hours, looking through a small periscope with no body armour or tin hats, knowing that at any time a shell could blow you to kingdom come - not a comfortable position.

'We were a lucky crew. When we were waiting for supplies, we saw a group of Frenchmen shaving the heads of young girls - this was their punishment for collaborating with German soldiers.

'The driver risked his life to bring our petrol and rations. There was still a lot of fighting. If the weather permitted we would sleep under the tank, but it was dangerous. We could be crushed.'

Bill Fisher, gunner-radio operator, 4th Tank Battalion, Grenadier Guards. *'We travelled through Belgium meeting only small pockets of resistance until we got to Holland. By Christmas we were at Helmond, where Dutch families were good to us. As we made our way to Eindhoven we ran into about 50 German infantry. A number of them didn't survive. But waiting for us around a bend was a well-camouflaged slit trench with a German Bazooka crew. They got a Canadian scout car that drove past us, but we got them. Heavy fighting continued around Nijmegen Bridge. Remains of burnt British gliders were in the fields - bodies of British soldiers still in them. There was the same smell of death in the air as there was in Normandy. Soon afterwards, I was given three days' leave. A family looked after me. I hadn't seen a real bed for more than two years. Then it was back to the war. We were issued with a small survival kit, the main thing being a cyanide tablet. It was a quicker way to die if the tank was hit and we couldn't get out. We slowly made our way into Germany. It was a long and dangerous journey with a lot of fighting on the way. We found our way to Hamburg. The destruction was terrible. Civilians were throwing flowers on the rubble. When we were about a mile from Kiel we heard that the war had ended. It was as if a cloud had been lifted from us. We were escorted to a building full of young German soldiers. They looked about 16. They were excited and some were crying. It was a sad day when we had to say goodbye to our tank, a faithful friend, out on the outskirts of Düsseldorf. We were among the lucky ones. We had survived. I got 10 days' leave and made my way back to Norwich. Painted on a wall near the railway track at Thorpe was a message. It said: 'Good old Tommy, you will want for nothing now it's all over.'*

'We reached the North Foreland Buoy, just north of Deal, at 2200. Just now the paratroops would be dropping. I wished them luck. Parachuting is rather a nerve-racking business. There must be many people in the Whitehall area walking about with their fingers crossed tonight, I thought. I was feeling detached about the whole thing now, but never let myself stray far from a piece of wood to touch. The wind freshened still more and it looked as if the landing was going to be really foul. There was an angry sky as the light faded and I was reminded of a somewhat fanciful picture of the Battle of Jutland that used to hang in my grandfather's house when I was a little boy. (At least they said it was Jutland). The sky was just like that.

'I warned everyone to sleep with a clasp knife handy, in case anything happened, so that they could cut themselves clear of the camouflage net, which was stretched over the tank deck. Then I went up on the bridge and waited for the shells to come over from Gris-Nez. None came. We were passing through the Straits at the not exactly breakneck speed of 5 knots. At 0330 I went below to turn in. The sub-lieutenant in charge of the mobile naval radar set which was with us had elected to sleep outside, in the interests of fresh air and space. Sleep came to us with difficulty. But it came. In addition to the two pongoes and me, there was also the flotilla engineer officer, a pleasant Canadian with a snore like the open diapason of an organ.

'At 0500 the sub came into the wardroom dripping wet from the rain. We cursed him sleepily as he fitted himself into the group on the wardroom floor like the last piece of a jigsaw puzzle. For some reason we all awoke exactly at 0725 and looked at one another.

'Did someone talk about an invasion taking place this morning?' asked one.

'Don't natter,' we answered.

'It was hard to realise that this was *Der Tag*.

'The wind was freshening and the old cow was waddling and ducking more and more disagreeably. So much water was coming over the bows that we couldn't get the hydro-cooker alight. The sub and I dived down into the starboard locker for some tins of self-heating cocoa to warm the shivering men. They were all pretty wet. So were we by the time we had finished.

'After breakfast we took turns standing by the gun pits as extra lookouts or sat in the wardroom reading. There was an air of complete unreality about the whole business and the bright sun and the cold wind and spray made me feel brittle for some reason. I finished reading *Humphrey Clinker*, which was perfect escapist literature and opened Triple Fugue, which was not. As we passed Beachy Head I began to wonder if my stomach wasn't full of butterflies. Up forward, a lot of the troops were being or had been seasick, some, I found, with a whole-hearted abandon not entirely admirable. I must try not to be sick in front of the pongos, I thought and climbed up to the bridge to talk to the 1st lieutenant. There were miles of LCT ahead and astern of us and the large LST at the head of our convoy looked like Roman triremes in the distance.

'At 1300 we disobeyed all rules and regulations and switched on the BBC, rather in the manner of one pinching oneself to make sure he is awake. Yes, there it was, sure enough. The airborne had landed and the first flight was doing well on the beaches. Our turn soon. Just before 1400 we turned south and were on the last leg of our journey. We were due to land in about five hours. 'I shall be sorry to leave the LCT', I thought; though she's so uncomfortable and dirty. If anyone had told me three days before I was going to be sorry to leave the old bitch I'd have laughed.

'We passed numbers of homeward-bound landing craft, all blackened from firing their rockets and scores of other craft. Large troop transports went proudly past, but we saw that only about half their LCA were still aboard. The remainder had been left on the beaches. A flotilla of fleet minesweepers passed three miles to starboard. Five miles to starboard something went up with a flash and left a pall of smoke. A sweeper detached herself from the flotilla and went to the rescue. We passed through several patches of oil where some poor wretches had bought it earlier on. A monitor [HMS *Roberts*] nosed past. There was a smug look about her, such as you'd expect to see on the face of a cat after a successful raid on the larder.

'Darkness came and we reduced speed. The wind freshened still more. We were three hours late already and still ten miles from the coast. The camouflage net was rolled back and the ramps were ready to lower. We began to see gun flashes ahead. I asked the skipper what he had been warned to expect in the way of opposition when we landed. He told me that several batteries would probably still be firing, mostly at random, as they were not among the First objectives.

'We crept slowly up to about a mile and a half from the beach. A big fire was burning just ahead. There was an air raid in progress over the beaches and strings of orange-red tracer climbed and wriggled slowly through the sky like chains of bright caterpillars. A deep rumble forced itself through the purr of our engines. Then German aircraft began to throb over us. There was a flash and a thud as a ship received a direct hit about a mile away. We all put our tin hats on and I sent the troops below for cover. A German aircraft flew down our column and all the Oerlikons in the Force stammered noisily into action. It was a relief almost, after so much inaction. Every now and then there would be bursts of tracer and flashes from the bigger guns of the now invisible myriads of ships lying off shore.

'A signal came from our escort, delaying our beaching until first light. Weather unsuitable, said the skipper. We dropped our hook. It was cold, so I gave the chaps a tot of rum each and talked to them about nothing in particular. We were all pretty excited but very annoyed it not landing exactly on D-day. Still, the intention had been good.

'At four the first light came timidly from the east. It was bitterly cold. There was a spasmodic air attack and I saw a Focke-Wulf dive out of the clouds over the column a couple of cables' length to starboard. Four bombs fell, each between a pair of the vessels for which they were intended. It was like a draughts-player going one-two-three-four across the board.

'The first Spitfires arrived at 0430 and an hour later we got the signal from the shore: Prepare to land. Two cruisers sat like broody hens surrounded by drifters and landing craft. As we passed their guns spoke from time to time. I hate the noise of a cruiser's guns. Widgeon and teal flew low over the water, looking like black tracer. Every now and then there was a big flash and clouds of smoke and a noise as some part of the beach was cleared of mines by sappers. We elbowed our way past many other craft. As one looked round there were so many thousands of ships that it was impossible to see the horizon and the eye became, so to speak, blasé. It was almost unimaginable, but it was true.

'It was an absolute skipper's nightmare; craft going ashore, craft leaving, barges, DUKWS, rhino ferries, LCT, all moving like slow and independent-minded insects over the surface of a huge pool.

'There was the coast; its shape and contours began to become recognisable. It was exactly as it had appeared in the low-level oblique photographs. Over to port was La Rivière, on the port bow was Mont Fleury, at the top of a rise. To starboard was Le Hamel. There only seemed to be about a couple of square inches of space to manoeuvre in and minor collisions happened from time to time. A LCT let down her ramps too soon and a 3-ton lorry slid gently and irrevocably into ten feet of water.

'It was possible to see the houses on the front in more detail. They looked a little knocked about. The emptiness in their windows was the emptiness in the eyes of a blind beggar.

'I took breakfast; dry biscuits and self-heated cocoa. There was no opportunity for further cooking.

'We could see tanks climbing up a little hill to their transit area, just short of the top. There were a number of LCA and LCT lying near the beach, some with their sides torn out, some on the bottom. One petrol barge was being unloaded with ill-concealed haste.

'It was 0830. My mother would be having breakfast. But somehow to think of normal things was just not on. It was hard to believe that one had ever come down to bacon and eggs and coffee and opened the Times and leaned it against the coffee pot. The 1st lieutenant handed us some packets of cigarettes each in an almost apologetic way. He wouldn't let us pay. I asked him to say good-bye to the skipper for us. We jumped into our vehicles. The ramps started to lower themselves. We ground on to the coast of France. We drove quietly ashore. That was all. There was no shelling, no excitement. It seemed very much of an anti-climax.

J. A. C. Hugill, aboard LCT 7073, one of 70-odd petrol-driven boats ordered hurriedly in November 1943. Most LCT were diesel-driven. HMS *Roberts* (15 in gun), whose lack of speed precluded her from sailing from the Clyde with other units of Force 'D', left at 1730 on 5 June, arriving Eastern task Force Area at 0525 on 6 June and expended 69 rounds of main ammunition by 1600.

'It wasn't until we got closer to 'Sword' beach and saw dozens of khaki-clad bodies that I realised the real danger. There was debris everywhere. Broken-down jeeps. Tanks. Absolute chaos. My job was to fill up the food dump on the beach. There were also dumps for petrol and ammunition. A bomb landed on one of the petrol dumps, sending a ball of fire thousands of feet into the air, setting alight all the ammunition. I was blown over, but escaped unhurt except for some bruising and some singed hair. What a spectacular firework display! For a while it looked as if we would have to evacuate the beach but one of the officers recruited a gang who made a corridor through the fire…I wouldn't have missed it for the world.'

Lieutenant John Avis, 27.

Order Of Battle 'Sword' Beach
3rd British Division
Major-General Thomas Rennie

8th Infantry Brigade
1st Battalion The Suffolk Regiment
2nd Battalion The East Yorkshire Regiment
1st Battalion The South Lancashire Regiment

9th Infantry Brigade
2nd Battalion The Lincolnshire Regiment
1st Battalion The King's Own Scottish Borderers
2nd Battalion The Royal Ulster Rifles

185th Infantry Brigade
2nd Battalion The Royal Warwickshire Regiment
1st Battalion The Royal Norfolk Regiment
2nd Battalion The King's Shropshire Light Infantry

Divisional Troops
HQ 3rd Division
7th, 33rd and 76th Field Regiments, Royal Artillery
20th Anti-Tank Regiment, Royal Artillery
246th Field Company, Royal Engineers
2nd Battalion The Middlesex Regiment (MG)

Units under command for assault phase
27th Armoured Brigade
13th/18th Royal Hussars
The Staffordshire Yeomanry
The East Riding Yeomanry
1st (Special Service) Brigade
3, 4 and 6 Commandos
45 (RM) Commando
2 Troops 10 (IA) Commando (French)

Elements of 79 Armoured Division
22nd Dragoons
5th Assault Regiment, Royal Engineers
218 Battery and HQ 73
Light Anti-Aircraft Regiment, Royal Artillery
1 Troop 318 Battery (of 92 Light Anti-Aircraft Regiment, Royal Artillery)
263 Field Company, Royal Engineers
629 Field Squadron, Royal Engineers
41 (RM) Commando (from 4 Special Service Brigade)*
3 Troops 5 Independent Armoured Support
Battery SP, Royal Marines

Beach Groups
5th Battalion The King's Regiment
1st Buckinghamshire Battalion

Units of 51st Highland Division which landed on D-Day and came under command of 3rd British Infantry Division
5th Battalion The Black Watch
1st and 5/7th Battalions, The Gordon Highlanders

Plus elements of:
Royal Corps of Signals
Royal Army Service Corps
Royal Army Medical Corps
Royal Army Ordnance Corps
Corps of Royal Electrical and Mechanical Engineers
Corps of Military Police
Pioneer Corps

* 41 RM Commando was an element of 4 Special Service Brigade, which was put under command of 3 British Division on landing on wrong beach.

'Two of my platoon were shot down by snipers. When the Germans came in, 'kamerading' my finger itched to pull the trigger, but it would have been too much like murder. I felt I had to work off my temper somehow, though, so I told them I was going to murder them just as my friends had been. To lend some truth to my story, I had them dig a hole and they broke down. They didn't know they were digging temporary graves for British and German dead.'

Sergeant William McPherson, a veteran of the North African campaign fighting with the 51st Highland Division. A month later he was shot dead while leading a patrol of the Gordon Highlanders - by a sniper.

'At 06.55 we opened fire at 11,000 yards, the rounds falling between the beach and 400 hundred yards inland. The rate of fire was three rounds a minute for each of the Division's 72 guns, so that about 4 tons of HE were arriving every minute on our immediate front. At the same time HE-filled rockets were being directed on to the same area from LCTs specially adapted to take them. They made a fearsome sight as they launched their missiles simultaneously.

'Amidst the hullabaloo a rending crash on our left flank where there was another LCT signalled the first return of shot from the shore. More enemy fire descended on the forward troops as they neared the beaches. There was a fierce satisfaction in calling out the fire orders and when we reached the end of the run-in, at H -5 and added 400 yards to the range, before emptying the guns, more than one additional round was shot off for luck. We turned away, having observed the shore, which looked for all the world like an English seaside and got ready to land.

Second Lieutenant Sidney Rosenbaum, troop officer, 33rd Field Regiment of self-propelled (SP) artillery equipped with American 105mm howitzers in tanks nicknamed 'Priests' from which the turret had been removed.

'Day after day, night after night, we'd rehearse our role for D-Day. On moonlit nights when every man and every vehicle was silhouetted against the backdrop of the silvered sky. On Stygian nights of impenetrable darkness, when a vehicle three paces in front suddenly disappeared at five paces. Rehearsals were practised under each and every condition, sometimes in silence, when the only sound was the click of a bolt as a live round was rammed home. Yes, absolute realism was essential. Month after month we practised to the state of exhaustion so that every detail, every movement, every tactic could be done automatically, without thinking, in our sleep; in fact, many rehearsals were done in our sleep, when exhaustion overwhelmed us. We were all impatient for the word GO. We'd trained to the peak of perfection - we were ready. When we left, as it happened, we passed by my wife's house, en route for embarkation. I kept my eyes front as we passed: I couldn't trust myself to look.

'The night was pitch-black; rain slanted down, hissing into turbulent, foam-flecked sea. The Landing Craft Transport, with our 3 Division badge painted on its funnel, wallowed its way through the sea. After several false alarms, we were on our way to the Normandy beaches. There was not a glimmer of light anywhere. It was impossible to see where the lowering sky ended and the sea began. Men whispered together - one wondered why, out here in the middle of the Channel? Perhaps because of the secrecy of the whole invasion we were reluctant to disclose our whereabouts by 'idle talk'. No smoking was a strict order to be obeyed, but it made a fag all the more desirable. We were in the last boat but one in our echelon, on the extreme left flank of the convoy, destined for

'Sword'-'Queen-Red' beach, the furthest spot on the left of the whole invasion force. The skipper's aim was to put us down alongside the Orne Canal east of Ouistreham. The boat behind us was the rescue launch; in front of us was an LCT loaded with lorries carrying fuel oil and all the other paraphernalia of modern warfare. We were loaded with composite loads of ammunition for direct supply to forward troops on D-night. It was comforting to know the rescue launch was so-close in spite of the explicit order we were given before sailing from Portsmouth: 'On no account will any craft stop to pick up survivors.'

'We ploughed our way through the night. Suddenly, without warning, all hell was let loose! The sound was as if some giant's hand had torn a large canvas sheet asunder, to be followed by a blinding flash of orange and white light as the LCT in front of us seemed to be lifted out of the water, throwing the vehicles and other equipment like children's toys into the air, before they cascaded down into the water.

'From a pitch black night it had suddenly turned into an aurora borealis of light: a rich orange colour with the stark silhouettes of human Catherine Wheels hurled into the sky against the tremulous motion of the streams of light. The horrendous screams, torn from shattered bodies, penetrated our eardrums, etching seared scars in our minds to return in the silent nights of future years. I shall never forget. Black evil-smelling diesel oil poured out over the sea - men frantically calling out for help from this turgid mass through which we passed. 'Just as our paralysed minds and bodies were recovering from the shock of the explosion, another cataclysmic explosive detonation came from our rear. The rescue launch disappeared skywards to rain down as a million disembowelled parts a few seconds later. Were we next? Against orders, our skipper hove-to. A boat was lowered. It rescued as many survivors as possible before the boat was ordered to return. These battered, bemused, shattered men, still covered in the thick clinging oil, which had so polluted the area with its stench that men on our boat were vomiting over the side. The poor devils, snatched from the sea, had swallowed this obscene oily liquid; it was in their lungs, their stomachs. Violent retches wracked their bodies as they made vain attempts to free themselves of this nauseous, loathsome liquid. They were covered in blankets and made as comfortable as possible. We gave them what succour we could - there was so little we could do.

'The skipper gave the order to 'GO AHEAD'. I looked over the side. We were alone, so alone. I knew how the Ancient Mariner must have felt. From the darkness ahead, miles ahead or so it seemed, appeared flashes, rather like sheet lightning on a midsummer's night. But we were alone, nakedly alone. Out of the dim shadows a ghost-like shape appeared: featureless, unidentifiable. Menacingly it approached. Were we to be the next casualties?

'The memory of the two craft so recently destroyed was too vivid in our memories not to cause us to catch our breath. A shiver ran through our bodies as the prow of the boat sliced through the water towards us. Suddenly the grey shape veered to our rear and a calm voice came over the Tannoy. 'I say, you're way behind the convoy ... press on. We'll stay with you until you catch up.'

'So it did. The Royal; Navy destroyer escorted us like a sheepdog shepherding a stray back into the fold. Our landing on D-Day seemed uneventful by comparison, or so we thought!'

Lieutenant Colonel 'Tiger' Tim East (27), Royal Army Service Corps. A farmer's son, born in the Cotswolds, he went to London University before joining the army as a private when war was declared. He was later Mentioned in Despatches for distinguished service.

'After an almost interminable sea journey in a rolling, lurching LCT dawn revealed the immensity of the operation we had embarked upon. There were ships everywhere. Closer to the coast of France, a smoke screen was laid. An escorting destroyer cut in two by torpedo attack, floated semi-submerged, forming a V with its bows and stern. This was H-Hour. The noise increased as the beach got closer, quite deafening now. To starboard a LCT (Landing Craft Rocket) fired a rocket salvo, which upon landing in unison shook every bone. My diaphragm oscillated in sympathy with shock waves, visible as they pulsed upwards through smoke and clouds. We started the 350 bhp engines of our Churchills, which contributed to the general noise. Lion-sur-Mer was in sight, the tide was out, revealing a beach covered with large tripod obstacles with mines attached. Seconds went by like hours, waiting to go down that ramp, or to eternity, we were carrying a large amount of HE. The tank preceding us was on the sea bed in 6 feet of water, when the rear louvre extension fell off, blocking our exit. Something, probably a mortar bomb, hit the 20 feet bridge we had attached to the front. We went down into the sea, missing the other tank as we pulled away, by now half full of water. My visor revealed green sea; at last we were on solid ground. Driver left, halt, reverse right. We went every way but sideways. When at last we emerged, a flail tank was leading us up the beach. The Atlantic Wall was not completed here rendering our bridge redundant.

'Once upon the promenade we drove through the chaos of what was once a town and dropped the bridge. A young woman wearing a Red Cross armband rode along the road on a bicycle towards the town undeterred by sporadic machine gun fire. When night came, the Luftwaffe dropped anti-personnel bombs to let us know that the war was not over yet. There was a lot more and worse to come.'

K. D. Budgen, 5th Assault Regiment, 1st Assault Brigade Royal Engineers, 79th Armoured Division.

'We were the first wave in on D-Day and the first to land on the Beach. Our Churchill Tanks were fitted with special mortars called Petards whose purpose was the destruction of the Pill Boxes and concrete defences. We had a very rough crossing and most of us were seasick. As we neared the French coast we encountered incoming fire and two of the escort ships were sunk. The LCRs (Landing Craft Rockets) opened fire and as we were the next to run in to the beach all the crew mounted the tanks through the turret, the front hatches being sealed so that the tanks could operate if needs be in up to six feet of water. The drivers mounted in first to start the engines. We beached safely. The ramp was lowered and the first two Sherman 'Crabs' fitted with flails went down the ramp. Both were knocked out immediately and burst into flames - it was not a very good sight-seeing your mates trying to bail out of their tanks on fire. I was Troop Officer's driver and drove the third tank down the ramp. There were mines everywhere on cross pieces about 2 feet off the ground. I picked my way through the mines the best I could. Just before I reached the edge of the beach we hit a mine, which blew a bogey off, but the track held. One of the crew put the windsock up. Our Troop Officer and Troop Sergeant had both been killed and we had lost over half the squadron.

'I drove behind a sand dune where we unsealed some of the hatches. By now the commandos were with us. The squadron leader who had lost his tank came up and took over command of our tank and directed us along a road where we came under small arms fire, which we returned until we came to a bridge over a canal. This was defended by a Pill Box on the other side. As our Petard Mortar had only a short range the Squadron Leader decided to cross the bridge to the other side to deal with it. On commencing to cross, the enemy blew the bridge, the section we were on held and I was able to reverse off, the commandos then took over.

'I was then directed into an open space where we were clear of the houses and where the Squadron Leader left us. The engine was running hot so I got out and commenced to unseal the hatches. I had just started when I heard an aircraft. I thought it was one of ours until I saw it release a bomb, which came straight at the tank. I promptly lay down on the engine hatches and prayed. All my strength seemed to ebb away and I felt terrible, however, the bomb just cleared the tank and burst in front of it. I lay there for some time until I had regained my strength and then got smartly into the driver's seat and closed the hatches.

'We stayed there all night, amidst bombs, shells, small arms fire and burning houses. We pulled back next day to regroup and maintain our vehicles.'

21-year old Private Edward 'Teddy' W. D. Beeton, 79th Assault Squadron, 1st Assault Brigade, Royal Engineers, Churchill Tank AVRE driver.

'On 2 June we were taken to Southampton, where we loaded our tanks onto landing craft. Other Divisions were loaded onto landing ships; the difference being landing craft are smaller and faster and lower in the water. The enemy could pick out a landing ship but not a tank landing craft until it had dropped its tanks up his nose so to speak. All along the French coast the Germans had used forced labour to build what they called Fortress Europe. Full massive Pill Boxes with dirty great guns pointing at us. The three divisions on the British sector all had special assault teams provided by 79th Armoured. Then came the glorious 6th of June. We hit the beach at La Brêche with my old friends from 4 Commando. We were to race as fast as we could to relieve 6th Airborne who had been dropped by parachute and glider to take the Orne Bridges. They had held out all day and we arrived with about two tanks left, so we joined the rest without tanks. In the village, not far from us some paratroops were holed up with some wounded. My troop officer, Mr. Duff said, 'Just take six blokes down there and get those chaps out'. I only had to find four blokes as I knew Jock would come with me. So we set off amongst shot and shell with a few little shots coming our way. But we all made it into the village. The first cottage had some paratroops, gear and a dead paratroop outside so we figured that's where our blokes must be. Jock kicked open the door and a British voice said, 'We are in here, wounded'. It was slightly dark inside so then when I asked how many wounded, a good old Norfolk voice said 'Six and who the hell are you'. I told him who I was and out of the darkened room he said, 'Bloody Ginger Oliver, for fuck's sake get us out of here'. Well we did get them out. The voice from the darkness was Ronnie Gant, my old mate from childhood. Were we pleased to see each other. We shared rations and found some French wine and drank our old toast, 'sod 'em all'. We were eventually relieved. Ronnie came home with an arm wound and we went on to more glory.'

Corporal Walter William Oliver, Reconnaissance Troop, Staffordshire Yeomanry.

'It was the worst 48 hours in my life on that landing craft. Worse than swimming 2 miles off the Dunkirk beaches in 1940 aged seventeen. 'Isn't it marvellous what fear can make you do!'

Platoon Sergeant Albert Pattison, 1st Suffolks.

29-year old Sergeant William Germanes returned to England after D-Day, knocked on his front door and expected a big welcome home. Instead, his mother's first words were: 'You shouldn't be here. You're supposed to be dead!' The Red Cross had wrongly sent a message to his home in Hackney, East London, saying I had been killed in the fighting after the Normandy landings. He had wanted to join the police, but at 5 feet 5 inches was not tall enough. Instead, he was called up to the Loyal Regiment (North Lancashire).

'At Gosport on the eve of D-Day we were ushered into this room and laid out on the floor was a map of the sea, beaches, roads, fields and buildings and told this was the layout of the place where we were going. But there were no names and no other information. It could have been anywhere for all we knew. On June 5 we were loaded with kit and ammunition and ready to go, but owing to the weather the whole show was cancelled. On the 6th, very early in the morning we got the order, 'It's on'.

'We were loaded onto a LCT with 100 other troops and six big Bofors guns. The tank was last on, first off and when we hit 'Sword' Beach, ready to storm up the sand with the infantry charging behind.

'One of my men was sick going across and as soon as we landed he went berserk - screaming, 'I want to go home, I want my mum, don't send me.' His nerve had gone. I was stuck with this man and an officer came along. I said: 'This man is no good to us. He's upsetting everybody. We have got to get rid of him.' He was taken away. I don't know what happened to him. Any men who were not afraid on that day were bloody fools or liars, but there are degrees of being afraid. I saw bodies and all sorts, but I thought if it came to me, I just hoped it would be over quickly.

'We got to the shore and the officer in charge of the tank said, 'Keep inside the white tapes, it has been cleared of mines. I will take you up the beach as far as I can.'

'Overhead there was whistling and gushing as our naval guns fired over us, sniping from the Germans, mortar fire ... planes going over, the noise was incredible. Going up the beach I saw a chap wounded severely in the legs. He was dragging himself along, crawling up the beach. Normally, we would stop to help him, but we were told he had to make his own way by the beach masters.

'I think I was lucky. I'm such a short person - perhaps all the bullets went over my head.'

'I saw in the first breaking light of dawn the outline of our escort destroyer close on our starboard side. My sickness and misery was suddenly added to by shock and dismay because of an explosion that lifted the destroyer out of the water amidships. I watched disbelieving as her middle went down, leaving her two ends upturned and floating. I rubbed my eyes as if it was an illusion or hallucination caused by sea sickness. The reality became all too evident when I saw over the side pieces of wreckage floating, some with figures clinging to it. Our ship appeared to me to sail over the drifting wreckage. I was horrified to see some of the wreckage and figures disappearing directly under our ship; and furious that nothing was being done to save the poor devils in the sea. They were obviously doomed to die.'

'We could see that we were in for a pretty hot reception, for already exploding spouts of water were appearing all around us. We received one hit on the stern of the craft which wounded a few of the troops before we got ashore. Perhaps it was that first hit that altered the Royal Navy craft commander's promise to land us in shallow water. When I dropped off the ramp, my Bren gun took me down like a stone, leaving me with several foot of water above my head. Only by underwater walking towards shore did I save myself from a watery end. I could see that some people were either drowning or drowned already. Some I could see screaming and waving their arms while going backwards and seawards. Many were wounded in the water and were unable to move in the advancing tide.

'I remember my first moments of dragging myself out of the sea holding on to my Bren gun, magazine boxes and other kit. I looked around to see death and destruction all around me. An absolute inferno: burning tanks, broken-down vehicles and very many dead and wounded lying about in a narrow strip between the sea and the barbed wire at the back of the beach. I sought cover behind an AVRE which had just been hit. I moved away quickly enough when I realised it was blazing away and that with its Petard explosive charges it could blow up at any second. I succeeded in making for the bank of the dunes at the high-tide mark. I hoped that somehow I could get my Bren gun into position to fire over and beyond the dunes in the enemy direction, wherever he might be.

'I remember - damned silly considering the circumstances - my annoyance and irritation at the sea lice or beach bugs that were crawling all over me as I itched to get my Bren gun alive and kicking to some good purpose. Our attacking position was not easy because of the mortars, shells and bullets that were hammering down on to a small and concentrated beach. I saw shells or mortars making direct hits on soldiers moving close to me. They literally disappeared in a flash.

'Until that time I had never seen a live or dead German soldier in my life. Here suddenly there were two of them almost jumping over me as I crouched low behind the sandbank at the high-water mark. One of the Germans appeared to throw a hand grenade as he came over the top to land on the beach, although it was difficult to know one explosion from the many others. A British

soldier managed to kick the German's behind to send him sprawling and then blast away with his Sten gun. I moved to a position to be able to view the ground over and beyond the sandbank. The area all around seemed to be covered by creeping barrages of small fire, raging and rolling over the ground, threatening to overwhelm us all.

'As night fell I found myself on guard duty on the far side of Pegasus Bridge. I settled in to my lonely foxhole position. It was getting to be late evening, with light failing fast and I cannot say that at that moment I was looking forward to passing my first night on foreign and hostile soil. I was not particularly charmed by the three corpses I found close to me. I could almost reach out and touch the most gruesome of the three, who was a German who had his brains blown out through a great jagged hole in his steel helmet. There were two Germans and one of our airborne. I pondered long and hard about the position of one of the corpses: it seemed almost impossible, the way it was laying on the steep river bank without rolling down. I concluded it could only be a very dead body indeed - rigid muscles, rigor mortis - that could cling on in such a way. I was, in truth, cold, frightened, confused, terribly tired and hungry: not a very brave young soldier. Before being swallowed up by the night I reflected on the long, long day and consoled myself with the thought that if D-Day plus one was perhaps just a tenth as bad, I should have only have to survive a mere ten possibilities of getting killed.'

Sapper Alfred Lane, an assault engineer in 263 Field Company, Royal Engineers.

The 'Jocks' and the Green Berets Forge Inland

'When a signal came saying we only had 2½ miles to go our troops put their packs on and got under cover. My crew also got down and I closed the armour plate covers of my cockpit and opened the slots through which I could see all around me. You could hear bursts of machine-gun fire from the shore and the wicked snarl of bullets ricocheting in the sea and over our boats. Some were uncomfortably close. Occasionally a column of water would shoot up near us and then we would hear the sound of the gun that had fired the shell. Then Jerry started lobbing over mortar shells and putting them very close indeed-None of the chaps were laughing and joking then. Suddenly we were up to the outer defences. Engines flat out. The obstacles were built of heavy timber forming tripods, on top of which were Teller mines. It would have been just too bad if we had touched one of these. I felt the craft sticking on underwater obstacles and in a moment we were up against the inner beach defences and could go no further. I gave the order to 'down ramp', our armoured doors were opened and our troops began to disembark. Mortar shells were bursting on the beach, which they had to cross and among our craft as Jerry had now got our range. On the sand, just clear of the sea, were the bodies of soldiers who had landed a few minutes before. Many others were in the sea itself; slowly moving back and forth as the waves rushed in and retreated. I watched our commandos as they slowly walked through the surf and up the beach. Some didn't reach us. They would fall quietly on their faces and lie there in the water. I saw one spin about suddenly and sit down, his face covered in blood. Some chaps would throw away their packs to drag their fallen comrades ashore. 'I didn't feel scared anymore - just numb as I wondered how much longer it would be before I got my 'packet'. It's a horrible feeling, the realisation that death is about to strike you.'

Newfoundland-born landing craft coxswain Bill Mills from LSI(S) *Prinses Astrid,* **a converted Belgian cross-Channel passenger vessel with a capacity for 507 troops and eight landing craft, which arrived off 'Sword' Beach at 0542 on 6 June with The Highland Light Infantry on board.**

'Will I need my water wings sergeant?'

'Tell the driver to wait, my good man. I won't be a minute.'

'Wait for you? How can you ask such a thing?... If there's any chance of our Astrid being raped, we'll be off.'

'At 0540 we anchored at the lowering position and at 0545 manned the craft. This proceeded in a most orderly manner, long practice having made each man familiar with his position in the different landing craft. As these were lowered at 0605, we of the ship's company silently sent them our good wishes for it will be remembered that these specially trained commandos had been with us over a period of many months and had grown to become part of the ship's company. There was a heavy sea running at the time and so it was with a sigh of relief that the craft were seen safely away without mishap, each soldier wearing full kit and extra ammunition.

'Opposite the place where our craft landed was an enemy stronghold and the beach was swept from end to end by machine gun and mortar fire. Many men never reached the beach and one craft had a mortar bomb fall in the centre of it while packed with troops, killing two and wounding others. Although one air raid warning was sounded during the time the ship was anchored off the beaches, no enemy aircraft could have survived in a sky so dominated by our own aircraft. Five of our landing craft returned by 1030 and we were genuinely pleased to see them: one had struck a submerged obstruction and returned without any steering gear. The sixth craft had been lost by enemy action…'

Extract from the LSI(H) *Maid of Orleans* **ship's log. A converted Southern railway cross-Channel passenger vessel with a capacity for 448 troops and six landing craft arrived off 'Sword' Beach two minutes earlier, at 0540 with 4 Commando on board.**

'The Highland Light Infantry and 4 Commando were carried across the English Channel on board *The Princess Astrid* and *Maid of Orleans.* Assault landing craft took No. 4 Commando ashore. My craft was hit and reared up almost vertically and I was jammed between my seat and the boat under a pile of men. The ramp was kicked open and the first commando out was practically ripped in half by a burst of machine-gun fire. Still trapped, I feared I would drown as the craft began to fall back and sink. A comrade, seeing my plight, dashed back and freed me. I jumped into the sea, now neck-deep. As I waded ashore, I saw men drowning in shallow water. Wounded, their 90lb ruck-sacks weighed them down.

'A Company of East Yorks had been landed earlier to clear the beach and lay white tape to mark a clear passage for us. They had not got ten yards before many had been cut down and they were ordered to dig in. It was an act of madness that only added to the carnage. I stepped over one wounded soldier whose stomach had been ripped open. I couldn't stop and help.

'I ended up in a building giving covering fire to troops attacking a German gun battery. I foolishly leant out of the window to get a better aim and was seen by a sniper who fired at me. As I ducked back inside to reload, a round whistled by me and hit the man behind me in the stomach. We carried him back on a door, but had to duck in a doorway when a German fighter flew over us with machine guns blazing. We left the wounded man there and marked his position with a small yellow pennant so he could be collected later.

'As we came back we found 30 East Yorks lying behind a hedgerow. All were dead, save one who was screaming for a padre. An oil bomb had dropped in the middle of them. It exploded burning oil and left a great black patch.'

20-year-old commando Private Bill Bidmead, A Troop, 4 Commando, part of Brigadier Lord Lovat's 1st Special Service Brigade.

'I was still at the River Orne when an ominous rumbling of tanks was heard at the T-junction near Pegasus Bridge and Major Howard sent for our platoon. We marched in regimental order to the bridge where I was given a PIAT - a tank-busting gun fired from the shoulder - and told to go up to the junction. I passed the Gondrée cafe crawled along a hedge on my stomach to get within 30 yards of the junction. My hands were shaking so much I could barely control them. It was 1.45 and I could hear two tanks moving about. Their commanders got out and exchanged words and then got back inside. I knew that I would have to act immediately.

'The lads behind me were only lightly armed with Bren guns, rifles and grenades. They wouldn't stand a chance if I missed and the whole operation would be over. I was so nervous I was talking to myself: 'This is it! You mustn't miss.' The first tank, a Mark IV, had begun moving slowly down the road. I pulled the trigger on the PIAT. It was a direct hit. Machine-gun clips inside the tank set off grenades which set off shells. There was the most enormous explosion, with bits and pieces flying everywhere and lighting up the darkness. To my delight, the other tank fled. We now had a breathing space and I suggested to Lieutenant Fox that we went along the canal banks to see if we could find any Germans. Sure enough, we discovered a bunker. We were amazed to see that five Germans were still asleep inside, oblivious to all the noise. Fox went to rouse the first one while I covered him with my Sten gun. He shook him and declared: 'You are a prisoner.' But the German seemed to think it was just one of his mates having a joke and turned around and went back to sleep. I started laughing and Fox said: 'Blow this for a lark! You take over.' I suppose I could have shot them all, but I don't believe in murdering people in cold blood so I put my Sten gun on to automatic and fired it along the bottom of the bunks. They moved like greyhounds!

'Meanwhile, some of the other lads had knocked on the door of George Gondrée's cafe. It became the first house in France to be liberated. He led them to the cellar where his wife Theresa and their children were sheltering and she hugged and kissed everyone so much her face became black with camouflage paint. George dug up 98 bottles of champagne he had buried in 1940, but unfortunately I missed out on the celebration! I had been with the other troops taking up defensive positions in a nearby field. By about 2pm I was wondering when I would see England again, when suddenly I heard the sound of bagpipes.

'You must be mad! Bagpipes in the middle of Normandy!' scoffed Lieutenant Fox.

'Out of the trees stepped commando piper Bill Millin followed by Lord Lovat, a tall man wearing a green beret and a white sweater and carrying a walking stick. He made his way onto Pegasus Bridge and shook hands with Major Howard with the words: 'John, history is being made today.' Meanwhile, we threw our rifles in the air and embraced the 20 or 30 commandos who had come through with him because we were so glad, to see them.

'In the early evening we sat in the field and saw the men from the 6th Airborne gliders being towed in by Halifax bombers and parachutists making their way down. Soon there were so many of them you could not see a bit of the sky. It was such a lovely sight that I broke down in tears. So did a lot of the others. It was a joy to behold but we had paid the price. Of the 181 men only 76 were without wounds.'

Sergeant Charles 'Wagger' Thornton, Ox and Bucks Light Infantry.

'That afternoon 4 Commando linked up with the Oxfordshire and Buckinghamshire Light Infantry glider force that had seized Pegasus Bridge. It was still under fire and the commandos ran across in twos and threes. One officer was killed crossing the bridge. A soldier accompanying him was deeply upset by his loss and came across three German prisoners sitting beside the bridge. 'One cried out for water. The soldier said, 'I'll give you water' and shot them. Nothing was said at the time, but the soldier was later killed himself. Funny thing; you usually found that if people went out of their way to kill someone, they generally ended up dead themselves.'

'I got my head down, but someone tapped on my helmet and whispered, 'Germans!' Moving forward out of a wood were dozens of coal-scuttle helmeted soldiers. Alongside me a Welsh Guardsman, Taff Hughes, picked up his Vickers K gun and opened fire. A stick grenade exploded in front of my trench. Shrapnel hit my lip and my mouth was smothered in blood. The force of the explosion flung me to the bottom of the trench and I heard someone say, 'Young Bid's had it'.

'The Germans made one last attack, but we cut them to pieces. We killed ten of them to one of us. A patrol went out and counted 250 German dead. Later, an 80-strong detachment of bicycle-mounted German reinforcements halted opposite our position. They were exhausted, having cycled all the way from Paris. As they dismounted and threw their kit down, we opened fire. It took 30 minutes to kill them all.'

Private Bill Bidmead, 'A' Troop, 4 Commando, who were shelled and mortared continuously for five days. 4 Commando remained in the front line for 83 days. Of its original 700-strong complement, only 70 remained unwounded.

'There were bodies - dead bodies, living bodies. All the blood in the water made it look as though men were drowning in their own blood. That's how it looked.

'The planners might have gone through a lot of campaigns at a very high level but nobody can know what it's like to be on a beach where you can do nothing. Where you're under severe fire and you've got to get off. And it's only a person who's been through it a number of times who can know - you stay and die or you get off and live. People doing it for the first time - no matter how many times you tell them - they don't realise it. And people didn't get off the beach. They were so transfixed with fright, they couldn't get off. I was transfixed with fright but I had the certain knowledge that either you stopped and died or you got up and got away. So I took the coward's view and got out of the bloody place.

'All the way along, you'd have snipers firing at you and by the time you heard the crack, it was too late. You couldn't really take evasive action from snipers other than to zigzag or to go behind a car or lamppost. And you couldn't stop. There was no point in stopping. You had to go on. The mortar-bombs were very frightening. You'd hear one whistle as it approached and then just before the loudest pitch as it reached you, you'd have to throw yourself on the ground. If you didn't get down quick enough, the shrapnel could hit you.'

Sergeant William Spearman, 4 Commando.

'In my rucksack at the bottom I had four two-inch mortar bombs, explosive, two smoke bombs and I carried six Mills bombs. I had, I think it was, near enough two hundred rounds for the Tommy gun and they would also fit the American automatic that I had. I had two smoke bombs; they were dangerous, they'd got phosphorus in them and I was worried about getting a bullet near them. Then every man in the unit from the colonel down carried two hundred rounds of rifle ammunition in a cloth bandolier. So it was a pretty good load. I would think about 70 to 80lbs in the rucksack. Then everybody carried a few personal bits and pieces, which helped to put the weight up again. There were no spare tunics or trousers, obviously. Everybody's boots were checked. You had to have thirteen studs in each boot with a steel toe piece and a steel heel.

'Once we left the shore and we were on our way, four of us played cards for hours in our LCT. We nearly wore the cards out. Our job was to get to the Orne bridges as quickly as we could, to relieve the paratroopers who were holding the bridge. When we got to the bridges, there were a lot of dead Germans around and some of our paratrooper fellows. Then I suppose the brigadier had a meeting with somebody and we set off over the bridge. There were snipers about and they were firing at us now and again and a fellow got hit - but the brigadier - Lord Lovat - he must have thought he was on his estate. He marched along with a bloody bagpiper playing alongside him. We went over the bridge and then the problems really started. We started to lose a lot of men, so we moved to a higher piece of ground and dug in. I didn't know what the hell was going on, other than I was digging a hole as fast as I could, because we were being mortared from a battery that had actually been taken, but our troops had moved on and the Germans had come back.'

Sergeant Henry Cosgrove, 45 (Royal Marine) Commando.

'As we progressed up the beach we saw that one of our tanks had gone over a mine and been blown onto its side. I recognised it at once as Sergeant Johnny Hardie's tank. We feared the worst. We approached it, expecting to find the five-man crew dead inside. To our amazement we discovered Johnny and his crew completely unharmed, sitting on empty ammunition cases in the lee of the tank, calmly drinking tea. They offered us some of the brew and we were about to join them when the beach marshal appeared and told us in real soldier's language what to do with our mugs of tea. When I asked Johnny why he and his men had stopped for tea in the middle of battle he shrugged, 'We're not infantry. We're not equipped to fight. What else could we do?

'Rather sensible when you think of it.'

Trooper 'Slim' Wileman, 24, 13th/18th Royal Hussars. 'Of the twenty tanks we landed, seven were still in operation by the end of the day. Eight men were dead.'

'We went to our air-raid shelter that evening and settled down. But at 1 am I awoke to a low, rumbling noise. At 5 am my brother left the shelter. Suddenly, he shrieked with excitement and we all ran upstairs. There, about a kilometre out to sea was a sight I shall never forget. The bay was black with ships - there was absolutely no sea left. Within minutes the earth began shaking with the constant hail of shells, machine-gun fire and bombs. And all the time thousands of soldiers poured out of landing craft. At 10 am three tanks rolled up outside our house and my father ran into the garden, ripped up the rose bush and gave it to the soldiers.

'I shall be grateful to the British for as long as I live.'

Prudent Boiux, 16 who lived on the seafront at Asnelles not far from Le Hamel with his fisherman father, mother and older brother. He saw the Second British Army land at 'Sword' beach. Madame d' Anselm, too had a house at Asnelles. A German gun was stationed at the bottom of the garden and the sector was manned by a unit of the 352nd Field Regiment.

'We had dug a little trench in the garden, just big enough to shelter the eight of us and a couple of others. It was not very well protected - or covered. When the bombing attacks started we were in the house, but it was so bad that we had to go into the garden and take refuge in the trench which was fortunate, because the windows and parts of the house were soon smashed. Then, somewhere between three and four o'clock, two of the children took advantage of a pause to go back to the house to fetch something. One of them seized the opportunity to climb on to the garden wall to see what was happening. There was a German gun just on the other side of the garden wall. Suddenly he shouted excitedly, 'Mummy, Mummy! Look - the sea - it's black with boats!'

Madame d'Anselm had been urged four days before to take her seven young children to a place of comparative safety by a friend who had had a 'presentiment' that invasion was imminent. Mme d'Anselm refused to leave the family home; her husband and eldest son fighting with the Maquis in the south would not expect her to desert. Her friend and children were killed as they fled inland on the night of 5 June.

'On Sunday 4th June the battalion moved by MT along the now familiar route to Newhaven, our port of embarkation. It was blowing fairly hard that day and the one fear in everyone's mind was that sailing would have to be postponed again. It had already been postponed once and further postponement would mean a delay of something like three weeks. Tides would not be right again until then and the delay would have had very serious repercussions on the troops and would have jeopardized our chances of success. The battalion was split between three LGIs (Landing Craft Infantry) and LGTs (Landing Craft Tanks). The latter carried our assault scale of vehicles, also the Adjutant and his little party. It was so worked out that in the event of any of the three LGIs being hit, the battalion could still function as a battalion on landing, command and vital staff being split between the three craft.

'On Monday morning the armada sailed. It was rough outside the shelter of the harbour and soon the troops were feeling it pretty badly. It was not until we were well at sea that the signal came over the naval wireless that the landing was 'on' and that we could now open our proper maps and for the first time know where we were going to land. And so the final briefing took place in the minute cabin of the LGI, with each member of the group every now and then rushing out, to come back not quite so green as when he left. And so darkness fell before the most historic day of our generation.

'At dawn on D-Day the battalion was almost within view of land. The array of little ships had to be seen to be believed. In the background there was the comforting sight of the destroyers and battleships. Overhead there was a never-ending stream of aircraft. I don't think anyone saw an enemy machine on D-Day. We were certainly never bothered by them and that has been the same throughout this campaign. How right Field-Marshal Montgomery was when he said, 'Win the air battle first.' Without this overwhelming air superiority we should probably still be fighting in France.

'After what seemed like an age, but was in fact two and a half hours, the signal came for us to land. Many precautions had been taken to ensure we got a dry landing: waterproof overboots and leggings had been supplied; every weapon and wireless set had a waterproof cover and even watches becoming waterlogged by a preventative designed for another purpose.

The captain of the craft had been well primed to drive hard for the shore and he was true to his word. With a thud and a shudder the LCI had done its job and the rest was up to us. All three craft had made a good landing and no one was hit; also the steepness of the shore made it possible for everyone to get a really dry landing, a thing we had never achieved on any exercise.

Many people have said the landing and forming up on D-Day were like the many exercises we had done. It was not really so. To begin there was the usual mass of material of all sorts on the beach. Then e scrum to get through the beach exit, struggling to avoid the usual bunching and finally trying to find out where you were and make sure you were heading in the right direction for the right RV. In the back of everyone's mind was the thought that the nearer to the sea one was the more likely one was to get shelled - the 'shorts' only should catch one inland. Thanks to good navigation and the excellent way in which the lie of the country had been presented on the briefing, there was not much difficulty in getting to the prearranged assembly area. After passing one or two dead Englishmen and several dead Germans and after having a few mortar bombs and a Nebelwerfer flung at one, everyone realized that this was the real thing and feeling ran accordingly.

'Everything had gone according to plan up to the assembly area: our only losses being one wireless set, which had got stuck in some boggy ground and about four of the airborne bicycles which formed part of our assault equipment. 'The plan was for our brigade to pass through the assault brigade (who were to capture and hold the main dominating feature from which the beach exits could be observed), cross an anti-tank obstacle, push on to some high ground overlooking Caen and if possible capture the town itself. An ambitious plan, but by no means an impossible one if all our intelligence was correct. The intervening country was chiefly standing crops and was good tank-going except for a few woods here and there.

'After a prolonged wait at the assembly area, the battalion eventually received orders to advance along the pre-planned route. All went well until the village of Granville was reached. Here we suffered our first casualties, as we were under direct observation from a dominating feature which was much more strongly held than had been anticipated. This feature later proved to be a very sharp thorn in the flesh and when eventually overrun it was found to be a proper 'hedgehog' with feet of concrete, mines, anti-tank guns and the rest. (It is still wired off as a place to be avoided.) This was the feature which should have been captured by the assault brigade. It is no discredit that they failed in this task and it was not until flails, AVREs and tanks could be brought up that the place eventually fell. An interesting sideline here is that the weapon which finally persuaded the defenders to surrender was the flail. On being questioned, they said they couldn't stand this mechanical spider crawling up to them and exploding the mines as it advanced; fortunately a blind spot was chosen from the devastating effect of the 88s, that ubiquitous and most effective of all German guns.

'From Granville the battalion was told to push on to the feature behind the one described above. In order to do this a wide detour was necessary and accordingly the two leading companies, 'A' (Captain A. M. Kelly) and 'B' (Major E. A. Cooper-Key) were sent off under the 2 IC. Things were going quite nicely when the enemy spotted this movement and turned two MGs on to the leading company, which was 'A'. Both companies became engaged in a fire fight which lasted for 2½ hours. The 18 sets were hit and touch with Battalion HQ was lost. Meanwhile the rest of the Battalion moved farther round the left flank and captured the feature which was to become known as Norfolk House. Finally 'A' and 'B' companies succeeded in disengaging and rejoined the Battalion. 'On our right, things had gone a little quicker and the KSLI had actually got one company up to the high ground which overlooked Caen - a remarkable feat in the light of future events. The Warwicks were just short of a village called Blainville on our left, but there were still many snipers about in this village. By this time the whole battalion had collected at Norfolk House, but it was too late to do anything more that day. And so ended D-Day - successful in that the bridgehead was formed, but the line was not as far forward as was hoped. However, our job was to defeat the enemy - the capture of ground being a secondary object for the moment...'

History of the 1st Battalion, the Royal Norfolk Regiment 1939-1945.

'After leaving our camp enclosure we boarded our ship, an armed merchant cruiser converted to a landing ship infantry. We were told the invasion date was June 5 but, owing to the atrocious weather conditions, it was delayed for 24 hours. Even then the weather didn't improve much at all, so it was to be June 6 at early light. We knew that it was France, as we had been paid out in francs (invasion money). We could only take ten shillings English currency with us, any other having had to be changed into francs. Of our beach signal section, combined operations, only myself and a sergeant were accompanying the assault troops of The Queen's Own Rifles. Another seven members of our section were to follow later. This was to be repeated on the other two sectors, plus the CO (28 in total). The sergeant and myself shared a cabin with two QOR sergeants.

'Reveille was about 3:30 am on June 6 and before breakfast we all lined up for our rum ration, after which it was absolution, followed by a short service conducted by the Canadian padre. We then boarded our LCA's (Landing Craft Assault]. Boarding the LCA's in that kind of stormy weather and the heavy swell was a very risky situation. It was a case of climbing down the scrambling net and judging when to drop into the landing craft. You can imagine the ship rolling one way and the LCA the other. If it was not timed accurately, it was possible to drop between the ship and the LCA and be crushed to death. In any case you wouldn't survive in that heavy sea, not being able to ditch your equipment (50lbs plus a 46 wireless set). Together, with troops of the Queen's Own Rifles, we were seated along the sides of the LCA under a steel overhang about 30 inches in width.

'We pulled away from the 'mother ship' and nearing the coast we heard the guns from the warships pounding away at the coast and the rocket ships lighting the sky where previously the air force had had been softening up the shore defences. By this time things were really 'hotting' up with the shells and bullets splattering all around. We were now nearing the shore, approaching the crystal defencer, concrete pyramids and angle iron set in concrete with mines fixed to them plus barbed wire and pointed metal staves capable of ripping out the bottom of landing craft. Fortunately our craft managed to squeeze between these obstacles more by luck than judgment. Others weren't so fortunate and there were many casualties. The rough seas didn't help at all. Then came the shout 'Down doors!'

'The ramps went down and we raced down the ramp quite orderly only to find ourselves up to the waist in water. On reaching 'dry' land we raced to reach the sea wall (quite high). Actually not being a good sailor and a bit queasy, I was relieved to get my feet on the ground in spite of the horrific circumstances. All hell was let loose, with heavy machine gun fire from beyond the seawall, which we climbed and crossed over and the coastal railway line with more barbed wire obstacles, plus mines.

'I count myself very lucky to have survived firstly the assault and then the rest of the war.'

Cyril Crain was a wireless operator with the UK. 19 Beach Signal Section, Combined Operations and he landed with The Queen's Own Rifles at Berniéres-sur-Mer on D-Day. He was good friends with Sergeant Freddy Harris, one of the many riflemen to die on the beach that day.

'I was stood on the steps of the boat and was telling the boys what I could see. I was bloody terrified, but the adrenaline had started to kick in and we were all ready to go. The noise was incredible. The shelling sounded like a demented woman screaming. I could see the shells like big metal canisters coming through the air towards us. One of our ramps was hit and destroyed. The fear started to kick in and from my position I could see lots of bodies floating face down in the water with their packs on their backs. Time seemed to stand still, but at the same time everything happened so quickly. It was hard to get your bearings with the noise of the shelling and the screaming. We must only have been about 20 yards from the beach houses, but it seemed like miles.'

Private David Davies, a rifleman in Number 5 section, 14 Platoon, Royal Norfolk Regiment.

'We came ashore with dry feet but just as the disembarkation started a shell blew the left hand ramp off so we all had to come down the right hand side. I had a Bren gun to carry and only got 100 yards with my bike before an officer told me to dump it.

'The noise of it all didn't worry me as I had lived through the Blitz.'

Private Fred Howell, 13 Platoon, 'C' Company, Royal Norfolk Regiment. He had joined as a boy soldier in 1942 with a group of 12 mates from Hackney who played together in their own football team. They were only 17 but when they were asked for documentation they told the Army that they had been bombed out in the Blitz and hadn't got anything. Seven of them survived the war. His closest friend, who he had known since they were three; lived next door and went to school with, was killed at Lebisey. Soon

after D-Day Fred was seriously wounded by a burst of machine gun fire. 'A bullet got me in the arm and another in the leg but I also had three bandoliers of bullets wrapped round my body and the machine gun bullets hit that and set them on fire. If not the machine gun bullets would have been in my guts and I probably would have died.' He spent 8 weeks in hospital and the next two years in India, guarding Italian prisoners.

'We had a hell of a baptism - I was detailed to go with 8 Platoon across cornfields where the Brigadier put us in front of our own tanks and we got slaughtered. We had so many wounded and killed I was the only stretcher-bearer left. Of the other ones, Private Woolf was killed and two, 'Fanny' Grimes and 'Tricky' Power were badly wounded. I and one of the riflemen to help me, bandaged and carried them down to an old track across the fields where RAMC ambulances picked them up. At midnight that night, a padre joined the eight of us left and we buried the dead. Then he took us back to his HQ for a cuppa and we rejoined the Battalion just in time to attack Lebisey Wood for the first time. I shall never forget that attack. We had a lot of dead and wounded again. We had one man on the stretcher. Another man with a broken leg had his arm round my shoulder and was running down the hill. The second time we went up there I had to clear all our dead up from the first encounter after they had laid there for four or five weeks with booby traps on them.'

Lance-Corporal E. Seaman MM who was in charge of the stretcher bearers of 'A' Company, Royal Norfolks on D-Day. 'During an attack on 16 October 1944 the battalion was suffering heavy casualties. This NCO was in charge of 'B' (Assault) company stretcher-bearers and throughout showed quite outstanding coolness and personal courage. On one occasion, whilst attending to a casualty, he came under direct machine-gun fire. His own equipment was torn by bullets in two places, but he continued working in the open and then called up the other stretcher-bearer and carried off the casualty. Throughout this time he was under heavy enemy mortar and shell fire. Later in the day an officer was sniped in the next-door company area. There was only one stretcher-bearer left in that company and Lance-Corporal Seaman at once answered the call. He worked on a very nasty wound whilst under fire and while sniping was continuous. He then placed the officer on a stretcher and with the other man carried him off in full view of the enemy and under indirect fire to the advanced RAP. His devotion to duty, personal courage and extreme coolness were of an outstanding nature throughout the battle. The confidence in this NCO, who has worked unceasingly since D-Day, is a fine tribute to his personal conduct and his services to his battalion and company are beyond praise.'

'On D-Day, late in the afternoon, the RAP was hit by a mortar bomb. The medical officer and several stretcher-bearers were wounded and medical treatment and evacuation temporarily at a standstill. Lance-Corporal Ballard quickly took control, organized a new RAP, collected some men to act as stretcher-bearers, treated many men and saw to their safe evacuation (including the medical officer). By his coolness and organizing ability under adverse conditions Lance-Corporal Ballard undoubtedly saved several men's lives and kept morale at a high level when there was a grave danger of it dropping.'

Lance-Corporal E. Ballard received a mention in dispatches. He was KIA on 25 July 1944.

'My unit, the 1st Battalion The Royal Norfolk Regiment, along with the 2nd Battalion The Royal Warwickshire Regiment and The 2nd Battalion The King's Shropshire Light Infantry, made up the 185 Brigade. The plan was for the 8th Brigade to land at 19:30, capture the beach and coastal defences then press on inland and capture high ground (Périers-sur-le-Dan) from which the enemy could bring fire to bear on the beach and beach exits. The role of the 185 Brigade was to pass through the 8th Brigade positions on the line of the road to Caen and establish a bridgehead over the river Orne by nightfall.

'For most of us, still in our teens, it was the first time in combat. Our baptism by fire, as our Platoon Sergeant so dryly observed: 'This is what sorts the men from the boys.' The months and months of training were over, the war games had finished and this was for real.

'We boarded the Landing Craft Infantry at Newhaven on June 5 and were herded down below to our deck areas. I say herded as each of us was loaded down like a pack mule. We had been issued with special assault jerkins, a sort of thick canvas waistcoat with pouches on the outside and pockets on the inside. Into these we packed ammunition, grenades, Bren gun magazines, 2-inch mortar bombs plus emergency rations and many other items a front line soldier required. We estimated each of us was carrying at least 80lbs.

'We left the shelter of the harbour and headed into the Channel. It was soon evident that the sea was not on our side, it was quite rough and it was obvious many of us would feel decidedly groggy by the morning. Darkness fell and sleep was out of the question for me, we were all keyed up and I spent the small hours dozing and pondering what the morning had in store. All sorts of thoughts were running through my mind. Had I learnt my craft well? Were my comrades just as scared as I was? And my family were foremost in my mind. 'My thoughts were suddenly shattered by a shout: 'Stand to and get your kit on'. The night had passed and we were making our run to the beach. We were two hours behind the assault Brigade so when we beached the enemy had ample time to range on the beach with their artillery and 'Nebelwerfers' (multi-barrelled mortars).

'Down below deck one could hear very little above the throb of the ship's engine. Suddenly there was a violent bump as our ship beached and I was up on deck. Before me was the most incredible sight I had ever seen. The sea was covered with the biggest armada of ships ever known. There were battleships, cruisers, destroyers, minesweepers and landing craft of every description. The thunder of gun fire was absolutely ear shattering. Struggling down the gangway I blessed the captain who had kept his promise to take us in as close as humanly possible. It was ironic that during our practices prior to D-Day we never had any waterproof clothing at all and got soaked wading shore. Now here, I was virtually stepping straight onto dry land. Once ashore I had to discard the waterproof suit and this is where I ran into trouble. My suit got hooked on my entrenching tool on my back.

'I thought I would get clobbered before I even got off the beach which was by now a most unhealthy place to be. Shells were bursting all around. Over to my left a knocked out Sherman tank was burning fiercely, the beach was littered with discarded equipment of all kinds, abandoned vehicles and supplies were everywhere. I finally struggled free of my suit, aged 10 years in as many seconds, then ran up the beach to join my section who were making for the exit leading from the beach to the beach road. I turned and looked back down to the beach. The landing ship which we had just disembarked from had received a direct hit on the bridge. I often wondered if our skipper who looked after us so well had survived.

'We scrambled through the gap in the barbed wire defences making sure we kept within the two white marker tapes which told us this track was clear of mines. The shells were constantly shrieking overheard and we would hit the ground and get bawled at by our sergeant, shouting: 'On your feet. That one landed a mile away.' There's an old saying you never hear the one that gets you but I must admit it gave me little comfort at the time.

'Most of the houses on the beach road were in a sorry state. Roofs missing, gaping holes in the walls; some on fire. This was the price of liberation, the havoc of war. Moving between the houses I saw my first dead men. Two German soldiers lying on the floor in a room where the wall had been blasted by a shell. I could see no wounds but they were covered by a fine layer of plaster dust, a most uncanny sight, probably killed by the blast of the shell.

'Once clear of the beach area we got ourselves sorted out and headed for the assembly area, having checked around the platoon there did not appear to be anyone missing, which was most reassuring for all concerned. Everything seemed to have gone to plan and we prepared to push on inland in the wake of the 8th Brigade. I could hear huge shells fired from the off shore battleships screaming overhead on their way to inland targets. Was I glad I wasn't on the receiving end of those! Each shell weighed a ton so I could imagine the destruction they caused among enemy positions.

'Moving through the Normandy countryside we were constantly reminded by the sharp crack of snipers' rifles that this was not to be a walkover. Then we were in Hermanville, a small village about half a mile from the coast. This had been taken by the 8th Brigade and some villagers were out waving the Tricoleur and giving out glasses of Calvados. What wouldn't I have given for a mug of tea just then!

'A short halt was called and I was glad to get the weight off my feet for a few moments and enjoy a cigarette. I lived for each minute as it came. Orders came through and it was 'On your feet lads, we're moving forward'. I struggled to my feet and we marched en route for Colleville-sur-Mer. As we cleared the outskirts of Hermanville we lost the cover of the buildings and trees and emerged into open country. We were soon spotted and it wasn't long before the 88's (German field guns) and mortars were giving us a pasting. We didn't hang about too long but we lost several lads on that stretch of road. As we approached the western outskirts of Colleville-sur-Mer we could hear stiff opposition on the far side of the village. In the village itself there were several knocked-out vehicles, German dead sprawled out on the road and several lads from the Suffolk Regiment lying dead in various places. One lad had been shot down in the middle of the road and a tank had run over him. It was a gruesome sight but war is a gruesome business. It was unbelievable how quickly one got hardened to the sight of death and accepted it with very 1ittle emotion; except when it was one of your own particular friends. Perhaps it's the way it had to be if you wanted to survive in a world gone mad?

'News came back that the road leading out of the village of Colleville-sur-Mer was blocked. This was the road that ran eastwards to Caen - our final objective. We detoured north out of the village and then into the cornfields. The object was to try to bypass the huge German heavy machine gun underground fortification (codenamed 'Hillman') which was holding up our advance. We made some progress but soon came under heavy fire from the enemy strong point which dominated all the surrounding countryside. We lost no lime diving for cover in the standing corn. Crawling through the corn on one's belly with all the gear we were carrying was a punishing experience, the sweat poured down my face and I thought to myself 'what the hell am I doing here? Why hadn't I joined the Royal Artillery like my elder brother?'

'The advance had come to a standstill. It was obvious that we would have to call up tanks and armoured conveyance to that heavily fortified strongpoint if we were to make any further progress. Laying there in the corn I was dirty, hungry and tired to the point of exhaustion. It seemed like an eternity before the supporting armour arrived. A fierce battle followed and the enemy position was finally over-run. I was mighty glad to see the last of that cornfield but several very brave lads were laying still and silent in that sea of corn. Our battalion had roughly 50 casualties both wounded and killed in this attack.

'We were now on the move again. We had not achieved all we had planned and the day was coming to a close, so we consolidated around the farmhouse (code named 'Rover') which we aptly named 'Norfolk House' and dug in. We were determined to hold what we won and a counter attack was on the cards. I dug my slit trench at the bottom of a hedgerow and making sure when laying down I kept my head below the top of it, thus developing what we all laughingly called the Normandy crouch. I smiled to myself when I recalled some of the most ridiculous things I had taken cover behind when coming under fire; small mounds of earth and clumps of grass that would not have concealed a rabbit. I even tried to squeeze my frame into a rut made by a cartwheel. Self preservation is a very strong instinct, believe me.

'Everyone 'Stood to' as dusk approached. I strained my eyes to peer into the gloom. I was having my own private battle now trying to keep my eyes open. My thoughts wandered back over that historic day, thankful that me and many of my pals had made it safely. We had gained a foothold in Normandy. What would tomorrow bring?'

Private Geoffrey Duncan, 10th Platoon, 'B' Company, 1st Battalion The Royal Norfolk Regiment. It took six hours to overcome the defenders of 'Hillman', the code name for Stützpunkt Höehe (Stp 17) or Wiederstandnest 17, also the command post for Oberst Ludwig Krug, commanding the 736th Grenadier Regiment. It was also signal centre to maintain communication with the other

units of the regiment and with General Wilhelm Richter at the 716th Infantry Division in Caen. WN 16 'Morris', the other strongpoint on the Périers Ridge, which had four 105mm guns, was taken quite quickly, its defenders surrendering after an hour. 'Hillman', which was manned by more than 150 men, proved far more formidable [51.] Spread out over 400 yards by 600 yards, it had twelve concrete bunkers, some for anti-tank guns while others were for machine-guns and steel cupolas, with a complete system of connecting trenches which permitted wide fields of fire (2,500 square yards) and was therefore hard for part of the 185th Brigade to bypass on its advance. Lacking the planned naval gunfire support, because the RN forward observation officer had been killed on the beach coming off the landing craft with his signaller, the 1st Battalion of the Suffolk Regiment faced a monumental task crossing minefields and barbed wire covered by artillery and machine guns. The Suffolks requested tank support and two troops of Shermans of the 13th/18th Hussars were diverted to help but the 17 pounder anti-tank shells just bounced off the steel cupolas. Twenty men of the Suffolk Regiment were killed in the assault. The Norfolks lost 150 men. In certain cases, the defenders had to be blown out of their emplacements by heavy explosive charges laid by the battalion pioneers. Krug held out until the morning of 7 June before surrendering, with his son Hans and grandson Christian and during his captivity was promoted to Generalmajor. The extra forces sent to capture 'Hillman' diverted armour from the push toward Caen. Most of the city was not to fall to the Allies until 9 July. The city was bombed no less than 26 times between D-Day and 8 July.

Geoffrey Duncan was wounded in the second major attack on Lebisey Wood and he was evacuated to England.

'On June 7 - D-Day plus one we had got as far as Norfolk House but the following morning we had information that the Warwickshires were held at Lebisey Wood and we had to go and relieve them. We made our way through the corn to where the 21st Panzers held the high ground. We moved forward for around 1,000 yards and they allowed us to get within 20 yards before they opened up. Men were slaughtered. The officers got it first. I heard one crying out all day. Stretcher bearers were sent but they were slaughtered by the German machine guns as well. We had to leave them and the officers and thought the Germans would move their bodies. But when we returned eight weeks later our men were still lying there.'

Private David Davies, a rifleman in Number 5 section, 14 Platoon, Royal Norfolk Regiment.

51   A few miles to the west at Douvres-Ia-Delivrande was a Luftwaffe night-fighter radar station that became operational in August 1943. Its radars were located in two linked strong points to the west of Douvres-la-Delivrande, the larger one about half a mile to the south of the other. Strongpoint 1 to the south was defended by five 50mm anti-tank guns, a 75mm field gun, flak, mortars and machine-guns in bunkers, tobruks and open emplacements, while the smaller northern strongpoint was only defended by machine-guns in tobruks and by light flak. The site was fiercely defended and it took several days for the 8th Brigade of the 3rd Canadian Infantry Division to capture it. Most of the bunkers have long since gone but a Würzburg radar dish has been reinstalled as part of a museum in Strongpoint l. *Hitler's Atlantic Wall* by Anthony Saunders (Sutton Publishing 2001).

'We boarded our landing craft at Newhaven and set sail at about 1800 on 5 June. The sea was a bit choppy and a lot of the lads were very seasick, including me. I was a very bad sailor. I had my hair cut on board, as did so many more of the lads, as we did not know when we would be able to get another one. We were not a pretty sight I can tell you!

'After all night at sea we approached the Normandy beaches at about 07:00 on 6 June. One could not hear one another speak for the noise that was going on around us. Almost every warship in the Navy must have been firing their guns at the same time. Shells were screaming over our heads in every direction. Also, the Germans were firing at us in our assault craft. We were ordered to get prepared to land. One could hear the German machine gunners hitting the side of our landing craft (LCI). We were pretty scared. Except for one or two old soldiers we were all young men. I was a lance corporal at the time I/c of the Bren gun in my section. We hit the beaches at about 07:15. We were expecting a very wet landing but the skipper of the craft got us in close, which we were very glad, as there was nothing worse than getting wet up to one's waist or above.

'Once we were on the beach we had quite a long run to get to cover, of which there was not much. We lost a couple of the lads but most of us made it to the dunes, which we were glad to see. Once the Germans realised what was really going on they started to shell us continually with mortar fire. We got up to the roadway where some of our tanks were. I got the side of one and advanced with it, as did others. We thought that if we were going to get hit the tank would get it first.

'When we got ourselves together we started to move towards the built-up area, which gave us a bit more protection. Our objective on D-Day was the city of Caen. We knew we had a long way to go before we got there and a lot of fighting and bloodshed would come but we kept going the best we could, losing a man here and there. Shrapnel from the mortar bombs wounded lots of our boys. Sometimes, one or two of our own shells would drop short causing a bit of panic. We got into the open country and we had fields of corn to go through which we did on our hands and knees as the German bullets were whistling through the corn. We kept our heads down! There was a lot of sniping going on at the same time. The German soldiers were very good at sniping. Many times our officer had t call in the artillery to try to stonk him out.

'As we got nearer to our objective we were stopped by a German counter-attack. We were getting a bit close to the German dugouts and I think he liked it much. All this occurred on a hill called Lebisey Wood, where a lot of our men form the Norfolk's and from other regiments lost their lives. We met stiff opposition but as our objective was Caen we had to gain this dominating ground to give us a clear view of our objective. So this was a very sad day. We retreated a mile or so back and dug in.

'We went out on patrols at night to try and locate the enemy, which we did several times, sometimes losing a man or two with anti-personnel mines, which were everywhere, but we overcame this as the engineers came in and cleared most of them. When we contacted the Germans we reported back to HQ and the artillery gave him a good stonk but he was very well dug in.

Before we went out on patrols we had our first hot meal since we landed. Our quartermaster came up to our lines in a Bren gun carrier to dish this meal out to us. Nothing went back to the cookhouse I can tell you. It was what we called an all-in-stew (a bit of this and a bit of that). It went down very well. As we were all very hungry we all sat in our trenches to have this meal as there was still the odd mortar bomb being fired at us. After a chat and a smoke we heard the sound of aircraft above and when we looked up we could see that these were gliders being towed to make a landing only a few miles away from us. A lovely sight but I am afraid that those glider lads got really cut up, as they were sitting ducks for the enemy.

This day was the longest day of my life but I was spared to fight another day thank God. I suppose one could say I was one of the lucky ones. After dark fell upon us we felt sure that the Germans would counter-attack us that evening or in the morning but nothing happened, thank God. The word got around that we had no need to worry about being pushed back into the sea. We didn't want another Dunkirk, when Montgomery sent word around that if anything happened he could lay down a artillery barrage of a 1,001 guns and believe me that would be quite assuring and we all felt better for this news. That was providing none of the shells fell among our boys. Some did sometimes but that's war.

Lance Corporal Peter H. Gould, 1st Battalion The Royal Norfolk Regiment. Lebisey was the holding point for 25 tanks of the 1st Company and HQ of 21st Panzer Division commanded by Hauptmann Herr at 15:00 on D-Day. By dusk leading tanks led by Lieutenant Colonel Jim Eadie had advanced six miles from the beaches and were on the summit of the wooded hills around Lebisey. On D+1 the Warwicks were ordered to take Lebisey Ridge and village but after heavy fighting the Germans beat them back with machine guns in the woods. The area was finally captured by the 185th Brigade of the 3rd British Division early on 8 July.

'Dawn brought a wonderful sight. At 6.40am we could see smoke and shell bursts on the beach in our sector. There were a lot of fighter aircraft about and we were delighted to see they were ours - the Army had enormous faith in the RAF. Our time for landing was 7.45am. Well before then we were all ready. 'C' Company was equipped with folding bicycles which were to taken them inland quickly. As the starboard ladder had just been lowered, it was immediately hit by either a shell or a mortar which squarely put it out of action but, by good fortune, no one was hurt, so down the port side we all had to go.'

Major (later Lieutenant Colonel) Humphrey M. Wilson MC, the Battalion Second-in-command.

'I landed with 'B' Company and we had just moved off the beaches when I saw Major Humphrey M. Wilson MC surrounded by a group of jabbering Frenchmen. Humphrey had spent many years in India and Urdu was second nature to him. He was regaling the French in Urdu and when he saw me he turned round and said,

'Eric, these bloody fools can't even speak their own language!'

Major (later Lieutenant-Colonel) Eric A. Cooper-Key MC, commanding 'B' Company, 1st Battalion, the Royal Norfolk Regiment.

'The first clear recollection is of being on board a LCI and setting sail from Newhaven. Four hours later, when we were allowed up on deck, I was absolutely staggered by the vast armada, which had gathered. Wherever you looked there were ships of all shapes and sizes. The storm clouds were gathering but they had not completely blotted out the sun, which was sending low shafts of sunlight across the surface of the sea, throwing everything into silhouette. Against this silvery background the ships looked sinisterly black.

'We spent a wretched night. Not many of us were good enough sailors to withstand the heavy sea we encountered and sick bags soon became inadequate! By morning the deck was about an inch deep in vomit and I wished I were dead! At daybreak we were allowed up on deck and never has fresh salty sea air smelt so good! The opportunity was taken to swill down and clear the foul smelling decks below, though some of the smell lingered because the leather soles of our boots had become impregnated.

'We were ordered to complete the Next of Kin and Will sections of our pay books and a 'Field Service Post card' for transmission to our next of kin. We were issued with condoms to provide waterproofing for watches and Francs and overtrousers/leggings to try to keep dry on landing. Being short my leggings could only be described as a tight fit under my arms!

'Suddenly we were told 'This is it, up on deck and prepare for landing!' Up we went and took up positions on the port side of the bow superstructure. This was not really the time for sightseeing but of course we all had a good look round and truly it was a staggering sight to see so many ships so close together - literally hundreds! One or two were on fire but most were busy putting people or equipment ashore while others, having performed their task, were reversing out to sea ready to take on whatever task was next. Our ship's captain had a full set of ginger whiskers. He did us proud. In fact, he went so far on to the beach that when his ratings lowered the ramps for us we stepped off into only about two feet of water, which was marvellous.

'Major Brinkley, our Company Commander, ordered us ashore and down the ramps we went. Ashore on the Continent at last! It was my job to see that the No.18 wireless set was close by the Company Commander at all times to try and maintain radio communication and not to be involved in the 'Blood and Gore'. I carried a standard rifle as my weapon, to the barrel of which I had tied two signalling flags in case I should need them to maintain communication. My mate Private 'Tuff' Tuffield and I went wherever the Company Commander went, just a pace or two behind. Following Major Brinkley across the beach was difficult. In addition to the weight we were carrying we had the problem of bypassing broken down or burning armoured vehicles of all sorts. Dead bodies and wounded made an additional difficulty over and above the occasional mortar shell landing nearby. This short journey didn't really take very long but to me it seemed like an eternity. But at last we were clear of the clinging sand and we hurried up over the sea wall of the little French seaside town, which was just as the photographs had said it would be, crossed the road and turned away from the beach up a track alongside some houses, heading in the general direction of Caen.

'The over-riding memory is of so many of my colleagues who through various causes did not see the campaign through to the end. Tuffield and I had reached the edge of Lebisey Wood in the late afternoon of Day 2 when eventually the order was given to withdraw for regrouping. As 'Tuff' and I retraced our steps down the sloping field we became the target of a German rifleman firing from the wood. Fortunately the field was very uneven and our withdrawal was thus somewhat erratic, which put the rifleman off a bit. We reached a gap in the hedge and made for the other side. Poor old 'Tuff' was wounded in the hand but we managed to scramble to safety on the other side. He was the first of ten signals colleagues who were to serve with me during the campaign to be replaced! I remember the awful carnage among the animals during the first two three months of our assault. I don't think I shall ever forget the sight of horses and cows bloated and putrefying but having to be left because of enemy pressure. I also remember the awful stench, which developed in the heat of that summer as a result of the carnage.'

Private (later Lance-Corporal) Nevil Griffin, Regimental signaller, 'D' Company, The 1st Battalion The Royal Norfolk Regiment. That evening 1 Royal Norfolk was firmly established in a wooded area at the top of a gentle rise, code named 'Rover', around a single building, which came to be known

'I left the beach, crossed the dunes and proceeded along the beach road to join up with Battalion HQ. I was driving nicely through the grain, sussing out the ditches, when some Jerries decided that I looked too much of a sitting duck to be left alone and started taking pot shots at me and dropping the odd mortar bomb around. 'That's when I discovered how fast the little thing would go. Rather hair-raising though, doing a hand-brake turn from something in excess of 50mph and on the edge of a six-foot deep ditch. The things that stick out most about Norfolk House are, in the early days, dodging the sniper fire when visiting the loos in the wood.'

Lieutenant Dennis Bell, who landed some tides ahead of the Carrier Platoon, driving a little amphibious vehicle, the CO's run-about called a 'Weasel'; much smaller than a carrier, it had rubber tracks, a screw and rudder at the back and went 'like a bat out of hell.'

'After spending many hours on a landing craft crossing the Channel and being seasick like many others, I was glad to get on the beach. It was like manoeuvres that we had done so many times before. I could not believe it was the real thing. We had no trouble on the beach. Once off the beach we slowly advanced along narrow dusty roads with Jerry snipers banging away at us. So far we had covered two or three miles and rare doing well until we came to a cornfield. Then Jerry machine guns in a small Pill Box opened up. The lads were soon being cut to pieces as the machine guns, with their tremendous rate of fire, scythed through the tree foot high golden corn. I remember one of the Company cooks behind me getting a bullet in his neck. That was the day I first saw the red poppies of France in the cornfields, diving to the ground out of the machine gun fire. My nose was stuck right amongst them! They reminded me of the hell and horrors of the 1914 war which my father had talked about so often.'

Private W. Evans, 12 Platoon, 'B' Company, 1st Battalion Royal Norfolks.

'I was driving the Bren gun carrier when we came across this figure lying in the road. He was covered in his gas cape. We couldn't run over him and I stopped to move him. When I pulled back the cape I saw who it was. It was Sergeant A. H. Wilson an old friend. His parents and mine lived less than 100 yards apart. A well-known boxer, he was 27, known as 'Tug'; Herbert to his family. There were no marks on his body and he had lain there during all the shelling. It seems that his luck had run out at the wrong time. I remember thinking, what on earth I was going to tell his parents when I next saw them. It never crossed my mind that I wouldn't get home to do that.'

Private Bill Holden, 1st Battalion Royal Norfolk Regiment. Bill fought on to the end up in Germany in 1945. His elder brother Corporal Bert Holden, was killed on 20 March 1945 while serving with the 2nd Battalion, Royal Norfolk Regiment in Mandalay, Burma, aged 32.

'My men and I had to bury a dozen men - not a pleasant job. The sergeant's gold fillings were brilliant in the sun.'

Lieutenant E. G. G. Williams. (In the period to the end of June 1944 the total number of battle casualties suffered by the 3rd British Infantry Division was 3,505, approximately one seventh of the total battle casualties of 2nd British Army, which by that time comprised the equivalent of almost twenty divisions.
'

We sailed to war not knowing what to expect. We were transferred from our transport ship on to a landing craft, which also had on board two 3-ton army trucks and we headed for the beaches. All went well until the time came to disembark and wade ashore. We went close in but then they decided to let the trucks off first into about 3 feet of water, which was no problem, but after the trucks went, that made the landing craft lighter and it also started to move into deeper water of about 6 or seven feet. The skipper was scared to go in any closer in case he ran aground. Now comes more Army stupidity. This idiot of an officer ordered us to take a 5-gallon can of petrol in each hand and jump. We refused. If we jumped into the deeper water we would have sunk to the bottom and drowned but the day was saved by one of the sailors on the crew. He tied a rope around his waist and dived overboard fully clothed and swam ashore. The craft went a bit nearer and holding ONE can of petrol and the rope in the other hand we went into about 5 feet of water and waded ashore, soaking wet and landed in France in one piece. From then on it became a hard job just to stay in one piece and not get killed. It became a test of survival, which the lucky made and the unlucky didn't. We never got the chance to thank that sailor for what he did. I just hope he survived the war. He deserved to.

'We left the beaches and were on our way to join the battalion and then saw our first sight of the enemy. Two German planes swooped over the beaches but they did not bother us, thank goodness. When we left the beaches, there were bundles lying on the beach all covered in army blankets, which we realised, were our dead waiting to be buried. A sad sight, but a common one in the future. Being British or German they had one thing in common, they all looked the same, DEAD, what for? War is so stupid.

'I was soon to get a rude awakening as on my first night the Germans decided to give me a nice welcome as they plastered our positions with mortar and shellfire. I was absolutely terrified and crouched in my duver shaking like a leaf. I really thought my end had come but the shelling finally stopped and I was still in one piece. But you could hear the cry for stretcher-bearers so some poor sod had copped it. I then understood why I was told to dig deep and if your luck was in you survived. If not, then your duver became your grave.

'The worst thing was a mortar the Jerries had named Moaning Minnie. It was a six barrelled mortar and they landed in a straight line so if your duver was in line with the first bomb, then, if one of the next five had your name on it, that was your lot. They just filled in your duver and stuck your rifle on top of it with your name and number. I had had my first baptism of fire, but many more to come.

'Jerry kept up with his shelling and we were told to be prepared for an attack, which happened shortly after the alert. Jerry put in a big attack with infantry and tanks and we were all standing by ready to fight them off... Bill Norrie was killed. Jim Glennie and Ron Macintosh were missing with most of 'A' Company. Jim and Ron had only lasted about three days but we learned much later that they were taken prisoner and we met again after the war. Jerry was pushed back thanks to our superiority in artillery, tanks and of course us, the poor bleeding infantry. We always got the dirty end of the stick.'

Stan Bruce, 5th/7th Battalion, The Gordon Highlanders.

Dear Mother,

As I write this letter to you, we are lying just off the coast of France, pouring 15-inch shells into the enemy positions. It's god to see the orange flame belch forth from the muzzle of our gun. It's great to hear the one-ton shells whistling through the air, to see the clouds of dust and smoke rise where they fall and then, to think of the destruction and panic they cause amongst the Hun and how the morale of our troops jumps even higher that what it is when they know the Royal Navy is not far away backing up every move they make.

Perhaps I'd better explain how we felt something in our blood as every warship in the harbour weighed anchor and slowly steamed out to sea. After being at sea for about half an hour we heard the click of our loudspeakers. You could have heard a pin drop. Then came news we had been waiting for. The captain told us we were about to make history - we were going to take part in the Second Front. I felt thrilled and perhaps a little nervous. Each of us was given a signed order from General Eisenhower. He told us how important we were and wished us God speed.

HMS Ramillies ploughed through the water until I saw a fleet of every kind of ship the size of which I have never seen before and am never likely to see again. The mighty battleships were in the centre, cruisers on either side, with destroyers nipping around guarding the mighty brood. At the front were the all-important minesweepers and at the rear hundreds of barges carrying troops and ammunition. During the night we split into three squadrons and by daybreak we could see the rugged coast of France. There were many enemy batteries to be silenced before the barges could get inshore. I shall always treasure the honour that fell to my ship and to my gun of firing the first shot in the colossal engagement and it thrills me beyond words to think that I had the pleasure of loading that first shell. The Germans did almost everything except hit us.

The first hour will always be imprinted vividly on my mind. But it was no time for inward emotions. There was work to be done and we did it – our guns blasting enemy destroyer as they approached to attack. The thing that struck me most was our vast sea and air superiority. Where was the Luftwaffe?

The great landing came at 7.30 am. Thousands of barges began to move towards the beach while our planes circled overhead. An army like this could not possibly be beaten.

I had been closed up at my gun all day. I was still there at 7 pm, just standing meditating over the day's events. Then what seemed like a dark cloud appeared on the horizon. As it came nearer I could make out that it consisted of thousands of planes. They seemed to fly in pairs but as they moved closer I could see that attached to each plane was a huge black glider. This was the most awe-inspiring sight of the day. The enemy flak was terrific. As each plane passed over our ship the gliders began to detach themselves and glide to earth. It is easy to imagine the fear, which must have seized the enemy.

All that night we could hear the battle raging. It is raging as I write but the gunfire becomes less audible as the German war machine is driven slowly further inland.

John McLaughlin, HMS *Ramillies*

'We sailed from England on the evening of 5 June on the *Princess Josephine Charlotte*, a Belgian packet. Our task was to land at 'Sword' Beach and to break out on to Port En-Bessin. Our commando officer, Captain Walton, took us through to a junction on a coast road and told us to dig. We exposed a telephone junction box, which connected all military telephones and we blew it up. Later, as we advanced, we had some skirmishes with the Germans. A machine gun opened up on us, injuring some of the lads. 'Shock', the cry rang out from one of the wounded. As I tended to the lad, I realised I couldn't do all the necessary first aid in a prone position, but as I stood up the machine gun opened up again.

I could see the bullets hitting the hedgerow but as they came nearer to me, the gun must have lifted. Although the firing continued, the bullets were flying about and above my head. We put in a flank attack and captured the machine gun and crew. The gunner had a right shoulder injury. I had to treat him. When I'd finished he hugged me.

A Scout car with six Germans in it suddenly rounded a bend in the road. We dealt with it. Soon after we heard a horse galloping down the lane. As it came in view we saw it had a German rider. Sergeant Hooper stepped into the lane and fired his Tommy gun. The horse galloped off with the dead body still on its back.

Later, we approached a small village. An elderly woman was crying by the roadside. I could see the old lady was wounded in the arm, so I tended to her and wanted to get her in the house. While I was trying to get her to understand that she should be in bed, she slapped my face! I realised she had completely misunderstood. I had no choice but to give her a morphine injection and carry on.'

Marine Commando Percy 'Shock' Kendrick MM, an army medic who got his nickname because most of his patients were shell-shocked.

'When dawn broke we saw the coast of France and the great fleet around them and our morale soared. Our ships opened fire on the beach - it was a terrifying spectacle -then an explosion under our craft stunned my legs. We stopped 100 yards from the shore and were ordered into the water, not knowing how deep it was. A Sherman tank sank beneath the waves and two-crew scrambled out. The rest must have drowned. Next was our Bren gun carrier. Its wheel got stuck in the tank. My four pals plunged in but I couldn't swim so I stood on the carrier with water up to my chest. I put my life belt on and prayed. After what seemed like an eternity, my feet touched soft sand. Half drowned. I waded through the breakers and saw men lying on the sand. I stumbled towards the nearest one and saw that his chest had been torn open. We had lost our Bren gun so I took his rifle, ammo and steel helmet. Then I just ran for cover. Dead and wounded lay scattered all over the beach. I had swallowed a great deal of water and was violently sick. I lay in the dunes for a while. A war photographer came over to me with a packet of cigarettes. He said he had shot some film, which would be amazing, if he ever got back to England. After dark, German planes came over dropping hundreds of anti-personnel bombs. I had no sleep at all but I was still alive. God knows why, but I was.'

Private T. Platt, 1st Battalion South Lancashire Regiment.

'I was only 20 years old on D Day. They called it the Longest Day and I shall never forget that very sad day. Each June, I look out of my window and see the blossoms on the trees. France was very like England. I was stationed at Berwick On Tweed and then we moved down to Holt in Norfolk, before being sent to Ickworth Park near Bury St Edmunds. I thought 'Now is my chance to get some extra leave.' My wife was very worried about me at the time as she didn't know where I was. One day she was taking a walk in Ickworth Park late in the afternoon, when she saw something moving in the trees. It wasn't soldiers at all- it was a lot of deer but my wife didn't stop long, she soon made off! They then sent us to a camp 'Somewhere in England. It put me in mind of a Concentration Camp as it was surrounded with barbed wire. We had plenty of entertainment but nobody knew what was going to happen. We were shut out from the whole world and sworn to secrecy at that time. One afternoon we were all called together in the Big Tent and told 'The waiting is over'. D-Day, hoped for and at the same time feared, was no longer a rumour. The greatest invasion of all time was about to begin. When we heard this, I don't mind telling you, we all got the wind up. In the afternoon we were taken in trucks to Little Haven in North Wales. As we jumped out of these trucks we saw those huge landing craft. They told us they were American craft. As we got on to these craft the sailors were quite good to us. We had plenty to eat. We didn't know what was going on. The sea was very rough. I had never been on a boat before and I had never been to war before. Our hearts were very heavy and I shall never forget that June night. All of a sudden we had the order to push off. Yes, the time had come at last. We pushed off at midnight and the sea was very rough going over.

They told us it would be dawn when we hit the Normandy Beach Head and that it would be every man for himself; and that was quite true.

'We were struck with seasickness and when I arrived I felt pretty bad. We were very glad to get off the landing craft. We arrived about 20 past 7 and they let us down on a ramp at the side of the landing craft. As we came down Jerry was hitting quite a lot of us boys. We had to catch hold of a rope to wade ashore. As we came down this ramp there was a landing craft sinking at the side of us. It had the top knocked off. As I was making my way through to the beach, I just managed to put my head down away from this Jerry machine gun fire. I heard a shout behind me and looked round quick. We weren't supposed to look behind us: it didn't matter what happened to your other mates. He called out to me; 'Benny, save me'. I was just about to pull him from drowning in the sea. Poor boy, I felt very sorry for him, he was badly wounded in his leg and ripped up with machine gun bullets. I do hope he was brought back safely.

'As I got to the end of the beach, I came face to face with a Jerry prisoner who was helping us boys to come ashore. He was holding the ropes and seemed very happy to have been captured. We heard afterwards he was a White Russian. Jerries were running with their hands up. We had to move off the beach. I saw a dead Jerry being carried away on a stretcher. A little further I saw one of our boys, he was dead; I thought to myself 'I'm going to catch it soon', but I didn't. There were Military Policemen near the beach telling us what to do. I was told to jump into the Jerry trench which I soon did. I was very glad to get my head down to rest after that journey in that landing craft. As soon as I was in my trench, I decided I would make some tea. So I took out my Tommy Cooker, put it in the bottom of the trench, took out a cube and lit up, found a tea cube and put it in my mess tin. I was just about to mix the tea cube when all of a sudden, a shell fell short. Up went the sand in my trench and knocked my Tommy cooker over - that was my tea gone!

Private Benstead, South Lancs Regiment.

'We went first on to 'Sword' Beach and took a terrific number of casualties. There were bodies and wounded everywhere, in the sea, on the sand - so many that we had to walk and crawl over them. The commandos who followed us were surprised at the mortality rate and put it down to inexperience. This wasn't the case. We had been well trained. But heavy artillery and machine gun fire was pouring down on us. There just wasn't anywhere to go. I lost a lot of good mates that day. Men who gave their lives for others.'

Private Ronald Major, 21, East Yorkshire Regiment, who survived a bullet on 'Sword' Beach and the torpedoing of a landing craft taking him and other wounded to a waiting destroyer. He still managed a smile as he was snapped by famous *Picture Post* photographer Bert Hardy. The picture of Ron on a train, one arm in a sling, the other hand clutching a mug of tea, was blazoned over the front cover in June 1944.

'As we came off the beach we started coming across bodies - British bodies. I remember the first one I saw was an infantryman and what fascinated me was that he had no head. He was just lying there, with no head. There was no sign of his head, but I don't think I was particularly shocked. It sounds a cruel thing to say, but I was quite surprised at not seeing much more carnage. Then, as we started to get to the little sand hills, which were just below a concrete promenade - we did start seeing bodies and some wounded fellows. I was out of the half-track by this time and I started taking pictures of the troops coming ashore. Then I suddenly spotted two very tiny infantrymen marching along with a very tall German soldier who was absolutely terrified. He had a bandage round his face and there were these two rather cheerful- I think they were cockneys - on either side of him. I said, 'Just a minute!' and they posed as though they might be posing in Piccadilly Circus for their picture, with this German in between them.'

Francis O'Neill Photographer, Army Film and Photographic Unit.

'I was driving a Churchill tank and when I got to where we had to drop the fascine I said to our tank commander, 'Jim, I can't see the culvert.' He radioed back to Captain Ewart who was on the beach, but our orders were to carry on so I put the tank in first gear. As soon as I started to move we went straight down, because the Germans had flooded the area. Water started pouring into the turret. Everybody had to get out a bit sharpish but with me being the last, I started to swallow water. As my co-driver got out he put his knees round both sides of my head and dragged me with him. There was quite a bit of water in my stomach by then. When I got outside, Bill Hawkins hit me once in the stomach. We hadn't time for any niceties, he just brought the water up and that was it.

'We just lay down behind the sand dunes and Jim Ashton started to sing 'Kiss me Again'. He was a father figure, he was a good man and he always did this to settle us all down. I was the youngest one in the tank crew and he'd just started to sing when a mortar-bomb came and dropped between us, which killed three, outright. I was wounded; the co-driver had a hole in his back I could have put my fist in. But he was so brave and said 'I'll crawl for help.' I saw him roll over when he got a hundred yards from us and that's where he died.

'I rolled down into a minefield. There was a big board - Achtung Minen - straight above my head. I thought 'Cor blimey'. I managed to get up on to my feet and I ran about fifty yards, then my legs gave way and I collapsed. Two lads came and dragged me back and gave me a cigarette and a drink. I was left there for quite a while and the first one to come on the scene after that was a Canadian medical officer who gave me an injection of morphine. He told me that I couldn't possibly have run because I had five compound fractures in one of my legs. I said to him, 'Well, when you're fighting and there's bullets flying around, that makes you do queer things.'

Corporal William Dunn 26th Assault Squadron, Royal Engineers.

'I spotted an airman in the water. We tried to rescue him but he was numb with cold. The boat got stuck on a mud bank and my skipper shouted to let the airman go. He threatened to shoot me if I didn't. He had a gun trained on me. 'Then the ship turned and sliced the chap's head off.'

Seaman, G. E. Jacques aboard a landing craft at 'Sword' Beach.

'On the night of 5 June we lay off Spithead surrounded by the 'vehicles of war'; grey battleships, heavy cruisers, sleek destroyers, the heavily laden sea transports and the multitudes of different types of landing craft. The night was cold and wet and the sea was swelly and inclined to be a bit choppy further out. We waited aware that final decisions were being taken; the time of estimation was about to cease and history was about to be made. I was by now accomplished in assault landings having been in on 'Torch', [52] in Pantelleria, Syracuse in Sicily and at Salerno in Italy. France was the next target. The LCI on which I served was American-built and designed to carry about 200 troops in three separate apartments. The craft had a speed of about 15 knots, but did not float on the water like the other assault landing craft, which were flat-bottomed, but cut through the water. As a result the ship was almost constantly awash on the upper deck. The troops did not like this type of vessel for they had first to clamber to the top deck and then descend steep narrow ramps on either side of the bows and hope that the water was not too deep from then on. All the previous landings I had taken part in had begun under some secrecy, but in southern England it was obvious that major landings were sure to take place. In fact I think that this tremendous concentration of troops was in itself a great morale builder. The actual victory was 50 per cent won before the first commencement of battle. I understand that as the troop convoys left Portsmouth civilians lined the coast cheering the departure, loud-hailers aboard some of the ships played military music and ships' sirens sounded, almost like the farewell that had been for troops off to fight some colonial war during the previous century. Morale has never been higher amongst troops of any nation. 'How did I feel as we left Spithead? I don't think that any of us felt fear for we had trained for this great operation and all felt confident that our leadership had been supreme. Then, there was great comfort in the vast numbers and the knowledge that great forces were on our side. The comfort also of one's comrades, although most were new to me. But they looked up to me with some respect due to my previous experience and that fact alone did much for my own morale. How could I disgrace myself when many of those around me looked to me for support. Most of us kept up our good spirits during those early hours. We were spoken to by our Troop Commander and at this point we were told that our destination was to be France; that and nothing more. We knew that 48 Commando was to land with us to perform a pincer movement in order to connect the groups separated by a beach unsuitable for landing on. We were told that ours was to be 'Sword' Beach, Peter Sector and we were assured that by the time we landed the fortifications would have been softened as a result of heavy air and sea bombardment.

'We were closely packed together, not just because of our numbers. Our equipment weighed individually above 90lb. I also carried a rifle and a radio transmitter weighing about 30lb to be shared between me and another of my comrades. Our task was to make contact with 48 Commando and French civilians. To ensure mobility we were to use folding bicycles which were stored in racks in the stern of the craft. I cannot now remember the hour we actually landed but it

---

52 The invasion of French North Africa in November 1942.

was certainly after dawn. A tremendous bombardment was taking place almost up to the time we were to land and always it has been a fear of being caught in one's own fire. I could see the sector we were to land on. Later I was to learn that we were far from our allotted place. A tremendous battle taking part on our right flank was, so I learned later, 48 Commando, which lost half its numbers in that fight. By now I was on the deck of the craft with the folded cycle as addition to my load while my signaller comrade was struggling with our transmitter. Then the disembark signal was given - I think it was probably a combination of flashing lights and sirens. The ramps were lowered and we surged towards the beach. We were still a long way from the beach when it finally stopped. I would have felt much better landing from a craft with wider ramps instead of the crazy, steep, ladder-like gangways fitted to our vessel.

'The beach was clearer now, despite the smoke and fog which enveloped it. I saw what appeared to be several large houses on some kind of promenade and then a vivid streak of tracer shell streamed out of the windows towards some object to the left of us. I recall being surprised that anything could have survived the barrage from the sea. This had now stopped. I was first down the portside ramp with my comrade immediately behind me. .It was no dash ashore as Hollywood might portray. Instead I remember it as an agonizing stumble down the steep ramp under my heavy load. I jumped into the sea and immediately sank into deep water that came over my head, although thinking about it now it might have been the choppy sea that gave that impression. I scrambled eventually to the beach around the bows of the craft. The bicycle was beneath the waves but I still had all my equipment and rifle as I dashed up the beach to shelter behind some rocks. The rest of the Troop seemed to be some distance from me all lost in the gloom of the morning. The fire from the houses was joined with heavy mortar fire and big bursts which suggested artillery shells. There were a great many bodies strewn around the beach. At that stage they gave the impression of being soldiers other than my comrades. Some Beach Marshals and Redcaps were trying to organize exits from the beach. I looked for my signaller comrade but could see him no more. I found out later that he had been badly wounded on getting ashore. He had had the transmitter so our combined contribution was not to be.

'A sergeant of our Troop was gathering his men together and I joined him in an attempt to get a foothold to the right of the houses. My mind is very confused from that point. I remember perhaps thirty of us leaving behind a beach of great confusion and gathering in a field behind the houses. I remember also some Canadian soldiers who appeared to be in some confusion and leaderless.

'We were eventually joined by a lieutenant and about twenty Marines. He told us that the remainder of the Troop had now regrouped and had moved to the left against Lion-sur-Mer. We were to attack a large house or château which had been his original objective. The distance seemed a long one and the roads were strewn with German dead. We gained our objective, but the proposed link-up with 48 Commando was never achieved. A big counter-attack was supposed to be prepared by the Germans, but this never took place. In any case there was no strength left in 48 Commando and most never left the beach alive.

'During the actions of the next three days we took many prisoners. They seemed to be a mixture of Asiatic-type Russians who had been recruited from PoW camps as well as some young and frightened German boys. Many were suffering from shell-shock following the intense bombardment and I saw little to indicate the fanatical resistance that was to come further inland. It was at this time I was sent back to England with German prisoners and our own wounded; many from 48 Commando. I was treated with great care and consideration on my return to the barracks at Eastney; white bread, well-cooked food and white sheets and most important of all, leave. I suppose we had achieved something on that day, but success is seldom witnessed by the ordinary soldier. That is for the planners and manipulators of the General Staff to enjoy. Victories are things we are told belong to us long after they have taken place.'

Jack Brewin, signaller.

'Our vessel was an American boat, quite small and converted for our landing by the simple addition of long wooden ramps that could be lowered on each side of the bows. Since we had reduced our first stage needs to items that could be carried on foot, the only awkward ones were the company and platoon's bicycles which had been retained for message taking along the road we knew ran behind the dunes of Ouistreham Beach. We spent a not too uncomfortable night on the deck. I did notice one of the men, sleeping like a baby on the steps of the engine room ladder. 'Early next morning, the engines started and we cast off for our short voyage. As we reached the open channel, the sight was truly amazing. As we were on the left flank of the whole expedition we could see a series of naval vessels patrolling to ensure that German MTBs could not interfere should our armada be detected. The RAF had ensured clear skies from the Luftwaffe and so, to our right as far as the horizon, we could see on this clear, sunny summer's day orderly lines of vessels of all shapes, sizes and types. They seemed no more than 500 yards apart and steadily we ploughed our way through a gentle swell towards the French coast. The total discipline and control fired enormous pride in those who were privileged to be a part of this mighty venture.

'Alongside me was a marine who had been placed on the vessel for liaison duties. 'You have to watch these skippers, Sir', he said, 'they've got tanks in the bows which they can fill with sea water to increase their depth, then blow clear to ensure they do not get stuck on the beach. I suspect he's windy and likely to put you in out of your depth.'

'He may have exaggerated, but we certainly had to cope with water up to our armpits and I noticed my 'runner' struggling with the bicycle, which insisted on floating horizontally until he could get some weight in it to force the tyres down.

'Our beach appeared as per models. However, the row of houses behind the dunes looked like the teeth of a very bad lower jaw, with black gaps where fire had followed the bombardment and shattered roofs and walls. High explosives had done the damage. As we ran in, I could see the planned two exits had been started and engineers were laying Somerfeld metal track to help get vehicles through the fairly steep passage through the dunes. There was a fair amount of small arms fire, particularly from a large pillbox which obviously had not been cleared to our right. The men swore that some of the sniping was from

French women, 'collaborateurs' during the German occupation who were none too pleased that we had arrived to chuck their boyfriends out!

'It was now 3pm and the tide was low, giving a wide expanse of wet sand over which all manner of men and machines were struggling to carry out their appointed duties. As Page and I were a little way up towards our destination beside the right hand exit, we were surprised to hear the sound of planes to our left. Coming in low were the only two Messerschmitt dive-bombers [sic] that evaded the RAF that day, I believe. We heard the rattle of their guns and saw the spurt of bullets in the sand ahead of us, apparently doing little, if any damage. But as they were nearly overhead, we could clearly see the two wretched little bombs they carried released from under their wings to sail in a gentle curve down towards us. We flopped down on our bellies and the bombs plopped into the sand a short distance away. Fortunately, the sand and mud which the River Orne had deposited over time immemorial was far too soft to detonate them on contact and they sank, to explode after a second or two and squirt up a column of disgusting mud which broke up and came pattering down all over our backs. We did feel that to be excessively drenched on landing and then covered in mud into the bargain was a bit much!

'We crawled forward cautiously for a while, then I got fed up, stood up and started to walk forward, whereupon I was dragged down by Page who swore the snipers would get me. Eventually, we reached the dunes without mishap and established headquarters in a section of a German dugout. The one large pillbox that remained (about half a mile to our right) the Canadians had not been able to clear. Its fate was sealed, however, by the calling up of a large assault landing craft that had been lying off shore after discharging its troops and tanks earlier. This had a Bofors gun mounted on each side of its front ramp. The Canadians drew back, the guns were depressed to fire horizontally and proceeded to discharge, with their slow automatic thump, thump, thump, a clip of shells at point blank range. Temporarily the bunker disappeared in a cloud of smoke, the gunners with their second clip loaded, waited for this to clear. As it drifted away, some half a dozen Germans were observed staggering out with their hands up, thoroughly shell-shocked. They had decided they had had enough.

'Two factors greatly affected the plan for our stay on the beaches. First, due to stiff resistance by the Germans, our advance through Caen was halted and there was always the threat of a counterattack. We were to organise temporary dumps of ammunition, petrol and food in the sand dunes to back up immediate needs, then large depots nearer Caen would be established on a permanent basis - this the Germans prevented. Secondly, in spite of the brave and brilliant capture of Pegasus Bridge over the River Orne and its parallel canal by our Parachute Regiment supported by another Oxford and Bucks Unit trained as airborne troops who crash-landed in plywood gliders, only a small bridgehead was maintained and some high ground on the far side of the river mouth remained in German occupation.

'Every night we could hear the engine of their truck as it climbed to deliver rations and a little ammunition for a mortar they were manning. Every day, with German precision, at exactly midday, they lobbed half a dozen bombs into

Ouistreham town on our side. Needless to say, at a minute or two before noon, everyone took cover. The only fatality reported was that of a poor old Frenchman who decided to cycle across the square on the hour and was killed instantly by a bomb landing in it.

'Every day we sweated away keeping the constant flow of men, machines and materials moving up through the exits towards the hinterland. By night, this slowed and we took cover to await the curious throbbing note of German bombers trying to penetrate the defences. As they came over, the fireworks display was incredible. Shore-based anti-aircraft guns, combined with naval vessels offshore and search lights, produced an umbrella of tracer lines and brilliant beams topped with the flashes of bursting time-fused shells in the sky above. Steel helmets were essential, since the amount of shrapnel falling from these aerial explosions was nearly as lethal as any bombs that fell. Most of the planes were driven off course, but a few persisted and dropped mainly anti-personnel bombs.

'One day I had a disagreement with a signals officer who occupied the dugout next to our headquarters. As we sheltered in our respective hovels, a most tremendous explosion occurred, sand descended everywhere and as the bombers' engines faded away, we went out to investigate damages. In the dim moonlight, it was obvious that our neighbours had suffered a direct hit.

'I heard a sound like a sheep baa-ing and as I made my way into the remains of the dugout, I could see the form of a man slouched against the side. The sound was his weak call of 'HELP!' I realised he was wounded and tried to drag him out, whereupon he swore at me for causing him pain. I assured him I would contact medical and went off to report to our MO's tent in the dunes. Next morning, Page, always a source of all local information, told me the soldier had been patched up and put on a returning craft for Blighty, but a piece of shrapnel from the bomb had decapitated the signals officer. I felt very bad at having parted on bad terms, as it were, but that is death for you - it is always wise to try and avoid regrets.

'None of our experiences were pleasant, least of all perhaps the regular journey for the morning session at Battalion HQ, having to pass a stack of rigid German corpses awaiting burial by Pioneer Corps detachments whose miserable duty it was to undertake this task. They did not arrive for some ten days, as this priority was naturally well down the list. By this time the top body, staring steadily out to sea, had been named Nelson, since he only possessed one dead eye, the other being a black hole where a bullet or a piece of shrapnel had abruptly finished his career in the Wehrmacht.

'In time, almost worse, however, was the frightful stink from numerous cattle carcasses killed by the primary bombardment and dotted about all over the place in fields adjoining the beaches. In the hot June sunshine, these Norman moos began to decompose rapidly, producing an all-pervading and very offensive odour. Due to their bulk, a bulldozer was required to dig holes big enough to bury these massive ladies, so it was some weeks before hygiene could supersede the demands of combat.

'Fortunately, any guns on the German defences over the river had been sited to fire seawards and only their Short-range mortars could be brought to bear on our most easterly positions, so with tremendous anti-aircraft defence and Air Force superiority, the primary dumps, now packed with enormous quantities of ammunition, petrol and diesel fuel due to the Caen hold-up, had survived intact.

'On about the tenth morning, I arrived at the entrance to the deep Battalion HQ bunker and was surprised to hear the noise of airplane engines just across the river. Pausing, I spotted a two-engined bomber approaching at low altitude, surrounded by exploding shell bursts but obviously on a suicide mission. I froze as I saw the tail disappear in a cloud of smoke and the plane go into a nosedive. I suddenly realised it was going to land very much nearer than I had imagined and started for the shelter of the bunker. Three steps down, a tremendous roar smote my eardrums and a blast of hot air hit the back of my neck and hurled me, unhurt, to the bottom of the entrance.

'Hell on earth ensued. The aircraft, with its bomb load, had landed smack between the ammunition and fuel dumps, creating destruction that is not difficult to imagine. Camouflage nets draped, as instructed, on the stacks, spread the fire among wooden boxes and hot jerry-cans. The 'whole bang shoot'; had to be left to die out. Fortunately, with the 'Mulberry' harbour and 'Pluto' (Pipe Line Under the Ocean) established, supplies of ammunition and fuel were soon replenished and I do not think the combat troops suffered any lack of backup.

'About a week after landing, my flank platoon guarding the entrance to the canal and the mouth of the Orne reported that, in moonlight, movement could be seen on the beach below their positions. These were still behind German barbed wire on which hung, as usual, the yellow signs with black skull and cross bones signifying 'Minefield' - (Achtung Minen, in German). Some were genuine and some dummy, but one could not tell which!

'Orders were issued that we should open an entrance to allow patrols to descend and check the reported movements in case the enemy was planning a counter-attack and had landed reconnaissance parties across the water. We decided to cut the wire after darkness had fallen and make the way down. At about 11 pm, I presented myself at the chosen point and found a lot of whispering but little movement in progress. A gap in the wire could be seen and the NCO holding a detector turned to me with the words 'We think it's a mine, Sir.' Silence. It was clearly a case of 'where the buck stops'.

'I put on the earphones and sure enough, when pushed forward the detector pad generated the telltale whistle in my ears. Thinking hard, I started the routine we had rehearsed. Feel gently over the surface - no booby-trap wires. Scrape away the sand to expose the top of the mine casing - no smooth casing as demonstrated by Royal Engineers in our training sessions. Somewhat heartened, I dug deeper and soon felt the raw edges of a large chunk of shell casing, deposited no doubt in the preliminary bombardment. Triumphantly I held it up as the cause of the detector's warning. It proved to be a dummy field, of course and the required path was soon cleared of wire, giving access to the beach.

'Regular patrols at night established that no German activity existed, proving the point that if you are a weary sentry and stare long enough at a dark object in pale moonlight or worse still, starlight, you will see it move and be appropriately alarmed. About a week after landing we noticed a strange vessel moving towards the low cliffs beyond the river where the remaining Germans were entrenched. To our surprise, it did not head into the shore as a large landing craft, which it resembled, but swung to lie parallel to the land. It hove to and immediately disappeared in a huge cloud of fire and smoke. We thought it had been hit and exploded - not so.

'Out of the smoke sailed a huge line of rockets, followed by a roar as the sound of their launching reached us. A few seconds later, the German positions disappeared in a similar but far larger cataclysm - to our considerable satisfaction. As the original cloud of smoke cleared, we realised that the rocketeers had been busy re-loading because the performance was repeated twice, then the rocket ship quietly moved away and disappeared beyond the line of our 'Mulberry' harbour.

'The stubborn defence of Caen was causing a good deal of embarrassment to the High Command who handed the 'baby' to Bomber Harris. One morning, we heard the sound of engines and were about to take cover when we saw a wave of aircraft coming in from over the sea. As soon as the first line drew near, a second appeared and then another and another until the whole sky appeared full of big four-engined bombers heading inland. The Luftwaffe had been rendered powerless, of course, so they flew in quite low and entirely unopposed.

'A few minutes after the first wave had passed; we heard a rumble like thunder that went on and on as a great cloud of smoke and dust rose up above the inland horizons. Caen was being flattened. Even after this, it was reported that some German resistance was encountered, but the plug had been pulled and the mass of attacking power flooded through to meet up with the Canadians and Americans now wheeling around to drive north towards Germany.

'Prior to this, we had been able to move off the beach into a better grade of billet in the town, into a house that still boasted a roof. One disadvantage applied, however, as lying offshore was the navy's only monitor, a flat sort of vessel equipped with a pair of enormous guns. From time to time, troops inland would call on support against a specific target, whereupon the sailors would loose off two mighty shells which could actually be seen, glowing red, as they sailed overhead. These somehow seemed to coincide with our breakfast or lunch, now being served by Page and co, in a civilised manner at a dusty table. 'The double 'crack' of the missiles would be heard speeding aloft. The drill was to cover one's plate and count one, two, three, four, five - pause! After this delay, the blast from the discharge of 14-inch armament reached shore. Walls shook, cracked ceilings showered chips and plaster dust as we stopped our ears against the noise. We then gave a cheer and uncovered our plates, knowing it would be some time before the guns had cooled enough to be reloaded in anticipation of further potential destruction.'

Major R. G. H. Brocklehurst of the Bucks and Oxon Light Infantry.

Bob Littlar, meanwhile, had moved inland with the rest of the 2nd Battalion King's Shropshire Light Infantry: 'We were supposed to assemble in an orchard and I was concentrating on that. Eventually we moved off inland, on the road to Caen. We walked past what must have been lovely seafront houses in peaceful days. We were moving south towards our assembly area and suddenly I could see a German plane coming from my left. He was dropping what I could only describe as oil bombs. I could see them bursting and the flames going up and spreading. We were carrying Bangalore torpedoes and I turned to the lads and said, 'Dump those in the ditch, quickly and lie on the road - it's our only hope if they explode.' Fortunately the bomber missed the road. We decided to leave the Bangalore torpedoes behind. We eventually got to the orchard where our battalion was gathering and were organised into company groups. We were getting shelled, I have no idea where from. A piece of shrapnel hit my lance corporal, it cut his boot open and you could see flesh and blood sticking out through the hole. 'That's it,' he said to me. 'Cheerio, I'm off with the stretcher-bearers.' That left me without a lance corporal.

'We were meant to ride forward onto Périers Ridge with some tanks, but the tanks never showed up so the decision was taken that the battalion would move forward without the support of the tanks. My company was to be the first one going up the left hand side of the road and W company was to go up the right hand side. The concentration of fire on this ridge was incredible and to this day I have no idea whether it was our boys or the enemy firing. Whoever it was, it wasn't nice.

'We left a space of at least five yards between each man as we moved up the hill, as we had been trained to do. This is to avoid a cluster of men being hit at once. The first bit was all right, but then we got closer and closer to this massive concentration of fire. I was so scared I got down on my hands and knees and then onto my stomach. It was a baptism of fire. I had never seen anything like it. I think some of the fire was German, but some of it was our ships firing onto the ridge. We eventually made it over the ridge and onto the southern slope, where the fire eased off a bit. What I didn't know at this time was that there was a German battery of six guns on the right-hand side of the road at Périers-sur-le-Dan. The brigadier had ordered our colonel to send a company to deal with that and that reduced us to just three companies.

'We carried on towards Beuville and in the distance I could see what I would call a wadi, with a small stream running through it. It was now coming up to midday and we had been going since 4am. I was feeling tired and decided that I would cross the stream at a bridge. We could see the village on the other side of the river, but as we rounded a corner near the bridge, BAM! A chap from W company was hit by an incendiary and killed instantly as the bandoliers of ammunition around his waist exploded. I thought the fire had come from a farm on my left so I turned around and started shooting at the farmhouse. Took all the windows out. But of course, they fire from ground level. I wasn't to know that - these things you learn on the job. I saw another company commander taking a hit in his shoulder, then tossing a grenade over a wall because he thought the fire had come from there, but in truth none of us had any idea where it had come from.

'By this time three tanks had caught up with us and one of the captains was leaning out, telling our lieutenant that he'd seen about 40 Germans going to a farm 3,500 metres away. My platoon commander ordered me to go across the road and around the right-hand flank of the village, to the meadows at the back of the buildings. We scrambled up the banks, heading for the back of the village. All the while we were being fired on by snipers. A corporal in charge of one of the other sections (a company is made up of three platoons and each platoon has three sections, each one of them commanded by a corporal) came up to me and told me who had been hit by snipers. Most of them were other NCOs. We both got our jack knives out and removed the stripes from our uniforms and put them in our pockets. We rubbed some dirt onto our uniforms where the stripes had been. We never wore our stripes again during that campaign.

'After we crossed the road to the village of Epron, our deployment was halted and the order came to dig in. Some anti-tank guns were moved into the area, so we were expecting German tanks, but I hadn't seen any of them at that point. Four German tanks soon showed up but they were deterred by our anti-tank guns and swung away to the west. We had 20 minutes to dig in, so we paired up and got our shovels and picks out. We were in an orchard so the soil wasn't too bad. You dig in roughly to shoulder-height. By about 5pm we were dug in and we stayed in that position during the night-time for five days, moving around during the day. That night, a few Messerschmitts flew over and machine-gunned us and there was some intermittent shelling as well.

'Our objective had been to reach Caen by the end of the day, but we realised that we wouldn't be able to do that. We did do a few patrols forward, but the battalion stayed put for the night. In the end, we only reached Caen more than a month later. We had known that D-Day would be something huge and I felt proud to have been a part of it. We felt it had been an honour to have been selected, but we were only a small cog in a very big machine.'

'I'm looking towards the bay now. It is really an almost unbelievable sight. It's stiff with shipping. Warships, landing-craft, merchant vessels - everything right down to motor-launches and small boats. There they are, their signal lights winking in the late evening sun, an occasional siren hooting. Overhead, the sky - there's hardly a cloud to be seen anywhere; but the sky's picked out with silver barrage balloons, as thick as currants in a pre-war Christmas cake. And of course we've got our air cover; they're up there now, as they are every moment of the day. And so, on this ground where a fortnight ago the Germans were masters, tonight the Allies are in complete control. I stood by the roadside yesterday and watched the men and machines and supplies rolling in. And a soldier beside me - I don't know who he was - just turned and said: Once you've seen all this, you know we just can't help winning this war.' That's just how we all feel here.'

Frank Gillard, BBC Broadcast, 18 June.

The Road To Victory – Normandy to Berlin

These pictures record one soldier's personal journey from invasion beach to German capital.

After the chaos of coming ashore, inland was the wreckage of the airborne invasion.

On 10 June 1944, 2nd Lieutenant John A. Weese of the 386th Fighter Squadron, 365th Fighter Group was flying P-47D 42-76279 D5-H as 'tail end Charlie' in a four-ship flight on patrol over the Cherbourg Peninsula. Separated in the broken cloud deck, he radioed he'd been hit; with his engine oil pressure falling and a malfunctioning propeller, he reported he could see the Normandy beachhead, and thought he could belly-land behind friendly lines. He made no mention of being wounded, but was apparently killed in action. The wreckage of the Thunderbolt remained at the high water mark, amongst the other wreckage of war.

Wrecked Waco gliders and C-47s'.

The wrecked French village of Villers Bocage...
The battle for the village took place on 13 June, one week after the Allies landed in Normandy to begin the liberation of German-occupied France.

The battle was the result of a British attempt to improve their position by exploiting a temporary vulnerability in the German defences to the west of the city of Caen After being severely damaged by the fighting of 13 June and subsequent bombing raids, the town was finally liberated by a patrol of the 1st Battalion Dorset Regiment, on 4 August 1944.

The road to Berlin was littered with hastily scrawled roadsigns warning of enemy attack.

The village of Aunay-sur Odon was virtually destroyed by shelling.

The village of Cahagnes was a commune in the Calvados department in the Basse-Normandie region in northwestern France.

Cahagnes was also to suffer severe damage during the days of fighting.

The agony and the ecstasy.

The face of despair. A French woman sits among the debris of her devastated Normandy village home...while the face of Victory can be seen on the face of a French woman who is overjoyed to welcome Allied troops to the town of Gisors.

Below: A French family rests in the cloisters of Caen Cathedral, one of the few large buildings left virtually unscathed in the city during the Allied bombing.

A British soldier helps an elderly French lady through the ruins of Caen.

French civilians meet British commanders after the Allies finally captured Caen.

A French woman looks down on a column of British Army vehicles moving down a street in Bayeux

Brigadier General Charles de Gaulle leads Free French troops through the streets of Bayeux, the first French town to be liberated after the invasion.

French civilians welcome British troops with glasses of cider as they stop at a Normandy farmhouse.

British infantry advance inland from Gold Beach.

A flail tank squeezes through the narrow streets of Cahagnes.

Left: Caumont

Below: An abandoned German tank at Thaon.

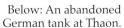

Burnt out German vehicles, such as this troop carrier burnt out at Gheel.

The Basilica of St. Thérèse of Lisieux, dedicated to the saint. The incomplete building was little damaged by the war.

88mm gun

A dummy
German tank.

Crossing the
Seine

The destroyed railway line at Lens

There was still time for sightseeing, such as here at the memorial to the First World War dead at Vimy Ridge

The devastation at St Silvian

Crossing the French-Belgian border on the road to Brussels

Mechelen (Malines): Grote Markt (Large Market square), St. Rumbold's Cathedral

The Town Hall at Mechelen

A destroyed German tank in the town square at Gheel.

The main square in Brussels.

The wreckage of a German V-1

Left: the remains of the
Reichstag in Berlin.

The badly damaged and burnt
out Reich Chancellry, showing
Adler's Balcony.

Below: journey's end - the
Brandenburg Gate in Berlin.

Chapter 4

A Foothold On The Continent Of Europe

'Joy Howard, the wife of John Howard who had led the glider attack on the Caen Canal bridge, was feeding her baby at home in Oxford, too busy to switch on the radio, when a kindly neighbour came in and asked her to spend the day with her and said somebody had given her a brace of pheasants which they could have for dinner. Joy was surprised by this sudden invitation and her mind flew to the problems of taking the pram for the baby and the high chair for the two-year-old, 'We thought you'd like company on a day like this,' the neighbour said; and then, seeing her bewilderment she added: 'Oh, haven't you heard the news?'

John had told her weeks before that by the time she heard of an airborne attack, his own part in it would be over; and so it was, for the moment. Just about then, in fact, he was finding time to laugh. Two Italians had reported for duty at the bridge. They had been working for the Germans, digging the holes and putting up the anti-glider posts in the meadow by the bridge where his gliders had landed. They had finished the holes, but not the posts. Now they did not know what to do, but after they had argued it out between them, they decided they had better carry on. So they went into the field and started putting up the anti-glider posts, all round the gliders which were already there.

Connie Bowes, who had just got engaged to Ivor Stevens of the Beach Control group, heard the news on the radio in the factory where she worked at Hawick in Scotland. It was a stocking factory, turned over to making jettison fuel tanks for aircraft and all the workers were women; and almost all of them had a son or a husband or a lover who had not told her for months what he was doing and had not written at all for weeks. Work stopped for a bit and then went on with extra energy. Almost everyone in the factory was in tears. Connie Bowes kept her feelings to herself, but she wondered what Steve was doing.

Perhaps it was just as well she did not know, because just about then he was lying in a slit trench on top of another man and thought his last moment had come. All morning, since Neville Gill had been wounded, Steve had been looking after his exit from 'Sword' Beach, not caring about anything except to see that traffic kept moving through it. Suddenly he saw men scattering for cover on the beach and looked behind him and saw a row of German bombers tearing along the beach at the height of the villa roof-tops. He dived for his trench and as he fell in on top of the man who had got there first, he saw the first plane hit and swerve towards him. It went over the trench so low that he felt the heat of it and it hit the dune a few feet beyond him and burst into flames. Expecting to be burnt alive, he jumped up to get out, but the first of the bombs in the aircraft exploded with the heat and he quickly lay down again. Bombs went on exploding one by one. It was a long time before Steve and the man underneath him agreed that *the last had gone off.*

Sylvia Ogden-Smith, whose husband was the man who swam ashore to sample sand, was also at work in her factory in Wales when she heard the news and understood why Bruce was not coming to Buckingham Palace that afternoon to get his Military Medal, though nobody had told her what he had done to earn it. On June 6th she had already put on her best hat and was on her way to the railway station in Wales when she had a telephone message to say that her husband was unavoidably detained and would not be turning up to meet the King. Nothing surprised her by then. She went home and sadly put the hat away again, hoping she would need it to go to the Palace one day.

As welfare supervisor, she had been given notices to be posted when the invasion had started, urging the staff to work even harder to support the men at the front. She went round and stuck them on the notice-boards, but they were not at all necessary. She saw a stout elderly mother sobbing over her capstan lathe, but the lathe was still running and her hands were moving as fast as ever. She went to talk to her and found most of the other women weeping at their work. She tried to cheer them up and then she went away to have a cry herself.

Her husband, just about then, was trying to help to rescue the crew of a landing craft which was burning furiously aground on 'Omaha' Beach; and somewhere quite close to him, Henry Meyers, the schoolmaster from Brooklyn, who had landed in conditions worse than any of the women had imagined, was waiting to advance with his telephone wire; and his wife Molly, who operated an accounting machine in a New York store, was given time off and went to church to pray for him, with her friends from the office who had husbands and lovers overseas in England.

Dawn of D-Day. [53]

In the morning, the House of Commons was packed by members waiting eagerly for a statement by Mr. Churchill; but nothing whatever disturbs the routine of Parliament. Question time was first. A Communist member made a plea for the abolition of banks and an independent asked the Secretary to the Treasury if he would arrange that members of the Government Minor and Manipulative Grades Association of Office Cleaners should be referred to in future as such and not as charwomen or charladies. When many matters like these had been disposed of and Churchill rose to speak, he added to the atmosphere of impatient expectancy by talking for ten minutes about the fall of Rome which had been announced the day before. Of course that was only fair to the men who were fighting in Italy; but he seemed to members to be taking a mischievous delight in keeping them on tenterhooks and his own account confirms that he enjoyed it. When at last he announced the invasion he added: 'So far, the commanders who are engaged report that everything is proceeding according to plan. And what a plan! This vast operation is undoubtedly the most complicated and difficult that has ever taken place.' That afternoon, in a second statement, he reminded the House: It is a most serious time that we enter upon. Thank God we enter upon it with our great Allies all in good heart and all in good friendship.'

Dawn of D-Day. [53]

53 By David Howarth (The Companion Book Club 1959).

> The annual meeting of the Channel Tunnel Company was held that day in London and the chairman reported that the future of the tunnel was impossible to foresee.

'Everything has started well. The mines, obstacles and land batteries have been largely overcome. The air landings have been very successful and on a large scale. Infantry landings are proceeding rapidly and many tanks and self-propelled guns are already ashore.'

Churchill in a telegraph to Marshal Stalin on the afternoon of 6 June.

'My colleagues and I cannot but admit that the history of warfare knows no like undertaking from the point of view of its scale, its vast conception and its masterly execution. Napoleon in his time failed ignominiously to force the Channel. Only our allies have succeeded in realizing with honour the grandiose plan. History will record this deed as an achievement of the highest order.'

Marshal Stalin.

'Our convoy of ten tank landing craft arrived on the evening of D-Day. The battleships and rocket craft were firing continuously. There was a scare while we were under a smokescreen as a plane flew overhead, but it turned out to be a Spitfire. We landed early next day… Unfortunately, my mate, Fred Bone from Chesham, had to endure many months of torment. He had lost his false teeth overboard.'

Sapper Harold Merritt 689 Road and Airfield Construction Company, Royal Engineers.

'I never kept a diary in peacetime and in wartime my particular duties forbade it, but on going through some notes recently I came across a piece of paper on which I had scribbled some impressions on what I imagine must have been about D+5. I quote them exactly as I jotted them down:

'I am standing outside Naval Headquarters about half a mile inland. Wheeler (N.O.I.C.) has just gone in to deal with an urgent signal.

'The church bells are ringing and the villagers are going to Evensong in their Sunday best... Nuns in their wide white hats. Tanks and lorries are roaring by, but no one takes any notice... Children are giving Nazi salutes... how could they know otherwise. All look remarkably clean and comparatively well fed... Their shoe leather is good.

'Looking out to sea from slightly high ground, Cherbourg peninsular stretches out to the left, Le Havre away to the right. Criss-crossing the beach and along the roads leading up from it, are long lines of dust... lorries, tanks, bulldozers and heaven knows what. At their sides the infantry are marching to lorry embarkation points. Many are wet through from wading ashore. Prisoners are going down to the beaches and either side of the roads... miserable and downcast.

'Sand dunes at top of the beaches are dotted with people hurrying hither and thither like industrious ants. Large coloured beach signs for incoming landing craft, wind sleeves and barrage balloons give a Derby day atmosphere.

Burnt out tanks and beached landing craft - relics of D-Day - give the opposite impression.

'Shipping as far as the eye can see. Transports, supply ships, 'Mulberries' on the way over, more and more landing craft in never ending stream.

'Lights flashing from HQ ship... freighters and small tankers beached on sand. Mobile cranes on beach moving overturned vehicles.

'Clouds at 4,000 - overcast. Spitfires overhead. Cruisers with guns angled right up, bombarding. Rodney firing salvos from further out at sea.

'Mines going off in sea, more mines exploding on beaches, 'Achtung Minen' and deaths head signs all around me.

'Anti-U-boat destroyers patrolling outside anchorage. More ships, including hospital ships, coming in.

'Two peasants late for Evensong.

'What a change from school holidays. Only two things the same - villagers going to church and waves lapping up on the beach.

'Wind rising.'

'It was only a few days before an unexpected gale swept the Channel and did untold damage to the prefabricated ports upon which the whole operation depended. Had that gale come a little earlier and before we were as strongly established ashore, I shudder to think what might have happened.

'Shades of Dunkirk, North Africa and Sicily! We have a lot to be grateful for in our prayers.'

Anthony Kimmins.

'We boarded a Danish ship in Swansea, Wales on 5 June and sailed around the tip of England on the 6 June, arriving at 'Omaha' Beach at about noon. We stayed aboard ship that night and were both strafed and bombed. Finally reaching our assembly point on 7 June we relieved units of the 1st Division North of Trevières. We were greatly harassed by German sniper fire all the way. That got us off the beach. Of the three Regiments of the Second Infantry division; the 9th and the 38th were the first to come ashore. At the time a multitude of things that would float - gas masks, back packs, life preservers, dead bodies, body parts, spare tyres and - was floating in the surf. We were catching a lot of artillery fire from shore batteries that had not yet been knocked out. The surf was rough and the landing craft was pitching wildly and making it hard for the coxswain to get the craft ashore in the appointed place. Our landing craft hit a sandbar 50 yards out and thinking we were at the beach they lowered the ramp. I was intending to be the first one off because it was rumoured aboard ship that the German gunners would zero in on a landing craft and as soon as the ramp came down they would try to put a round in the landing craft. We were told on one occasion they succeeded killing all except one of the 100 men aboard that craft. When the ramp went down I went off to the side going in over my head holding my rifle and ammo high. Finally straightening up I could hold my head back and wade ashore. For the first two hours it was utter chaos and confusion.'

Pfc James Branch, HQ Company, 1st Battalion, 38th Infantry Regiment, 2nd Division. 'Our first baptism of fire came on 9 June when we were ordered to attack south at High Noon. We encountered stiff resistance around

Trevières. We were attacking without our heavy weapons, as they were to come ashore yet. We crossed the L'Aure River. After house-to-house battling in Trevières we then moved to take Cerisy. We captured a road junction near Haute Littee cutting the Ste-Lô-Bayeux highway and then one our companies took the village of Vaucrevon. On our first two days in combat we advanced a total of 17 kilometres. Not bad for a first time in combat Infantry Regiment without its Heavy weapons. Our aim was Ste-Lô via Hill 192, which is another story in itself.

'...They took us to an apple orchard. The orchard looked lovely, the blossom smelt lovely and there was also honeysuckle and orange blossom. We were dug in near an old farmhouse. I shall never forget that very warm June afternoon. We'd been shelled a number of times. We decided to take a rest. We didn't take off our clothes for three weeks but we changed them when we went back to a rest camp. While we were in the apple orchard we lay in our trench one afternoon taking it easy. Private Dean, who was only 18, was reading some books his sister had sent him. All of a sudden I heard this shell coming over; it fell short and I just managed to duck my head down in the nick of time. It killed this young soldier in the trench next to me. His mate was very upset at that time: he never got a scratch on him. How lucky can you be? We had to lift this boy out of his trench and lay him against a tree ready to be picked up by the stretcher bearers. Perhaps someday I will manage to visit his grave.

'We had to crawl through cornfields a number of times. We had to look for a wounded Bren gunner and we found him all right sitting under a tree but his foot was nearly blown off. He was very pleased we saved his life. That evening Jerry had turned the Tiger tank on them and they had fled leaving the Bren gunner alone badly wounded. We lost another of our Bren gunners in a wood near Caen. We had to put our attack in about 3 o'clock in the afternoon. We all had some rum to sip: I thought this is my lot now. We had to crawl along by these trees and then make a mad dash to this wood. As I was running I ran past one of our men who had been killed. At the end of the wood I had to help my Bren gunner pull his Bren gun up. As we lay there the Jerries opened up on us. The bullets were hitting the trees behind us and we were getting wounded. I shall never forget my Bren gunner as long as I live. He was a very brave soldier. He took his gun, stood up and let them have it, right into the Jerry strongpoint. I thought to myself 'I hope he knocks them out' but as he was firing he was shot and fell with his head down. I was lying behind him waiting to see what would happen. There was another of my mates behind me; I looked at him and thought he was dead as well. He had a great big cut across his forehead and was in a pretty bad way. I decided to stand up to see what was going on. All of a sudden I was hit in my leg by a piece of shrapnel. It was bleeding pretty bad. I couldn't see many of my mates about. I expect they were lying at the ready with their rifles at the alert. I thought to myself; 'What shall I do? It's either got to be me or the Jerry. So I went forward and noticed that Private Taylor the Bren gunner was dead; so I took the Bren gun off him and tried to do my best to keep up the covering fire. As I was firing I was hit in both arms. My left arm was badly hurt but I didn't seem to care what happened to me after I saw the

Bren gunner fall before my very eyes. Somebody had been watching us boys - our Corporal. He came across to see me and knew I was in a bad way. He told me 'Lay still. Don't worry, you'll be picked up. You've done your share today. Give me that Bren gun.' He had seen what happened and said he would recommend me for the Military Medal when I got to Caen. I don't think I deserved that: I think the Bren gunner who I was with should have had that.

'They picked me up and took me in a tent where we all had labels put on us. General Montgomery should have shaken hands with us but I missed seeing him which I thought was a shame. I sailed on a hospital ship and landed at Southampton. I spent some time in Bradford Hospital. We had plenty of entertainment while I was there. The nurses were very kind to us. I was discharged from Hospital on 24 May 1945.

Private Benstead, South Lancs Regiment.

'We had arrived in England - or rather, Valley, Wales - on D+1- via ATC. The airport was just a runway in the Welsh farm country. Upon deplaning, knowing the invasion was in progress and wanting some information about the war, I walked over to a welsh farmer not far from the runway and asked if there was any news from the Continent.

'Aye, 'tis a great contest going on over there. 'Tis a great contest.' These were the first words to greet my ears in the ETO.'

Lieutenant Eugene Fletcher, pilot of B-17 *Government Issue,* **assigned to the 412th Bomb Squadron, 95th Bomb Group at Horham, Suffolk.**

'Shortly after daybreak on D+1 a troop transport, the USS *Susan B. Anthony,* flashed its signal light at us. I was surprised, but I flashed the go-ahead signal. His message was 'come alongside, we need help.' I should have called the skipper, but I figured he needed the rest and just answered, 'Sorry, we have other orders and we can't change them.' His response was 'We are sinking.' Then I saw life rafts being launched and there was a column of smoke pouring out of the starboard side. I ran down off the bridge and shouted into the skipper's cabin: 'Get up! Get up, quick!' And then with hardly pausing down into the engine room, I started the engines. I rushed back up to meet some of my sleepy mates and the skipper and I shouted, 'That SOB over there is sinking!' We got into action almost before the anchor cleared the bottom and slammed alongside the *Susan B. Anthony,* which turned out to be carrying part of the 79th, Cross of Lorraine Division, one of the reserve divisions. Within a few minutes the rescue efforts were joined by plenty of other craft. Actually, the *Susan B. Anthony* was a victim of one of the mines that had dropped the night before. Our first instruction was to land the troops on the beach, but a colonel got on the radio and raised hell, saying that his men had lost equipment, were disorganized and in no shape to take on the German Army. So, including our two wounded men we put them aboard another empty transport.

'That afternoon we were ordered to help off load a cargo of 81mm mortar shells on a liberty ship, which gave us our first opportunity to return to the beach. The beach was really a mess. It was littered with discarded life belts, bodies, wrecked landing craft including two LCIs, destroyed tanks and jeeps and small craft; it was just terrible. The end of the beach was near the perimeter of the US lines. We helped with the unloading and there was enemy shelling close by. We could see those shells landing perhaps 400 or 500 yards away so we didn't get to stay around very long. At the beach party's urging, we got off as quickly as we could and headed back for another load. With little rest for about five straight days now, the skipper got approval from the flotilla commander to anchor and do some more clean up, but mainly for rest. We lay to and did nothing but clean the craft and then get to bed early.

'Next day we again picked up a cargo of ammunition and returned to the north-eastern end of 'Omaha' Beach. The beach engineer and the Navy demolition teams had been hard at work disarming and removing obstacles. Bulldozers were at work laying roadways and flattening the dunes. Bodies were being collected and there was a steady stream of landing craft of all types, including LSTs landing on the beach and retracting. There was just a mass of men, materials, weapons and ammunition being piled up along the beach.

'Much of an artificial harbour was formed by placing the concrete caissons that had been towed over from England and also by scuttling old ships; all this to shelter the beach from rough weather. The pontoon causeways which were also under construction were quite useful because they extended out several hundred yards from the high water mark. Larger craft like LSTs could come in and tie up to them and lower their ramp and rapidly disembark their vehicles and they didn't have to be concerned about getting stranded on the beach if the tide dropped too quickly. But unloading was really slow and most of the craft, particularly the ones like LCTs, had to stay on the beach through a high tide and low tide cycle. This wasn't really a problem because the beaching vessels all had flat bottoms and we merely sat safely on the hard sand. The only discomfort was that without a source of cooling water, generators and engines had to be shut down.'

William Thomas O'Neill, LCT 6-544. [54]

54 On D+3, we picked up a cargo for delivery to Isigny-sur-Mer, perhaps to test LCTs for river transport. My only recollection is the hoards of mosquitoes we encountered on the river. Shortly after D-Day a raging storm tore up the beach area. The artificial harbour was severely damaged, the causeways were swept away and many landing craft were beached. We were lucky. Although we were dragging anchor like crazy, we started our engines and ran them in reverse - full speed at times - and that was just enough to keep us from dragging anchor and joining the other unlucky ones on the beach. So, for the LCT (6)-544, its part in the European operation settled down to a routine and boring existence of going out to the cargo ships, picking up a load and then bringing it down to the beach. Our two casualties returned after some time. They went back to the UK to a hospital there and we were happy to see them again. We did lose another one of our crew members, one of the veterans from the Mediterranean, who became depressed and we transferred him to a hospital ship. The crew had some tangible rewards for D-Day. The cook received the Navy and Marine Corps medal with a 'V' for valour. Stiegmeyer, the seaman who had volunteered to be the human depth finder, even though he didn't get to take his walk, was awarded the Silver Star and nobody begrudged him that. Our flotilla commander recommended the LCT 25, the 305, the 544, and the 545 for a Presidential Unit Citation, but nothing ever came of it. In September the Mediterranean veterans - Don Gray, Harry Hulscher, Bob Fusic and me were relieved and returned to the United States. The 544 remained in Normandy, continuing to unload cargo which diminished as Channel ports became available. It eventually was hit by a storm similar to the one that we had encountered in June and was destroyed, but most of the original crew was off the LCT by that time.

'The small number of American troops in London yesterday saw few outward changes in the life of the Allies' invasion capital. There were no hooters or noisy celebrations, but on practically every street corner long queues, mostly women, stood awaiting the latest editions. American and Allied soldiers in non-combat jobs quietly read their papers and went to work. Their sentiments the same as those of the MP on guard duty at a headquarters building who said fervently. 'Christ, I wish I was over there with them.'

G I Joes and London's - reaction was, 'We've waited a long time for this, now let's make it good.'

There was a new tenseness among the people in the buses and busy thoroughfares but everyone seemed to be waiting for the next fellow to show how excited he was. Yanks in London who expected to see the population get het up remembered that most of them had fathers or brothers fighting with the invasion troops.

A girl bus conductress said the only difference she had noticed was that passengers were more polite than ever before.

One policeman, on his beat in Piccadilly, compared yesterday with Sept. 3, 1939 - the day Britain declared war. 'We waited and worried a long time then before we knew for certain whether we had to fight,' he said. 'We've waited a long time for the invasion. Now it's here I think everybody will be calmer than ever before. It's the waiting and worrying that gets you down.'

American MPs patrolled with orders to send soldiers on pass and furlough from camps more than 25 miles out back to their stations.

Most London Red Cross clubs were half-empty and everywhere the conversation of American and British workers was of the soldiers, now fighting, who have swarmed through the buildings during the last year and more.
Arthur W. White *Stars and Stripes* Staff Writer, Wednesday 7 June.

'The first infantry and tanks moved in along the main road and already French tricolours and Union Jacks were flying from roof tops and balconies. All our vehicles were brought to a dead stop by crowds of old men, women and children packing the main street. The whole town was hysterical with excitement and joy and many of the old people simply stood there and cried. But all around there was a roar of cheering and shouting and waving; our troops were embraced, kissed, showered with roses and carnations, bottles of wine and glasses brought out and toasts drunk in the streets. The children were clambering over the jeeps and asking for souvenirs. Odd pennies and sixpences were produced and handed round. Then gradually the crowds split up and groups of our men were taken off to cafes and hotels and the celebration started all over again with much piano playing and singing of God Save The King and the Marseillaise.'
The British Liberate Bayeux; BBC news bulletin, 8 June.

'The first British woman arrived in Normandy as early as D-2. She was twenty two year old Corporal Lydia Alford of the WAAFs, who flew over to tend eight wounded soldiers who were being evacuated that same day to England. The wounded were reported to be surprised to see women so close to the front.

Corporal Alford saw nothing of the fighting, but LACW Sylvia Carter, who followed her the next day, did; her Red Cross plane landed in the middle of a German barrage and she was forced to take cover with the soldiers until it was time to load up the new casualties.'

Charles Whiting, British Liberation Army 1944-45.

At Hethel Bob Sherwood noted the sense of anti climax after the thrill of D-Day. The 389th was alerted to fly every day after 6 June. Every day Hall's crew was slated to fly; each day there was a stand down. The weather was impossible. Fog and rain. Anything that was not paved turned into brown mud. The crews stayed in their damp, dark huts. They dashed out only to get meals. The humid mess hall smelled of powdered eggs, stale grease and wet wool.'

The Little Gramper's Tour, Certified Brave **by Robert H. Sherwood.**

'The stench of war was everywhere. The scene on the beach was one of destruction, with houses alight and knocked-out tanks burning. I saw a commando first-aid post with quite a few wounded lying out on stretchers. The commandos were clearing houses of sniper and odd pockets of Germans. The captured Germans looked as if they had suffered badly and some were helping their own badly wounded down the road. We were on the extreme left of the seaborne forces at Ouistreham, on the River Orne. The area faced high ground and we were shelled heavily. But one enemy tracked vehicle showed itself and was quickly disposed of. Suddenly the most magnificent sight appeared in the sky - swarms of bombers towing gliders. Many were hit and were crash-landing. My first day in France ended in a noisy night, with incessant gunfire.'

Les Barber, tank driver.

'I was ploughing fields when above the noise of my tractor I heard a strange drone in the sky. It was a sight I'll never forget. Over the horizon were so many aircraft they blotted out the sky. As the sound got louder I was so afraid that I hid in a ditch. That evening they were bringing casualties into a nearby army hospital and we land-girls volunteered to help the wounded. One American soldier insisted on giving me a little present to show his appreciation. He said it was something to remember D-Day. It was a Purple Heart medal awarded to US soldiers wounded in action.'

Patricia Gent, a land-girl near Blandford, Dorset.

'I was doing war work in a local factory when the radio programme 'Workers' Playtime' was suddenly interrupted soon after 10 o'clock and news of the D-Day landings was announced. Everybody cheered - including me. It was only later that I learned that by the time I heard the announcement my husband was already dead.'

Jessie Mosley, twenty years old and who had been married for only two months to a paratrooper.

'I knew something desperate was happening and wasn't surprised when the radio announced landings on the Normandy beaches. It was D-Day. I felt sure that my husband was in that terrible affray... we were told on the radio that we would receive a card from the troops who had gone over on D-Day. The next day all my husband's letters that had been held up arrived. In one of them he begged me to keep writing. I wrote to him every day for three anxious weeks. Every day I waited for the postman to bring me that longed-for card. The card never came. Instead a letter arrived from the War Office telling me that it was their 'painful duty to inform' me that my husband had been killed on D-Day. Mrs. F. Jones of Birkenhead who was married to a corporal.

'After 24 hours off, Ward 1, women's medical had changed beyond recognition. As I opened the ward doors I could hardly believe it. First of all it was the untidiness that hit me. Every bed and locker was overflowing with khaki; Greatcoats, kitbags, remnants of tattered uniforms and army boots under every bed. The beds themselves were filled with the pride of the army - glider pilots, parachutists, commandos, soldiers of the first wave of the assault troops to land on or behind the beaches. They were all so masculine. Splintered arms and legs stuck out from the beds at the most peculiar angles. I can remember the faces of many of them: The four Cockneys who each spoke a different London dialect. I can even remember their wounds. The tank sergeant with the burnt hands, the young football fanatic with a shattered knee, the quiet, older, glider pilot who survived three days and nights wounded in a dyke but soon to die of a coronary. And there was the boy who became one of my favourite patients. He was only 19 and one of his feet had been blown off. But he was always so cheerful and nearly drove us mad singing: 'Mares eat oats and does eat oats and little lambs eat ivy.'

19-year old Marjorie Jefferson, probationer nurse, Leeds General Infirmary.

'It was about two o'clock when Miss Hobbs, my nursing commandant, came into the office where I was working and said I was needed up at QA, which was Queen Alexandra's Hospital, that there were so many wounded coming back from the beaches that they desperately needed help. I ran home to tell my mother, got my uniform and then rushed up the hill to the hospital.

'Another girl who I saw once a week at lectures checked in shortly after I did and we reported to Matron together. She checked our names and told us to go to this particular ward. It took us some time to get there because all the corridors were laid end to end with stretchers. Lorries were corning up from the dockyard so quickly that there wasn't room for all the wounded. The army stretcher bearers knew who was badly wounded and those who were less seriously wounded were put on the floor.

'When we got to the ward we were told to start cleaning people up, giving them drinks and things. Many of them were filthy - well, they were quite young and when you're frightened you know what happens, you're all messy and dirty - so the main thing was to clean them and bed-bath them. We didn't have to treat their wounds or anything, if you took somebody's filthy battledress off and found something bad and then you would call a sister.

'Mostly they were conscious but not talking much; they were mostly really, really tired and later on in the day we were told that these were the first exhaustion cases. A lot of them were so completely exhausted they didn't care one jot what happened to them. They had been on standby since the day before. 'Some of them could speak, but when you are completely exhausted, not just very tired, when you are too tired to care about anything, you just want to be cleaned up and have something to drink. They weren't hungry.

'As I worked with these poor exhausted soldiers, I was thinking, 'How long will it go on? If I come tomorrow and the next day, will I still be doing this?'

'While I was washing and cleaning up filthy and dreadful and horrible messes and giving out water and cold milk to people who were allowed such things, two sisters came round and asked if I would be willing to work in the German prisoners' ward. They needed the same kind of help, but some nurses refused to go into their ward.

'I had to go and see Matron first. I went with my friend, Win. Matron said, 'You know we have a lot of German prisoners - they were picked up very early from the beaches.' I said I didn't know, but had just been told. She said, 'Well, a lot of people won't work with them, they are either walking out or refusing to work with them. Will you do what you're doing, for them?'

'Well, I was a bit meek and mild and I didn't say anything and Win looked at me and Matron said, 'Hurry up and make up your minds, because if you are not going to do it, I'll try somebody else.' Win looked at me and said, 'Oh, come on, Naina. My Eddie is out there and if somebody said they wouldn't clean him up, Mum would feel terrible.' So with that, I felt that if Win was going to do it, I'll do it. We would do it together and protect each other! I also couldn't bear the thought of my commandant saying to me, 'One of my girls wouldn't even give a prisoner a cup of water?'

16-year-old nurse, Naina Beaven.

'Sister was a young girl from London and she looked at us and said: 'When my boys come in, you girls might be the last thing these boys see on earth … I want a gentle smile and when you bend over my boys have a nice look in your eyes and don't let your eyes reflect what you see.' One chap, who was very badly burned, said to me: 'I'm quite good-looking really, you know, Nurse.' I said, 'Your eyes are not bad now, they're quite saucy.' So he said, 'You wouldn't like to give us a kiss, would you Nurse?' We weren't allowed, but I looked around and I bent down and kissed him on his horribly burned lips with the awful smell coming off his burns.'

Mary Verrier, Hants 12th Detachment, VAD, Portsmouth.

'…And then the casualties came. I was an operating room supervisor. We started out with one operating room theatre and then we required another because we just couldn't handle all the casualties. When I say theatre I mean several rooms, each room with its own surgeon and nurse and corpsman [enlisted Navy medical personnel]. It was one big unit. The first casualties came into my downstairs operating room and kept on coming. We had no place to put them so we put them out in the halls and everywhere. We never thought about food, sleep or anything else. The doctors, as well as the nurses and corpsmen were taking care of patients. Finally sleep had to be rationed because no one would leave their work. We lived on sandwiches and coffee for a long time. As the casualty load lightened, things got back to a decent pace.'

Nurse Helen Pavlovsky USN stationed at The Royal Victoria Hospital at Netley.

'A lot of the casualties were suffering from 'shell shock.' Some of them didn't know who we were. They thought we were Germans and they wouldn't tell us anything except their names and serial numbers. They were classified as mentally ill. Some of them were just farm boys and the shock of war was just too much for them.'

Sara Marcum, a ward nurse originally from rural Kentucky, who after graduating nursing school in January 1943 joined the Navy Nurse Corps.

'I had a 30-bed surgical ward; 27 of my patients who had been severely wounded on 6 and 7 June were critically ill. All were 19 and 20 years old - younger than I was. Some had fingers and arms blown off. One had his buttocks blown off. Some had stomach wounds. It was one almost constant nightmare. We were fighting death. One 19-year-old boy from Texas had been in a tank and all but his face and the top of his head and the palms of his hands were burned. Before he was picked up he had lain there so he was covered with maggots. He told me, 'I can stand the pain of the burns but the crawling maggots are driving me almost insane.' The doctors, the sergeant and myself immersed him in warm, sterile, saline solution but never got them all. A tall young black man read from the Bible to him. This white Texan and the black Southern soldier talked about God together. I had the Miraculous Medal and I asked him if I could put it on his finger. I so wanted him to live. He whispered to me, 'Don't worry, don't worry, I am ready to go and when I die, I want you to write to my parents and tell them I was prepared and I knew I would see God.'

'So I did.'

Elizabeth Hillmann, American Army Nurse.

'The paratroopers fought their way down to the beachhead. They had captured 214 German Prisoners of War, many of which were wounded. It was my duty to put them on a tank deck, take them back to England to treat them for their wounds. For one example, one German had a hole in his chest. I asked the doctor, 'What do we do with him?' He said, 'Oh, put some peroxide on him and slap a bandage on him.' So I did. I also had charge of feeding the prisoners and passing out the water to the prisoners. In the corners of the tank deck, there were paratroopers with machine guns guarding the prisoners. We had about 50 paratroopers on our LST on one trip we made across. We were in the worst storm that lasted for three days, which is the worst storm in recorded history for over 60 years. Finally, as we get the beachhead under more control, they landed the troops and they were as glad to get off our ship as we were to be on the ship and not have to go onto shore at that time. After we loaded the paratroopers, we could still hear the machine guns firing up in the hedgerows. Finally, the storm ended, after three days. The odour was terrible from having so many people aboard the ship with no facilities. We took them back to

England to get more supplies. There was a great fear that we would not be able to get back in time to reinforce the troops so that they could continue going forward. We made six trips across the Channel before the time came to be sent back to Norfolk, Virginia.'

Maro P. Flagg, Chief Pharmacist's Mate US Navy.

'We got off the Normandy coast late in the day of D-Day. There were armadas of ships, boats of all sorts. There was a great deal of gunfire on shore. It was maybe a couple of weeks after that before I put my feet on shore. Our ship was assigned to the British beaches sort of on loan. Their LSTs had one doctor for a group or flotilla but they did not have the Liberty ships of the kind that I was on to look after the personnel so we were sent to 'Sword' and 'Gold'. I saw actually more British personnel during the weeks and months of the landing than I did Americans. I did not see any severe casualties of war. We had minor accidents, illnesses and a fair amount of venereal disease. If I had anything severe, I took them by small landing craft to a hospital ship of which there was almost always one in sight. They came over and anchored a few days and picked up a load of casualties and took them back.

'We stayed anywhere from one to four miles offshore depending on where we were and what the tides were like. There was a time when we ran aground and we got off in a high tide into deeper water. We mainly watched the boats and ships that brought the supplies ashore. We actually swung an anchor there for four months until late September before I was taken back to England. During that time later on after the Cherbourg had gotten secure and Normandy beaches had all cleared, I went ashore many times to take men that had problems that I couldn't handle to bigger hospitals ashore and that sort of thing.

'When our ship was hit by flak falling from the sky one of our cooks looked up and apparently with his jaw sagging, one of his sets of false teeth fell out on the deck. He reached down to pick it up and the other set fell out and both burst in two. Well, to have a cook with no teeth was a minor disaster. A hospital ship took the teeth back to England on their next trip. When it returned after a number of days and much complaining by the cook, I picked up his teeth and from then on our food improved considerably.

'I guess my most exciting thing was one time in very foul weather when I did an appendectomy on somebody that had an absolutely red hot case of acute appendicitis. I had no way of doing a blood count on him so I had to make the diagnosis purely clinical. None of my five pharmacists' mates had ever been in an operating room for a major operation so we had two or three rehearsals! I did the operation on him under general anaesthesia, having one pharmacist mate, drop ether on an open ether mask under my direction. Another pharmacist mate did nothing but kill flies throughout the procedure. One more or less held me to the table because the ship was rolling terribly and one assisted and one handled the non-sterile instruments as they came back and forth from the autoclave. We took the appendix out, kept the fellow for two or three days and when the weather was calm shipped him off to a hospital.

'Another fellow came down with gonorrhoea. Again, no way of diagnosing by microscopic examination, because I didn't have a microscope. I was not given any penicillin. I did have sulphur, which I started him on, but I knew some penicillin would be a very helpful so I got a boat and we started off from ship to ship to ship begging penicillin. It was my only time to board some real British men-o-war. I'll never forget the curious look they gave me when I asked permission to go to the sick bay to seek out a doctor and ask him if he could give me some penicillin. I got 10,000 units here and 10,000 units there and 10,000 or so from a hospital ship, all together making up I guess 50 or 60,000 units which I gave this man. The gonorrhoea germ was not as resistant to penicillin as it is now and the man was successfully cured.

'When things quieted down, I made several rather pleasant trips up and down the Normandy coast. I very much wanted to go to Paris, but it would involve being away from my ship overnight and I was never willing to do that. I was given leave, though, at one time and went back to England on a ride back on an LCI. We spent a couple of days at Solcombe. None of the five other doctors at St. Elmo Hospital had ever left. They were still seeing some casualties but never had any very acute activity in the war. I think they sort of envied me having been on the coast and seeing some of the action. So after swinging in anchor for four months, seeing a good deal of medical problems, I got orders and was shipped back to the States with the idea of being sent to the Pacific.'
Lieutenant (J.G.) Simon V. Ward, US Navy Medical Corps, ss *Woodward*.

'Veronica and I are gloating over the stories about Shimi. His commandos refused to wear helmets and went into the attack in their green berets, with Piper William Millin leading the way. 'Give us *Highland Laddie*, man!' Shimi yelled as he plunged into the sea up to his armpits. Once on shore the piper paraded up and down the beach playing *Road to the Isles* oblivious of the shells and shouts of 'Get down you silly bugger!' Relieving the bridge over the River Orne, he strolled along in his plimsolls, as if he were inspecting a herd of bulls, with his inevitable pipers - who, I think, really deserve a medal - playing *Blue Bonnets over the Border*. The Scottish papers gave him a colossal spread on the lines of 'Tall, handsome Lord Lovat, a leader any man would die for, strolled up to the bridgehead in an open-neck pullover,' and so on. Veronica and I are, of course, lapping it up. It even consoles her for the awful fact that she has got piles!
Joan Wyndham, a WAAF stationed near Inverness who had discovered that she was 'a sort of distant cousin' of the Lovat family and frequently spent her free time at Beaufort Castle and with Simon ('Shimi') Lovat's sister, Veronica.

'In England we had been told that we would be driving on the left side of the road like in England. I soon discovered this was incorrect. As I drove my load of radio equipment up the hill from the beach I noticed other six by six trucks with stretchers placed from bench to bench with soldiers on them. At first I thought they were wounded GI's being taken back to England, Then I realized they were the dead GI's being removed from the battlefield. Also I noticed six-foot high piles of bloodied blankets all around. As I drove on farther I met a truck heavily loaded with German bodies piled in a criss-cross; helter-skelter fashion being taken to a bull dozed burial place. Inland the road was lined with dead soldiers and also dead bloated cattle with their legs outstretched. One dead soldier with curly hair really hit me emotionally. He looked just like a dear friend from high school days.'

Orv Iverson, 9th Tactical Air Command Signals Section.

'We were to be thrown into the battle to establish the beach heads on the Normandy coast. Our part was to prevent movement of enemy reinforcements from the rear of their defences through into the battle area. Along with thirteen other crews we were briefed on 6/7 June to attack bridges in Caen over which there were enemy troop movements. O-Oboe carried eighteen 500lb GP bombs. The flight out to the target was uneventful and we made our attack from 5,000 feet as briefed. Then without any warning the aircraft was raked with cannon and machine gun fire, with a short reply from the rear gunner. Ron Walker put the Lancaster into a dive to starboard and commenced to corkscrew away from the area. There was no more fire from the enemy aircraft, identified by Flying Officer Crombie from the astrodome, as a Ju 88. Ron called all members of the crew to check if all was well. There was no reply from Pilot Officer Tom Quayle, the mid-upper gunner so I went back along the fuselage to see what the problem was, only to find that Tom had been killed in the action. His wounds were such that he must have died instantly. I told Ron of Tom's fate. Flying Officer Ken Bly, our Canadian Air Bomber, came back from his place in the nose of the aircraft, not believing what I had said and obviously taken aback by the event. I persuaded him to return to his place in the nose position and with Ron's permission, I advised base of the attack made upon us by the enemy fighter and the death of the gunner. From the inside of the fuselage, it was obvious that we had sustained a lot of damage from the cannon fire from the fighter and care in landing would be required, particularly as the aircraft was not handling too well. The reply from base said that an ambulance would be ready to receive us.

'It was nearly 5am as we circled the airfield and headed down wind when we were given permission to land. Although we made a not too bumpy landing, a tyre burst, the starboard wing broke open and out came the dinghy, which inflated and was dragged along the runway. We headed towards the waiting ambulance and the medical team led by the Station Medical Officer. On entering the aircraft they looked at Tom and quickly confirmed my original diagnosis that he had lost his life when we were hit by the cannon and gunfire from the enemy fighter. Furthermore the Lancaster was in a mess. Both gun turrets were damaged, the bomb bay had been hit, there were many cannon and machine gun bullet holes in the fuselage and the port, tail and mainplane were damaged. A sad night indeed. After the debriefing, we met the Medical Officer who prescribed drugs to get us all off to sleep for the day. I slept well into the next day and felt much rested when I awoke. With the rest of the crew, I was stood down from flying for a few days, although the squadron was still active with attacks on the enemy in support of our land forces in Normandy.'

Flight Sergeant Roland 'Ginger' A. Hammersley DFM, **RAF Lancaster air gunner, 57 Squadron. On 6/7 June 1,065 RAF bombers dropped 3,488 tons of bombs on nine rail and road centres used by the enemy to bring reinforcements to the Normandy battle area. Ten Lancasters and a Halifax were lost.**

On 6/7 June 1,065 RAF four engine bombers and Mosquitoes dropped 3,488 tons of bombs on nine choke points including bridges and road and rail centres behind the Normandy battle area. Important road and railway bridges at Coutances were badly damaged by five squadrons of Halifaxes of 6 Group who bombed visually onto red and green TIs dropped by two Lancasters and three Mosquitoes of 8 Group. But much of the town was hit and set on fire and 312 civilians were killed. Two Lancasters were lost and a Halifax III on 426 'Thunderbird' Squadron, which was hit by a bomb while over the aiming point, was later abandoned over Slapton Sands off the south coast of Devon and crashed near Torquay. A 408 'Goose' Squadron Halifax landed damaged at Melbourne. Four Lancasters were lost on the 5 Group attack on Caen where the Main Force of bombers had to wait for the target to be properly marked and then fly over an area teeming with German units and guns at bombing heights below 3,000 feet. At Dunholme Lodge two Lancasters were missing; one on 44 Squadron with the entire crew and one on 619 Squadron whose pilot Flight Lieutenant Kimberley Roberts DFC RAAF and four of the crew were killed. Two men who survived were taken into captivity. There were only four survivors on the two other missing Lancasters; Q-Queenie on 630 Squadron at East Kirkby and B-Baker on 83 Squadron at Coningsby. Among the dead was 1st Lieutenant C. J. Van Horn USAAF, the navigator on B-Baker flown by Flying Officer George Mervyn Kennedy RNZAF who also died.

Four Lancasters were lost on the 5 Group attack on Caen where the Main Force of bombers had to wait for the target to be properly marked and then fly over an area teeming with German units and guns at bombing heights below 3,000 feet. On 83 Squadron at Coningsby Flight Lieutenant Bill Siddle's crew had volunteered for a second tour and when asked if he was coming with them Clayton C. Moore, Siddle's Canadian rear gunner, could see little point in refusing. His second tour began at thirty minutes past midnight on Wednesday June the 7th when the squadron had lifted off for the hastily called attack on the marshalling yards at Caen.

'Because of the considerable confusion caused by the swift and unpredictable arrival of the Allied armada, we encountered only moderate opposition over the target area. This was to be expected in the circumstances. Because of the vast area of coastline to be defended against possible invasion, the German resources in guns and troops were scattered and sparse and would remain so until these could be concentrated in the area of the attack. In the initial stages of the invasion, we could expect to be called upon frequently to attack these important road and rail centres so that the transportation of vital enemy troops and equipment to the front could be delayed. The attack on Caen turned out to be a fairly easy one for us and it was the first operation I could recall during which I had not seen a single aircraft being shot down.'

The centre of Caen was left in flames, the river barrage over the Orne was destroyed, four other bridges were destroyed or had their approaches blocked and the main roads from the town to Falaise and Bayeaux were badly cratered. At Vire two of the three Lancasters lost were shot down by enemy fighters, the other to flak. The attack, by 1 Group, was over in about five minutes, during which time the bombers hit all the choke points and partly destroyed the railway station. The centre of the town was in ruins with rubble blocking the roads. 5 Group's Lancasters attacked Argentan and another force bombed Lisieux and Conde. At Achères near Paris about half of the 97 Lancasters of 1 Group did not bomb as Campbell Muirhead recalled: 'Duff weather, heavy cloud and rain. Was map-reading my way quite easily up to the target had even selected and fused my bombs, when the Master Bomber of the Pathfinders Force came on the air and ordered us to take our bombs back to base. Having real finger trouble the PFF, not being able to identify the railway junction. (Yet, to be fair, perhaps the cloud beneath the Master Bomber was much thicker than the stuff below us.) Was annoying, really, to be able to identify that rail Junction so clearly, even to see it sliding so steadily up my bombsight towards the graticule (as you get it on to the graticule you press the tit) then to be told not to bomb it. Felt inclined to press the tit despite the order, but thought better of it. Not that I'm becoming 'bomb-happy' or anything like that, but for all I know, because we didn't bomb, a German troop train, maybe even carrying Tiger tanks which can knock hell, so we understand, out of any tanks we or the Yanks possess, bound for Normandy might, as a result, be able to pass through that junction before dawn.

'So we returned to base with our bomb load. Our turn over Achères brought us over the outskirts of Paris. They don't have a black-out there; it's a form of 'blue-out' and you can see, dimly, the outlines of certain streets. Now and then torches could be seen flashing 'V'. Suppose the French would have to stand on roofs to do that, otherwise the Germans would shoot them. No flak or searchlights over Paris. In fact, this evening we haven't had flak or searchlights anywhere. Wonder if I'll ever visit Paris. Before the war only the comparatively rich could afford to visit France (when everything was very cheap, a bottle of wine, I'm told, costing about a tanner). Maybe my turn will come after the war.

'Seven aircraft missing from this operation, though none from Wickenby, which shows that there must have been quite a few night-fighters knocking around. Surprising they made so many kills what with all that heavy cloud and without searchlights to guide them. Reckon their victims must have been Lancs who got out of the bomber stream and were then sitting ducks, easily picked up by the radar sets the night-fighters are supposed to be able to use with great accuracy once the German ground control has guided them to the vicinity of the wandering Lanc. It's the old, old story; allow yourselves to get out of the bomber stream and almost certainly you have had it; even on a five hour round trip into Northern France.'

A Lancaster which failed to return crashed at Eragny with the loss of all seven crew. More than 1,060 aircraft had attacked and dropped 11,500 tons of bombs. F/L J. S. A. Marshall RAAF recorded in his log book a tragic moment on returning from the trip to Argentan: 'On crossing the Channel the Navy (ours) shot down a Lanc about 200 yards on our port. Trigger happy bastards.'

The centre of Caen was left in flames, the river barrage over the Orne was destroyed, four other bridges were destroyed or had their approaches blocked and the main roads from the town to Falaise and Bayeaux were badly cratered. At Vire two of the three Lancasters lost were shot down by enemy fighters, the other to flak. The attack, by 1 Group, was over in about five minutes, during which time the bombers hit all the choke points and partly destroyed the railway station. The centre of the town was in ruins with rubble blocking the roads. The last of the initial raids was on the rail centre at St-Lô by 103 Halifaxes of 4 Group without loss. Wing Commander 'Pat' Daniels the Master Bomber on 35 Squadron controlled the attack well. Having dropped his markers from 4,000 feet, just below the cloud, he was able to observe some good, concentrated bombing on the town and railway yards. The locomotive depot was partly destroyed.

Argentan, Conde and Lisieux were next. 5 Group's Lancasters attacked Argentan with more than 100 aircraft and everything appeared to go well. But at 02.28 hours, A-Apple and 23-year old Flight Sergeant Cliff King's crew on 9 Squadron at Bardney contacted Waddington direction finding (DF) believed asking for a weather report. Due to the weak signal, Waddington reported back the message and at 02.42 hours sent a weather report. Neither message was acknowledged. Later it was learned that A-Apple had collided with trees and crashed near Belvoir Castle in the Leicestershire Wolds not far from Grantham. Only the rear gunner survived. King, whose commission had come through the day before and who had a wife in Boscombe, died at the controls of the Lancaster. The other five men on his crew, which included the navigator, 20-year old Flight Sergeant James Morton Stevenson RCAF were killed. Stevenson's parents had emigrated from Scotland to the USA and had gone to live in Parkchester in the Bronx district of New York. Their son had completed his first trip on 28 May when the squadron flew a feint towards the German battery at Ste-Martin-de-Varreville at Cherbourg. He too would not get to wear his Pilot Officer rings on his sleeves or enjoy the modest increase in pay, still way short by USAAF standards; but it went without saying that few if any of the American volunteer airmen in the RAF were in it for pounds, shillings and pence.

About 100 aircraft each of 3 and 6 Groups attacked Lisieux and Conde. The Canadian Group suffered no losses but at Lisieux a 115 Squadron Lancaster was lost. At Châteaudun in clear conditions 100 Halifaxes in 4 Group were directed by the Master Bomber, Squadron Leader E. L. Chidgey of 35 Squadron. It took five attempts to mark the rail junction using 'Oboe' and Chidgey could see that his back-up markers had landed some way from the Aim Point so he ordered the Main Force to bomb on those dropped by his deputy, Flight Lieutenant Lambert. A 578 Squadron Halifax which was hit by flak failed to return. To the east, at Achères near Paris about half of the 97 Lancasters of 1 Group did not bomb. Thick cloud covered the target and the markers that were dropped could not be seen. A few of the crews took it upon themselves to drop below the cloud and start bombing but Squadron Leader G. W. Godfrey the Master Bomber decided that the risk to French civilians was too great and ordered the raid to be abandoned. A Lancaster which failed to return crashed at Eragny with the loss of all seven crew. More than 1,060 aircraft had attacked and dropped 11,500 tons of bombs.

On the night of 6/7 June heavy He 177 Greif ('Griffon') bombers of II./KG 40 took off to raid Allied shipping off the Normandy coast with Hs 293 guided bombs but strong Allied night-fighter forces prevented the bombers' operations. The Australian 456 Squadron shot down four He 177s in the area of Cherbourg and Cap Barfleur.

Raids on the communication targets continued on the night of 7/8 June when 337 aircraft were dispatched to bomb railway targets near Paris at Achères, Juvisy, Chevreusse and Versailles-Matelet and an important road and rail junction at Massy-Palaiseau about 14 miles south of Paris. This target was very well marked with red and green TIs and bomb bursts were concentrated amongst them. The railway track could be seen in the light of explosions. Crews bombed from 6,000 feet and at this height they encountered intense light flak. On the leg into the target they also met considerable fighter opposition and eight bombers failed to return. Twenty-eight Lancasters and Halifaxes were lost on the raids on the road and rail targets. At Mildenhall where 25 Lancasters had been dispatched for the operation on Massy, no word was received from three of the four missing Lancasters on XV Squadron and the two on 622 Squadron. The Lancaster piloted by Flight Lieutenant W. J. Bell DFC on XV Squadron was badly shot up by a Me 410 and the navigator, Sergeant Charlie Kirk, was killed by a cannon shell. Bell crash-landed at Friston on Beachy Head where the aircraft immediately burst into flames but the crew all escaped with minor injuries.

On the raid on Chevreusse 115 Squadron at Witchford lost six Lancasters, one of which exploded over Paris. On the raid on Juvisy 78 Squadron at Breighton lost three Halifax IIIs and a fourth crashed at West Malling. The raid on Achères resulted in the loss of three Halifaxes and a fourth, piloted by Squadron Leader William Brodie Anderson DFC RCAF on 429 'Bison' Squadron RCAF was hit by flak as the Halifax passed Dieppe and would not make it back to Leeming. Anderson was mortally wounded and while still conscious, ordered his crew to bail out. Three did so over enemy territory. At this point Flight Sergeants John Mangione the mid-upper gunner and Gordon Ritchie the rear gunner dragged Anderson to the rear escape hatch, attached a static line to the pilot's parachute and pushed him out. Sergeant G. E. J. Steere the flight engineer had taken over the controls and he managed to fly the Halifax back across the Channel to reach the Oxfordshire area where he and the rest of the crew abandoned the aircraft before it crashed near Benson. The gunners' efforts were in vain and Anderson died. Mangione and Ritchie were awarded the DFM and Steer received a CGM.

In another attack, which was requested by the US 1st Army, 112 Lancasters and ten Mosquitoes of 1, 5 and 8 Groups carried out a raid on an important six-way road junction in the Fôret de Cerisy half way between Bayeux and Ste-Lô. The area was believed to contain fuel dumps and German tank units preparing to attack 1st Army units. The bombing was not successful however, as the Main Force bombed on a stray marker, which had been dropped in error six miles from the target. A Lancaster on 101 Squadron failed to return.

The night following 483 aircraft attacked rail targets at Alençon, Fougères, Mayenne, Pontabault and Rennes to prevent German reinforcements from the south reaching the Normandy battle area. Three Lancasters and a Mosquito failed to return. The raids created so much devastation that much of the 3rd Paratroop Division, which had arrived in Rennes from its bases around Brest on twelve trains before the attack closed the station, was soon bogged down; the approach road to St-Lô, the final destination, was cratered heavily over its last twenty miles. By the evening of 9 June, most of the 3rd Paratroop Division had got only as far as Brecey, east of Avranches. At Fougères the leading train transporting the 265th Infantry Division from Vannes and Quimper on the Brest Peninsular was bombed and cut in two and the rear half, which contained the Division's horses, rolled back down the line for four miles. When the wagons came to rest finally, the French released the horses and a 'Wild West'-type of round-up followed in which the German soldiers wasted much time acting as cowboys! [55]

'Wednesday 7 June. We crossed the invasion coast on the way to bomb a railway bridge over the Loire River at Nantes. The English Channel was positively jammed with ships and boats of all descriptions. Several landing craft were burning on the beaches. The fields near the coast were littered with Horsa and CG-4 gliders, all painted with the same black and white invasion striping we carried on our fuselage and wings. We took flak at Tours and then began our bomb run from the south of Nantes. Halfway down the bomb run, it became apparent we were on a collision course with a B-24 group. The enemy was beginning to pound us with 88s so we elected to do a '360' and came up behind another B-24 group. The second bomb run was good. We hit the target just at the southern approach to the bridge and there was a very large ball of flame in the marshalling yard - gasoline! We took more flak on the way out at Rennes and at Guernsey Island, where we were clobbered at only 11,000 feet.'
Diary entry, Lieutenant Abel L. Dolim, navigator, 332nd Bomb Squadron, 94th Bomb Group.

'21 Squadron was out whenever weather permitted patrolling behind the battlefront looking for anything that moved. The night of D-Day we were briefed to patrol the Caen-Lisieux-Boisney road to stop German reinforcements reaching the beachhead. We were told that there was a corridor across the Channel in which every aircraft must stay on outward and return flights. Our night-fighters were patrolling on either side of the corridor and were likely to regard any plane that was found outside the designated area as hostile. As we left the English coast a hail of flak went up from a ship in mid-Channel right where we were headed. Pretty shortly down went an aircraft in flames - it looked like one of our four-engined bombers. It seemed that one of our own ships (the Royal Navy got the blame) had parked itself right on the path that every aircraft going to and from the Continent that night would be following. And, in true naval fashion, it let fly at everything that went over. We decided to risk the night-fighters rather than

---

55 See *Point Blank and Beyond* by Lionel Lacey-Johnson (Airlife Classic 1991)

fly through that lot and did a wide detour. Whereas before D-Day there had been almost total darkness, now over France there were lights everywhere and most of the Normandy towns burned for several nights. Navigation was much easier; you just flew from one fire to the next.'

Les Bulmer, pilot, 21 Squadron.

Due to a last-minute alteration in the arrangements, legendary American war correspondent Ernie Pyle did not arrive on the beaches in France until the early morning after D-Day aboard a landing craft. His first report from 'Omaha' Beach entitled *A Pure Miracle* was 'pooled' - made available to all newspapers and news agencies: 'By the time we got here the beaches had been taken and the fighting had moved a couple of miles inland. All that remained on the beach was some sniping and artillery fire and the occasional startling blast of a mine geysering brown sand into the air. That plus a gigantic and pitiful litter of wreckage along miles of shoreline.

'Submerged tanks and overturned boats and burned trucks and shell-shattered jeeps and sad little personal belongings were strewn all over these bitter sands. That plus the bodies of soldiers lying in rows covered with blankets, the toes of their shoes sticking up in a line as though on drill. And other bodies, uncollected, still sprawling grotesquely in the sand or half hidden by the high grass beyond the beach. That plus an intense, grim determination of work-weary men to get this chaotic beach organized and get all the vital supplies and the reinforcements moving more rapidly over it from the stacked-up ships standing in droves out to sea.

'Now that it is over it seems to me a pure miracle that we ever took the beach at all. For some of our units it was easy, but in this special sector where I am now our troops faced such odds that our getting ashore was like my whipping Joe Louis down to a pulp...'

Pyle was not supposed to write the news of what was happening; that was for 'the boys at SHAEF' so, he began simply to walk. Over the new day or two Pyle, who described every war front he visited - from the Battle of Britain, to all the great American campaigns of World War II, in a plain yet poetic style reminiscent of Mark Twain and Will Rogers, provided powerful mental images of Normandy for his readers.

'I took a walk along the historic coast of Normandy in the country of France. 'It was a lovely day for strolling along the seashore. Men were sleeping on the sand, some of them sleeping forever. Men were floating in the water, but they didn't know they were in the water, for they were dead.

'The water was full of squishy little jellyfish about the size of your hand. Millions of them. In the center each of them had a green design exactly like a four-leaf clover. The good-luck emblem. Sure. Hell yes.
'I walked for a mile and a half along the water's edge of our many-miled invasion beach. You wanted to walk slowly, for the detail on that beach was infinite.

'The wreckage was vast and startling. The awful waste and destruction of war, even aside from the loss of human life, has always been one of its outstanding features to those who are in it. Anything and everything is expendable. And we did expend on our beachhead in Normandy during those first few hours.

Ernie Pyle described the material wreckage that lay in the surf-ruined trucks and barges: swamped boats and landing craft, burnt jeeps and tanks, abandoned rolls of barbed wire and steel matting and 'half-tracks carrying office equipment that had been made into a shambles by a single shell hit, their interiors still holding their useless equipage of smashed typewriters, telephones, office files... smashed bulldozers and big stacks of thrown-away lifebelts... and stacks of broken, rusting rifles.' [This wastage] 'was enough for a small war ... And yet we could afford it. We could afford it because we were on, we had our toehold and behind us there were such enormous replacements for this wreckage on the beach that you could hardly conceive of their sum total. Men and equipment were flowing from England in such a gigantic stream that it made the waste on the beachhead seem like nothing at all, really nothing at all.

'But there is another and more human litter. It extends in a thin little line, just like a high-water mark, for miles along the beach. This is the strewn personal gear, gear that will never be needed again, of those who fought and died to give us our entrance into Europe.

'Here in a jumbled row for mile on mile are soldiers' packs. Here are socks and shoe polish, sewing kits, diaries, Bibles and hand grenades. Here are the latest letters from home, with the address on each one neatly razored out-one of the security precautions enforced before the boys embarked.

'Here are toothbrushes and razors and snapshots of families back home staring up at you from the sand. Here are pocket-books, metal mirrors, extra trousers and bloody, abandoned shoes. Here are broken-handled shovels and portable radios smashed almost beyond recognition....

'I picked up a pocket Bible with a soldier's name in it and put it in my jacket. I carried it half a mile or so and then put it back down on the beach. I don't know why I picked it up, or why I put it back down...

'I stepped over the form of one youngster whom I thought dead. But when I looked down I saw he was only sleeping. He was very young and very tired. He lay on one elbow, his hand suspended in the air about six inches from the ground. And in the palm of his hand he held a large, smooth rock.

'I stood and looked at him a long time. He seemed in his sleep to hold that rock lovingly, as though it were his last link with a vanishing world...'

Ernie Pyle. [56]

'After D-Day floating bodies were plentiful off the Normandy coast. One, in particular, had been washed to and fro in the anchorage for days. We manoeuvred alongside and got lines round it and heaved it inboard. The head was nearly skeletonised and things crawled on the deck from the sodden bundle that had once been a RAF pilot. Everyone, even my coxswain, felt pretty sick.

'Come on you bastards,' I said. 'Rip off those clothes; let's see the poor devil's papers.' Then we weighted his feel and I forgot all about that lovely

---

56   See *Ernie Pyle's War: America's eyewitness to World War II* by James Tobin (The Free Press 1997).

prayer book of mine down below. As we slid him into the sea I just said: 'Oh Lord God, we commit these sorry remains to the sea from whence they came.' 'There was a silence in the wardroom. We could see that Denis was deeply moved and we knew the moral courage it had taken to perform that act.

'I sent the papers to NOIC Arromanches,' he went on, 'so some poor mother will know what happened to her son. And afterwards I issued a tot of' rum all round and entered the fact and the reason therefore, in the log.'

'What about your crew?' I asked.

'Oh,' said Denis, 'they just said 'You can offer us as much rum as you like, Sir, but we don't want any more jobs like that.' But it did the bastard's good.' 'Denis's eye beamed, our glasses clinked...'

Lieutenant Denis J. M. Glover DFC RNZNVR, **Commanding Officer, HM LCI(S) 516, recalling a conversation in the wardroom of LCI(S) 519 alongside a sunken block ship in the Arromanches Gooseberry.**

'...There were a lot of bodies we never identified. You know what a direct hit by a shell does to a guy. Or a mine. Or a solid hit with a grenade, even. Sometimes all we have left is a leg or a hunk of arm. The ones who stink the worst are the guys who got internal wounds and are dead about three weeks with the blood staying inside and rotting and when you move the body the blood comes out of the nose and mouth. Then some of them bloat up in the sun, they bloat so big that they bust their buttons and then they get blue and the skin peels. They don't all get blue, some of them get black. But they all stink. There's only one stink and that's it. You never get used to it either... And after a while the stink gets into your clothes and you can taste it in your mouth.

'You know what I think? I think that if every civilian in the world could smell this stink, then maybe we wouldn't have any more wars...'

Technical Sergeant Donald Haguall of the US 48th Quartermaster Graves Registration Company.

'I had never seen anything like these wounds. We would see a large hole in a man's chest with bits around and hear the sound of air going in and out. We saw a section of the abdominal wall blown away with bowel protruding. Limbs might be all or partially absent... I learned always to have a package of morphine syrettes in my pocket, as well as a pack of cigarettes and a lighter. Cigarettes were often the first request of a wounded soldier. I wore a cartridge belt which I kept loaded with chunks of chocolate supplied by my father. Somehow the large Hershey or Nestle bars which he sent got through. I also fed this chocolate to the tired me working on the wounded.

'...When I finally got to my bed, to my surprise, I slept. Occasional flares lit the sky in almost daylight. Heavy shells fired by our ships offshore and by our heavy artillery went over our heads sounding like freight trains. Incoming, we could hear the snap of bullets and the crunch of German 88s. Occasionally, we heard the whistle of descending mortar shells and we were to hear much more of them in the future. But the spot which we had chosen for the collecting company was perfect from a military point of view and only rarely did a shell hit near us.'

Combat Medic World War II by John A. Kerner MD. [57]

'On D+2, I noticed a man in a correspondent's suit - an overbearing, big man with a beard and kind of a foul mouth. I said to somebody, 'who in the hell is that fellow?' And they said 'That's Ernest Hemingway.' Well, I changed my mind about him. Just before I went into the service I had been to the movies and saw his story *For Whom the Bell Tolls.* I had a different impression of him after seeing what a foul-mouthed guy he was.'
 Robert Bogart, a medic on 'Omaha' Beach.

'NORMANDY, June 1944. - Our front lines were marked by long strips of colored cloth laid on the ground, and with colored smoke to guide our airmen during the mass bombing that preceded our breakout from the German ring that held us to the Normandy beachhead.

'Dive bombers hit it just right. We stood in the barnyard of a French farm and watched them barrel nearly straight down out of the sky. They were bombing about half a mile ahead of where we stood.

'They came in groups, diving from every direction, perfectly timed, one right after another. Everywhere you looked separate groups of planes were on the way down, or on the way back up, or slanted over for a dive, or circling, circling, circling over our heads, waiting for their turn.

'The air was full of sharp and distinct sounds of cracking bombs and the heavy rips of the planes' machine guns and the splitting screams of diving wings. It was all fast and furious, but yet distinct, as in a musical show in which you could distinguish throaty tunes and words.

'And then a new sound gradually droned into our ears, a sound deep and all encompassing with no notes in it - just a gigantic faraway surge of doom-like sound. It was the heavies. they came from directly behind us. At first they were the merest dots in the sky. You could see clots of them against the far heavens, too tiny to count individually. They came on with a terrible slowness. 'They came in flights of 12 three flights to a group and in groups stretched out across the sky. They came in 'families' of about 70 planes each.

'Maybe these gigantic waves were two miles apart, maybe they were 10 miles, I don't know. But I do know they came in a constant procession and I thought it would never end. What the Germans must have thought is beyond comprehension.

'Their march across the sky was slow and studied. I've never known a storm, or a machine, or any resolve of man that had about it the aura of such a ghastly relentlessness. You had the feeling that even had God appeared beseechingly before them in the sky with palms outward to persuade them back they would not have had within them the power to turn from their irresistible course.

'I stood with a little group of men, ranging from colonels to privates, back of the stone farmhouse. Slit trenches were all around the edges of the farmyard and a dugout with a tin roof was nearby. But we were so fascinated by the spectacle overhead that it never occurred to us that we might need the foxholes.

57 Creative Arts Book Company (Berkeley, California 2002).

'The first huge flight passed directly over our farmyard and others followed. We spread our feet and leaned far back trying to look straight up, until our steel helmets fell off. We'd cup our fingers around our eves like field glasses for a clearer view.

'And then the bombs came. They began ahead of us as the crackle of' popcorn and almost instantly swelled into a monstrous fury of noise that seemed surely to destroy all the world ahead of us.

'From then on for an hour and a half that had in it the agonies of centuries, the bombs came down. A wall of smoke and dust erected by them grew high in the sky. It filtered along the ground back through our own orchards. It sifted around us and into our noses. The bright day grew slowly dark from it.

'By now everything was an indescribable cauldron of sounds. Individual noises did not exist. The thundering of the motors in the sky and the roar of bombs ahead filled all the space for noise on earth. Our own heavy artillery was crashing all around us, yet we could hardly hear it.

'The Germans began to shoot heavy, high ack-ack. Great black puffs of it by the score speckled the sky until it was hard to distinguish smoke puffs from planes.

'And then someone shouted that one of the planes was smoking. Yes, we could all see it. A long, faint line of black smoke stretched straight for a mile behind one of them.

'And as we watched there was a gigantic sweep of flame over the plane. From nose to tail it disappeared in flame, and it slanted slowly down and banked around the sky in great wide curves, this way and that way, as rhythmically and gracefully as in a slow motion waltz.

'Then suddenly it seemed to change its mind and it swept upward, steeper and steeper and even slower until finally it seemed poised motionless on its own black pillar of smoke. And then just as slowly it turned over and dived for the earth - a golden spearhead on the straight black shaft of its own creation - and it disappeared behind the treetops.

'But before it was done there were more cries of, "there's another one smoking and there's a third one now.'

'Chutes came out of some of the planes. Out of some came no chutes at all. One of white silk caught on the tail of a plane. Men with binoculars could see him fighting to get loose until flames swept over him and then a tiny black dot fell through space, all alone.

'And all that time the great flat ceiling of the sky was roofed by all the others that didn't go down, plowing their way forward as if there were no turmoil in the world.

'Nothing deviated them by the slightest. They stalked on, slowly and with a dreadful pall of sound, as though they were seeing only something at a great distance and nothing existed in between. God, how you admired those men up there and sickened for the ones who fell.'

IT WAS THE HEAVIES by Ernie Pyle who on 18 April 1945 was killed on Ie Shima by a Japanese machine-gunner.

'The month we spent before Caen was a pretty bloody one in more ways than one. Those who had fought in the 1914-18 War told me that the battles before

Caen came up to anything they had ever experienced and I know that of the 212 casualties suffered by my regiment in the campaign in north-west Europe, at least seventy-five per cent were incurred during this month in Normandy.'

Brian Thatcher. The massive air raids succeeded only in creating piles of rubble which served the defenders but impeded the attackers. General Montgomery ordered 7th Armoured Division to drive south-east from Bayeux to Villers-Bocage. Once they had reached and consolidated around that area the German position would be untenable. The thrust from Bayeux by 7th Armoured was countered along the line Verrieres-Tilly by the newly arrived Panzer Lehr Division which forced the British formation to seek alternative routes to the objective. By 13 June part of 22nd Brigade had worked its way round 2nd Panzer flank and begun its move towards Villers-Bocage. Orders were issued that once the little town had been reached, 4th County of London Yeomanry and 'A' Company of 1st Battalion, The Rifle Brigade, were to push on and to take Point 213, the high ground which lay about a mile to the north-east. By 09.00 hours the point unit of 22nd Armoured had reached the little town.

"My first action was in Normandy. We landed on 10 June and I was surprised to see so little destruction. From BBC reports we all expected to see the place looking like the pictures of the Western Front - all mud and tree stumps. They tell me that Caen was a mess, but I never saw it so I cannot say. The countryside was very green with high hedges running along little roads. Some of the roads had hedges which were more than twelve-foot high and so thick you could not see through them. They were good defensive positions and the units that had been fighting in this sort of countryside deserve every credit. It must have been a real hell. There were lots of little cemeteries we passed as we moved up the line. Four or five graves in a group - an infantry Section perhaps, or a Sherman crew, because the place was littered with knocked out Shermans. And some of them stank. There were more than likely bodies still in them. So far as I remember from what we were told in 'O' groups, 7th Armoured was to capture a little town called Villers-Bocage. If it could do this it would have trapped the Jerries in Caen. They would have to pull out or be destroyed and if they pulled back we would have them on the run. Things turned out a bit different from what we were told was going to happen. The Jerry opposition was quite strong and it took us a couple of days to reach the little town which was our objective. '...We were in the town centre, a little square and not much else. There were a few shops open, cafes I think and we were just standing about waiting for orders when we heard the sound of gunfire coming from the road out of town. There seemed from the noise to be a big battle going on and presently we saw black clouds of smoke in the air. One of our soldiers said they were tanks blowing up. This did not sound so good as we had one of our armoured brigades on the road ahead. Then, all of a sudden our anti-tank platoons were ordered into action - to take post. The ammunition trucks were driven into side streets and all the rifle sections were told to take up positions in windows of houses on the 'enemy' side of the village, as it was called. To be honest, I saw nothing of the battle which followed, although I was in it. My memories are of the noise and the solid shot that smashed through the walls of the room in which I and a group of other Queensmen were positioned. I suppose, when you are excited or frightened noise sounds louder in some way. Also the narrow streets seemed to hold the noise in so that it sounded really loud. There were several loud bangs which were our 6-pounder anti-tank guns going off and then one very loud explosion. I learned later that this was a Bren-carrier of ammunition that went up. Then we heard tank tracks squeaking and squealing and these must have been Jerries because the sound seemed to be coming from the 'enemy' side. Then there was a whooshing sound and a sort of flashing light behind us in the room. We all turned round and there was a hole in the outside wall and another in the inside one. A solid shot had passed through the whole house - in one side and out the other. It had been an AP round, I suppose, from a Jerry tank. There was a lot of plaster dust in the air, but none of us had been hurt. We didn't think of it at the time, but if that shall had struck a couple of feet from where it did, all of us in that room would have been killed.

'The firing seemed to spread and I believe that Jerry infantry [Panzer Grenadiers] were working their way into the town. Then there was some more tank gun fire, some machine-gun fire and then dead silence. We all waited. Nothing happened for about ten minutes or more. Then an officer came up the stairs and told us to fall in outside. The street was a mess. Bricks and rubble all over the place. A couple of hundred yards up the road there was the biggest tank I had ever seen. It looked undamaged. One of our 6-pounders was lying on its side, just opposite our house. Up came the unit transport and we moved back up the road which we had been along first thing that morning.'

Albert Kingston, the Queen's Brigade, part of 7th Armoured Division. SS Obersturmführer Michael Wittman, a veteran of the Eastern Front (where he had destroyed 137 tanks) and his 'Tiger' tank crew in the 101st SS Heavy Tank Battalion destroyed 25 tanks, 14 half-tracks and 14 Bren-gun carriers. In the narrow streets of Villers-Bocage a shot fired by one of the 6-pounder anti-tank guns of the Queens blew off the track of Wittmann's 'Tiger' and he and his crew were forced to abandon the vehicle. After a bitter fight 7th Armoured Division withdrew towards Tilly. Wittman, who had received the Ritterkreuz (Knight's Cross) with Oak Leaves, was eventually killed on 8 August.

'My Company entered Caen the morning after it had been reduced to a heap of rubble by allied bombers. Buildings leaned at crazy angles and we had to use bulldozers to make a passage through the streets. There had been heavy casualties among the French civilians and those who survived to see us enter regarded us without enthusiasm. Nearly all of them had lost their homes and dearest possessions. Furthermore, the Germans had only withdrawn across the river and there was every probability that they would return in a few days to drive the British out.

'The heavy hand of the Nazis had lain on Caen for a long time and one could be sure that, in the event of their return, severe punishment would fall on any who had helped the invaders. The sublime confidence of the British soldiers, however, admitted no such possibility and in a very short time various units established themselves in what remained of former German billets.

'Most of these had a really elaborate and solid air-raid shelter or bunker attached. Civilians could not use these shelters during the German occupation and fearing their return (after all, they were only a few hundred yards. away), few would use them now. I occupied one of them, well below ground. It was about eighteen feet long by six feet wide, with steps at each end. Close by it stood a wooden shed in which I stored the Company's rations for which I was responsible.

'For a few days things remained quiet. I made daily trips from Caen to the beach-head to obtain supplies. Those trips were not without interest, for German artillery shelled ahead of dust clouds raised by trucks though few were hit. Returning to Caen with a load of rations one evening I gave a lift to an infantry corporal who was trying to rejoin his unit somewhere along the River Orne. It was late when we reached Caen and after he had helped to unload the boxes of rations into the wooden shed he asked if he could stay the night with our Company and try to find his unit in the following day. He was a small man with a quiet manner. I was mildly surprised, later in the evening, to hear him carrying on a conversation in fluent French with an old man near our billet.

'When darkness fell we prepared to sleep. People slept in strange places in Caen. Immediately facing the entrance to my shelter and about fifty yards away was a large open garage. The doors had been blown off and were lying some distance away.

'The garage was now occupied by fourteen or fifteen French children, up to about ten years of age, who slept there on the floor. A middle-aged man who had gathered them together in the hope of one day returning them to their parents kept a fatherly eye on them. They went to 'bed' early, but tormenting flies and mosquitoes kept them awake. Also, they were hungry and several times I had heard them talking late into the night. Tonight, however, all were peacefully asleep. It was a glorious evening and as darkness fell and covered the ruins around us it was possible to forget the war for a few moments. The Corporal and I smoked a cigarette together before we entered the shelter to sleep. It was quite dark down there of course, but I had a small electric torch and our preparations for sleep were not elaborate. We lay on the floor and chatted a while.

'And then the Germans across the river decided to complete the destruction of Caen. They opened up a terrific bombardment; shells whistled and crashed into the ruined city. I put on my boots and went to look out from the door of our shelter.

'It was dark, of course, but fires and flashes lit up the space around the shelter. My store of rations received a direct hit and the boxes flew through the air. It was very noisy as shells poured in, but we were safe enough in the shelter. A pinging, humming noise puzzled me for a while until I saw that a long row of iron railings had been blown down. They now lay around like so many deadly spears and each shell-burst sent them flying through the air with awful force.

'At about this time the Corporal joined me in the doorway. A Dunkirk veteran, he was not unduly perturbed about the shelling, but as the bombardment intensified he thought that perhaps it might be the prelude to a counter-attack and decided to put his boots on. It was then we heard the terrified screams of the children and caught glimpses of them rushing around in the open. The Corporal left my side and dashed out into the darkness. The shells screamed and the iron railings hummed and whistled through the air with appalling force. The Corporal brought back four children, thrust them into the shelter and then rushed out again. Crazy with hysteria, the children tried to follow him and I had difficulty in restraining them. The Corporal returned with four more children. The others, he said, could not come. I knew why.

'Down in the shelter we tried to calm the children. It was difficult in the darkness and presently the Corporal took an electric torch and ventured out again. Into the shelter he flung some empty ration boxes. He followed them down hurriedly and arranged them along one side of the shelter.

'By the light of the torch he seated the children on the boxes. He himself sat on one box and by his side he placed a pile of chocolate bars salvaged from the ration store.

'The Corporal's manner calmed the children. He asked which of them had seen the film *Snow White.* I had noticed posters in the town advertising it. Most of the children had seen it but there were three mites who had not. To each of these three he gave a bar of chocolate. Already they were less afraid and gradually, in his quiet voice, he persuaded the others to tell him about the film. Breaking into their excited chatter he told them that he would give chocolate to each one who could sing a song from the film. The others must join in the chorus. A bold spirit started and the others followed. What matter that each one sang the same song? They were singing. They were eating chocolate. Their eyes were bright - and not with fear. There was no war and they were safe!'
The Children of Caen, **E. J. Madden.**

'In the days following D-Day, I experienced some of the hardest fighting I had seen in the war. Involved were the 9th Parachute Battalion, 1st Canadian Parachute Battalion and 5th Battalion Black Watch. Imagine what it was like for a 9th Battalion soldier. These men had never seen a shot fired in anger until forty-eight hours before. Their average age was twenty. They had suffered an appalling night drop on D-Day. They had stormed the Merville battery and attacked Le Plein. They arrived on the ridge on the 7th June, 90 strong, having set off from England with over 600 officers and soldiers. They were minus their equipment and not exactly fresh. In the first eight days of the Battle of Normandy my brigade, which started around 2,000 strong, lost about 50 officers and 1,000 other men.

'...A narrow road ran along the ridge. We had to hold this ridge at all costs. If the Germans had secured it, the bridgehead at Ranville would have been untenable. Alistair Pearson and his 8th Battalion were denying the enemy the approaches to the ridge from the south. The 9th Battalion, whose numbers fluctuated during the battle, held the wooded area and the road adjoining the Château-Ste-Côme. Brigade HQ and their defence platoon were in the middle. The Canadians held the Mesnil crossroads area immediately to the south. My Brigade HQ with their strong defence platoon, numbering some 150 and the Canadians with some 300 men were concentrated over a front of about one mile, astride the Bréville-Troarn Road, running north to south on top of the ridge.

'Enemy attacks concentrated first on the Canadian battalion at Le Mesnil then swung against the 9th Battalion after the Germans had occupied Bréville on D+ 2. It was then that I realised we were up against a first-class German infantry division - 346 Grenadier Division - supported by tanks and self-propelled guns. During this period, some six attacks were launched against the 9th Battalion from Bréville and the east - three of which were coordinated with attacks on the Canadian positions at Le Mesnil. There was constant patrolling activity and on one occasion, my defence platoon accounted for 19 Germans.

'My room was on the top floor of a barn with access only from the outside staircase. I sat on the top step with my left backside overhanging the steps which was good as I smelt of gangrene poisoning - I had lost most of my left backside during a mortar attack on D-Day. From my position, I had a bird's-eye view of the German break-out from Bréville on D+4 and their attack on Peter Luard's 13th Battalion holding the north-east perimeter of Ranville. The 13th held their fire until the last moment and then mowed them down. For the next two days the Germans filtered back through the rear of our positions. I knew it was irregular to see Germans creeping about, but we had neither time nor resources to chase them.

'It was about this time that we were strafed by our own Typhoons. Unfortunately the lady of the château, walking in the garden with her husband, was hit and killed. Our doctors tried to save the baby, to no avail and we buried her in a shroud in her garden with what dignity we could muster under such circumstances. Soon after that, the husband and housekeeper left and my Brigade HQ occupied the château.

'Sitting on my steps, looking down on the bank below, I saw the adjutant of the 9th Battalion, Hal Hudson, lying on the bank looking like a shrivelled parchment, waiting to be operated on by my Field Ambulance unit in the adjoining building. His story was unusual. He received 18 shrapnel wounds in his stomach during the capture of the Merville battery. He thought, 'I must kill one German before I die.' He imagined he saw a figure looming up and he shot it with his Sten gun. It was in fact his foot. The pain was such that it took his mind off his much more severe wounds and thanks to that and the treatment he received from the Field Ambulance; he lived to tell the tale.

'On D+5 the 5th Battalion of the Black Watch were put under my command to capture Bréville. The attack went on in the early hours of the morning and was repulsed by the Germans with heavy losses. I then told them to hold the Château Ste-Côme itself and coordinate their defence with the 9th Battalion. At this juncture, the German Divisional Commander decided that our positions at Ste-Côme-du-Mont and Le Mesnil must be liquidated for once and for all and a major attack was launched on D+6 on both the 9th Battalion and Black Watch positions and the Canadians. This attack was in strength, preceded by a heavy bombardment lasting three hours and it went on supported by tanks and self-propelled guns. The Black Watch were driven back and came back through the 9th Battalion and my defence platoon positions.

'At 1600 hours, I received a message from Terence Otway commanding the 9th Battalion to say that he was doubtful whether he could hold out much longer. I knew that he would not send me this signal unless things were urgent and that something must be done about it. I had no bodies to spare so I went

to Colonel Bradbrook, whose HQ was 200 yards away at the end of our drive and asked him to help. At that moment, German tanks had overrun the road to his right and were shooting up his company HQ at close range. To his eternal credit, he decided that he could deal with this problem and he gave me what was left of his reserve company under Major Hanson, a very tough commander, together with cooks and any spare men and we set off to the 9th Battalion area.'
Brigadier James Hill DSO MC Commanding Officer, 3rd Parachute Brigade.

'…It had happened! Excitement in Paris was at fever pitch. The news was patchy, because the BBC stations were jammed. People rushed round in the streets telling everyone they met the latest news. Soon it would all be over - unbelievable. There were rumours that all the water supplies for Paris were going to be blown up, as well as the gas mains and electricity. Diana and I spent a whole day frantically filling empty wine bottles with water, adding one grain of permanganate to each one. We were unaware that the General in charge of Paris, General von Choltitz, was having a bitter struggle with Hitler and the Gestapo. He too loved and appreciated Paris and felt it should be left intact, whereas Hitler wanted to raze it to the ground.

'The rest of June was glorious, making up for the bad weather of the landings. Diana and I prayed and hoped and willed the Allied Armies to succeed in their advance. All over France, Resistance organizations were doing all in their power to help by disrupting communications. For a week or so it had appeared to be touch and go, but now the advance seemed to consolidate. I wondered if my father was with them. Everyone hoped the British would liberate Paris, though that was still a long way off.'
Antonia Hunt, an English girl, who aged 14, was left behind by her parents in Nazi-occupied France.

'After D-Day, the radio in the mess did a roaring trade, especially with the French crews. We were all eager to know how the Alit front was moving although a few of us semi-privileged people cot walk into the ops room and see the current situation chalked up chinagraph on the talc-covered large-scale map. I shall, however, never forget the day when the liberation of Paris was so dramatically announced. I was standing by the radio looking out into anteroom. There was a large circle of attentive faces; French, British, Canadian, Australian and New Zealand all-agog for latest news. After the pips the announcer, in calm measured tones, said, 'It has just been announced that Paris was entered this morning by American troops; Paris is liberated…' There was a moment pause, during which a pin would have been heard if dropped, broken by the first strident but stirring notes of the *Marseillaise*. Look round the sea of faces I saw many an unashamed tear. I, too, had a lump welling in my throat. It was truly a wonderful moment.'
Mike Henry DFC air gunner, 107 Squadron, Hartford Bridge June 1944.

'Our destination turned out to be Gosport with its 'Mulberry' Harbours where there were a large number of flat-bottomed Tank Landing craft awaiting us. We drove our wagons right on to the far (stern) end of the craft and chained them down. The tanks followed us on and we chained these down as well. The fumes, perspiration and stench were multiplied tenfold and the condensation dripped from the underside of the upper deck so much that it resembled being in a thunder storm. We were still completing these tasks when we set sail and we did not see the leaving of our shores. When we had finished chaining we were allowed to our quarters, a long passage, about 3 feet 6 inches wide, running the length of the craft with bunks in tiers of three joined at the foot and head. From end to end there was the stench of sweaty bodies. I had just taken off my boots when buckets of steaming hot tea came round. A cheer went up and we all filled our pint mugs. I took my first gulp. It was made with 'connie onnie' (condensed milk). I made a hasty dash topside and spent the rest of the crossing hanging over the rail wishing that I had never been born.

'As we neared the Normandy coast we were ordered back on to our vehicles ready to disembark. A shudder went through the landing craft as we hit the beach. The ramps dropped down, the tanks thundered off and then it was our turn. 'Juno' beach was littered with wrecked and abandoned tanks, trucks, jeeps, guns and even clothing and personal effects; all evidence of the hellish time that they had experienced. Hundreds of army personnel were busy extricating gruesome remains from the wreckage. It was enough to make you sick. Our sight of this was very brief and up the beach into a very narrow country lane we went. Progress was rather slow. We had to be very cautious because our front line was still only about 6 or 7 miles ahead and we could hear the noise of gunfire up ahead.'

Bill Stafford 2nd Tactical Air Force advance party.

British 'Mulberry' Harbour Project

The first designs are made at Kingswood School in Bath. The codeword came from a tree standing in the grounds. Up to 45,000 workers, based in companies all over Britain, were involved in the construction of the 'Mulberries', round the clock. Most of them had no idea what they were building.

'Mulberries' consisted of four miles of piers and six of floating roadway from 15 pier heads. They were towed in sections and submerged on D plus 1. Each enclosed more than five square kilometres of water with a breakwater of concrete caissons each five storeys high and weighing 6,000 tons. 200,000 tons of old ships known as 'Gooseberries' were towed from Scotland and sunk alongside the 'Mulberries' to act as breakwaters.

From drawing board to construction 'Mulberry' took less than a fifth of the time it took to build Dover harbour which had half the capacity. In eight month's two artificial harbours and five 'Gooseberry' breakwaters including: 400 'Mulberry' units totalling 1.5 million tons and including up to 6,000-ton 'Phoenix' concrete breakwaters, were built.

59 old merchantmen and warships are sunk in line as block ships for the 'Gooseberries' to provide protection to the innumerable small craft immediately after D-Day before the 'Mulberries' were properly laid and in operation. All were in place by 10 June.

The 'Mulberries' were designed to deal with up to 12,000 tons of stores and 2,500 vehicles a day, as well as Atlantic storms and dramatic tide differences.

The largest 'Phoenix' caissons weighed more than 6,000 tons and were 60 feet tall. More than 200 different types were made, using more than 1 million tons of concrete and 70,000 tons of steel.

Steel pontoon bridges, which rose and fell with the tide, created the roadways and piers. Vertical columns 90 feet tall and weighing 36 tons anchored them to the sea bed.

Admiral Tennant had a force of over 15,000 men to tow the harbours over,' plant' and maintain them. It took 160 tugs to tow the 'Mulberries' across the Channel.

By D+ 2 the block ships were in position and the 'Gooseberry' harbours were operating. The placing of the million and a half tons of gear for the 'Mulberries' was under way and by D+13 the major work was done. By the end of June 1944 they had landed 875,000 men on the beaches.

19-22 June a storm (the worst during any June for 40 years) batters the 'Mulberries' and they start to break up. The weather wreaks five times the amount of damage caused by enemy bombardment after D-Day. Many landing craft and DUKWS are lost and a total of 800 are driven ashore. American 'Mulberry A' off St. Laurent is wrecked and its parts used to repair the more carefully laid British port at Arromanches off 'Gold' beach, which is gravely damaged. It is to last another ten months, landing 2½ million men, 500,000 vehicles and four million tons of supplies

30 June 'Neptune' officially ends in the British sector.

Construction of 'Mulberry A' at 'Omaha' began the day after D-Day with the scuttling of ships to form a breakwater. By D+10 the harbour became operational when the first pier was completed; LST 342 docking and unloading 78 vehicles in 38 minutes. Three days later the worst storm to hit Normandy in 40 years began to blow, raging for three days and not abating until the night of June 22. The harbour was so completely wrecked that the decision was taken not to repair it; supplies being subsequently landed directly on the beach until fixed port facilities were captured. In the few days that the harbour was operational 11,000 troops, 2,000 vehicles and 9,000 tons of equipment and supplies were brought ashore. Over the 100 days following D-Day more than 1,000,000 tons of supplies, 100,000 vehicles and 600,000 men were landed and 93,000 casualties were evacuated, via 'Omaha' Beach.

3 July 'Neptune' officially ends in the American sector. However the shuttle service of men and supplies continues unabated. By these dates, ships had conveyed to France more than 800,000 personnel; in excess of 130,000 vehicles and at least 400,000 tons of stores. In the words of 'Neptune's commander-in-chief - Admiral Sir Bertram Ramsay - it was 'the greatest amphibious operation in history'.

'After D-Day, we organized very rapidly and we set up the Beachmaster communications as we were supposed to. I did duty on ships communicating from ship to shore through the Beachmaster's office. The Beachmaster's office was a bunker on the beach where all the communications were concentrated - telephone, radios, messengers and a message centre where they decoded messages and so on. The job was to get the cargo out of the holds of these ships and onto the beach. By that time they were installing the 'Mulberry' harbour. They had taken old ships and sunk them in a semi-circle around the beach, so that it was like a protected harbour. I remember them blowing these ships and sinking them. The ships, many Liberty ships, pulled into the harbour. They unloaded them with DUKWs. These were floating trucks, trucks that would drive into the water and then operated on land. Drove into the water, had propellers and acted as motor boats. They pulled alongside the ships, the cargo was unloaded, they came back, drove up on land, there were ramps constructed of wood with cranes where the cargo was lifted out of these DUKWs and into regular trucks. The trucks were operated by the black Quartermaster outfits and they were later known as the Red Ball Express.

'And they took it right up to the front lines. My job was to maintain regular communication with the Beachmaster and pass statistics about unloading, also request more stevedores and whatever radio traffic had to be handled by the ship's captain, the commander of the stevedores, to shore. It was very pleasant duty because I got to eat in the crew's mess which was fantastic compared to the chow we got on shore. But at night it was very uncomfortable. Every night from D-Day on, I would say, relentlessly, the Germans were over the beach with airplanes. They still had enough air power left. The nearest German airfield was still only 5 minutes or 10 minutes flying time away and they were constantly overhead. All night long it was the ack-ack going off and to be on an ammunitions ship with 5000, 8000 tons of ammunition was scary. Even the fallout from the ack-ack could set off an explosion. I had seen one explosion which was like an atomic bomb going off on the horizon. Some ship blew up. They did not have black-out, there went all through these air raids with the lights on because we had to move the cargo, it was a matter of life and death for the front troops. So they kept the lights on, even during the air raids, making us a terrific target.'

Technical Sergeant Fritz Weinshank, 293rd Joint Assault Signal Company. In August he went home and was reassigned to the Pacific Theater in a Quartermaster outfit. He landed on Lingayen Gulf on 16 January 1945.

PLUTO

'As the preparations for D-Day gathered pace, I remember being open-mouthed at some of the equipment that was being assembled. Part of PLUTO that looked like an enormous bobbin floated about in Southampton Water. We didn't know what that was. We saw pieces of 'Mulberry', some with cranes, some without. Again, we'd no idea what they were. We saw the crabs, the scorpions and the flails. We didn't know what any of it was, but we knew we'd be on our way very soon.'

Lieutenant William Jalland Platoon commander, 8th Battalion, Durham Light Infantry

Early 1942 construction begins on a network of pipe lines, 1,000 miles long, to carry petrol brought across the Atlantic to the relatively safe ports of the Mersey and Bristol Channel to London and the South and East coasts. PLUTO (Pipeline Under the Sea) a 3-inch diameter steel pipeline, is laid to carry fuel across the Channel.

REs and RASC troops are trained to operate the pumps, which are camouflaged as garages, bungalows and teashops

Special ships with large holds carry the huge heavy coils of pipeline. Barges join the main line to the beaches. By D-Day the PLUTO Force has over 100 officers and a thousand ratings.

PLUTO covers 770 miles of the seabed and pumps 210 million gallons of fuel from England to the Allied forces.

Once Cherbourg falls and sea-lanes are cleared through minefields, a submarine pipeline is laid from the Isle of Wight and petrol pumped to France. Later, as the British and Canadian Corps move north along the coast, more lines are laid across the Channel until the point is reached when over a million gallons of petrol a day passes through PLUTO to the Allied Armies in France. In the days after D-Day more than 112 million gallons were pumped through.

PLUTO cost £3,000 per mile to construct and once salvaged after the war was sold at £2,400 per mile. It supplied the plumbing needs of 50,000 houses and yielded 75,000 gallons of high-octane petrol.

'On 8 June we got orders to unload our cargo on 'Omaha' Beach. There was just chaos and confusion everywhere. I don't think we hit the right part of the beach. We saw a lot of people completely lost who didn't know where they were. I didn't see any Navy corpsmen or Navy aid stations. But I did see a lot of Army medics. They established their aid stations wherever they could. We saw bodies - some were our troops, some were theirs. I saw people with arms and legs missing, parts of bodies. You just couldn't understand it - guys not even making it to the beach, some of them impaled on iron rails that were in the water. Some were washed ashore. It was complete mayhem, terrible.

'After unloading our cargo, our LST was filled with wounded. We treated the wounded, mostly by applying tourniquets and giving morphine. Then we would mark the patients as to what time you had given the morphine to tell when they were due for the next shot. I remember one soldier. I knew he was in pain so I checked him right out. His leg was missing. He had stepped on a mine right on the beach. I gave him a morphine shot and told him he would be okay for a couple of hours. He jumped up and looked at the stump. I don't know where he got the strength. He said, 'I'm a farmer. What am I going to do?' I pushed him back and told him he would be okay. He just screamed. He was only 20 years old.'

19 year old Pharmacist Mate Frank R. Feduik, USS LST 338.

The Beachhead Is Won	
6 June-31 August	21st Army Group suffers 83,825 casualties.
7 June onwards	65,000 men and 19,000 vehicles leave Weymouth and Portland to reinforce the initial landings.
8 June	'Omaha' and 'Gold' beachheads joined. 12th SS Panzer attacks Canadians at Port-en-Bessin and Bretteville l'Orgueilleuse.
9 June	Counter attacks on British by elite German Panzer Lehr

	Division beaten back.
10 June	'Utah' makes contact with 'Omaha'. Montgomery establishes his HQ in Normandy. First RAF base established on French soil.
12 June	Carentan liberated, joining up 'Utah' and 'Omaha' landings. All five beachheads joined up. British 7th Armoured attacks towards Villers-Bocage. 330,000 men and 50,000 vehicles are ashore. As US Seventh Corps fights its way across the Cotentin, the rest of US First Army thrusts forward around St Lô. Further east the British and Canadian Corps of British Second Army battle their way around Caen against fierce German counter-attacks.
30 June	By the end of June 875,000 men have landed in Normandy, 16 divisions each for the American and British armies. Although the Allies are well established on the coast and possess all the Cotentin Peninsular, the Americans have still not taken St Lô, nor the British and Canadians the town of Caen, originally a target for D-Day. German resistance, particularly around Caen is ferocious, but the end result will be similar to the Tunisian campaign. More and more well-trained German troops will be thrown into the battle, so that when the Allies do break out of Normandy the defenders will lose heavily and lack the men to stop the Allied forces from almost reaching the borders of Germany

'In August, a regular tent camp was established and we slept on folding cots. The food improved markedly also. While in this camp, I had one day off and was able to visit Caen. It was an interesting experience; they had a beautiful cathedral. This was my first opportunity to see public urinals out in the middle of the street. They were set up and situated so that you could see men's feet and legs and their heads, of course, which was kind of unusual. There was very little to eat in the town although they had raised a lot of potatoes and you could get what they called potato sandwiches. I guess the sandwiches were nourishing, not terribly tasty but you could survive on it. They also made something they called coffee, which somebody said was made out of poached barley. It tasted much like Postum that I remember having as a child.'

Roy Aron Ford, 111th Naval Construction Battalion. 'On September 15 our battalion was relieved by the 69th Construction Battalion and we returned to Plymouth. We soon returned to Camp Endicott in Rhode Island, given leave and I observed both Thanksgiving and Christmas of 1944 at home.

'Sometimes, too, they sang as they went; *'Now this is number one and I've got her on the run/Roll me over, lay me down and do it again...'* They sang of *'Madamoiselle from Armentieres who hadn't been fucked for thirty years...'* about the spider which approached little Miss Muffet while she was sitting on her tuffet: *'... He whipped his old bazooka out and this is what he said: There's big balls, small balls/Balls as big as yer head; Give 'em a twist around yer wrist and wing 'em over yer head...'* and naturally that old, old song with its mocking refrain: *'What did yer join the army for? Yer must have been fuckin 'well barmy...!'* As for the veterans of the Big Red One, they sang a newer ditty about *'Dirty Gertie from Bizerte,'* who *'hid a mousetrap beneath her skirtie'* - with predictable results.'

Charles Whiting.

'We were soon given a taste of what our fate was to be in the coming weeks, when a rain of fire suddenly came pouring down. Such an unrelenting concentration of material had never been seen in such a restricted area in the whole of the war. The enemy's artillery was far superior to ours in numbers, excellently positioned and they had observation aircraft. But the unforgettable factor for anyone who was there was lying just off the coast and battering the division thunderously. The whistling of the heavy shells and the explosions was just devastating.

'I came across a young lad who had been very badly wounded in the back and chest. My driver and I heaved him into my car and laid him on our coats, trying to make him comfortable. He knew he was dying and with his last breath he asked me to find his company commander and ask him to pass a message to his mother. He said, 'Tell her I died for my beloved Fuhrer and for my Fatherland and that I tried to be brave. Tell her she shouldn't cry because she can be proud of her son.'

'I am not ashamed of the tears I cried. The boy gave me his hand and I held it until he died. I then went to sleep. When I woke, I saw we were parked under a great oak and there were several fresh graves under it. I saw from the date on the boy's cross that he had fallen on his 18th birthday. I cried my eyes out. In the Falaise pocket, I tried to escape. My driver was burning and I had a bullet in the arm. As I ran along a railway track, I was hit in the leg and then, 100 metres further, again in the back of the neck, like a hammer blow below my right ear. The bullet came out through my cheek.

'I was choking on blood and there were two Americans and two French soldiers looking down at me. The French wanted to finish me off but the Americans bandaged my leg and then operated on me for more than five hours. They removed 13 bullets.

'I know one thing; it the army had not been left by the Luftwaffe and the navy to fight alone, the invasion would have turned out very differently. But we had run out of planes.'

22-year-old Leutnant Herbert Walther, 12th Waffen-SS Armoured Division Hitler Jugend (HJ). After receiving the Iron Cross he became an American PoW.

'…Every day another face would vanish…Jerry opened up, killing our Bren gunner, who was just a wee bit in front of me. We all hit the deck and returned fire into the woods where the firing came from. You did not aim but just fired where you thought Jerry was to make him keep his head down. The Bren gunner was a very nice chap called Bill Hughes, another Desert veteran. The Jerry who had opened fire came out with his hand up shouting, Kamerad, Kamerad. I just heard Bert shout, 'You Bastard' and he shot him dead. This kind of thing happens in the heat of battle. Your blood is up and you do things like that. I suppose Jerry did the same. Bill Hughes had paid the price. So had the Jerry, whose body was still lying there next morning.'

Stan Bruce, 5th/7th Battalion, The Gordon Highlanders.

'As a lovely morning dawned a lone German came out of the sunrise, an aerial torpedo hit our escort, the HMS *Boadicea*. Within seconds she sank. There was a mass of bodies and fuel oil in the water. Our captain ordered us into the lifeboats to pick up the survivors. There were only twenty out of 300 men.

S. Davies, one of 30 crew of the British MoWT (Ministry of War Transport) *Freeman Hatch* **making its second run to the 'Omaha' Beachhead with stores and ammunition on 13 June.** *Boadicea* **was hit in the forward magazine by an aerial torpedo at 0445. Fore part of the ship disintegrated and after part sank rapidly.**

'Field Marshal Wilhelm Keitel, head of Armed Forces High Command, rang me from Paris in a panic. 'What shall we do?'

'Make peace you fool.'

Gerd von Rundstedt, Commander-in-Chief West, 10 June, who with Field Marshal Rommel, urged Hitler on two occasions to make peace after the Allies had gained a firm foothold ashore. (Von Runstedt could make no decisions during the invasion - only Hitler could issue direct orders - 'As commander-in-chief in the West my only authority was to change the guard in front of my gate. I asked Supreme Command in Berlin for authority to commit two divisions into battle but the answer was 'no action'. Hitler was asleep in bed with Eva Braun at the Berghof and no one dared disturb him). Von Rundstedt and Rommel wanted to withdraw behind the Seine but Hitler decreed that 'There should be neither a fighting withdrawal to the rear nor a disengagement to a new line of resistance. Every man will fight and fall where he stands.' Von Rundstedt was dismissed on 2 July, news of which was 'accompanied by a Führer-sweetener' a small leather-bound case containing silver Oak Leaves to affix to his Ritterkreuz'. On 17 July Rommel was badly wounded when two Typhoons of 193 Squadron led by Wing Commander Johnny Baldwin attacked a convoy of German staff cars on an open road near Vimoutiers during the retreat from Caen. Rommel suffered serious head injuries and was convalescing at Herrlingen at the time of the July Plot against Hitler. Though not a conspirator, he was disenchanted with Hitler and the plotters had considered him as a potential Chief of State. Under torture, a conspirator blurted out his name and Hitler sent Generals William Burgdorf and Meisel to Rommel's home with poison on 14 October. They offered him the choice of suicide or a public trial which would involve his wife and son. He chose suicide. He died on 14 October 1944 and was buried with full military honours. He was 53.

'With the minimum of delay, we set out and left our unattractive beaches behind. We drove along the coast through Lion-sur-Mer, Luc-sur-Mer, Ste-Aubin and so on, to Courseulles. Most of the houses were damaged, with rubble lying about and Achtung Minen notices everywhere. At Courseulles I walked through the town to the beaches. The volume of craft and shipping lying off this beachhead is many times greater than 'Sword'. They are fortunate in having a kind of harbour; or rather a sort of tidal cutting, where large numbers of small craft could shelter. The mass of shipping to seaward is an incredible sight. We examined an immensely strong 'strongpoint', more complete than any of ours. We had to withdraw when craft started asking for orders from me and I had to say 'I was a stranger 'ere.' The town was pretty unprepossessing. We passed the local tart no less than three times in our wanderings, making a different date each time: she was most unattractive. The only shop we could find was full of sailors and soldiers and seemed to be selling the most awful trash in cheap jewellery and seaside souvenirs, so we went on. Another memory is of Courseulle's drains, which were evidently out of action. We picked up the car and drove west along the coast, past the edge of 'Gold' beach where there seemed to be an incredible number of DUKWS and then via a rather long diversion inland to the 'Mulberry' at Arromanches. This was impressive, though we would see it better from a boat. The combination of sunken merchant ships (Corncobs) and concrete towers (Phoenix) appeared to give a lovely shelter and it must be much 'steeper to' here as some of the coasters were right close in being unloaded rapidly by DUKWS. The Whale piers with their Spud pier-heads were interesting and when the second is complete there should be a great speed-up in unloading.

'We met one of our former American correspondents who told us about his first visit to the American beaches 'Utah' and 'Omaha'. The latter was apparently very hot and he said they had only succeeded in getting 150 yards inland by the evening of D-Day.'

Behind the lines in Normandy, 28 June 1944. **Lieutenant-Commander R. D. Franks DSO RN, Force 'S'.**

'I shall never forget what I saw and experienced that day. It was absolute hell. All you could see was dust and smoke and flames and the pungent smell of cordite hung in the air. We were lucky to survive. Every time I return to Normandy, I know what a fantastic feeling it is to be alive. Yet it is tinged with sadness and emotion when we visit the British cemetery where 4,000 men are buried. It was about survival, a case of kill or be killed, getting on with what you had to do. June 6 1944 was one of the proudest days of my life.'

AB Lol Buxton, Higher Gunner on HMS *Goathland.*

'We went straight into what became a veritable tank war of attrition. Landing on 21 June, by which time the allies were well established but being held up by German forces, we were to be quickly in action in the battle for the Odon River and the capture of Caen. The losses were hellish. After Caen, we were involved in the crossing of the Orne River, among other things supporting the 7th Battalion Royal Norfolks and then the crucial crossing of the Seine which effectively ended the Battle of Normandy. By this time, the pursuit of the Germans was swift, so the 'heavies' were switched to clearing up the channel ports like Le Havre and Dieppe. Still to come were Arnhem, the Ardennes,

Rosendahl and the corridor to the Rhine. Every time there was the fear of the unknown. There was the dreadful fear of moving into attack, though once in action you had to concentrate on the task in hand. Everyone had their own way of dealing with it. I liked to be alone. Normandy is a funny place. You never get over it. You can hear it, feel it. The smell never gets out of your nostrils. I went back in 1984 and when I went to the cemetery at Bayeux my mind went straight back to 1944. I could smell it then. I could see it all so clearly. I was not at the cemetery any more. I could suddenly smell the tanks burning, a terrible smell, the smell of death around you all the time. 'It was very traumatic. I'm not alone in feeling this way.'

Jack Woods volunteered for action on 23 May 1942, his 18th birthday. Two years later, as part of the 9th Royal Tank Regiment, he landed in a Churchill tank on a beach in Normandy.

'The French population did not seem in any way pleased to see us arrive as a victorious army to liberate France. They had been quite content as they were and we were bringing war and desolation to their country.'

Chief of the Imperial General Staff, General Sir Alan Brooke.

'Because my mother and father lived at Mentone, in the south of France and were cut off by the Occupation, I had not heard from them for over three years, Then in June 1944 I crossed the Channel with the rest of my unit, thinking I might soon be able to link up with them again. But the unit moved up toward Antwerp, where I had a miraculous escape from being killed by flying-bombs. 'It was not until December that the news came through that the Allies had linked up with the forces in the south of France. Right away I got fourteen days' leave to go down to Mentone and see what I could find out about my parents. I had to make my own way by hitch-hiking and what a journey! Brussels to Paris took me two days, owing to many bridges being down. I managed to get on a train from Paris to Lyons; that took twenty-four hours, as it was packed to overflowing and I had to carry fourteen days' iron-rations with me in a sack. 'From Lyons I made for Avignon, which took another twenty-four hours. I crossed the river by boat and went on to Marseilles. When I got there I made my way to the station and found there was an auto-diesel train going as far as Nice leaving at nine o'clock at night. But it carried only sixty people and there were about two thousand waiting to get on it.

'I had already spent five days of my leave and had nine days left in which to do all that I wanted, with another three hundred miles to go. But as soon as I reached the platform everybody made way for me; I was the first British soldier they had seen and my uniform was a passport in itself. We travelled all night to Nice and just outside Toulon were shot at by the insurgents who had not yet surrendered.

'I arrived at Nice at last, on 18 December, after six days' travelling, but still had another thirty miles to cover to Mentone. It was late, so I stayed the night at a hotel in the Promenade des Anglais which was occupied by the Americans.

'The other side of Monte Carlo was no-man's-land and to get there I had a special pass from General Mark Clark. When that was fixed an American sergeant took me in a jeep to the border at the bottom of a hill and a few hundred yards away from the top was a grand view of Mentone. The Italian frontier, still held by German forces, was five miles farther on.

'The American wished me luck and said he would not wait. So on I went until I reached the top, where I expect everybody could see me. They could and soon afterwards some shelling started, so I hid all my rations in the bushes and made a detour. I knew where my parents lived, not above three hundred yards away, not far from Cannoles.

'I made my way down carefully, with the shells falling heavily so that progress was slow. The shelling eventually stopped and then I saw it, the garden gate with letter-box, the home where my parents lived. I started to cry because I knew there was no hope of their being alive, for the house had been bombed and only part of it remained standing. There was no sign of anyone about, but in the letter-box were twenty-eight letters, from my brother and myself, which had been there for over five months. I returned to the border of no-man's-land, heartbroken and crying. The shells started to fall again and then I heard my name being called. I took no notice, but the calling grew louder. I saw a little old lady running toward me shouting:

'Alain, Alain! It's you! I know you! You came for your parents.' She burst into tears and she said no more. When she stopped crying she gasped out: 'Your mother and father are in prison, arrested by the FFI.'

'I said: 'Thank God they are alive.' Then she told me that they were in prison in Nice.

'It took me nearly three days to find out how my parents came to be in prison. I saw the Prefect of Police, who took me to the Palais de Justice and showed me my mother's dossier. She was supposed to have had a short-wave radio in her house and to have been communicating with the German Army, with which my brother and I were supposed to be serving. I was given documents authorizing their release but it was late in the evening so I waited till next day.

'I then went to the British Consul for help. He lent me his car and driver and we drove to the prison at St. Laurent du Var. There a guard took me to the Commanding Officer, who told me that because of the papers I had brought my mother would be freed.

'They fetched Mother from the top of a four-storey building and took her to a private room. It was nearly six years since I had last seen her and she never dreamt I would ever find her alive. I would never have recognized her, as she usually weighed about fourteen stone and here she was-just over seven stone. I saw her standing there with a nurse. Neither of us spoke for a moment and then, with a lump in my throat, I said: 'Hallo, Mum.' She just muttered my nickname, 'Fet' and passed out.

'When she recovered everything was all right. I explained that worse things than this had happened during the war. Mother came with me to see Father, very ill in the prison hospital. But poor Dad, though we got him out into a home, never recognized me and died a few months later.

'The day I liberated my parents was Christmas Eve, 1944. Though I was twenty-four hours late in returning to my unit in Antwerp my CO at once gave me four weeks' further leave to settle my mother in a little villa called Mon Reve, at Roquebrune Cap Martin.'

Liberation, **Alain Ferrucci.**

21 Army Group
Personal Message from the C-in-C
(To be read out to all Troops)

1. On this day of victory in Europe I feel I would like to speak to all who have served and fought with me during the last few years. What I have to say is very simple and quite short.

2. I would ask you all to remember those of our comrades who fell in the struggle. They gave their lives that others might have freedom and no man can do more than that. I believe that He would say to each one of them: 'Well done thou good and faithful servant.'

3. And we who remain have seen the thing through to the end; we all have a feeling of great joy and thankfulness that we have been preserved to see this day. We must remember to give the praise and thankfulness where it is due: 'This is the Lord's doing and it is marvellous in our eyes.'

4. In the early days of this war the British Empire stood alone against the combined might of the axis powers. And during those days we suffered some great disasters; but we stood firm: on the defensive, but striking blows where we could. Later we were joined by Russia and America; and from then onwards the end was in no doubt. Let us never forget what we owe to our Russian and American allies; this great allied team has achieved much in war; may it achieve even more in peace.

5. Without doubt, great problems lie ahead; the world will not recover quickly from the upheaval that has taken place; there is much work for each one of us. I would say that we must face up to that work with the same fortitude that we faced up to the worst days of this war. It may be that some difficult times lie ahead for our country and for each one of us personally. If it happens thus, then our discipline will pull us through; but we must remember that the best discipline implies the subordination of self for the benefit of the community.

6. It has been a privilege and an honour to command this great British Empire team in Western Europe. Few commanders can have had such loyal service as you have given me. I thank each one of you from the bottom of my heart.

7. And so let us embark on what lies ahead full of joy and optimism. We have won the German war. Lets us now win the peace.

8. Good luck to you all, wherever you may be.

   (Signed) B. L. Montgomery
   Field-Marshal C-in-C
   21 Army Group
   Germany
   May, 1945.

Index